day trips® series

day trips®
the carolinas

third edition

>>> getaway ideas for the local traveler

james l. hoffman

Globe
Pequot

Essex, Connecticut

All the information in this guidebook is subject to change. We recommend that you call ahead to obtain current information before traveling.

Globe Pequot

An imprint of Globe Pequot, the trade division of
The Rowman & Littlefield Publishing Group, Inc.
4501 Forbes Blvd., Ste. 200
Lanham, MD 20706
www.rowman.com

Distributed by NATIONAL BOOK NETWORK

British Library Cataloguing in Publication Information available

Library of Congress Cataloging-in-Publication Data
Names: Hoffman, Jim, 1963- author.
Title: Daytrips the Carolinas : getaway ideas for the local traveler /
   James L. Hoffman.
Description: Third edition. | Lanham, MD : Globe Pequot, an imprint of
   Globe Pequot, the trade division of The Rowman & Littlefield Publishing
   Group, Inc., [2022] | Series: Day trips | Includes index.
Identifiers: LCCN 2022014025 (print) | LCCN 2022014026 (ebook) | ISBN
   9781493065837 (paperback) | ISBN 9781493065844 (ebook)
Subjects: LCSH: Automobile travel—North Carolina—Guidebooks. | Automobile
   travel—South Carolina—Guidebooks. | North Carolina—Guidebooks. |
   South Carolina—Guidebooks. | North Carolina—Description and travel. |
   South Carolina—Description and travel.
Classification: LCC F252.3 .H638 2022 (print) | LCC F252.3 (ebook) | DDC
   917.504—dc23/eng/20220420
LC record available at https://lccn.loc.gov/2022014025
LC ebook record available at https://lccn.loc.gov/2022014026

∞™ The paper used in this publication meets the minimum requirements of American National Standard for Information Sciences—Permanence of Paper for Printed Library Materials, ANSI/NISO Z39.48-1992.

For Bonnie

contents

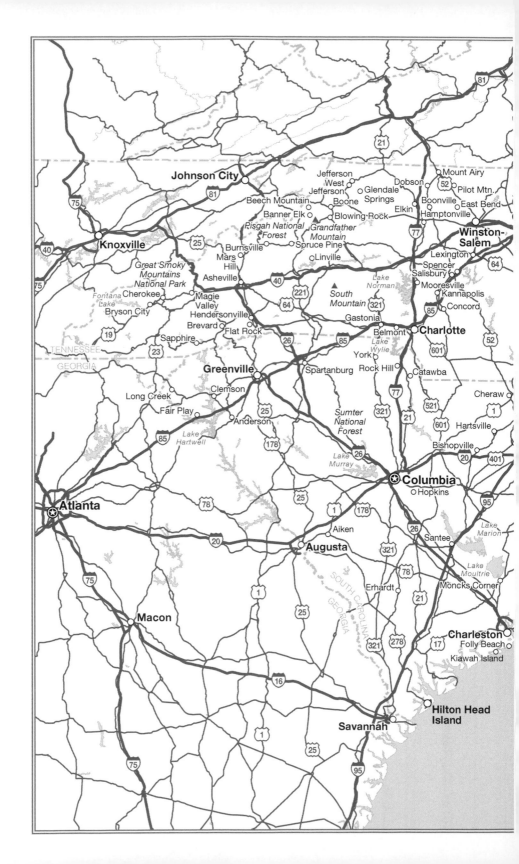

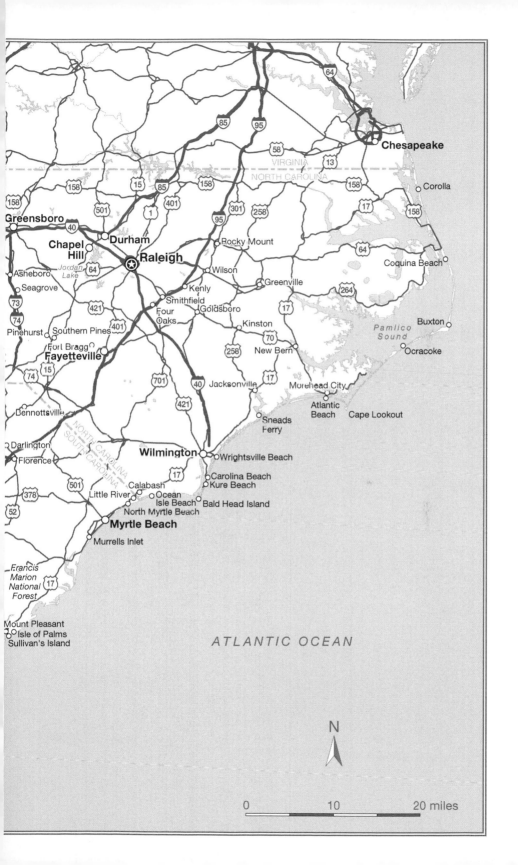

day trip 33

day trip 34

day trip 35

charleston, sc

day trip 36

day trip 37

day trip 38

day trip 39

day trip 40

food & drink

day trip 41

day trip 42

day trip 43

day trip 44

day trip 45

day trip 46

the great outdoors

historic trips

 # about the author

James L. Hoffman is a lifelong resident of North Carolina and grew up a few miles from the South Carolina line. A lover of nature and culture he's the executive director of the Museum of Coastal Carolina in Ocean Isle Beach and Ingram Planetarium in Sunset Beach. Hoffman has also been a newspaper reporter, columnist and editor and worked at Belmont's Daniel Stowe Botanical Garden and Charlotte's Discovery Place. He is the author of *Day Trips from Raleigh-Durham*, *Day Trips from Charlotte*, and *Fun with the Family North Carolina*, all published by Globe Pequot. Hoffman lives in Gastonia with his wife, Bonnie. They have five children and one grandchild.

acknowledgments

I gratefully acknowledge all those who contributed their thoughts, ideas, suggestions, and well-wishes that made this work possible. First and foremost I would like to thank my family for putting up with me during this project. It takes an incredible amount of time and concentration and would not be possible without their understanding. To Melissa, John, and Foster; Michael, Jessie, Michaela, Kaitlyn, and my beautiful and understanding wife, Bonnie, I offer not only my gratitude but my love and adoration.

Thanks to my editors at Globe Pequot Press. Your patience, advice, and guidance are irreplaceable.

Thanks once again to all my friends in the tourism industry for keeping me straight and informed. Many helped, but special thanks goes to my Charlotte area friends, Molly Hedrick, Laura Hill, Rachel Walker, Moira Quinn, Melissa McGill, Tracy Aldridge, Donna Carpenter, and Reine Smirz. I would also like to thank PR pros Susan Dosier, Michelle Yelton, Craig Distl, Allison Andrews, and Tammy O'Kelly for their invaluable suggestions. The folks at the N.C. Department of Tourism—Margo Metzger, Wit Tuttle, and Kathy Prickett—continue to provide invaluable support. In South Carolina a number of key people, including Amy Phillips and Dawn Dawson, made invaluable contributions to this work. Thanks also to Sondra Katzenstein and Judith Burgess for filling me in on Aiken and to Melissa DeLony and Joe, Karen, and Kelly Hoffman for their assistance from Hilton Head.

A number of other people in my professional life have contributed substantially to my ability to carry on this work, including GPP author Sara Pitzer, who helped start it.

introduction

I'm perpetuating a myth, but I didn't realize it until it was too late. When my New England publisher asked me to write the latest edition of its popular Day Trips series, I didn't realize until after I signed the contract that it may somehow support the belief among people who don't live here that North Carolina and South Carolina are one state—Carolina. The states were in fact one colonial province for about 100 years, but both became independent royal colonies in 1729.

There are still, however, similarities and certain truths that hold in the northern part of the Carolinas as well as the southern part. I submit: All things, including chicken, fish, okra, and Doublestuffed Oreos, taste better when coated in some sort of flour mixture and fried in vegetable oil; none of that EVO stuff. There really is no substitute for sweet tea. People (even those in the Carolinas) complain that temperatures in Columbia and Charleston are soooo hot, but is there really that much difference from Charlotte's average July high temperature of 90 degrees and Columbia's 92 degrees? It's the South. The forecast in the summer is hot, humid, and chance of rain.

There are also distinct differences in the two Carolinas. Some of this might be argued, but here goes. I submit that Carolina plays basketball at the Dean Dome in Chapel Hill, not football at Williams-Brice Stadium in Columbia. With its mountains to the coast mantra, North Carolina may be a vacation varietyland, as its license plates once noted, but South Carolina seems to have the more popular beaches. South Carolina might be the birthplace of a dance known as the Carolina Shag, but you have to go north of the border to Calabash to get the real version of the fried seafood. South Carolina gave birth to Hootie and the Blowfish, Dizzy Gillespie, and the Marshall Tucker Band, but North Carolina is just as proud of its James Taylor, Doc Watson, and Charlie Daniels. Andrew Jackson? We're not really sure if the place our seventh president was born was North or South, but the Carolinas can claim him.

Similarities and differences aside, nothin' could be finer than to be in Carolina, and this guide attempts to give credence to that. Four North Carolina cities and two in South Carolina provide home bases for our day trips that include places to go, shop, eat, and even sleep. The fact that there are more trips in North Carolina than in South Carolina is due solely to the fact that North Carolina is much larger. With 49,000 square miles and 10 million people, North Carolina has twice the population of South Carolina, which covers about 30,000 square miles.

We begin our exploration of the Carolinas in the northern capital of Raleigh and enjoy the cosmopolitan rewards of the Triangle, home of some of the state's great universities and museums. From there the coastal communities of the Cape Fear and Crystal Coast, where Blackbeard once roamed, provide a little more than a day trip. Using Wilmington and the beach community of Wrightsville as a home base, a whole world of day trip opportunity opens up from hanging out on the beach to examining our military history. From there we hit the city of Charlotte with big league sports, big-time entertainment, fine food, and a whole host of other experiences close at hand. From Charlotte you can touch the mountains, get back to nature, and even dip down into South Carolina. Experience the mountain life from the eclectic city of Asheville to the quaint Bryson City, a town named for a girl named Maggie, and Cherokee, where these Native Americans have finally settled.

The graceful South Carolina state capital of Columbia boasts culinary and cultural experiences anew after many years of revitalization. And close at hand are other artful experiences in the city of Greenville as well as abounding natural experiences at South Carolina's great lakes. The low country of Charleston and Hilton Head offer a taste of Gullah culture, resounding history, and remarkable culinary experiences while the popular Myrtle Beach offers much to fill a day.

Are you the kind of day-tripper who knows what kind of adventure you want on a given day? Check our themed trips. Sip your way through Yadkin Valley wine country or chug your way through a brews cruise in Asheville. Stop and fill up on barbecue, fish, or fresh food. Race to the cities of speed—Concord, Kannapolis, and Mooresville—or go skiing in the mountains of the Blue Ridge. Wet a line at Santee Cooper and one of the greatest freshwater lakes in the world, canoe on black water, and raft on white water. Play golf or see what you can learn by hearing stories from the darkest days in our country's existence. Dance the night away in the Shag Capital of the World or climb to the tallest lighthouse in America on the Outer Banks.

I may have been duped into perpetuating this Carolina myth, but if you only have a day, does it really matter if you are in North or South Carolina? Whether you are on the peaks of the Black Mountains in western North Carolina or the South Carolina foothills near Georgia, the view is just as nice. Whether you are at Wrightsville Beach or Folly Beach, the sand is just as soft and sun just as bright. Whether you are on Fort Sumter where the Civil War began or in Durham where it ended, the history you will realize—good and bad—made North and South Carolina the great states they are today. Begin discovering that for yourself.

using this guide

This guide includes day trips departing from six different cities in North and South Carolina—**Raleigh, NC; Wilmington, NC; Charlotte, NC; Asheville, NC; Columbia, SC; and Charleston, SC**—with all trips originating from the center of each of those cities. Each trip will suggest the best places to go within about a 2-hour drive, but are not intended to be all-inclusive. We've sought out the best places to go, the best and most popular places to eat, and even best places to stay should you want to extend your day trip. Following those trips are **themed trips** that focus on food and drink, the outdoors, and history.

hours of operation

Exact hours of operation are provided where available, but they are subject to change. Attractions often operate seasonally, and that is noted wherever possible. Always remember to call ahead.

pricing key

attractions

Exact pricing for attractions is provided where possible. However, facilities change prices and often charge for special events or may charge more in peak periods. You can assume all establishments listed accept major credit cards, unless otherwise noted. If you have questions, contact the establishments for specifics.

accommodations

The price code reflects the average cost of a double-occupancy room during the peak price period (not including tax or extras). Always ask if any special discounts are available. Occupancy tax in North Carolina is 6 percent; 7 percent in South Carolina. Some local authorities add a tax as well.

$	Less than $100
$$	$100 to $150
$$$	More than $150

restaurants

The price code reflects the average price of dinner entrees for two (excluding cocktails, wine, appetizers, desserts, tax, and tip). You can usually expect to pay less for lunch and/or breakfast, when applicable. If a restaurant mainly serves breakfast or isn't open for dinner, we list the price for the most expensive meal.

$ Less than $10
$$ $10 to $20
$$$ More than $20

driving tips

highway designations

Federally maintained highways are designated as US Highways (US 421) or as interstates (I-77). Other highways are roads maintained by the state and are indicated by SR. North Carolina does not have any county-maintained roadways. Local governments in South Carolina, however, maintain about one-third of its roads statewide.

travel tips

carry a map

This guide includes maps that are intended for reference. Find one at the front of the entire area and a map for each day trip. "Getting There" directions are also provided from each base city to each day trip destination, then from the first destination to the next. Some scenic routes and alternatives are also noted throughout the guide. Typically, a GPS will do nicely in getting travelers from Point A to Point B, but the more skilled, adventurous day-trippers will want to deviate from the beaten path. For that they need a map. The North Carolina Department of Transportation provides a fine map, available by going to visitnc.com, by visiting any one of North Carolina's nine welcome centers, or by calling (800) 847-4862. In South Carolina a road map can be ordered by going to discoversouthcarolina.com or to one of its welcome centers. Also consider purchasing a *Delorme Atlas & Gazetteer* for each state; it's good for back-road travel and hiking.

don't overload your travel itinerary in the mountains

Travel is often slow in the mountain regions, so if there is too much on the agenda, you will spend all your time driving and miss all the fun. The maximum speed limit on the Blue Ridge Parkway, for example, is 45 miles per hour. So while it is beautiful, it's not preferred for expeditious travel. In addition, parts of it and other mountain roads are closed during winter or during inclement weather. Also note that the parkway as well as many beach highways use mileposts (MP), not addresses, to mark specific points. Leaf-lookers come out to the mountains in droves in autumn, a great time for many day trips, and inevitably slow traffic. Travel information, delays, construction information, and so forth are available in North Carolina at ncdot.gov/traffictravel or by dialing 511. In South Carolina information can be obtained at 511sc.org.

fishing licenses

Fishing licenses are required to fish in any North and South Carolina waters. This includes the Atlantic Ocean. You can purchase a limited license, a year license, or a lifetime license by going to ncwildlife.org or dnr.sc.gov. Note that a trout stamp may also be required. Local vendors at bait and tackle shops may also sell licenses and can fill you in on other regulations. Even though you've booked a trip through a service, you may still need to purchase your license ahead of time.

where to get more information

North Carolina Division of Tourism   1(800) VISITNC
15000 Weston Pkwy.   visitnc.com
Cary, NC 27513

South Carolina Department of Parks, Recreation & Tourism
1205 Pendleton St.
Columbia, SC 29201
(866) 224-9339
discoversouthcarolina.com

raleigh, nc

day trip 01

raleigh, nc

>>> **capital city:**
raleigh, nc

raleigh, nc

Though it's not the largest city in North Carolina, the state's capital offers a diverse selection of things to see and do. Families can play at Marbles, the city's children's museum, and explore the state's museums of history, art, and natural sciences. For adults, culinary rewards, shopping, and other things to see and do abound.

Raleigh, Durham, and Chapel Hill form what is known as the Triangle. More than just points on an indistinct geometric-geographic shape, each has its own distinct cultural appeal, its own college sports favorites, and its own special set of things to see and do. In between is Research Triangle Park, a global center of research and innovation—many large companies such as IBM, Cisco Systems, DuPont, Glaxo Smith Kline, and hundreds of others have major sectors based here. Busy and bustling are the highways that run between these cities with Raleigh in the heart of it all.

Named for Sir Walter Raleigh, who sponsored the English settlement in what is now North Carolina in the 16th century, Raleigh is the "city of oaks" with a population of just more than 465,000 (people, that is; we're not sure how many oak trees there are). It was established as the seat of Wake County and the state capital in 1792, chosen in part because of its central location but also for its proximity to a tavern frequented by state legislators. It was planned, unlike other state capitals in the country, specifically to serve as the government seat. What it has become is so much more. For more information contact the Greater Raleigh Convention and Visitors Bureau at (800) 849-8499; visitraleigh.com.

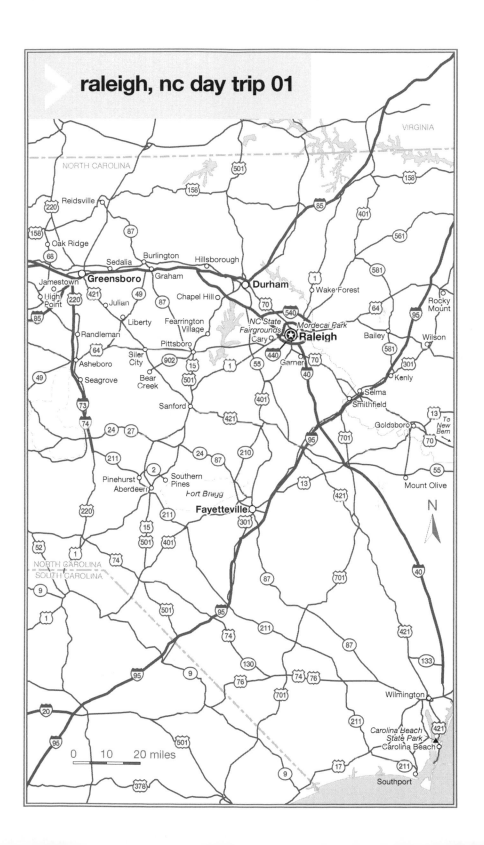

raleigh, nc day trip 01

getting there

I-40, fed by I-85 near Durham and Chapel Hill, pokes into Raleigh from the northwest and forms part of the inner loop along with I-440. I-40 then runs south out of Raleigh. An outer loop, I-540, forms an arc north of the city. I-95 runs some 50 miles east of the city and connects with US 64, I-40, and several less significant routes. US 1 provides access from the southwest from cities such as Sanford.

where to go

Carolina Hurricanes. PNC Arena, 1400 Edwards Mill Rd.; (919) 861-2323; carolinahurri canes.com. PNC Arena, formerly the RBC Center, has been the home of hockey's 'Canes since October 1999, and it is also home court for North Carolina State's basketball team. A perennial championship contender, the Hurricanes reached the Stanley Cup finals quickly in 2002 and brought the famed trophy to North Carolina in 2006. When there's no b-ball or bodychecking, the center is host to other large-scale concerts and events.

Contemporary Art Museum. 409 W. Martin St.; (919) 513-0946; camraleigh.org. Opened in 2011 CAM stirred up the capital city's museum scene with new, rotating exhibitions of modern art and programs designed to engage a variety of audiences. Works range in mediums from film and digital art to more traditional forms, but unexpected works by local and national artists remain this museum's specialty. Admission is free. for children 10 and under. Free admission is offered the first Friday of the month. Open Fri 4 to 8 p.m., Sat and Sun noon to 5 p.m.

Dorothea Dix Park. 1030 Richardson Drive; (919) 996-3255; dorotheadixpark.org. Located on more than 300 acres in the heart of the city, Dix park was created out of an innovative partnership between the city of Raliegh and the non-profit Dix Conservancy. The state's first mental health facility was founded here 150 years ago until it closed in 2012. Its expanses include a chapel, fields of sunflowers and daffodils, a dog park and space for special events from the Acorn Live Music series to yoga,. Generally open during daylight hours.

Executive Mansion. 200 N. Blount St.; (919) 807-7950. An impressive mansion built in the Victorian style of architecture, the Executive Mansion was constructed largely of handmade bricks and has housed 30 families since its completion in 1891. Self-guided tours of the home are permitted on an irregular basis. The Capital Area Visitor Center, located in the North Carolina Museum of History, also conducts guided tours with advance notice. Free. Call for hours or other information.

Historic Oakwood. Delson, Edenton, Boundary, and Watauga Streets; (919) 832-9712; historicoakwood.org. This 20-block area of homes of varying architectural styles in downtown was built in the late 1800s. While most of these are private homes typically not open for touring, the Historic Oakwood Preservation Society plans an annual holiday candlelight tour each winter and a garden tour each spring. The adjacent Oakwood Cemetery, 701

quirky carolina

A giant copper acorn sculpture stands sentinel over downtown Raleigh's Moore Square district, the capital city's arts district. The 10-foot-tall, 1,200-pound acorn is dropped from a crane every New Year's Eve.

Oakwood Ave., holds the grave sites of 2,800 Confederate soldiers, 5 Civil War generals, and 7 governors. Get a walking tour map at the Capital Area Visitor Center at City Plaza on Fayetteville Street or download it from the website.

Joel Lane House Museum and Gardens. 728 W. Hargett St.; (919) 833-3431; joellane .org. Built in the 1760s west of downtown is Raleigh's oldest dwelling. In 1782 representatives of the newly formed legislature selected this site as the capital and purchased 1,000 acres of the Lane plantation to create the city of Raleigh. The furnishings in the home are authentic to the period. Beautiful gardens feature pomegranate trees, a grape arbor, and stately brick walkways. An herb garden features medicinal and culinary herbs. Admission to the garden and grounds is free. Guided tours are $8 for adults, $7 for seniors, $4 for students, free for children under 6. Gardens are open during daylight hours. Tours offered Wed through Fri, on the hour at 10 and 11 a.m., noon and 1 p.m.; Sat at 1, 2, and 3 p.m., Mar 1 to mid-Dec. Jan and Feb, tours are offered Sat at 1, 2, and 3 p.m.

Jordan Lake State Recreation Area. Southwest of Raleigh on State Park Road, off US 64; (919) 362-0586; ncparks.gov. One of the largest summertime homes of the bald eagle in the eastern US, Jordan Lake is a great place to study nature, a welcome refuge from man and beast in the middle of one of the state's busiest areas. The 15,000-acre recreation area offers a full-service marina as well as opportunities for hiking, camping, fishing, and swimming at 9 separate recreation areas. An exhibit hall at the visitor center includes displays on the environment and bald eagles. Hours vary according to season.

Marbles Kids Museum. 201 E. Hargett St.; (919) 834-4040; marbleskidsmuseum.org. Marbles is a big, open, and active children's museum that focuses on child development through communication, creativity, and play. Interactive experiences with fun, energetic names include Splash, Around Town, Moneypalooza, KidGrid, and Power 2 Play. While most of the exhibits focus on children under the age of 10, the museum also has an IMAX theater that presents documentary and feature films. Admission is $9 for everyone over the age of 1. IMAX films start at $7, but combo packages are also available. Open Mon 9 a.m. to noon, Tues through Sun 9 a.m. to 5 p.m.

Mordecai Historic Park. 1 Mimosa St.; (919) 996-4364; raleighnc.gov/parks. Andrew Johnson, the 17th president of the US, was born at this historic site that was a home for five generations, beginning with the Joel Lane family in 1785. It was named for attorney Moses Mordecai, who married into the Lane family in 1817. What was once an antebellum plantation opened as a village-type park in 1972. Today visitors can see any number of historic buildings or take a trolley tour through the property. Johnson, who became president when Abraham Lincoln was assassinated, was born in a small cabin here in 1808. Guided tours are $7 for adults, $4 for seniors and youth, and free for children under age 7. Open Tues through Sat 10 a.m. to 4 p.m., Sun 1 to 4 p.m. Trolley tours offered Sat, Mar through Dec, are $10 for adults, $4 for youth, and free for children under age 7.

North Carolina Museum of Art. 2110 Blue Ridge Rd.; (919) 839-6262; ncartmuseum .org. The spectacular North Carolina Museum of Art houses the permanent art collection of the state as well as changing exhibits. The museum contains paintings and sculptures dating back 5,000 years that come from across the Americas, Africa, and Europe. Included are works by Raphael, Monet, Botticelli, and others. Of note are sculptures by Rodin and a significant collection of African art. The newest part of the museum includes a stunning contemporary building constructed with techniques that utilize natural light to enhance exhibits and conserve energy. It is a work of art in and of itself, and along with it the museum opened Museum Park, which includes sustainable landscaping intertwined with newly acquired outdoor sculptures. Notable are the works of Wilson farm equipment repairman-turned-artist Vollis Simpson. Free, with a charge for special exhibitions. Guided tours are conducted at 1:30 p.m. daily. Open Tues through Thurs 10 a.m. to 5 p.m., Fri 10 a.m. to 9 p.m., Sat and Sun 10 a.m. to 5 p.m.

North Carolina Museum of History. 5 E. Edenton St.; (919) 807-7900; ncmuseumofhis tory.org. Open and unexpectedly unstuffy is the North Carolina Museum of History, which leads visitors through the story of the state through exhibits depicting a part of North Carolina's history. Included are displays that present a chronological history, the role of women in the state's history, and folk life. Artifacts tell North Carolina's story from the earliest settlements on Roanoke Island as well as the state's role in the Revolutionary and Civil Wars. One of the newest permanent exhibitions is the 20,000-square-foot "Story of North Carolina," which tells the history of the state in two parts. One group of artifacts and interactive displays takes the visitor from the 16th century to the 1830s. Part two begins in the 1840s and covers slavery, textiles, and North Carolina's involvement in all the period's wars. A replica of a drugstore gives insight to early 20th-century Carolina life while the North Carolina Sports Hall of Fame delivers artifacts and audiovisual displays about North Carolina's sports greats. Free. Open Tues through Sat 9 a.m. to 5 p.m., Sun noon to 5 p.m.

North Carolina Museum of Natural Sciences. 11 W. Jones St.; (919) 733-7450; natural sciences.org. Also located in the capitol complex is this massive collection of exhibition spaces devoted to the study of natural history that spans 5 stories of exhibits. Visitors here get an opportunity to explore the natural world by learning about things that are unique to North Carolina. Among the exhibits is Prehistoric North Carolina, including Willo, a sixty-six-million-year-old dinosaur with a fossilized heart and the only acrocanthosaurus (known as the Terror of the South) on display in the world. Giant whale skeletons hang in multistory galleries and turtles lounge on rocks in the aquarium. Live animals are part of the Mountains to the Sea exhibit that presents North Carolina's 5 distinct habitats. Escalators carry guests systematically through the well-designed building. It ends with the arthropod zoo and a butterfly house. In 2012 they opened a new wing of the museum called the Nature Research Center. In addition to housing working scientists who regularly interact with visitors, the center includes public labs, a 10,000-gallon aquarium, a science theater, and other resources to help demystify scientific research. Free, with a charge for special exhibitions. Open Tues through Sun 10 a.m. to 5 p.m.

North Carolina State Fairgrounds. 1025 Blue Ridge Rd.; (919) 821-7400; ncstatefair.org. North Carolina's State Fair is a traditional festival featuring rides, games, and farm-related events and exhibitions. It is usually held for 10 days in the middle of October and attracts nearly a million people. When the fair isn't in town, the grounds are host to a flea market on the weekends and a variety of other shows, including livestock and pet shows. Rodeos are also periodically held here.

North Carolina State University. (914) 515-2011; ncsu.edu. With almost 35,000 students, this is the state's largest institution of higher learning. The university is almost a town unto itself, noted for its redbrick walkways and buildings and as host to Wolfpack basketball, football, and other sports. In addition, it provides venues for concerts, theater, and the arts. The NCSU J.C. Raulston Arboretum (919-515-3132), which features 6,000 different kinds of plants from 55 countries, is one of the state's most renowned public gardens. Located off Old Hillsborough Street at 4301 Beryl Rd., the arboretum also includes a Victorian gazebo and a Japanese garden, with guided tours at 2 p.m. Sun from Mar through Oct. Admission is free. Surrounding the university are shops and restaurants, pubs and coffee shops typical of a college town.

Pullen Park. 520 Ashe Ave.; (919) 831-6468; raleighnc.gov/parks. Part of Raleigh's Parks and Recreation Department and the first public park in the state, Pullen Park offers a train ride through the amusement park, a kiddie boat ride, pedal boats, and a 1912 Dentzel Menagerie Carousel. Of course, you'll find standard park attractions such as tennis courts, softball fields, a swimming pool, and picnic and playground areas as well as an arts center. Pullen Park is also home of the TV Land's tribute statue of Andy and Opie Taylor honoring *The Andy Griffith Show*. Generally open during daylight hours. Free, with fees for some attractions.

State Government Complex. Raleigh's downtown Bicentennial Plaza creates a link to all the major downtown museums and government buildings. It's a gathering spot, a starting point, and a place to grab a hot dog from a street vendor. The State Capitol (919-733-4994) is located in the geographic center of downtown. Built in the late 1830s in Greek Revival style, it houses the governor's office, cabinet offices, historic legislative chambers, and the state library. It was once nearly destroyed by fire but since has been restored to its original condition. Free. Open Mon through Fri. 8 a.m. to 5 p.m., Sat. 10 a.m. to 4 p.m. The state Legislative Building (919-733-7928) is located across Bicentennial Plaza and is home to the North Carolina General Assembly. Devoted solely to the legislative branch, the General Assembly gives visitors an opportunity to see the legislative process with viewing galleries that overlook both chambers of the legislature. The building was designed in 1960 by famous architect Edward Durell Stone, who also designed New York's Radio City Music Hall, the Museum of Modern Art, and the Kennedy Center. Free. Open Mon through Fri 8 a.m. to 5 p.m., Sat 9 a.m. to 5 p.m., Sun 1 to 5 p.m.

where to shop

Cameron Village. 1900 Cameron St.; (919) 821-1350; shopcameronvillage.com. Six blocks of specialty stores, boutiques, and cafes line the village-like streets of this quaint shopping center. Jewelry, home decor, fashions, and sporting goods are all to be found here. Eateries feature dining alfresco.

City Market. 220 Wolfe St.; (919) 821-8023; citymarketraleigh.com. Streetlamps and cobblestone streets create a special ambience for this shopping experience. The region's supermarket of the early 20th century is now the renovated home of Artspace, a nonprofit working studio, Blake Street Studios, collectibles shop, clothing boutiques, and more.

where to eat

Angus Barn. 9401 Glenwood Ave.; (919) 781-2444; angusbarn.com. The Angus Barn is known far and wide for its quality steaks and has been in continuous operation here for 50 years. Located in a red barn just off the interstate, its decor includes barn items, and the Wild Turkey Lounge, where you will ultimately wait, includes a collection of Wild Turkey decanters and Colt revolvers. Chef Walter Royal of *Iron Chef* fame offers a monthly culinary class, but don't plan on dropping in; they sell out early. Open Mon through Fri 5 to 10 p.m., Sat 4 to 100 p.m., Sun 4 to 9 p.m. $$–$$$.

Bida Manda. 222 S. Blount St.; (919) 829-9999; bidamanda.com. "Let's go out for Laotian food" has likely become a more popular phrase in Raleigh since Bida Manda hit the restaurant scene. Vansana and Vanvisa Nolintha, a brother and sister team, opened this restaurant in 2012 to honor their parents, its name taken from the Sanskrit term of endearment for father and mother. It has become a local sensation. Lettuce wraps, curried food, noodles, and fresh fish dishes are recipes from the Nolinthas' parents. Open for dinner Tues through Thurs 5 to 10 p.m. and Fri and Sat 5 to 11 p.m. $$.

Caffé Luna. 136 E. Hargett St.; (919) 832-6090; cafeluna.com. Tuscan-style Italian is served in the beautiful and bright restored historic building in downtown. Fish and penne are more common on the menu here than spaghetti and meatballs. It's also a popular wedding-ceremony and rehearsal-dinner spot. Open Tues through Thurs 5-9 p.m. Sat 5 to 10 p.m. $$$.

The Pit. 328 W. Davie St.; (919) 890-4500; thepit-raleigh.com. Whole hog barbecue comes out of the smokers here. Famous throughout the city, The Pit is more upscale than the typical barbecue joint, and it also serves Texas-style barbecue brisket, ribs, barbecue turkey, and fried chicken. The Pit's Brunswick stew has also acquired some notoriety throughout the state. Open Sun through Thurs 11 a.m. to 9 p.m., Fri and Sat 11 a.m. to 10 p.m. $$.

Poole's Diner. 426 S. McDowell St.; (919) 832-4477; poolesdowntowndiner.com. Poole's started as a pie shop in the 1940s. Now it's one of the city's most popular downtown dining locations. It is sleek and contemporary but still features chalkboard menus that change so often it's hard to note examples. Look for hearty comfort food with a contemporary twist. Open Tues through Sun 5:30 p.m. to midnight. $$.

Second Empire Restaurant and Tavern. 330 Hillsborough St.; (919) 829-3663; second-empire.com. Possibly the best fine dining restaurant in the capital city, Second Empire is located in a restored historic home in downtown. Lamb, fillets, fresh fish, and fine wine star on the menu at the full restaurant. A tavern-style dining room offers a more casual setting, salads, pasta, and a big selection of beer on tap. Open Tues through Sat 5 to 10 p.m. $$$.

where to stay

Longleaf Hotel. 300 N. Dawson St.; (919) 867-5770; thelongleafhotel.com. A nod to the state tree of the ole north state, the Longleaf Hotel and Lounge Is conveniently located near tho state capital and Red Hat Amphitheater. Its mid-century inspired vibe may take you back to long drives with Mom and Dad, but the modern décor, in-room Bluetooth speakers and other amenities place you squarely In the 21st century, $$

Origin Hotel, 603 W. Morgan St.; (984) 275-2220; wyndamhotels.com. Operated by Wyndam, trendy décor and "camping gear" for kids make this hotel, located in the warehouse district, a little more special than a typical hotel stay. The hip restaurant located here offers a large selection of plant-based offerings. $$$

day trip 02

raleigh, nc

tobacco road:
durham, nc

durham, nc

Today anchored in the medical industry, Durham's Brightleaf Square stands as a reminder of the roots from which it sprouted. Durham was a city born of the tobacco industry and James B. Duke's once famous Bull Durham tobacco. Now one of the state's most culturally diverse cities, Durham is the home of Duke University and the famous Durham Bulls baseball team, and it tells a dramatic historical account. The university opened its medical school in 1930, and today the city boasts five major hospitals, numerous pharmaceutical research companies, and other health-related companies. For more information: Durham Convention and Visitors Bureau, (800) 446-8604; discoverdurham.com.

getting there

Take I-40 west from Raleigh and arrive in Durham in about 30 minutes if you don't have to contend with much traffic, which can be extremely heavy at rush hour. Take exit 279B, SR 147 north, which leads downtown via US 15/501.

where to go

Bennett Place State Historic Site. 4409 Bennett Memorial Rd.; (919) 383-4345; nchis toricsites.gov. It was at Bennett Place State Historic Site that the Civil War effectively ended. Union general William T. Sherman and Confederate general Joseph E. Johnston met at this

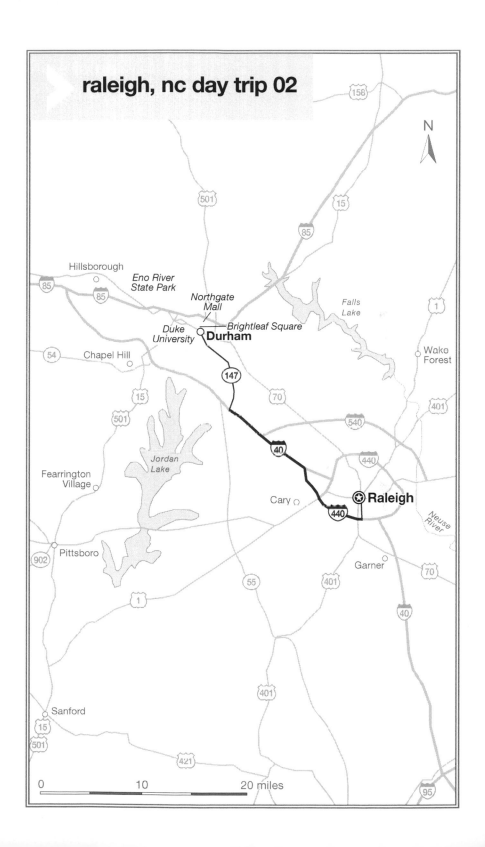

raleigh, nc day trip 02

N

158

501

15

85

Hillsborough

Eno River
State Park

85

85

Falls
Lake

1

Northgate
Mall

Duke
University

Brightleaf Square
Durham

Wako
Forest

54

Chapel Hill

147

70

540

401

15

501

40

440

Jordan
Lake

Fearrington
Village

Cary

Raleigh

440

Neuse
River

902

Pittsboro

Garner

70

55

401

40

1

Sanford

401

15

501

421

95

0   10   20 miles

farmstead in 1865, 17 days after Confederate general Robert E. Lee surrendered at Appomattox. Following meetings in Hillsborough, the Durham meeting set up the largest surrender of the war. Although fighting continued in the west, this was the conclusion to the bloody War Between the States. Today the simple farmhouse and outbuildings have been restored, and the grounds also include a museum and interpretive center, exhibits of uniforms, flags, weapons, and more that focus on North Carolina's role in the war. A surrender reenactment is presented each April. Free. Open Tues through Sat 9 a.m. to 5 p.m.

Carolina Theatre. 309 W. Morgan St.; (919) 560-3030; carolinatheatre.org. This renovated 1926 Beaux Arts–style building includes a small live performance hall with about 1,000 seats and 2 cinemas. It hosts small musical acts and locally produced plays. The movie halls host film festivals and other annual events.

Duke Homestead State Historic Site. 2828 Duke Homestead Rd.; (919) 477-5498; dukehomestead.org. Long before Durham was a medical center, its roots were deeply embedded in the tobacco industry. Duke Homestead connects the two. The site includes the home of Washington Duke, constructed in 1852, plus tobacco barns and 2 early tobacco factories. The museum chronicles the history of the tobacco industry and production, and cigarette manufacturing. A moving mannequin plants tobacco and helps bring the industry into perspective, as does a film about the Duke family and their tobacco empire, which consequentially helped establish many of today's humanitarian and cultural establishments that bear the Duke name. Open Tues through Sat 9 a.m. to 5 p.m.

Duke University. Duke University's stately architecture complements its rich history and legacy as one of the leading private universities in the country. More than the home of the Cameron Crazies, whose antics have led the university's men's basketball team on to more than its fair share of victories memorialized in the Duke Basketball Museum and Hall of Fame located here, the campus brings to mind those of the Ivy League. It is the city's largest employer with researchers and abounding cultural gems. Found at Duke University are a number of interesting attractions, most notable of which is Duke University Chapel in the west campus. This 1,800-seat chapel, constructed in the 1930s, was the last of the great collegiate Gothic projects. It features a 5,033-pipe organ with 5 keyboards and a 50-bell carillon. Its 77 intricate stained-glass windows depicting stories from the Bible are also noteworthy. For more information the university website is duke.edu.

Duke Lemur Center (all ages). 3705 Erwin Rd.; (919) 489-3364; lemur.duke.edu. This is the world's largest sanctuary for rare and endangered prosimian primates. It was established in 1966 on 85 acres in Duke Forest to help study and preserve these adorable animals that live naturally on the island of Madagascar. Family-oriented tours take visitors around the facilities to learn about these fascinating animals. A separate tour, costing $95 per person, takes participants ages 10 and over behind the barriers to get up close and personal with the lemurs. Regular guided tours are $14 per person. Reservations required and no self-guided tours are available.

Nasher Museum of Art at Duke University. Located on Campus Drive in the east campus; (919) 684-5135; nasher.duke.edu. Opened in this contemporary location in 2005, the Nasher Museum of Art at Duke University is most notable for its fine collection of medieval sculpture, but it is also host to a lovely collection of stained glass and an extensive collection of pre-Columbian exhibits and classical objects. The Chinese jade is one of the museum's smaller holdings but quite unusual. A collection of contemporary art focuses on the African diaspora. American and European paintings, prints, and drawings round out the trip to the museum. Admission is $5 for adults and free for children ages 15 and under. Open Tues, Wed, Fri, and Sat 10 a.m. to 5 p.m.; Thurs 10 a.m. to 9 p.m.; Sun noon to 5 p.m.

Sarah P. Duke Gardens. 420 Anderson St.; (919) 684-3698; garden.duke.edu. Fifty-five acres of beautifully maintained gardens here range from the natural to meticulously sculpted landscapes. The walk through this spectacular garden leads visitors over bridges, through grottoes and court lawns, past waterfalls and pavilions. Such a wide variety of plants exists here that you'll find color in bloom practically all year long. More than 900 species of native plants can be found along 5 acres of wooded trails. Iris, roses, and formal lawns are featured through much of the garden while the Asiatic arboretum features a peaceful pond among more unusual horticultural holdings. Free. Hours for the grounds are 8 a.m. to dusk daily. The visitor center is open Mon through Fri 9 a.m. to 6 p.m., Sat 9 a.m. to 5 p.m., Sun noon to 5 p.m.

Durham Bulls Athletic Park. Blackwell Street; (919) 768-6000; durhambulls.com. The famous boys of summer play at this downtown stadium in what has become a Durham institution. The Durham Bulls are a Class AAA baseball affiliate of the Tampa Bay Rays

black wall street

In the early 1900s black-owned businesses prospered on Durham's Parrish Street. With a larger than average African-American population, Durham has played prominently in the struggle for Civil Rights and is noted for one of the first sit-ins that would later begin a much larger movement. Notably, Martin Luther King Jr. visited Parrish Street, where he coined his rallying cry, "Fill up the jails," during a meeting with a local minister.

and perhaps the best-known minor-league team in the country. The Bulls received national attention in 1987 with the release of the movie *Bull Durham*, starring Susan Sarandon, Kevin Costner, and Tim Robbins, filmed largely at the Bull's original 1926 stadium about a mile from here. In 2002 the team was featured in the film *The Rookie*, staring Dennis Quaid. The brick ballpark, also host to Duke University baseball games, is designed to be reflective of major-league stadiums including Camden Yards in Baltimore and Boston's Fenway Park.

Durham Performing Arts Center. 123 Vivian St.; (919) 680-2787; dpacnc.com. Known as D-PAC, this state-of-the-art, 2,800-seat theater in the former tobacco district hosts Broadway series plays, intimate concerts with big-name stars, and family performances. It opened in 2008 and quickly became one of the Triangle area's most popular performance venues. Among the many shows have been appearances by Neil Young, Bob Dylan, B.B. King, and Mickey Mouse.

Eno River State Park. 6101 Cole Mill Rd.; (919) 383-1686; ncparks.gov. Just minutes from Durham and the center of the Triangle is access to this secluded wilderness area. A rocky bottomed, swift-moving stream cuts through Durham and parts of surrounding counties for 33 miles. Ruins of mill sites, fords, and homes established by early settlers are still evident in this state park. The landscape is rugged but manageable for the less-skilled hiker. There are also access areas for canoes and kayaks, but no facilities for leasing them. Fishing is also permitted in the park with an appropriate state license. West Point on the Eno is a notable historic park and grist mill located on the southern bank of the river just off North Roxboro Street. Free. Open typically during daylight hours.

North Carolina Museum of Life and Science. 433 Murray Ave.; (919) 220-5429; life andscience.org. This great interactive museum features a range of exhibits from railroads to aerospace. Included is a display of the *Apollo 15* and *Enos*, the first US spacecraft to orbit Earth. The museum's nature center offers indoor and outdoor exhibits that allow visitors to observe a variety of wildlife and learn more about it through hands-on activities. Hold a box turtle or hear a rabbit's snappy heartbeat and peruse black bears, red wolves, and other large animals on display in attractive, well-maintained displays. A farmyard allows young and old to pet the animals, a tropical butterfly house is renowned statewide, and a half-mile-long dinosaur trail of life-size replicas offers a trip through the past. Young visitors are encouraged to conduct experiments in The Lab or build their own flying model in the Launch Lab. Admission is $23 for adults, $21 for seniors, $18 for ages 3 to 12. Open daily 10 a.m. to 5 p.m.

where to shop

American Tobacco Campus. 305 W. Pettigrew St.; (919) 433-1566; americantobacco.co. DPAC and the Durham Bulls stadium are located here and thus, the emergence of shopping and dining experiences. The Pettigrew Street address will place you in a convenient walking distance to much of its offerings.

Brightleaf Square. Gregson Street at Main Street; (919) 682-9229; historicbrightleaf.com. Renovated brick tobacco warehouses now house shops and restaurants in this downtown area. Clothing boutiques, a trendy bath and body shop, jewelry shops, and antiques can all be found in the district.

The Streets at Southpoint. 6910 Fayetteville Rd.; (919) 572-8808; streetsatsouthpoint .com. *USA Today* named this one of the top 10 super malls in the country. The massive contemporary complex features more than 100 stores, an IMAX theater, and 20 restaurants, anchored by Nordstrom, Macy's, and the Apple Store. Open Mon through Sat 10 a.m. to 9 p.m. and Sun noon to 7 p.m.

where to eat

Bull City Burger and Brewery. 107 Parrish St.; (919) 680-2333; bullcityburgerandbrewery .com. Bull City's own brews pair well with one of the more unusual list of burgers. Choose from the Over Easy Burger, the Green Monster, or the Joan Jett Bean Veggie Burger. $$.

Bullock's Bar-B-Que. 3330 Quebec Dr.; (919) 383-6202; bullocks-bbq.com. Check out the pictures of the famous folks, including actor Robert Duval and Presidents Joe Biden and Ronald Reagan, who have dined here on what is in the running for the best eastern barbecue in the state. Though it has changed locations, it is the oldest restaurant in Durham. Note that Bullocks is a cash-only operation. Open Tues through Sat 11:30 a.m. to 8 p.m. $$.

Dames Chicken and Waffles. 530 Foster St.; (919) 682-9235; dameschickenwaffles.com. Chicken and waffles gained notoriety during the Harlem Renaissance in the 1920s, but it didn't take that long to catch on here. The Durham location is one of four that serves the sweet and savory dish as well as other palate-pleasing comfort foods. $$.

Elmo's Diner. 776 9th St.; (919) 416-3823; elmosdiner.com. At one of the most popular spots in Durham, find everything from breakfast to burgers, shakes, and malts. It's also a prime location for breakfast or Sunday brunch. $–$$.

Foster's Market. 2694 Durham-Chapel Hill Blvd.; (919) 489-3944; fostersmarket.com. Sara Foster opened this as a specialty and take-out food store, but you can also grab a bite on the porch. Find soup, sandwiches, casseroles, and more here. Open daily 7:30 a.m. to 8 p.m. $$.

where to stay

21C Museum Hotel. 111 N. Corcoran St.; (919) 956-6700; 21cmuseumhotels.com/dur ham. The first such hotel in the Carolinas, 21C is a contemporary boutique hotel located in a restored building. It includes a contemporary art museum complete with docents and a collection of its own, as well as temporary special exhibitions. $$$.

Arrowhead Inn Bed and Breakfast. 106 Mason Rd.; (919) 477-8430; arrowheadinn.com. This is a AAA 4-diamond B&B on a plantation estate just outside the city limits. White columns stand tall beyond the manicured lawns and gardens that match the meticulous care offered by the well-appointed rooms. $$$.

Blooming Garden Inn. 513 Halloway St.; (919) 687-0801; bloominggardeninn.com. This simple, yellow, Queen Anne–style home has comfortable porches for relaxing immersed in mature southern perennial gardens. Period antiques adorn the home, which offers only 4 guest rooms. It is within walking distance of D-PAC and the ballpark. $$.

Washington Duke Inn and Golf Club. 3001 Cameron Blvd.; (919) 490-0999; washington dukeinn.com. This is a 4-star hotel with impeccable service and first-class amenities. Expect to pay for it. This is clearly the most desirable place to stay in Durham and one of the best resorts in the state. It's set among familiar pine trees and offers daily tea service. $$$.

day trip 03

raleigh, nc

>>> **go heels!:**
chapel hill, nc

chapel hill, nc

The home of the nation's oldest state university is noted for being an idyllic college town, just 7 miles away from its great basketball rival in the neighboring city of Durham. Campus amenities are full and varied, and the adjacent Franklin Street rounds out the experience with coffee shops, art galleries, pizza joints, and fine dining.

Chapel Hill was named after the New Hope Chapel, which stood on a hill at the crossing of two primary roads in the late 1700s. Construction of the university began in 1793 with the Old East building that still stands today. Delayed by the Revolutionary War, the university was chartered in 1789, and Hinton James arrived from a 170-mile walk to become the first student to enroll in this country's first state University. It would still be another 60 years before the town was incorporated.

Today part of the 16-campus University of North Carolina system, UNC–Chapel Hill is ranked among the great institutions of higher education in the nation. The campus covers 740 acres and provides education to more than 29,000 undergraduate, graduate, and professional students. While its offerings are typical of a college town, it's also a small town where you can sit at the soda fountain at Sutton's Drug Store or gaze at the stars of Morehead Planetarium. Visit the university, browse the shops, and have lunch or dinner at one of the many "institutions" that are now Chapel Hill landmarks. Planning ahead? Contact the Chapel Hill/Orange County Visitor Bureau at 501 W. Franklin St., Ste. 104 (888-968-2060;

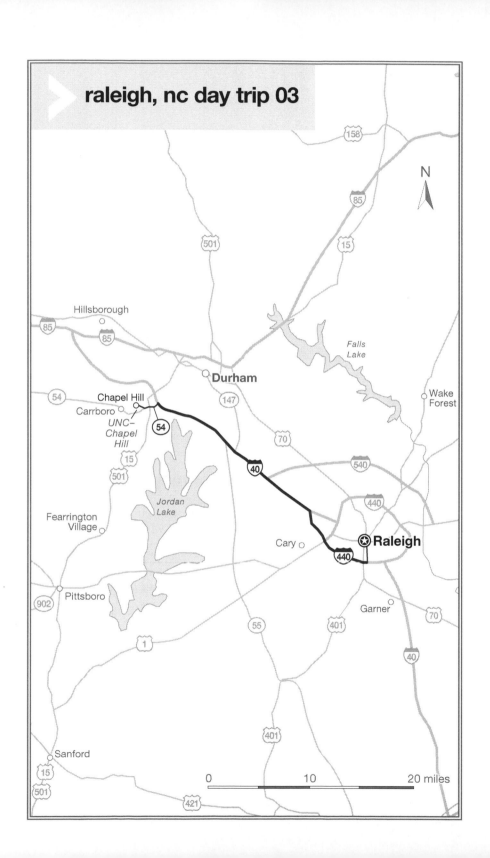

visitchapelhill.org). The UNC Visitor Center is located at 134 E. Franklin St. Contact folks there at (919) 962-1630; unc.edu/visitors.

getting there

From Durham, Chapel Hill is just minutes south on US 15/501, but from Raleigh, take I-40 west and take the exit for SR 54 (Raleigh Road).

where to go

Ackland Art Museum. South Columbia Street (off East Franklin Street on the university campus); (919) 966-5736; ackland.org. The permanent collection of more than 19,000 objects includes art from around the world and throughout the ages. The museum holds the most significant collection of Asian art in the state and one of the largest collections of works on paper in the Southeast. Long known for its strength in European painting and sculpture, the Ackland in recent years has focused on collecting contemporary art with a continuing emphasis on collecting works of Asian artists. More than half of the Ackland's space is reserved for changing exhibitions, so expect to see a dozen special exhibits each year. Free. Open Wed through Sat 10 a.m. to 5 p.m. and Sun 1 to 5 p.m. It is also open the second Friday of the month until 9 p.m.

Carolina Basketball Museum. 450 Skipper Bowles Dr.; (919) 843-9921; goheels.com. The story of Carolina's storied basketball program is told at this museum adjacent to the university basketball arena affectionately known as the Dean Dome, named for the late Dean Smith, the legendary men's basketball coach. Artifacts and highlight tapes of some of the greatest moments in the basketball program along with championship trophies, audiovisual displays, and exhibits are found throughout the facility. UNC's men's basketball team has won 6 NCAA championships, 32 Atlantic Coast Conference titles, and 21 conference tournament titles. Free. Open Tues through Fri 10 a.m. to 4 p.m. and Sat 9 a.m. to 1 p.m.

Charles Kuralt Learning Center. UNC School of Journalism; (919) 962-1204; hussman .unc.edu. The Kuralt Center is on the second floor of Carroll Hall on the UNC campus.

down on copperline

The James Taylor Bridge, named for the legendary singer-songwriter who grew up in Chapel Hill, runs over Morgan Creek on US 15/501. Taylor, whose father was dean of the UNC School of Medicine, references Morgan Creek in the song "Copperline." His song "Carolina in My Mind" is frequently sung (by just about everyone present) at UNC events including graduation ceremonies.

Much of Kuralt's TV work, including the famous *CBS News* "On the Road" episodes, has been digitized so that visitors can watch the programs using touch-screen technology. The contents of Kuralt's three-room office suite on West 57th Street in midtown Manhattan have also been re-created here. Open Tues and Thurs 2 to 4 p.m. and by appointment.

Horace Williams House. 610 E. Rosemary St.; (919) 942-7818; chapelhillpreservation .com. The only historic house in Chapel Hill open to the public, this facility features changing art exhibits in its octagon wing and throughout the house and hosts chamber music concerts on a regular basis. It is also the starting point for a self-guided tour that leads to a number of Chapel Hill's historic homes, as well as the oldest church in town. Free. Open Tues through Fri 10 a.m. to 4 p.m.; closed on major holidays and the first 2 weeks in August.

Morehead Planetarium & Science Center. 250 E. Franklin St.; (919) 549-6863; more headplanetarium.org. Once a training center of NASA astronauts, Morehead was the first planetarium in the South. Morehead Planetarium has been teaching space sciences education since 1950 and has been expanded in recent years into a full science center. The planetarium features public shows in the full dome digital theater, educational exhibits, the Rotunda Portrait Gallery, the Infinity gift shop, and outside facing Franklin Street a giant sundial rose garden. Admission is $11.95 for adults; $9.95 for children and $10.95 for senior citizens, and students. Building hours are Tues through Thurs 10 a.m. to 3:30 p.m., Fri and Sat 10 a.m. to 3:30 p.m. and 6:30 to 9 p.m., Sun 1 to 4:30 p.m. Public planetarium hours are typically Fri evening, Sat, and Sun.

North Carolina Botanical Garden. 100 Old Mason Farm Rd.; (919) 962-0522; ncbg.unc .edu. The largest natural botanical garden in the Southeast, the North Carolina Botanical Garden consists of 600 acres of preserved land, nature trails, carnivorous plant collections, and aquatic and herb gardens. Collections of plants indigenous to North Carolina and the Southeast are arranged by habitat in simulated natural settings. Playwright and Pulitzer Prize winner Paul Green's restored cabin, moved here from a site nearby, is also at the garden. A LEED-certified visitor center constructed of wood from the property hosts temporary exhibits of paintings, quilts, and other media. Free. Open year-round, Mon through Fri 8 a.m. to 5 p.m., Sat 9 a.m. to 5 p.m., Sun 1 to 5 p.m., and to 6 p.m. on weekends during summer months.

North Carolina Collection Gallery. UNC–Chapel Hill Louis Round Wilson Library, South Road; (919) 962-1172; library.unc.edu/wilson/gallery. The world's largest collection of resource materials related to Sir Walter Raleigh is here, including a document signed by Queen Elizabeth I in 1570. Located in one of three general libraries on campus, the North Carolina Collection is a treasure trove of historical material related to the state and the Southern Manuscripts Department. There are even obscure objects, such as a plaster death mask of Napoleon Bonaparte. Open Mon through Fri 9 a.m. to 5 p.m., Sat 9 a.m. to 1 p.m., Sun 1 to 5 p.m. Free.

where to shop

Carr Mill Mall. 200 N. Greensboro St., Carrboro; (919) 942-8669. Located just beyond walking distance from campus, Carr Mill Mall is a beautifully restored textile mill, built in 1899 and listed on the National Register of Historic Places. It houses many specialty stores, restaurants, a chocolate shop, a toy store, boutiques, and galleries. Also here is Weaver Street Market, a co-op of local farmers who bring together products at a continuously operating farmers' market.

Chapel Hill Downtown. 133 W. Franklin St. Both East and West Franklin Streets and East and West Rosemary Streets offer mostly locally owned and independent shops, including the Shrunken Head, Johnny T-Shirt, and Julian's, opened by the father of designer Alexander Julian in 1942, as well as a wealth of restaurants.

where to eat

Breadmen's Restaurant. 324 W. Rosemary St.; (919) 967-7110; breadmens.com. Popular with the college crowd that's on a budget, this is the place to get breakfast anytime, day or night, including specialty omelets. It's also a good place to get a big burger, sandwiches, fresh salads, and homemade soups and desserts. Open daily 7 a.m. to 9 p.m. $–$$.

Carolina Brewery. 460 W. Franklin St.; (919) 942-1800; carolinabrewery.com. Chapel Hill's first microbrewery and restaurant serves contemporary American cuisine and handcrafted beers, which also play a role as ingredients in many dishes. Live music is presented every Thurs. Open Mon through Thurs 11 a.m. to 11 p.m. , Fri and Sat 11a.m. to midnight, Sun 11 a.m. to 11 p.m. $$.

Carolina Coffee Shop. 138 E. Franklin St.; (919) 942-6875; carolinacoffeeshop.com. A place for quiet conversation, this Chapel Hill landmark established in 1922 has wooden church-pew booths where you can order a cup of coffee or a brew as well as a meal. Open daily 8 a.m. to 3 p.m. $$.

Lantern. 423 W. Franklin St.; (919) 969-8846; lanternrestaurant.com. Opened in 2002, Lantern is still new by Chapel Hill standards, but it quickly took a place of prominence on the local culinary scene and is holding strong; owner Andrea Reusing won a Best Chef Award from James Beard in 2011. Asian cuisine produced with locally found fare is the mainstay on the menu. Open Mon through Sat 5:30 to 10 p.m. $$$.

Mama Dip's Kitchen. 408 W. Rosemary St.; (919) 942-5837; mamadips.com. Until her death in 2018 cookbook author Mama Dip (Mildred Council) had been preparing down-home southern food since she was 9. She servied In Chapel Hill since the 1980 and now her family carries on the tradition. Her restaurant offers an abundance of traditional American food, especially vegetables, and the most popular menu item: fried chicken that can't be beat. Open Mon through Sat 8 a.m. to 9:30 p.m., Sun 8 a.m. to 9 p.m. $$.

Mediterranean Deli. 410 West Franklin St.; (919) 967-2666; mediterraneandeli.com. When Jamil Kadoura and his wife Angel opened their first deli in Chapel Hill in 1992 there were only 12 seats, now it is one of the most popular restaurants in town with huge offerings that include their very own gluten-free pita bread. $$.

Top of the Hill Restaurant & Brewery. 100 E. Franklin St.; (919) 929-8676; topofthehill .com. Overlooking downtown Chapel Hill from a large, third-floor outdoor patio, Top of the Hill offers casual, upscale dining and is a favorite among students and alumni alike. The restaurant continually wins "Best of Triangle" awards, including Best Restaurant in Chapel Hill, Best Microbrew, and Best Outdoor Deck. There's live music Thursday evenings. TOPO not only focuses on farm-fresh ingredients and its own brews, it also produces its own brands of vodka, whiskey, and gin. Open daily 11 a.m. to 2 a.m. $$–$$$.

where to stay

The Carolina Inn. 211 Pittsboro St.; (919) 933-2001 or (800) 962-8519; carolinainn.com. A historic, AAA 4-diamond, 184-room hotel, the Carolina Inn is the epitome of gracious southern hospitality and elegance. Located near UNC's fraternity row, 1 block from downtown shops and restaurants, the inn has many amenities, including a fitness center, room service, nightly turndown service, antiques, and a spectacular restaurant. The Carolina Inn is listed on the National Register of Historic Places and hosts many special events including an annual show of artistically produced birdhouses. $$$.

Graduate. 311 West Franklin St.; (929) 442-9000; graduatehotels.com. The former Franklin Hotel was completely renovated as a Graduate Hotel, a brand being introduced in college towns across the country. Rooms are decorated In Carolina Blue and pay homage to some of the University's most famous students, including Michael Jordan and Mia Hamm as well as campus landmarks like Old Well. $$.

The Siena Hotel. 1505 E. Franklin St.; (919) 929-4000 or (800) 223-7379; sienahotel.com. This elegant boutique hotel offers exceptional service amid fine antique furnishings. Classic Italian cuisine is served in Il Palio, the state's only AAA 4-diamond Italian restaurant. Rates include a full buffet breakfast and nightly turndown service. $$$.

day trip 04

raleigh, nc

going green:
greensboro, nc

greensboro, nc

With a bustling business district, the city of Greensboro is where you will find the International Civil Rights Center and Museum, influences from Quaker settlement, and a whole new series of places to enjoy the arts, restaurants, and shopping. The Saura and Keyauwee Indians were the earliest known inhabitants of the region, and Greensboro has had a unique role in American history from the Revolutionary War to the Underground Railroad and to the sit-ins that helped launch the national Civil Rights movement. Germans, Quakers of Welsh and English descent, and Scotch-Irish from the northern colonies were the first European settlers in the Greensboro area beginning around 1749. In 1774 a log courthouse and jail were built in a place called Guilford Courthouse, the site of a fierce Revolutionary War battle on March 15, 1781. The city was named in honor of Major General Nathanael Greene, who led the defensive that day to thwart a redcoat invasion.

Prior to the Civil War, Quaker antislavery advocate Vestal Coffin and his cousin Levi operated an underground railroad here to move slaves out of the state. During the Civil War, Greensboro was both a storehouse and a railroad center for the Confederacy, a vital source of supplies and troops for Robert E. Lee's Army of Northern Virginia. Civilian refugees and wounded soldiers were transported and sheltered here. Greensboro became the seat of the Confederacy on April 11, 1865, when Confederate President Jefferson Davis arrived here after Lee's surrender at Appomattox, to discuss the military situation of General Joseph E.

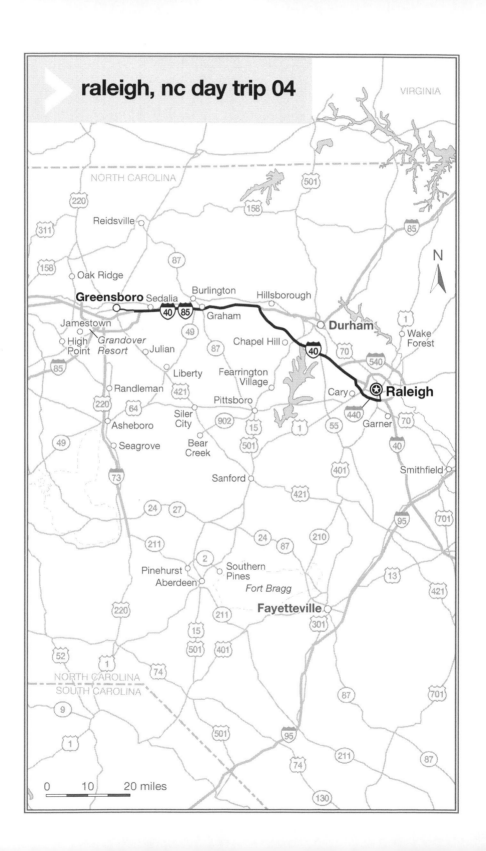

raleigh, nc day trip 04

Johnston and the weakened Army of Tennessee. Here Johnston advised Davis to enter into surrender negotiations with William Tecumseh Sherman. These negotiations led to Johnston's surrender to Sherman on April 26, 1865, at Bennett Place near Durham.

To get a jump on the Greensboro experience, contact the Greensboro Area Convention & Visitor Bureau, 2411 W. Gate City Blvd.; (336) 274-2282; visitgreensboronc.com.

getting there

Greensboro is an easy 90-minute drive from Raleigh that actually begins on I-40, which merges with I-85 just beyond Chapel Hill.

where to go

Blandwood Mansion & Carriage House. 400 W. McGee St.; (336) 272-5003; preservatoingreensboro.org. An elegant 19th-century farmhouse with Italian villa addition, Blandwood was home to prominent onetime North Carolina governor John Motley Morehead. The 1844 addition by renowned architect Alexander Jackson Davis contributed to Blandwood's designation as a National Historic Landmark. The addition featuring stucco walls and tower is considered the oldest existing Italianate structure in the country. Today Preservation Greensboro and the Blandwood Guild operate it as a museum. The carriage house is typically used for events. Admission is $8 for adults, $7 for seniors, and $5 for children under age 12. Open Tues through Sat 11 a.m. to 4 p.m., Sun 2 to 5 p.m.

Carolina Theatre. 310 S. Greene St.; (336) 333-2605; carolinatheatre.com. First opened in 1927, this restored vaudeville theater listed on the National Register of Historic Places was the first commercial building in the state equipped with air-conditioning. Today it serves as one of Greensboro's principal performing arts centers, showcasing the city's ballet, its community theater, and opera company. It also hosts comedians, musicians, and other small acts.

Charlotte Hawkins Brown Memorial State Historic Site. 6136 Burlington Rd., Sedalia; (336) 449-4846; historicsites.nc.gov. Located just outside Greensboro, this is North Carolina's first official historic site to honor an African American and a woman. The site is the former location of the Palmer Institute, a preparatory school for African Americans established by Brown from 1902 to 1961. Exhibits, both archival and audiovisual, tell the story of education of African Americans. Free. Open Tues through Sat 9 a.m. to 5 p.m.

The Greensboro Arboretum. Near Wendover Avenue at West Market Street and Starmount Drive; (336) 373-2199; greensborobeautiful.org. Fourteen labeled plant collections, special garden displays, and distinctive features are contained within a 17-acre portion of Lindley Park. An interesting combination of conifers, wetland plants, shrubs, and small trees provides year-round interest. Free. Open daily sunrise to sunset.

Greensboro Children's Museum. 220 N. Church St.; (336) 574-2898; gcmuseum.com. Elementary school students get their hands full at one of the state's first and best children's museums. Young visitors can swing by the kid-size ATM at the bank, drive a fire truck, sound the siren on a police car, and bring a DC-9 jet in for a landing. Kids can help with a house under construction or deliver the mail in a US Postal Jeep. "Our Town" is complete with a grocery store, bank, and theater, and early childhood exhibit areas. There is also an edible schoolyard with a teaching kitchen. Admission is $10 for anyone over age 1. Open Tues through Sat 9 a.m. to 5 p.m., Fri to 8 p.m., and Sun 1 to 5 p.m.

Greensboro Cultural Center at LeBauer Park. 200 N. Davie St.; (336) 373-4678; greensboro-nc.gov. Located in and around a 4-story building adjacent to this city-maintained park is a showplace with 12 visual and performing arts organizations, art galleries, rehearsal halls, a sculpture garden, a privately operated restaurant, Europa Bar & Cafe with outdoor cafe-style seating, and an outdoor amphitheater. It includes the African American Atelier (336-333-6885) that features original artwork by local African-American artists; the Green Hill Center for North Carolina Art (336-333-7460) with works in glass, ceramics, jewelry, and painting; the Guilford Native American Art Gallery (336-273-6605); and the Center for Visual Artists. Open Mon through Fri 8 a.m. to 10 p.m., Sat 9 a.m. to 6:30 p.m., and Sun 1 to 6:30 p.m.

Greensboro Historical Museum. 130 Summit Ave.; (336) 373-2043; greensborohistory .org. Stories of Piedmont people and events come alive in 12 galleries and 2 restored houses that make up the Greensboro Historical Museum. Accounts told here include the 1960 Greensboro Civil Rights sit-ins, Guilford native Dolley Madison's lasting legacy as first lady, and the popular short stories written by O. Henry (real name: William Sidney Porter) who was born in Greensboro. Displayed are 20th-century photography, a Model T, a world-class collection of Civil War firearms, and furniture created by Piedmont craftsmen. Stroll through a historic cemetery and check out the merchandise of an old-fashioned general store. Free. Open Tues through Sat 10 a.m. to 5 p.m., Sun 2 to 5 p.m.

Guilford Courthouse National Military Park. 2332 New Garden Rd.; (336) 288-1776; nps.gov/guco. More than 200 acres are dedicated to the March 15, 1781, battle that occurred here. That day, American Major General Nathanael Greene deployed 4,400 rebels in resistance to a redcoat invasion of North Carolina under Lord Cornwallis. Though Cornwallis held the site, he lost a quarter of his army, leading to defeat at Yorktown 7 months later. Twenty-eight monuments of soldiers, statesmen, and patriots of the American Revolution are here as memorial to those who gave their lives for American freedom. Park activities include a self-guided cell phone driving tour. In the visitor center are a dramatic 30-minute, live-action film, an animated battle map program, and information-packed museum exhibits featuring original Revolutionary War weaponry and artifacts. The park also provides paved walking trails and a bookstore. Free. Open daily 8:30 a.m. to 5 p.m. Memorial Day weekend through Labor Day. The rest of the year it is open Tues through Sat 8:30 a.m. to 5 p.m. Closed New Year's Day, Thanksgiving, and Christmas.

The International Civil Rights Center & Museum. 134 S. Elm St.; (336) 274-9199; sitinmovement.org. Though sit-ins had occurred in other American cities prior to February 1960, the four black students from North Carolina A&T State University are credited with starting a movement when they walked into the Greensboro Woolworth and ordered lunch. Their action started a national sit-in movement that literally changed the country. Today that store has been converted into a center and museum dedicated to telling the story of the Civil Rights movement. Central among archival displays is the lunch counter where those students and their classmates sat in peaceful protest over segregation, which was a way of life in the 1960s South. Through 90-minute guided tours, visitors begin to understand the history and the effects of segregation from 18th- and 19th-century slavery to the Jim Crow South. Three levels of exhibits document the efforts of those students and others who contributed to change a society. Admission is $15 for adults, $10 for students and seniors, $8 for children ages 6 to 12. Open Mon through Sat 10 a.m. to 6 p.m.

Natural Science Center. 4301 Lawndale Dr.; (336) 288-3769; greensboroscience.org. Roam through the Dinosaur Gallery and learn about gems and minerals at this hands-on museum, zoo, and planetarium. Visit snakes and amphibians in the Jaycee Herpetarium and explore Kids Alley. The science museum also has space for national touring exhibits. A small zoo with tigers, jaguars, bears, crocodiles, primates, a farm petting zoo, and many other animals is also open for visiting. The Wiseman Aquarium was added to the already sprawling facility in more recent years. Admission is $19.50 for adults, $17.50 for children ages 2 to 13 and $18.50 for seniors. Open Mon through Sat 9 a.m. to 5 p.m., Sun 12:30 to 5 p.m. The Animal Park is open Mon through Sat 10 a.m. to 4 p.m. and Sun 12:30 to 4 p.m.

Tanger Family Bicentennial Garden & David Caldwell Historic Park. 1105 Hobbs Rd., just north of Friendly Avenue; (336) 373-2199; greensborobeautiful.org. This beautiful garden features flowering trees, shrubs, annual displays, and the Bog Garden, a marsh of ferns, bamboo, and other plants. The adjacent park is named in honor of Caldwell, who served as a local minister and educator and owned much of this land.

Weatherspoon Art Museum. Spring Garden and Tate Streets; (336) 334-5770; weatherspoon.uncg.edu. This fine museum on the campus of UNC–Greensboro houses a nationally recognized collection. Within 6 galleries of open dramatic space and a sculpture courtyard, the museum has a collection of more than 5,000 paintings, sculptures, drawings, prints and photographs, and objects in miscellaneous media. Highlights include the Dillard Collection of art on paper and the Cone Collection of prints and bronzes by Henri Matisse, Picasso, and others. Free. Open Tues, Wed, Fri and Sat 10 a.m. to 5 p.m., Thurs 10 a.m. to 8 p.m.

Wet 'n Wild Emerald Pointe Water Park. 3910 S. Holden Rd., I-85, exit 121; (336) 852-9721 or (800) 555-5900; emeraldpointe.com. The largest water park in the Carolinas and one of the top 10 in the US offers more than 35 rides and attractions. Thunder Bay, 1 of only 4 tsunami pools in the country, makes massive, perfect waves. Dr. Von Dark's Tunnel of Terror drops 40 feet, spinning riders 360 degrees in total darkness. Traveling with younger children? Head to Happy Harbor and Splash Island. Tickets are $34.99 for those under 48 inches and $44.99 for those 48 inches or taller. Call or log on to their website for seasonal hours of operation.

where to shop

Four Seasons Town Centre. I-40 at High Point Road/Koury Boulevard; (336) 292-0171; shopfourseasons.com. The center's 3 levels include more than 200 specialty stores and eateries, as well as anchors Belk, Dillard's, and JC Penney. Stop by for a bite to eat in the food court, or enjoy free and regularly scheduled entertainment in the performing arts amphitheater. Open Mon through Sat 10 a.m. to 9 p.m., Sun 12 to 6 p.m.

Friendly Center. Friendly Avenue near the Wendover Avenue Overpass; (336) 292-2789; friendlycenter.com. This open-air shopping center, originally established in 1957, isn't as slick as modern malls, but it has a steady list of tenants and customers. Shops include Loft, Chico's, Old Navy, Banana Republic, Victoria's Secret, Gap, and anchors such as Belk, Macy's, and Sears. Also located here is a multiplex theater, the Grande. Friendly Center boasts several restaurants, including Harpers and the ever-popular Jay's Deli. Open Mon through Sat 10 a.m. to 9 p.m. and Sun 1 to 6 p.m.

Greensboro Farmers' Curb Market. 501 Yanceyville St.; (336) 373-2402; gsofarmers market.org. Homegrown vegetables, fruits, and other produce are only half the story of this farmers' market; fresh-cut herbs and flowers, baked goods, pottery, and crafts also are available. And the Piedmont Blues Preservation Society schedules regular performances here. Open Jan through Apr, Sat 8 to 11 a.m. May through Dec, Wed 7:30 to 11:30 a.m. p.m. and Sat 6 a.m. to noon.

Old Greensborough & the Downtown Historic District. 122 N. Elm St.; (336) 379-0060; downtowngreensboro.net. Mixed into this revitalized, century-old commercial, residential, and industrial district are more than a dozen antiques, art, and other shops and restaurants. A free guide is available at most merchant locations, the Greensboro Area Convention & Visitor Bureau, the Greensboro Historical Museum, and the Downtown Greensboro Incorporated office. The district is located in and around South Elm Street from Market Street to Lee Street.

Piedmont Triad Farmers' Market. 2914 Sandy Ridge Rd.; (336) 605-9157; triadfarmers market.com. Get to know some of the South's friendliest people while shopping for local Piedmont fruits, vegetables, flowers, baked goods, jams, honey, crafts, and more. Make sure you visit the garden center and Moose Cafe while you're there. Open daily 7 a.m. to 6 p.m.

State Street Station. Between North Elm and Church Streets, just north of Wendover Avenue; (336) 275-8586. Stroll through this relaxed neighborhood of 35 unique shops, restaurants, and boutiques housed in elegantly refurbished 1920s vintage buildings. Lots of locally owned shops, a consignment store, and jewelry shops are all located here.

where to eat

Barn Dinner Theatre. 120 Stage Coach Trail; (336) 292-2211 or (800) 668-1764; barndinner.com. This is one of Greensboro's oldest entertainment traditions. Since the 1960s it has produced popular Broadway-style plays and traditional buffets. Performances are presented seasonally throughout the year. Dinner is served on a buffet that features ham and roast beef along with a selection of veggies and sides. Matinees are offered on Tues and Sun while evening performances are presented on Fri and Sat. $$$.

The Green Valley Grill. 622 Green Valley Rd.; (336) 854-2015; greenvalleygrill.com. The owners refer to this grill, adjacent to the O. Henry Hotel, as "informally elegant zestful dining." Patrons enjoy internationally elegant dining with an old-world influence. Changing menus feature regional European recipes that may be from Provence one month and Tuscany the next. Open for breakfast Mon through Fri 7 to 10 a.m. and for brunch Sat and Sun 7:30 a.m. to 3 p.m.; for lunch Mon through Thurs 11a.m. to 2 p.m., Fri 11 a.m. to 3:30 p.m. and for dinner Mon through Thurs 5 to 10 p.m., Fri and Sat 3:30 to 10:30 p.m.1 and Sun 3:30 to 9 p.m.$$–$$$.

Liberty Oak. 100 W. Washington St.; (336) 273-7057; libertyoakgso.com. Liberty Oak pays homage to a 200-year old 78-foot tall tree that once stood near here. Rated 4 stars by Greensboro's *News & Record*, Liberty Oak offers casual elegance, a changing menu, extensive wines by the glass, and outdoor dining. Liberty Oak specializes in fish from trout to tuna. Open Mon through Sat starting at 11 a.m. $–$$.

Lucky 32. 1421 Westover Ter.; (336) 370-0707; lucky32.com. Changing menus every month or so, Lucky 32 offers regional American cuisine focused largely on southern tastes with locally available foods such as its famous collard greens. A Lucky 32 is also located in Cary. Open daily for lunch and dinner, Sun for brunch. $$–$$$.

Natty Greene's Pub & Brewing Company. 345 S. Elm St.; (336) 274-1373; nattygreenes .com. Philly cheesesteak is made all over, but this is the only place you can find an Elm Street Philly. Grinders, burgers, crab cakes, and the like fill up this filling menu. A dozen or more handcrafted brews, some of North Carolina's best-selling, are also available for sampling. Open daily 11 a.m. to midnight. $$.

Yum Yum Better Ice Cream Co. 1219 Spring Garden St.; (336) 272-8284. This 100-year-old Greensboro institution located near the UNC campus serves ice cream and hot dogs, all the way with chili, slaw, and onions if you like. It's still operated by the same family that opened it, and they still only take cash. Open Mon and Sat 10:30 a.m. to 5:30 p.m. and Tues through Fri 10 a.m. to 10 p.m. $.

where to stay

Biltmore Greensboro Hotel. 111 W. Washington St.; (336) 272-3474 or (800) 332-0303; thebiltmoregreensborohotel.com. Accommodations at this unique European boutique hotel, conveniently located in the heart of Greensboro, include a complimentary deluxe continental breakfast. The interior is warm, decorated with historic portraits and furnishings. There are only 26 rooms so service is attentive. $$$.

Grandover Resort & Conference Center. One Thousand Club Rd.; (336) 294-1800 or (800) 472-6301; grandover.com. Located on 1,500 spectacular acres just off I-85 is this AAA 4-diamond resort with 247 guest rooms in an 11-story tower. Though built in the last century and contemporary by design, it is intended to represent an old-world European castle. Amenities include spa facilities, a tennis complex, racquetball courts, an indoor/outdoor swimming pool, 5 food and beverage outlets, and lush gardens, as well as the rolling terrain of the resort's top-rated golf courses. $$$.

O. Henry Hotel. 624 Green Valley Rd.; (800) 965-8259; ohenryhotel.com. Located near Friendly Center, the stately AAA 4-diamond hotel evokes the grandeur of the original O. Henry, which stood in downtown Greensboro from 1919 to 1978. The new hotel was designed, as were hotels at the turn of the 20th century, to be a part of the community and blend into its surroundings. A great restaurant, the Green Valley Grill, and lounge are on the premises. $$$.

The Proximity Hotel. 704 Green Valley Rd.; (336) 379-8200 or (800) 379-8200; proximityhotel.com. A day trip to Greensboro can help the planet, too. The Proximity was the country's first LEED Platinum hotel—the US Green Building Council's highest recognition in the Leadership in Energy and Environmental Design (LEED) rating system, the nationally accepted benchmark for the design, construction, and operation of high-performance green buildings. The hotel received a 4-diamond AAA rating because of its custom furnishings and detail, commissioned art, and innovative, stylish design complemented by abundant natural light and carefully selected, green construction materials. $$$.

worth more time

Mendenhall Plantation. 603 W. Main St., Jamestown; (336) 454-3819. A bottomless wagon, used to transport slaves on the Underground Railroad, is housed and is on exhibit in the barn at Jamestown's Mendenhall Plantation, which in the 19th century became a symbolic opposition to slavery from an otherwise quiet people. The 1811 house is central to the complex of buildings that was the home of Quaker Richard Mendenhall. Much of the house, including the kitchen, remains as it was when the Mendenhalls lived here, with an obvious absence of slave quarters. One addition was made in 1840 to accommodate the growing family. While the only evidence that the wagon was used in transporting slaves from North Carolina to Ohio are the stories passed down from generation to generation, there is other evidence that Mendenhall also hid slaves in the basement of the home. Tours are conducted Tues through Fri 11 a.m. to 3 p.m., Sat 1 to 4 p.m., and Sun 2 to 4 p.m. They cost $5 for adults and $2 for children, students, and seniors.

day trip 05

raleigh, nc

>>>

primates & pottery:
asheboro, nc; seagrove, nc

Just about 90 minutes from Raleigh is North Carolina's outstanding natural-setting zoo and, just south of that, a spectacular collection of potteries that have turned this area into something of a tourist mecca. The area is located in the Uwharrie Mountains, rugged terrain and among the oldest mountains on earth sliced and over time shaped by the Pee Dee and Yadkin Rivers. Asheboro is smack-dab in the middle of the state, centrally located between the mountains and coast and Virginia and South Carolina. Unlike many a tourist area, however, it feels comfortable and welcoming. The 1,450-acre zoo could be a day trip unto itself, but Randolph County is clearly an area that's worth getting to know. Not only is it home to the king of the jungle, but it's also where the King of NASCAR, Richard Petty, grew up. In addition to new restaurants and other recreational opportunities, found here are one of the South's finest collections of vintage Harley-Davidson motorcycles and the North Carolina Aviation Museum, home to vintage military aircraft. The aptly named website heartofnorthcarolina.com can help you navigate these hills, roads, and skies.

asheboro, nc

The rolling hills of the Uwharrie National Forest were once hunting grounds for the Keyauwee Indians, who settled here 300 years ago as noted by celebrated explorer John Lawson in 1701. Strangely, it feels like the mountain country of the western part of the state, but geographically speaking it's technically on a plateau, resulting in a somewhat milder climate.

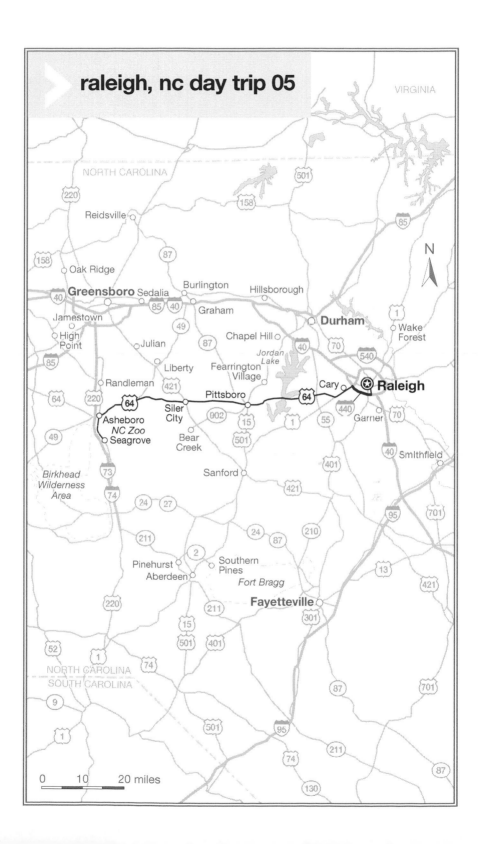

This made it a perfect locale for the state-run zoological park, which prides itself on allowing exotic animals to roam as if in the wild.

getting there

Pointing the car west on US 64 in Raleigh takes the driver across Jordan Lake, through—or around—the town of Pittsboro, and to Asheboro in less than 90 minutes.

where to go

American Classic Motorcycle Museum. 1170 US 64 West; (336) 629-9564. The American Classic Motorcycle Museum is also a working Harley-Davidson dealership and repair shop. Composed here is one of the South's finest collections of antique and classic Harley-Davidson motorcycles. More than 45 bikes in all date from 1936 to 1978. Free. Open Mon 6 a.m. to 2 p.m., Tues through Fri 6 a.m. to 5:30 p.m., and Sat 6 a.m. to 4 p.m.

Birkhead Wilderness Area. Access areas located at 3977 Lassiter Mill Rd. and 3091 Tot Hill Farm Rd.; (800) 626-2672. These 5,160 acres of the Uwharrie National Forest are the only ones in the Piedmont designated as a federal wilderness area. Formed by ancient volcanoes, the Uwharries are among the oldest mountains in the world. Centuries of erosion have left rock outcroppings scattered throughout the old-growth hardwood forest. Leading from the access areas are trailheads through the forest. From three trails along sparkling streams, hikers can spot foundations, chimneys, walls, abandoned mines, and other archaeological evidence of historic homesteads and even Native American settlements.

North Carolina Aviation Museum & Hall of Fame. 2222-6 Pilotsview Rd., Asheboro Regional Airport; (336) 625-0170; ncamhof.com. This museum, created for the preservation of military aircraft, is home to an impressive collection of airworthy vintage military aircraft. Featured is a 1941 Piper Flitfire flown by Orville Wright. The museum also houses exhibits of World War II military uniforms and a collection of World War II–era newspaper features. Admission is $10 for adults, $8 for seniors and $5 for students. Open Thurs through Sun 11 a.m. to 5 p.m.

North Carolina Zoological Park. 4401 Zoo Pkwy.; (336) 879-7000 or (800) 488-0444; nczoo.org. Founded in 1974 as a natural-habitat zoo, largely free of the obvious bars and fences that typically separate humans from exhibits, the NC Zoo is one of the first American zoos within which horticulturalists, zoologists, and designers work together closely to develop exhibits that leave animals as free to roam as they might be living on the American plains or African desert. The first permanent exhibit was the Forest Edge, home to zebra, ostrich, and giraffe, which opened in 1979 and exists today much as it did then. Today zoo guests travel from African habitats through North America, zoologically speaking, in just a few hours. Big animals such as elephants and rhinos highlight the African exhibits, not to be outdone by lions, gorillas, and other primates. As guests travel through North America, polar bears and playful otters aim to please the crowd as alligators linger in a swamp. Other exhibits allow visitors to get up close and personal with snakes and other reptiles.

An internal tram is available to transport visitors between exhibit areas, but most animals are not visible from the trams. You can enter or exit by either the North American or African gate; a shuttle bus transports visitors to the parking areas. Zoo officials recommend taking a minimum of 5 hours to explore all that the park offers at a comfortable pace. The zoo is open daily 9 a.m. to 5 p.m. Apr 1 to Oct 31, daily 9 a.m. to 4 p.m. Nov 1 to Mar 31, and closed Christmas Day. There are additional hours during special events and reduced hours during inclement weather. Admission is $15 for adults, $13 for seniors, and $11 for children ages 2 to 12.

Pisgah Covered Bridge. 6925 Covered Bridge Road. Take exit 49, just south of Asheboro off US 220 Business. Look for the historical markers that will direct you to the covered bridge, one of only two in North Carolina, which was built around 1910 at a cost of $40. Hiking trails, picnic tables, and parking are available. The bridge crosses the West Fork Branch of the Little River. Free.

Richland Creek Zip Line & Canopy Tours. 2728 Fairview Farms; (336) 629-9440; richlandcreekzipline.com. Though zip lines are popping up throughout the Carolinas, this is one of the more authentic canopy tours along Richland Creek and Purgatory Mountain. Four skywalks and 14 zip lines make up this wild ride. Cost is $40 per person. Open daily 9 a.m. to 6 p.m.

where to shop

Collector's Antique Mall. 211 Sunset Ave.; (336) 629-8105; collectorsantiquemall.com. More than 125 dealers offer antiques and collectibles in more than 35,000 square feet of retail space in the downtown antiques district of Asheboro. It occupies the former B.C. Moore Department Store and Big Bear Supermarket buildings. Open Mon through Sat 9:30 a.m. to 4 p.m.

where to eat

Flying Pig. 208 Sunset Ave.; (336) 610-3737; theflyingpigasheboro.com. The Flying Pig has quickly become the place to go in Asheboro for evening fun. The pub also serves sandwiches and wood-fired pizza. Give the spicy, fried angry okra (really fried jalapeños) a try. Open Mon, Thurs, and Fri 5 p.m. to 1 a.m.; Sat and Sun noon to 1 a.m. $$.

Heritage Diner. 1172 US Highway 64 W.; (336) 629-0853; Located in the level below the motorcycle museum, the heritage diner carries on the motorcycle theme. Breakfast is the specialty of the house, but sandwiches and other homecooked selections are available for lunch. Open Mon through Sat 5 a.m. to 2 p.m.

The Table Farmhouse Bakery. 139 S. Church St.; (336) 736-8628; thetablefarmbakery .com. Cookies and pastry made this place an instant hit in Asheboro when it opened in 2013, but sandwiches made from bread baked right here receive just as much praise. Pimento cheese, a Cuban, or healthier selections of salads and grain bowls make this as nice a stop for lunch as it is for breakfast. Open Tues through Wed 7 a.m. to 2:30 p.m., Thurs and Fri 7 a.m. to 10 p.m., and Sat. 7:30 a.m. to 10 p.m. $$

where to stay

Hunter's Run Lodge Bed & Breakfast. 1245 Mount Tabor Church Rd.; (336) 302-4107 or (336) 629-3074; bbonline.com/nc/huntersrun. Located just outside Asheboro is a traditional country inn on 68 acres of rolling green hills. Stroll by the lake, wet a line, sit by the fireplace, or unwind in a Jacuzzi. A stay here also features a complimentary continental breakfast on weekdays and a full breakfast on weekends. $$.

seagrove, nc

Whether it's a serving platter or piece of art you seek, you can find it in Seagrove. This town of 300 has garnered international acclaim for its potteries that produce both pragmatic and museum-quality pieces. Some crystalline-glaze works go for thousands of dollars while others give the beginning collector a good entry price. The more than 100 area potters have established other long-standing traditions and widely recognized styles. The historically based work of potter Mary Ferrell has been featured on the sets of films such as *The Patriot* and *Cold Mountain.* Art pottery produced at Johnston & Gentithes Studios is anything but historical. Their work, once exhibited at the Smithsonian, is contemporary, whimsical, unpredictable, and reflective of literature and nature. And there are many more.

The day-tripper is encouraged not only to get to know the pottery here, but also the people with the hands from which it is born. The history of Seagrove pottery dates to the Revolutionary War, when English and German immigrants made utilitarian pottery due to the quality of local clay. These practical pieces lost popularity, and the craft dwindled as the sale of mass-produced housewares grew. Potters began producing more artistic pieces in the 1920s, but their popularity would not catch on until the 1980s, when a group of local potters founded the North Carolina Museum of Traditional Pottery and organized the Seagrove Pottery Festival, an annual event still held each year on the weekend before Thanksgiving.

getting there

From Asheboro, take US 220 Alternate south until you reach the famed 705 in Seagrove. You'll come upon a handful of potteries en route. Departing directly from Raleigh, US 1 going south to US 15/501 to SR 22/24/27 will lead to the old Plank Road, which becomes SR 705. This route will take about 90 minutes.

where to go

Museum of North Carolina Traditional Pottery. 127 E. Main St.; (336) 873-7887. A good first stop on a trip to Seagrove; pick up maps and learn about different pottery before heading out to the shops. Free. Open Mon through Sat 9:30 a.m. to 3:30 p.m.

North Carolina Pottery Center. 233 East Ave.; (336) 873-8430; ncpotterycenter.org. Seagrove pottery is showcased along with permanent displays of North Carolina pottery, Native American pieces, historical items, and changing exhibits. On Saturdays a local potter is on site doing live demonstrations. Admission is $2.50 for adults, $1 for students in 9th through 12th grades. Open Tues through Sat 10 a.m. to 4 p.m.

Seagrove Pottery. 106 N. Broad St.; (336) 873-7280. This gallery represents more than 50 potters and artists from the Seagrove region. It offers a wide variety of face jugs, utilitarian and decorative pottery, basketry, candles, and hand-painted garden accessories.

where to shop

The potteries of Seagrove are more than places to shop. They are authentic museums of art and history—places of great folk traditions passed down from generation to generation. Often studios are the homes of the artists themselves. If your heart is set on visiting one particular pottery, you might call ahead to confirm their operating hours. While listing all of them isn't possible here, the following are a few stops to consider. The Randolph County Tourism Development Authority (800-626-2672) has a complete list of potteries at heartof northcarolina.com. Seagrove Area Potter Association maintains another helpful website: discoverseagrove.com.

Ben Owen Pottery. 105 Ben's Place; (336) 879-2262; benowenpottery.com. Ben Owen III is perhaps the most familiar of the Seagrove potters, largely because the Owen family and a handful of others living within a 5-mile radius are credited with starting this resilient industry. His studio, one of the oldest potteries, was founded by his ancestors six generations ago. Open Tues through Sat 10 a.m. to 5 p.m. Closed during the month of January and the week of July 4.

Johnson & Gentithes Studios. 741 Fork Mill Creek Rd.; (336) 873-9176; johnstonand gentithes.com. Though rooted in the southern folk tradition, this studio with a fair share of fanciful finds has definitive influences from around the world and mythical places beyond this world. Open Mon through Sat 10 a.m. to 5 p.m.

Jugtown Pottery. 330 Jugtown Rd.; (910) 464-3266; jugtownware.com. Jacques and Juliana Busbee founded Jugtown Pottery in 1921 just south of Seagrove in a log cabin that's on the National Register of Historic Places and where potters still work today. The Busbees also worked with the Owens and other families who started the pottery tradition here. Open Tues through Sat 8:30 a.m. to 5 p.m.

King's Pottery. 4905 Reeder Rd.; (336) 381-3090; kingspottery.com. This studio special-izes in wheel-thrown and hand-built utilitarian pottery—wood-fired and salt-glazed items include folk art, face jugs, and specialty pieces. Their work has been featured on *Antiques Road Show*. Open Mon through Sat 9 a.m. to 4 p.m.

Phil Morgan Pottery. 966 SR 705; (336) 873-7304. Morgan has gained recognition for a particularly elegant form of crystalline glaze pottery. These pieces are anything but practical. They are classic pieces that are the center of collectors' displays and even the displays of heads of state who receive them as gifts from US presidents. Open Mon through Sat 9 a.m. to 5 p.m.

Westmoore Pottery. 4622 Busbee Rd.; (910) 464-3700; westmoorepottery.com. The classic, historical pieces found at Westmoore can be seen in feature films, but the replicas can also be a part of your home decor. Open Mon through Sat 9 a.m. to 5 p.m.

where to eat

Seagrove Family Restaurant. 8702 SR 220 South; (336) 873-7789. Country-fried steak and other diner-style selections along with burgers and fries make this a nice choice for lunch, but the locals come here for breakfast. Peach cobbler is recommended. Open Mon through Sat. 5:30 a.m. to 2 p.m. $.

Westmoore Family Restaurant. 2172 SR 705 South; (910) 464-5222. Westmoore offers a full line of fried and broiled seafood, pit-cooked barbecue, and daily meat and veggie spe-cials. Open Thurs through Sat 11 a.m. to 9 p.m., Sun 11 a.m. to 8 p.m. $–$$.

where to stay

The Duck Smith House Bed & Breakfast. 465 N. Broad St.; (336) 873-7099; ducksmith house.com. This restored historic farmhouse is located within walking distance of potter-ies. The full country breakfast includes freshly picked fruits, jams, and other goodies from 50-year-old fruit trees on the property. $$.

Seagrove Stoneware Inn. 136 W. Main St., (336) 707-9124; seagrovestoneware.com. Owned and operated by potters David Fernandez and Alexa Modderno, the house features artwork from across the country. Rooms are decorated with pottery from both local and nationally known potters. $$.

day trip 06

raleigh, nc

>>> **tobacco fields & silver screens:**
smithfield, nc; selma, nc; kenly, nc

The tourist activity in this area appears to indicate people still remember sex symbol and actress Ava Gardner even though she died more than 20 years ago. She was born here, and people, particularly bus tours, still flock to the area just north of I-95 that hosts a museum of her life on the silver screen. North Carolina's rich agricultural heritage is remembered here, too, at the Tobacco Farm Life Museum in the middle of wilting tobacco fields looking for more prosperous crops for a new day. There are also more than one or two good barbecue sandwiches waiting to be consumed. In these parts, the smoky morsels differ from those found at points west. Here, they serve eastern barbecue, which lacks the distinguishing tomato-based accompaniment of western or Lexington-style barbecue. While the debate over North Carolina barbecue rages and is covered substantially in themed day trip 44, here simply noted is that the distinguishable difference between the two is in the sauce.

While you're in the area, take a short detour north of Selma to Atkinson's Mill, where cornmeal is ground to make the hush puppy mix used at some of the barbecue restaurants you can visit. Or stop by The Rudy Theater, to appreciate the sound that goes along with good barbecue.

smithfield, nc

Cast in many popular and memorable roles, Ava Gardner was born just 7 miles east of Smithfield. She is buried at Smithfield's Sunset Memorial Gardens on US 70. Smithfield was

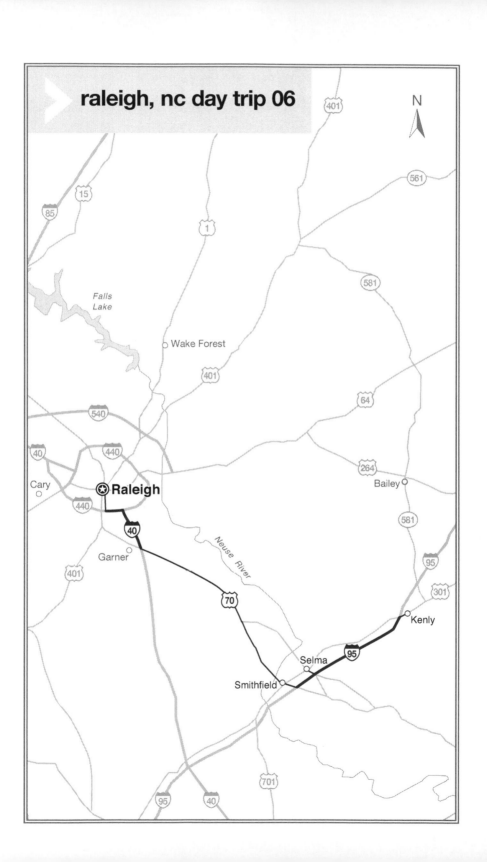

established on the banks of the Neuse River in 1777, making it one of the 10 oldest towns in the state. A classic southern town, Smithfield's downtown is the heart of this community of just more than 12,000 residents. It's a popular stop for bus tours and for the traveler looking for the simpler, slower pace of days gone by.

getting there

Reach Smithfield from Raleigh by traveling 15 minutes east on I-40 then east on US 70. Take exit 326 to merge onto 70 Business East to head into Smithfield.

where to go

Ava Gardner Museum. 325 E. Market St.; (919) 934-5830; avagardner.org. Gardner, who rose to fame as a sex symbol in 1940s Hollywood, was married to Mickey Rooney and Frank Sinatra. An incredible collection of items includes childhood memorabilia, film clips, costumes, domestic and foreign posters, black-and-white stills, film scripts, magazine covers, and scrapbooks. Stored and forgotten in a London attic, Gardner's childhood and career keepsakes were shipped to the museum in 2002. Among the items were teenage Ava's scrapbook with dance cards, cotillion invitations, and telegrams from a boyfriend, as well as three scrapbooks completed by Ava's sister that chronicle the actress's career up to 1953. Open Mon through Sat 9 a.m. to 5 p.m., Sun 2 to 5 p.m. Admission is $8 for adults, $7 for seniors and teens, and $6 for ages 6 to 12. Free for children under age 6.

where to shop

Brightleaf Flea Market. 2320 S. Bright Leaf Blvd.; (919) 934-4111; brightleaffleamarket .com. This is Johnston County's largest flea market. Its name is a throwback to its agricultural heritage, but the facilities at this flea market are more contemporary. In addition to antiques and other typical flea market finds, it conducts carnivals and other special events throughout the year. Open Fri through Sun 8 a.m. to 5 p.m.

Carolina Premium Outlets. 1025 Industrial Park Dr.; (919) 989-8757; premiumoutlets .com. The more than 80 factory-direct stores include Ann Taylor, Nike, Gap, Adidas, Carolina Pottery, Polo Ralph Lauren, Tommy Hilfiger, Reebok, and Fossil Company Store as well as the locally-based Clayton General Store. Open Mon through Sat 10 a.m. to 9 p.m., Sun 11 a.m. to 7 p.m.

Smithfield Ham Shop. 204 N. Bright Leaf Blvd.; (919) 934-8054; countrycuredhams.com. There are literally thousands of hams from which to choose here. Operated by Johnston County Hams, this company specializes in country ham rather than the style of ham that originated in Smithfield, Virginia. The shop also carries local favorite jams, jellies, sauces, and cheese. Open Mon through Fri 8 a.m. to 5 p.m.

where to eat

Becky's Log Cabin. 2491 US Hwy. 70 Business East; (919) 934-1534. Located outside of town in a rustic building, Becky's simply serves steaks and other grilled specialties. There is live entertainment on Saturday nights at the Peacock Lounge, so named for its large, stained-glass ceiling medallion. $$$.

White Swan Barbecue. 3198 US 301 South is the original location. A handful of White Swan locations are sprinkled throughout Johnston County with one in Atlantic Beach; (919) 934-8913; whiteswanbarbeque.com/smithfield.htm. The White Swan, which has been serving barbecue since 1959, also serves ribs, fried seafood, highly recommended fried chicken, Brunswick stew, hush puppies, slaw, potatoes, and desserts. Open Mon through Wed 10:30 a.m. to 7:30 p.m., Thurs through Sat 10:30 a.m. to 8:30 p.m., and Sun 10:30 a.m. to 8 p.m. $–$$.

selma, nc

The tiny town of Selma offers more than 20 shops and malls covering 100,000 square feet, all within walking distance in a 1950s small-town setting. Selma also hosts the East Coast Antique Show and Sale each October. It includes dealers, vendors, food, and entertainment. Selma boasts the very best fine-ground cornmeal around, ground by millstones at the 200-year-old Atkinson Milling Company.

getting there

Selma is just a few minutes from Smithfield north on I-95. Directly from Raleigh it takes no more than 30 minutes via I-40 South to US 70 East. Alternately, take SR 96 north from downtown.

where to go

Rudy Theater. 300 N. Raiford St.; (877) 843-7839; amjubilee.com. Formerly the American Music Jubilee Theatre, the Rudy offers a touch of Branson and Myrtle Beach in eastern North Carolina. the theater presents evenings of southern hospitality, American music, and down-home comedy each weekend. The Branson-style variety show entertains visitors with music from '50s rock 'n' roll to classic and contemporary country and gospel. Admission rates vary by season but begin at $19.50 per adult. Evening performances are at 7:40 p.m., matinees at 1:40 p.m.

Atkinson Milling Co. 95 Atkinson Mill Rd.; (919) 965-3547; atkinsonmilling.com. Built in 1757, this gristmill has been in continuous operation for more than 250 years. Today Atkinson's Mill is the only water-powered gristmill operating in the area. A wide variety of cornmeal products, including a selection of hush puppy mixes, is available at the gift shop. Open Mon through Fri 8 a.m. to 5 p.m. and Sat 8 a.m. to noon.

Country Tonight at The Ice House. 112 N. Webb St.; (919) 631-3797; icehouseselma .com. Bringing a bit more Branson to the Selma music scene is this country-music house. Regional bands play country classics from today and days gone by. Showtime is Friday night at 7:45 p.m. Admission is $12.

Selma Union Station. Railroad Street; (800) 871-7245; ncbytrain.org. Built in the 1920s, the new station serves as a working depot for passengers boarding Amtrak's Carolinian from Selma to Charlotte and Jacksonville to New York. Be sure to see the interpretive exhibits from the days when Selma was a major hub in the state.

kenly, nc

Kenly is located in the heart of North Carolina's tobacco country. The town, settled around 1875, was named for an executive of the Atlantic Coast Line Railroad, which would become Southern Coast Line. The town was incorporated a decade later and quickly became a center for producing flue-cured tobacco.

getting there

From Selma it is a straight shot northeast on I-95 to Kenly. From Raleigh, take I-40 east to US 70. Continue east on 70 to I-95. Follow I-95 north to reach Kenly in about 45 minutes total driving time.

where to go

Tobacco Farm Life Museum. 709 Church St. (US 301 North); (919) 284-3431; tobacco farmlifemuseum.org. This exceptional museum that spans 5 acres includes exhibits, building restorations, and modern facilities that depict a lifestyle gone by. That way of life was tobacco farming. Flue-cured tobacco became the first major cash-producing agricultural commodity for the region during the late 1800s. Now, a 6,000-square-foot exhibit hall displays artifacts from all aspects of farm life, along with a hands-on children's exhibit. Household goods, musical instruments, clothing, and agricultural tools are displayed. A restored farmstead with main house, detached kitchen, and smokehouse depicts rural life as it was during the Great Depression. Open Mon through Sat 9:30 a.m. to 5 p.m. Admission is $8 and free for children under 2.

worth more time
bailey, nc

Just 30 minutes east of the capital city is Bailey (population 529), settled in about 1860 and incorporated in 1907. It is significant for its **Country Doctor Museum** (6642 Peele Rd.; 252-235-4165; countrydoctormuseum.org). This is the only medical museum in the nation dedicated to rural physicians who practiced medicine in North Carolina and the South during the 19th and early 20th centuries. A composite restoration of 2 doctors' offices includes the Dr. Howard Franklin Freeman Office, built in 1857, and the Dr. Cornelius Henry Brantley Office, ca. 1887, which illustrates the early doctor's office with instruments and equipment of the day. In 3 century-old buildings and 2 modern ones, the Country Doctor Museum collects and preserves the medical instruments and tools of pharmacy used by country doctors, and the diaries, papers, and medical books of these rural physicians. Docents lead tours through the facility. Admission is $8 for adults, $6 for seniors, and $4 for ages 18 and under. Open Tues through Sat 9 a.m. to 3 p.m. with tours beginning at 10 a.m. and every hour thereafter.

day trip 07

raleigh, nc

>>>

military history:
fayetteville, nc; fort bragg, nc

Synonymous and eternally connected, Fayetteville and Fort Bragg, one of the country's largest military installations, are undoubtedly the best places for military buffs or historians to study this part of our country's past. With Fort Bragg and Pope Air Force Base nearby, Fayetteville has had to bear the brunt of carrying the moniker of "military town." True, it does live up to some of the rough-and-tumble characteristics of a town that holds a mostly transient population, but once you get beyond that perception, the Fayetteville area has much to offer the day-tripper.

Fayetteville is made up of four distinct historic districts: the downtown Historic District, Haymount Historic District, Liberty Point National Register District, and Market House Square National Register District. Nearly worth the trip alone is the city's Airborne and Special Operations Museum, the only museum of its kind in the country. Then, of course, there is Fort Bragg itself. Visitors may pass freely (albeit with security checkpoints) through the military installation. The Fort Bragg Welcome Center is at Randolph and Knox Streets (910-396-5401). A trip through the base will no doubt leave you with a true appreciation for the sacrifices made by our nation's military.

fayetteville, nc

Dozens of American cities and counties have been named after the Revolutionary War hero Marquis de Lafayette, but Fayetteville was the first and, reportedly, the only one he actually

45

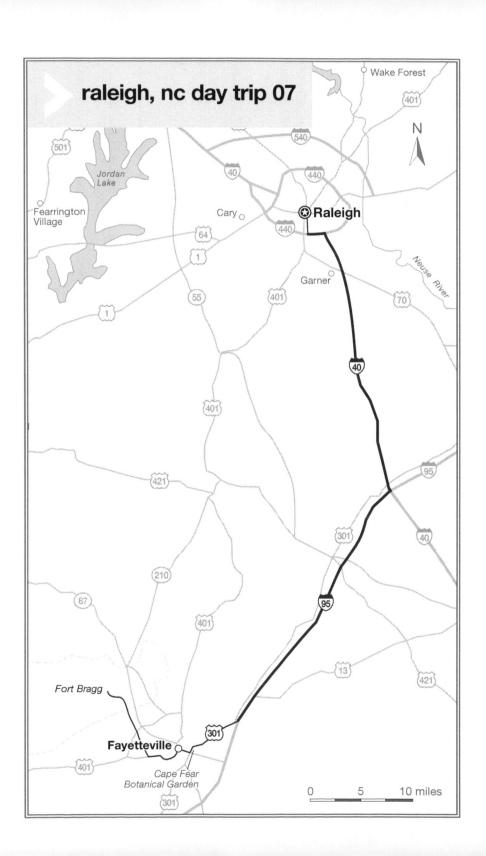

the babe

An 18-year-old baseball player named George Herman Ruth, the youngest player on the Baltimore Orioles, hit his first professional home run at the old Cape Fear Fairgrounds here on March 7, 1914. He, of course, would go on to become the Major League's all-time home run king until 1974.

visited, in 1825. The area was originally settled by Highlanders from Scotland in 1739; they established two early settlements, Campbellton and Cross Creek and later Liberty Point, which would become downtown Fayetteville. After the Revolution, with no permanent state capital, the state's legislature periodically met here, and in 1783 Campbellton and Cross Creek merged and were named Fayetteville. In 1789 in a State House that the city built on aspirations of remaining the state capital, North Carolina representatives ratified the US Constitution; they also chartered the University of North Carolina. The Great Fire of 1831 destroyed more than 600 buildings, including the State House, but Reconstruction resulted in many of the city's present-day landmark structures.

The Fayetteville Area Convention and Visitors Bureau (910-483-5311; visitfayettevillenc .com) operates 2 visitor centers. They are at 245 Person St., open Mon through Fri 8 a.m. to 5 p.m.; at the Fayetteville Area Transportation and Local History Museum, open 10 a.m. to 4 p.m. Tues through Sat.

getting there

Fayetteville is an hour from Raleigh south on I-40 and I-95.

where to go

Airborne and Special Operations Museum. 100 Bragg Blvd.; (910) 483-3003 or (866) 547-0649; asomf.org. More than 50 monuments to various units of the military line the entrance to this special museum. Part of the US Army Museum System, this museum is the only one of its kind in the nation. It explores the 60-year history of airborne and special operations units through dramatic, life-size, imaginative exhibits, a theater, and interactive displays such as a 24-seat simulator that nearly replicates what troopers experience when parachuting or flying at treetop level over rough terrain. Sometimes stark dioramas lead visitors through major U.S. conflicts from World War II to the Global War on Terrorism. Located on 6 acres in downtown Fayetteville, the museum is open Tues through Sat (and on federal holiday Mondays) 10 a.m. to 5 p.m., Sun noon to 5 p.m. Free.

Arts Center. 301 Hay St.; (910) 323-1776; theartscouncil.com. Built in 1910 as a US post office, the Arts Center houses the galleries and offices of the Arts Council of Fayetteville/

Cumberland County. The galleries feature rotating art exhibits. Open Mon through Thurs 8:30 a.m. to 5 p.m., Fri 8:30 a.m. to noon, and Sat noon to 4 p.m.

Atlantic Coast Line Railroad Station. 472 Hay St.; (910) 483-2658. Built in 1911, the station is a rare example of Dutch colonial architecture. The outside passenger and freight platform and shelter date to World War I. The depot serves as an Amtrak passenger station and houses the Atlantic Coast Line Depot Railroad Historical Center. Open alternating Saturdays, but visit the exterior during daylight hours.

Cape Fear Botanical Garden. 536 N. Eastern Blvd.; (910) 486-0221; capefearbg.org. The 85-acre garden, at the confluence of the Cape Fear and Cross Creek Rivers, contains an old farmhouse and heritage garden, perennial gardens, wildflowers, majestic oaks in an old-growth forest, nature trails, and numerous species of native plants. Among the 2,000 specimens of ornamental plants are 200 varieties of camellia that keep the garden beautiful even in cooler months. Admission is $10 for adults, $9 for seniors, and $5 for children 6 to 12. Open Mon through Sat 10 a.m. to 5 p.m., Sun noon to 5 p.m.

Cool Spring Tavern. 119 Cool Spring St.; (910) 433-1612. Built in 1788 and having survived the Great Fire of 1831, Cool Spring Tavern is the oldest structure in the city. The tavern housed the delegates who ratified the US Constitution for North Carolina. The city built it in an attempt to entice them to base the state capital here. With Federal-style architecture, it has double porches, a gabled roof, and brick chimneys. The interior is not open to the public.

Fayetteville Area Transportation and Local History Museum. 325 Franklin St.; (910) 433-1457. Located in the train station of the Cape Fear and Yadkin Valley Railroad Company, this museum details the development of the unique plank road system that made this area important throughout the state. From Native American trails to steamboats and trains, guests are invited to explore early trade communities and how they did business. Open Tues through Sat 10 a.m. to 4 p.m. Free.

Heritage Square. 225 Dick St.; (910) 483-6009. Owned and maintained by the Fayetteville Woman's Club, Heritage Square has 3 structures listed on the National Register of Historic Places: the Sandford House, built in 1800 and once home to artist Elliott Daingerfield and to the first US bank in the state; the Oval Ballroom, a freestanding single room built in 1818; and the Baker-Haigh-Nimocks House, constructed in 1804.

Liberty Point. Bow and Person Streets; (910) 433-1612. Here, on June 20, 1775, 55 patriots signed a petition declaring independence from Great Britain a year before the Declaration of Independence. The building at this site is the oldest known commercial structure in Fayetteville, constructed between 1791 and 1800. A granite boulder here bears the names of the signers.

Market House. Hay, Gillespie, Person, and Green Streets; (910) 483-2073. The focal point of downtown Fayetteville, the Market House was built in 1832 on the site of the old State House, where in 1789 North Carolina ratified the US Constitution, chartered the University of North Carolina, and ceded the state's western lands to Tennessee. The State House was destroyed by fire in 1831. Architecturally unique in North Carolina, the Market House is one of the few structures in America to use this town hall–market scheme traditionally found in England. Though slaves were periodically sold here, it was built as a meat and produce market. It is open periodically for special exhibitions.

Museum of the Cape Fear Historical Complex. 801 Arsenal Ave.; (910) 486-1330; museumofthecapefear.ncdcr.gov. Museum exhibits chronicle the history of southern North Carolina from Native Americans to the 20th century. The 1897 E. A. Poe House (not the poet) examines the lifestyle of upper middle-class families from 1897 to 1917. Arsenal Park reveals the history of a Federal arsenal, commissioned in 1836 by the Federal government and taken over by the Confederacy at the outset of the Civil War. General Sherman seized Fayetteville in 1865 and ordered the arsenal to be razed by fire. Its foundation remains. Free. Open Tues through Sat 10 a.m. to 5 p.m. and Sun 1 to 5 p.m.

North Carolina Veterans Park. 300 Bragg Blvd.; (910) 433-1537; ncveteranspark.org. Opened in 2011, this memorial park and visitor center is a contemporary tribute to North Carolina Veterans of armed services. Notable tributes include a fused-glass ribbon wall and a chandelier made of more than 33,000 dog tags. A Story Garden outside allows visitors to listen to stories on North Carolina residents' involvement in armed struggles. Free. Open Tues through Sat 10 a.m. to 5 p.m., Sun 1 to 5 p.m.

St. John's Episcopal Church. 302 Green St.; (910) 483 7405. Reconstructed in 1833, after Fayetteville's Great Fire of 1831, the church has 10 pyramidal spires and stained-glass windows made in Munich, Germany.

where to shop

The Shops at 123 Hay Street. 123 Hay St.; (910) 920-2146; theshopsat123haystreet .com. More than 20 vendors occupy the more than 5,000 square feet of this tidy antique mall. Glassware, vintage clothing and upcycled items can be found from booth to booth.

As you may expect, the Fayetteville area has its share of military surplus and collectibles stores. Here are a few, but call ahead to confirm hours.

> **Ed Hicks Antiques, Guns & Military Collectibles.** 819 Hope Mills Rd.; (910) 425-7000.

> **Memory Lane Antiques & Collectibles.** 2838 Owen Dr.; (910) 433-4395.

> **Tarbridge Military Collectibles.** 960 Country Club Dr.; (910) 488-7205.

where to eat

Huske Hardware House. 405 Hay St.; (910) 437-9905; huskehardware.com. This restaurant/microbrewery is located in a renovated hardware store, spacious and artfully restored. Its location makes it a good choice for combining a visit with the Airborne and Special Operations Museum; appropriately, the microbrewery offers a signature Airborne Ale. The lunch menu has a variety of soups, salads, and "starters," as well as sandwiches and specialties, including such items as pesto chicken and Cajun shrimp. Dinners include a selection of pasta, seafood, and beef. $$–$$$.

The Mash House. 4150 Sycamore Dairy Rd.; (910) 867-9223; themashhouse.com. The Mash House is known for its award-winning microbrewed beer—with 10 varieties on tap at last count plus seasonal selection—served in a chilled pint glass with a pretzel on a straw. Begin dinner with the steakhouse salad and follow it with one of the delicious entrees, such as wood-oven-roasted filet mignon, served with fried sweet onions, asparagus, roasted potatoes, and béarnaise. Open Mon through Thurs 5 to 10 p.m., Fri 5 to 11 p.m., Sat noon to 11 p.m., Sun noon to 9 p.m. $$–$$$.

Pharoah's Village. 2425 Hope Mills Rd.; (910) 323-2425; This Mediterranean restaurant gets high marks for its gyros, but the Greek salads and lentil soups are also recommended. Vegetarians will also find plenty to please their palate. $$

Rude Awakening Coffee House. 227 Hay St.; (910) 223-7833; rudeawakening.net. In the historic downtown district, this coffee shop offers all varieties of coffees, including specialty cappuccinos, as well as breakfast, lunch, and desserts. Check out the courtyard at the back. Open Mon through Sat 7:30 a.m. to 9 p.m., Sun 9 a.m. to 8 p.m. $.

fort bragg, nc

Named for General Braxton Bragg, a native of Warren County who served in the US Army during the Seminole and Mexican Wars and in the Confederate Army during the Civil War, "Camp Bragg" was established by Congress in 1918 as an Army field artillery site. Five years later the camp was renamed Fort Bragg, and in 1934 the airborne tradition began with the first military parachute jump, which used artillery observation balloons as platforms. In 1952 Fort Bragg became headquarters for the Army's Special Forces (Green Berets) when the Psychological Warfare Center, now the Special Operations Command, was established here.

With a total area of more than 138,000 acres (about the size of an average North Carolina county), Fort Bragg today is home of XVIII Airborne Corps and the 82nd Airborne Division, as well as of thousands of non-jumping troops totaling more than 45,000 military personnel. It is one of the largest military reservations in the US; because of the number of troops it houses, it is considered to be the state's tenth-largest city.

getting there

Fort Bragg is a few minutes from Fayetteville. Take US 401 west and then travel north on the All American Expressway.

where to go

82nd Airborne Division War Memorial Museum. Ardennes and Gela Streets; (910) 432-3443; 82ndairbornedivisionmuseum.com. The museum chronicles the history of the 82nd Airborne Division from 1917 to the present through featured photographic exhibits, static displays, and more than 4,000 artifacts. Outdoor equipment displays, including dozens of military aircraft and an hourly film provide additional insights into this historic unit and its famous Green Berets. Free. Open Tues through Sat and federal holidays, 10 a.m. to 4:30 p.m.

John F. Kennedy Hall of Heroes. Ardennes Street. Located across the street from the John F. Kennedy Special Warfare Museum, the JFK Hall of Heroes honors 19 Special Forces, 3 Rangers, and 10 Indian Scout Medal of Honor recipients.

John F. Kennedy Memorial Chapel. Ardennes Street; (910) 432-2127. Beautiful stained-glass windows are dedicated to Special Forces soldiers. There's also a monument given by John Wayne to the Special Forces for assistance during the filming of *The Green Berets*.

John F. Kennedy Special Warfare Museum. Ardennes Street, Building D-2502; (910) 432-4272. This museum provides a behind-the-scenes look at unconventional warfare, with an emphasis on Special Forces (Green Berets) and Special Operations from World War II until today. It houses a collection of weapons, military art, and cultural items from all over the world. Free. Open Tues through Sun 11 a.m. to 4 p.m.

Main Post Chapel. Half and C Streets; (910) 396-8016. Established in 1932, the chapel features stained-glass windows that were handcrafted with 14,000 pieces of antique glass from around the world.

day trip 08

raleigh, nc

>>> **second city of firsts:**
new bern, nc

new bern, nc

As North Carolina's second-oldest town (Bath Is the oldest), New Bern holds tremendous historic significance as the state's first capital and the location of the first state legislature. It's also the birthplace of Pepsi and holds close its Swiss sister city of the same name. In New Bern you'll visit historic Tryon Palace and stroll the pleasant picturesque riverfront downtown. Fine southern homes with wraparound porches, some that date to the 1700s, look out on the Neuse and Trent Rivers. But there are still more firsts: home of the state's first four-faced clock; originator of the state's first celebration of both Independence Day and George Washington's birthday; home to the first steamboat in North Carolina; the first incorporated public school in the state; the first public school for African Americans in North Carolina; the first printing press and published newspaper in the state; the first torpedo put into practical use; the first motion picture theater built in the state; and the first postal service in the Carolina colony.

A Swiss baron settled New Bern in 1710 and named it for Bern, his home in Switzerland. Like the Swiss capital, New Bern's symbol, the black bear, is ubiquitous throughout the town. There are no real bears in town, but rather artistic representations of them. By the middle of the 18th century, the port city had grown in size and importance. The colonial assembly often met here, so when British Royal Governor William Tryon saw the need for a permanent capital in the growing colony, he selected New Bern as the site and built Tryon

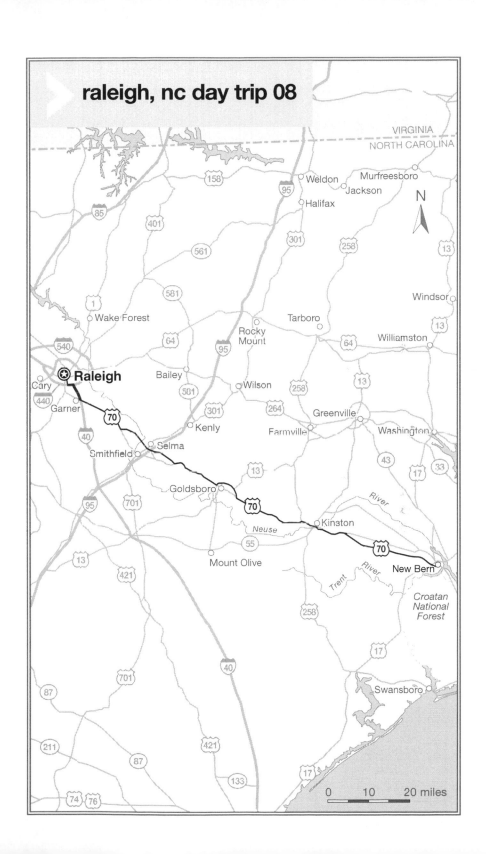

raleigh, nc day trip 08

Palace here in 1770. Union forces captured the town early on in the Civil War and occupied it until the end of the war. Hence, New Bern survived with less damage to its homes and buildings than many other small southern towns.

New Bern's city center fell into decline in the 1970s, when the sprawl of shopping malls and suburban housing drew citizens away from the business district. But in the 1980s city leaders founded the Swiss Bear Downtown Development Corporation and systematically began breathing new life into the downtown in the form of art galleries, specialty shops, antiques stores, restaurants, and other businesses. The Craven County Convention and Visitor's Bureau (216 S. Front St.; 800-437-5767; visitnewbern.com) can help with information before you head out or after your arrival.

getting there

From Raleigh, New Bern is 113 miles, after a short leg on I-40, traveling eastward on US 70; the drive across the Neuse River Basin is a pleasant one.

where to go

Croatan National Forest. 141 E. Fisher Ave.; (252) 638-5628. Hike, swim, boat, hunt, fish, camp, and picnic at the spectacular 157,000-acre Croatan National Forest, with access 9 miles south of New Bern just off US 70 East. Bordered by the rivers, it runs all the way to Bogue Sound east. Look for the rare Venus flytrap, real black bear, osprey, and alligators. The site of a Civil War battle, the recreation area has been nationally recognized for the quality of its offerings.

The Firemen's Museum. 408 Hancock St.; (252) 636-4087; newbernfiremuseum.com. Peruse displays in this 1928 fire station that include century-old hose wagons, an 1884 Button steamer, and an assortment of 18th- and 19th-century firemen's hats, leather fire buckets, and hand-drawn reels. Don't miss (as if you could) the mounted, stuffed head of Fire Horse Fred, who pulled the Atlantic hose wagon for 17 years and died answering a false alarm. Admission is $7 for adults, $4 for children ages 6 to 12. Open Mon through Sat 10 a.m. to 4 p.m.

Ghosts of New Bern. Departing from the Black Cat Shoppe at 246 Middle St.; (252) 365-1410; hauntednewbern.com. These ghost tours are a fun way to learn about New Bern's rich history and heritage. Mysteries, myths, and legends, passed down through the generations (and probably just made up for entertainment purposes), provide a 90-minute-long tour through the streets of the Historic District. Basic tour tickets are $17 for adults and $6 for children under age 12.

Historic Downtown District. (252) 637-7316 or (800) 849-7316; newberntours.com. For a dose of history and charm, walk the downtown district, then board the New Bern Tours trolley, across from Tryon Palace Visitor Center, for a 90-minute narrated tour. From

literary walk

Fans of Nicholas Sparks, the best-selling novelist who bases many of his stories on locales and people of coastal North Carolina, may want to take the "Walk to Remember Tour." The visitor center offers a self-guided tour that takes day-trippers to 15 landmarks from 3 of Sparks's most popular books. The center offers suggestions for more traditional tours, too.

the comfortable open-air (but covered) trolley, you will see such sites as the Coor-Gaston House, a Georgian-style home built around 1770. Its most famous resident was Judge William Gaston, the first chief justice of the North Carolina Supreme Court and composer of the state song, "The Old North State." Purchase tickets on the trolley ($18 per adult, $9 for children 12 and under). Departure times vary with the season but are typically at 11 a.m. and 2 p.m. Apr through Oct. Also offered on a weather-permitting, seasonal basis are horse and carriage tours. Call for times or to make reservations.

Tryon Palace Historic Sites and Gardens. 610 Pollock St.; (252) 514-4900 or (800) 767-1560; tryonpalace.org. Completed in 1770, then burned to the ground in 1798, Tryon Palace was rebuilt in the 1950s. That's right; the Tryon Palace you see today is a replica of the original palace. The 27-room, brick, Georgian-style mansion and its furnishings were painstakingly reproduced from meticulous records kept by British Royal Governor William Tryon. In addition to serving two royal governors, the palace was used by four state governors before the capital was moved from New Bern to Raleigh in 1794. Guides in period dress conduct informative 45-minute palace tours on which you learn, among other things, that George Washington not only slept but also danced here. The tour continues with the 18th-century-style English gardens surrounding the palace that you view on your own. Built in more recent years, the North Carolina History Center located here provides space for rotating exhibitions, waterfront dining, and shopping. Open Mon through Sat 10 a.m. to 5 p.m. and Sun noon to 5 p.m. The last guided tour begins at 4 p.m. daily. The gardens are open until 7 p.m. in summer. Visitors can purchase tickets until 4:30 p.m. Admission for adults is $20 ($10 for students through grade 12) to tour the palace, buildings, and 14-acre grounds.

John Wright Stanly House. Included with admission to Tryon Palace, this Georgian-style home was built in the early 1780s. On his southern tour in 1791, President George Washington slept here—twice. The Stanly House remains one of the finest examples of Georgian architecture in the South.

Robert Hay House. Also part of Tryon Palace, this unimposing house features character interpreters, who greet and respond to you as if it were 1835. Ask questions of the staff to learn about what life was like for the early colonists.

New Bern Academy Museum. Nearby, and part of the Tryon Palace complex, New Bern Academy was the first established school in North Carolina. During the Civil War, the building was converted to a military hospital to treat the victims of spinal meningitis, smallpox, and yellow fever epidemics, as well as casualties of war. The building has 4 rooms that chronicle the history of New Bern: its founding and early history, architecture, Civil War and Reconstruction, and education.

where to shop

Birthplace of Pepsi-Cola. 256 Middle St.; (252) 636-5898; pepsistore.com. This restored pharmacy marks the spot where Caleb Bradham invented Pepsi-Cola in 1898. Be sure to see the 35-minute video about the history of Pepsi, narrated by Walter Cronkite. Also offered is a 20-minute video that chronicles the history of Pepsi through commercials. The store sells fountain Pepsi in a cup and Pepsi collectibles, such as T-shirts, drinking glasses, coffee mugs, key chains, and caps. Open Mon through Sat 10 a.m. to 6 p.m.; Mar through Dec, it is also open noon to 4 p.m. on Sun.

Mitchell Hardware. 215 Craven St.; (252) 638-4261. This hardware store opened in 1898, the same year Bradham invented Pepsi. Jam-packed with everything from nuts and bolts to dishes, it is as much a museum as it is a store. Spend a good hour browsing the mix of hardware, garden tools, and yard equipment. You might even want to take home one of the store's country hams. Open 6:30 a.m. to 5:30 p.m. Mon through Sat.

Tryon Palace Museum Store/Craft and Garden Shop. 610 Pollock St.; museum store, (252) 514-4932; garden shop, (252) 514-4927. Tryon Palace Museum Store carries New Bern and colonial memorabilia. The Craft and Garden Shop carries just what the name implies: heirloom plants, crafts, gardening books, and more. Both shops are open daily.

where to eat

Bakers Kitchen. 227 Middle St.; (252) 637-0304; bakerskitchennb.com. Breakfast, complete with Baker's own butter syrup, is served here all day. Their breads, pastries, pies and more are also made fresh daily in the upstairs bakery. Go light with Twigs and Berries or go big with the Hungry Farmer—2 pancakes, 2 slices of French toast, 2 eggs plus a protein, plus grits or home fries or Dutch potatoes (and a nap!)

Captain Ratty's Seafood Restaurant. 202 Middle St.; (252) 633-2088; captainrattys .com. Captain Ratty's specializes in seafood, plus you can dine on the rooftop deck and wine bar. Then you can come back in the morning for breakfast. $$–$$$.

The Chelsea. 335 Middle St.; (252) 637-5469; thechelsea.com. Pepsi inventor Caleb Bradham used this building as his second drugstore. Now it's modeled after an English-style pub. The Chelsea's excellent food is fusion cuisine, and the atmosphere is comfortably sophisticated. For an appetizer that won't leave you hungry for dinner, try the Blue Chip Dip, a blend of blue, cheddar, and cream cheeses, bacon, and scallions served hot with home-made chips for dipping. Open Mon through Thurs 11 a.m. to 9 p.m., Fri and Sat 11 a.m. to 10 p.m. $$–$$$.

Morgan's Tavern & Grill. 235 Craven St.; (252) 636-2430; morganstavernnewbern.com. From a bottomless soup and salad to fish or shrimp tacos, you should have no problem finding something to please your palate here. You can also grab one of Morgan's Tavern ales produced In partnership by St. George Brewing Co. Open Tues through Thurs 11 a.m. to 9 p.m., Fri and Sat 11 a.m. to 10 p.m. $–$$.

where to stay

The Aerie. 509 Pollock St.; (800) 849-5553 or (252) 636-5553; aeriebedandbreakfast.com. This beautiful pastel blue 2-story, 1880 Victorian house, located a block from Tryon Palace, has 8 guest rooms with private baths, a cozy parlor with player piano, and a library with an extensive Civil War collection. A full breakfast with a choice of 3 hot entrees is served. Herbal flower gardens cover 1,500 square feet, and spa services can be secured on-site. $$.

Hanna House Bed and Breakfast. 218 Pollock St.; (252) 635-3209 or (866) 830-4371; hannahousenc.net. Listed in the National Register of Historic Places and designated a his-toric home, Hanna House is furnished in fine antiques and Oriental carpets. Gourmet break-fast and an in-room massage should be on the agenda here. Built In 1896, it was recently renovated, but many of the turn-of-the-century details have been retained. $$.

Harmony House Inn. 215 Pollock St.; (252) 636-3810 or (800) 636-3113; harmonyhouse inn.com. Purchased by Benjamin Ellis in 1850, Harmony House began as a 4-room, 2-story Greek Revival home. During the Civil War, Harmony House was occupied by Company K of the 45th Massachusetts Volunteer Militia. The house, located in downtown New Bern, has 7 guest rooms and 3 suites. Breakfasts include such specialty entrees as the inn's unique stuffed French toast. All are served with home-baked coffee cake and breads, fresh fruit, coffee, tea, and juice. $$–$$$.

Meadows Inn. 212 Pollock St.; (252) 634-1776 or (877) 551-1776; meadowsinn-nc.com. Formerly the King's Arms Bed and Breakfast, the Meadows Inn is located in the heart of the historic district. John Alexander Meadows built the home in 1847, 4 years after a fire destroyed most of the structures on Pollock Street. The inn was a private residence until 1980, when it became New Bern's first bed-and-breakfast. Each of the 9 spacious guest rooms has a nonworking fireplace. $$.

wilmington, nc

day trip 09

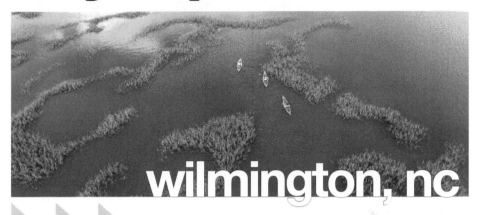

wilmington, nc

cape fear:
wilmington, nc; wrightsville beach, nc

At the mouth of the Cape Fear River is a pretty port city, bubbling with history and a bit of Hollywood. One of the 20th century's greatest battleships is moored here against a riverfront backdrop that offers day-trippers much to see and do. This city blends seamlessly into the coastal community of Wrightsville Beach where vacationers gather at Johnnie Mercer's Pier and surfers from a nearby university hang ten.

Located at the mouth of the Cape Fear River, Wilmington was important through the Revolutionary War and became a major shipbuilding center. With the construction of the Wilmington and Weldon Railroad early in the 19th century, it became the world's largest cotton exchange, the importance of which is still evident in downtown attractions. The surrounding communities flourished with the establishment of plantations, some of which travelers can still visit.

The city's economy has at times struggled, but in the 1970s city leaders committed to downtown revitalization, striking a remarkable balance between preserving history and establishing an economy for the future. Downtown is bordered by a charming riverfront where jazz bands play free concerts at sunset and street vendors offer their wares for sale.

Between the riverfront and coast are shopping malls, chain restaurants, a handful of established attractions, and a spectacular garden. Screen Gem Studios, the largest motion picture studio on the East Coast, made this city the Hollywood of the East when it was established here in 1980. Only 15 minutes away from downtown is Wrightsville Beach. Located on an island, the small town attracts tourists a plenty but still retains much of its turn-of-the-19th-century charm—a nice family getaway.

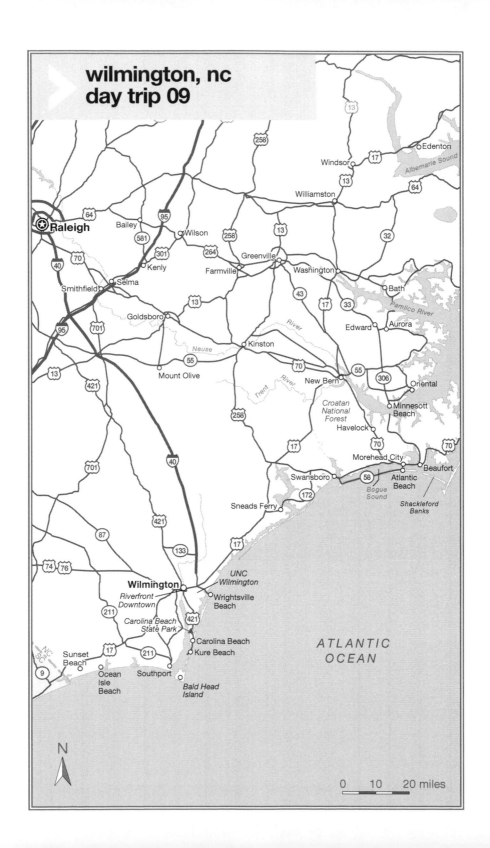

wilmington, nc
day trip 09

wilmington, nc

Wilmington was established as a trading post in 1729, originally referred to as Dram Tree and later New Liverpool, New Carthage, New Town, and Newton. When colonial Governor Gabriel Johnston took office in 1749, he incorporated it as the City of Wilmington, naming it after Spencer Compton, Earl of Wilmington. General Cornwallis and British forces would occupy the city for a year during the Revolutionary War, but when he withdrew and his armies fell, the area would flourish as a shipbuilding port and a center for export of cotton. Completed in 1840, the Wilmington and Weldon Railroad, the world's longest rail line, would be a critical link for the cotton industry and for more than a century would make Wilmington one of the state's largest and one of the country's most economically stable cities. In 1910 the railroad merged into the Atlantic Coast Line, but its headquarters remained in Wilmington. Surviving the Great Depression and world wars, the city was dealt a major blow in 1960 when the Atlantic Coast Line moved its headquarters. Its 1,000 employees and their families relocated to Jacksonville, Florida, the largest single move of employees ever staged by a southeastern industry.

Resilient downtown developers began a strong revitalization effort in the 1970s while preservationists sought protection for the historic downtown homes and buildings. Their combined efforts resulted in a reborn downtown that still attracts visitors, who take carriage rides and walking tours to learn about the city's history. For information about these joys and others, contact the Wilmington/Cape Fear Coast Convention and Visitors Bureau (1 Estell Lee Place.; 877-406-2356; capefearcoast.com). The CVB also operates a kiosk on the river at the foot of Market Street, but to get started read on.

getting there

US 17, which runs along the Carolina coast, US 421, and US 74/76 merge on the Cape Fear River as drivers enter Wilmington. I-40 enters the city's center from the north.

where to go

Airlie Gardens. 300 Airlie Rd.; (910) 798-7700; airliegardens.org. Designed in the early 1900s, Airlie Gardens encompasses 67 acres of post-Victorian, European-style gardens, with 10 acres of freshwater lakes. Offered is a 1-mile walking tour amid 100,000 azaleas, camellias, statuary, a butterfly garden, and the historic and amazing Airlie Oak that is believed to be nearly 500 years old. Also significant is the whimsical Minnie Evans Sculpture Garden that includes the Bottle Chapel, a small structure made of bottles, metal sculptures, mosaics, and ceramics. Admission is $9 for adults, $3 for ages 4 to 12. Open daily 9 a.m. to 5 p.m.

Cameron Art Museum. 3201 S. 17th St.; (910) 395-5999; cameronartmuseum.com. Formerly St. John's Museum, this well-established 42,000-square-foot museum highlights two centuries of North Carolina artists such as Minnie Evans, Romare Bearden, Claude Howell, Mary Cassatt, Jugtown potters, and more. Its permanent collections are displayed on a rotating basis. An outdoor exhibit includes a compelling collection of contemporary sculptures. Admission is $10 for adults, $8 for children ages 5 to 18, and free for children under age 5. Open Tues through Sun 10 a.m. to 5 p.m. and until 9 p.m. on Thurs.

Cape Fear Museum of History & Science. 814 Market St.; (910) 341-4350; capefear museum.com. Established in 1898 as a Confederate museum, this is the state's oldest history museum. Explore regional history in the exhibition Cape Fear Stories, featuring a model of 1860 Wilmington and a diorama of the historic battle of Fort Fisher, and through the Maritime Pavilion. Discover regional ecology in the Michael Jordan Discovery Gallery or examine the skeleton of a giant ground sloth. Admission is $8 for adults, $7 for seniors, $5 for children ages 6 through 17, free for children under age 6. Open Mon through Sat 9 a.m. to 5 p.m., Sun 1 to 5 p.m.

Children's Museum of Wilmington. 116 Orange St. (910) 254-3534; playwilmington.org. Spread among three historic buildings you will find an obligatory stop for travelers with children. A playful pirate ship, water wonders, animal alley and more offer fun ways for parents and children to learn together. Admission Is $9 for children and adults. Open Mon-Sat 9 a.m. to 5 p.m. and Sun 1 to 5 p.m.

azalea festival

NC Azalea Festival (910-794-4650; ncazaleafestival.org) is one of the state's biggest and best celebrations. It has been listed multiple times as a top-20 event by the Southeast Tourism Society since the coastal city began holding the festival in 1958, and now it attracts more than 300,000 people. Appropriately, it's held in early April over several days and features big-time pop and country music stars. It begins with the arrival and coronation of the Azalea Queen at the opening on Wednesday and continues with a circus, gospel concerts, a coin show, a horse show, and an air show. At its core, however, is an opportunity to view Wilmington's gardens—Airlie Gardens, Greenfield Lake Gardens, Orton Plantation Gardens, and as many as eight others associated with historic sites; public buildings are included in the events. Discount tickets good for the entire festival are offered for all gardens on the tour. "Azalea Belles" from the Cape Fear Garden Club are dressed in colorful antebellum hoop skirts and act as hostesses on the guided tours. Speakers and plant sales complete the event.

wilmington's finest

NBA superstar Michael Jordan was born in Wilmington. He helped the University of North Carolina win an NCAA basketball championship before moving on to the Chicago Bulls, where he would lead the team to six NBA championships. Jordan went on to become majority owner of the Charlotte Hornets.

Ghost Walk of Old Wilmington. For location and reservations, call (910) 794-1866 or visit hauntedwilmington.com. Explore Wilmington's haunted alleyways and cemeteries while learning engaging details of the city's history from an entertaining and sometimes mischievous actor. Under the shadows of moss-draped live oaks, stories of pirates, murder, mayhem, and betrayal come to near-life. Offered Apr 1 through Oct 31, 6:30 and 8:30 p.m. nightly; Nov and Mar, nightly at 6:30 p.m.; and Dec through Feb, Thurs through Sat at 6:30 p.m. Admission is $17 for adults, $15 for seniors and children, under 7 free.

***Henrietta III* Riverboat.** Board at Dock and Water Streets; (800) 676-0162; cfrboats.com. Boat captains narrate the history of the Cape Fear River as North Carolina's largest riverboat makes its way downstream and back. Narrated sightseeing tours are at 11:30 a.m. Tues through Sun from Apr through Oct. Sunset cruises are offered through Dec. Also scheduled periodically are murder mystery tours and other special events. Tickets are $17 for adults and $5 for children ages 2 through 12.

Historic Downtown Wilmington. Protected as North Carolina's largest historic district, within these 230 blocks are beautiful homes on cobblestone streets dating from the late 1700s, some of which are open for touring. The core of the hilly but walkable downtown is made up of restaurants, inns, bed-and-breakfasts, and specialty shops.

Bellamy Mansion. 503 Market St.; (910) 251-3700; bellamymansion.org. Built as the city residence of prominent planter and doctor John D. Bellamy, this home is one of the state's most spectacular examples of antebellum architecture. Wrapped by stalwart Corinthian columns, the restored 22-room home features white marble mantels, ornate cornice moldings, and elaborate brass chandeliers. It was occupied by Federal troops in 1865. Some of its history and details of the lives of free and enslaved blacks are covered in a visit here, but the site also functions as a museum of design arts. Admission is $14 for adults, $7 for children ages 5 to 12. Open daily 10 a.m. to 4 p.m.

Burgwin-Wright House. 224 Market St.; (910) 762-0570; burgwinwrighthouse .com. The Burgwin-Wright House originated as the city's jail but was adapted as a home in 1770 by John Burgwin, planter, merchant, and treasurer of the colony of Carolina. In 1781 Lord Cornwallis occupied the home shortly before his defeat and surrender at Yorktown. Joshua Grainger Wright purchased it in 1799 for 3,500 Spanish milled dollars. Occupied as a residence until 1937, the National Society of the Colonial Dames of America bought it thereafter. Beautifully restored, the Burgwin-Wright House is the oldest museum house in southeastern North Carolina. Examine fine details of Georgian-style architecture, a formal or parterre garden, a terraced garden, and an orchard that grace the house. Tunnels used to transport prisoners to and from the jail still run under it. Guided tours from costumed guides are $14 for adults and $7 for children. Open Mon through Sat 10 a.m. to 4 p.m.

Latimer House. 126 S. 3rd St.; (910) 762-0492; hslcf.org. Prosperous local businessman Zebulon Latimer chose the popular Victorian Italianate style for his new home in 1852. Designed to be symmetrical, the 14-room home is now the office of the historical society and displays more than 600 historical objects, including furniture, jewelry, tableware, tools, and more. Admission is $10 for adults and $5 for children. Open Mon through Fri 10 a.m. to 4 p.m., Sat and Sun noon to 5 p.m.

Springbrook Farms Inc. Water and Market Streets, (910) 251-8889; horse drawntours.com. Costumed drivers narrate the journey through past and present downtown. It's a great way to get acquainted with the rich history of this port city. Adults, $14; children under 12, $6. Carriage tours are offered year-round, but call ahead for schedules in Jan and Feb.

Thalian Hall. 102 N. 3rd and 310 Chestnut St.; (800) 523-2820; thalianhall.org. Built in 1855 for combined government and theater use and restored in 1909, this classic 19th-century opera house hosted such famous performers as Buffalo Bill Cody, Lillian Russell, John Philip Sousa, and Oscar Wilde. Renovated again in 2010, Thalian Hall holds a variety of performances from plays to concerts as well as showing classic films.

Wilmington Adventure Walking Tours. At the foot of Market and Water Streets; (910) 763-1785. Offers tours at 10 a.m. daily.

Hollywood East Tour. Before leaving home head to the wilmingtonandbeaches.com website to find 6 separate tours on the film and TV sites of Wilmington. If you were a fan of *One Tree Hill* or *Dawson's Creek* TV series, the tour Is a must. But you'll also discover the latest of the popular *Scream* films was made here, and the area is perfect backdrop for those romantic Hallmark films.

Jungle Rapids Family Fun Park. 5320 Oleander Dr.; (910) 791-0666; junglerapids.com. Cool off in the one-million-gallon wave pool or on the lazy river. This water park and entertainment facility features waterslides, go-kart tracks, jungle golf, laser tag, a climbing wall, more than 100 arcade games, a kids' indoor playground, a cafe, and a pizzeria. Open year-round; water park open seasonally. Waterpark tickets start at $41.99.

Poplar Grove Plantation. 10200 US 17 North; (910) 686-9518; poplargrove.org. Poplar Grove was the homestead of a successful farming family in the mid- to late 19th century. The home and outbuildings are typical of an 1800s-era working community. The 628-acre plantation, self-contained and self-sustaining, produced mainly peanuts, peas, corn, and beans and held some 64 slaves. Admission is $12 for adults, $10 for seniors, and $6 for ages 6 to 15. Open Wed through Sat 9:30 a.m. to 3:30 p.m. Closed Easter Sunday, Thanksgiving Day, and Christmas week through Jan.

Tregembo Animal Park. 5811 Carolina Beach Rd.; (910) 392-3604; tregemboanimalpark .com. This attraction was first opened in 1952 by the Tregembo family. They sold it but bought it back in 2005. Visitors can stroll down shady walkways to see African animals, including lions, tigers, and even a giraffe. In all, visitors can see 100 species of animals throughout the park. Admission is $12 for adults, $8 for seniors and children ages 2 to 11. The zoo is open daily 10 a.m. to 5 p.m. and is closed Dec through Feb.

USS Battleship *North Carolina*. US 17; (910) 251-5797; battleshipnc.com. Moored in view across the river from downtown Wilmington, this 1941 vessel played a part in every major naval offensive in the Pacific during World War II and at the time was the world's greatest sea weapon. On her decks and below, guests begin to get an idea of what life was like upon the great battleship. It's both a museum and memorial to those who served. Stories of the sailors who lived and worked on the massive vessel are told through audiovisual displays and memorabilia. Visitors can touch the heavy metal mid-century equipment, walk into the living quarters, and sit at the counters where sailors dined. Admission is $14 for adults, $10 for seniors and active military duty, $6 for ages 6 to 11, free for ages 5 and under. Open daily from 8 a.m. to 8 p.m. mid-May through mid-Sept, to 5 p.m. the rest of the year.

Wilmington Railroad Museum. 501 Nutt St.; (910) 763-2634; wrrm.org. For more than a century, railroading was Wilmington's chief industry and this museum highlights that history. Visitors explore extensive displays of model trains, photographs, and artifacts, ranging from a conductor's 4-ounce timepiece to a 150-ton locomotive. Displays include artifacts and memorabilia from the Wilmington and Weldon Railroad, which ran on 161 miles of track, making it the longest rail line in the world in the mid-19th century. A steam locomotive (be sure to clang the working bell) and caboose may be boarded, and there's a hands-on children's corner. Admission is $10 for adults, $9 for seniors and active military, $6 for children ages 2 to 12. Open Mon through Sat 10 a.m. to 5 p.m. and Sun 1 to 5 p.m. mid-Apr through Labor Day; Mon through Sat 10 a.m. to 4 p.m. the rest of the year.

where to shop

Cotton Exchange. Front and Grace Streets; (910) 343-9896; shopcottonexchange.com. Once home to the largest cotton-exporting company in the world, the 8 buildings that date from the 19th century have been converted into boutiques, specialty shops, and restaurants. Brick walkways and open breezeways connect apparel stores, shoe stores, jewelry shops, health food stands, and more. Open Mon through Sat 10 a.m. to 5:30 p.m., Sun noon to 4 p.m.

Old Wilmington City Market. 119 S. Water St.; (910) 763-7349; oldwilmingtoncitymarket .com. The restored historic market located in the heart of the downtown waterfront is now occupied by a flower shop, a bookstore, a pottery studio, and a variety of other retail shops. It's a bustling area with great restaurants and other shops.

where to eat

Circa 1922. 8 N. Front St.; (910) 762-1922; circa1922.com. Located in the waterfront district, the Circa 1922 offers a wide selection of tapas as well as traditional entrees along with great wine selections. Exposed brick and dark wooden booths provide a warm atmosphere. It is part piano bar on Saturday evenings. Open daily 5 until $$–$$$.

Chops Deli. 130 N. Front St.; (910) 399-6503; chopsdeli.com. With locations downtown, in Monkey Junction, and at Wrightsville Beach, Chops is the perfect place to grab a sandwich made with fresh, healthy selections when you are on the go. Menus vary a bit by location but the combinations vary far from typical ham and cheese. $$

Elijah's Restaurant. 2 Ann St.; (910) 343-1448; elijahs.com. Located on the Cape Fear River where the big ships run, Elijah's offers a great selection of fish and steaks; it's just the right place for crab cakes or fish and chips. Open for lunch and dinner. The main dining room closes from 3 to 5 p.m., but the oyster bar is open all day. $$–$$$.

Front Street Brewery. 9 N. Front St.; (919) 251-1935; frontstreetbrewery.com. Drop in at this brewery for a quick brat or for shepherd's pie or even fish tacos. Enjoy one of their local brews from the tap or get one in a growler to go. It's also a great place to nurse a glass of whiskey or bourbon. $$.

Paddy's Hollow Restaurant & Pub. 10 Walnut St.; (910) 762-4354; paddyshollow.com. Located in the lower level of the Cotton Exchange, Paddy's Hollow has a great casual atmosphere. Paddy's does burgers as well as they do steaks. $$–$$$.

where to stay

Graystone Inn. 100 S. 3rd St.; (910) 763-2000; graystoneinn.com. Luxurious rooms await the traveler at this AAA 4-diamond property. The Graystone Inn was chosen by American

Historic Inns Inc. as one of the "Top 10 Most Romantic Inns in the US." Originally "The Bridgers Mansion," the Graystone Inn was built in 1905–1906 by Elizabeth Haywood Bridgers, widow of Preston L. Bridgers, a local merchant and son of Robert Rufus Bridgers, who was past president of the Atlantic Coast Line Railway, founder of the Wilmington and Weldon Railroad, and two-time representative to the Confederate Congress. A historic landmark and one of the most elegant structures in Wilmington, the inn has been completely remodeled and returned to its original grandeur. $$$.

Hotel Ballest Willmington. 301 North Water St.; (877) 214-9174; hilton.com. Located on the downtown waterfront, the Hilton has 274 guest rooms, with half overlooking the river. The Poolside and Cabana Bar, adorned with ceiling fans and palm trees, is a great place for a sunset cocktail, and on Friday evenings in the summer, the pool deck is the scene of the Sunset Celebration, a popular live-music party. $$$.

Stemmerman's Inn. 130 S. Front St.; (910) 763-7776; stemmermans.com. Located downtown, Stemmerman's has a classic Victorian storefront style. Inside, remodeled suites and rooms are contemporary with exposed bricks and beams. $–$$.

The Verandas. 202 Nun St.; (910) 251-2212; verandas.com. This elegant, 8,500-square-foot Victorian Italianate mansion was originally built in 1853 by Benjamin Beery. The structure suffered extensive fire and water damage in 1992. Boarded up and decaying, the mansion was restored to provide a comfortable weekend retreat for tourists. Hurricane Florence In 2018 also did some damage, but once again its back to its original grandeur All 8 guest rooms are large corner rooms. Guests may choose from a selection of king, queen, or twin beds in corner rooms with luxurious private baths. $$$.

wrightsville beach, nc

Settled in 1889 and incorporated in 1899, the summer resort of Wrightsville Beach is a small island community that still retains its village charm, though the secret of her charms is becoming more well know thus is attracting increasing numbers of tourists. A variety of accommodations and restaurants can be found at Wrightsville, the weeklong summer home for many Carolina families. Students from the University of North Carolina at Wilmington, 10 minutes away, flock to the island's south end in warmer months. Some study while sunbathing; others surf, hugging the beach's second and now defunct fishing pier.

getting there

From Wilmington, take US 76 (Oleander Drive) east until it merges with US 74 (Eastwood Road) to go over the Intercoastal Waterway and reach Wrightsville Beach.

where to go

Johnnie Mercer's Pier. 23 E. Salisbury St.; (910) 256-2743; johnniemercersfishingpier .com. With access at the town's main beach, Johnnie Mercer's Pier is the center of activity in Wrightsville Beach as it has been since the 1930s. The only exception was after the original pier was destroyed by a double punch from hurricanes Fran and Bertha in 1996. The old wooden pier was rebuilt—this time in concrete—and reopened in 2001. In addition to fishing and buying fishing supplies you can grab lunch or ice cream, or play in the game room. Pier management charges a fee even to walk its 1,200 feet.

Wrightsville Beach Museum of History. 303 W. Salisbury St.; (910) 256-2569; wb museum.com. The tiny beach cottage museum houses various exhibits on Wrightsville Beach history and depicts the lifestyle at Wrightsville Beach ca. 1900. One of the oldest cottages on the island, the house was built by the Tidewater Power Company in 1907 as part of a plan to encourage residential development. Free. Open Weds through Sat 10 a.m. to 4 p.m., and Sun 1 to 4 p.m.

where to shop

Lumina Station. 1900 Eastwood Rd.; (910) 256-0900; luminastation.com. For several decades near the turn of the 20th century, Lumina was the social center of this region. People came to dance to the sounds of such greats as Cab Calloway, Benny Goodman, Guy Lombardo, and "Satchmo" Louis Armstrong. Today's Lumina Station remains true to the original landmark's style and spirit. Fine dining and shopping are to be found in the 27 shops.

South End Surf Shop. 708 S. Lumina Ave.; (910) 256-1118; southendsurf.com. A UNCW graduate opened this surf shop to cater to the number of surfers heading to this area. In addition to equipment and supplies for the surfer, you can also find T-shirts and other beach items or rent paddleboards.

where to eat

Bluewater Waterfront Grill. 4 Marina St.; (910) 256-8500; bluewaterdining.com. Overlooking the Intercoastal Waterway, the 2-story Bluewater provides panoramas and great food. Try the hot crab dip for an appetizer. For entrees the coconut shrimp plate and the seafood lasagna or the lump crab cakes are excellent choices. Sit indoors, on a waterside patio downstairs, or on an intimate covered terrace upstairs. The restaurant offers live entertainment on Sunday afternoons during the summer. Open daily 11 a.m. to 11 p.m. $$.

The Bridge Tender. 1414 Airlie Rd.; (910) 256-4519; thebridgetender.com. Overlooking the Intercoastal Waterway on the mainland side, the Bridge Tender has enjoyed a reputation for its prime rib and seafood since opening in 1976. Open Mon through Fri 11:30 a.m. to 2 p.m. for lunch, nightly for dinner from 5 p.m. $$–$$$.

The Oceanic. 703 S. Lumina Ave.; (910) 256-5551; oceanicrestaurant.com. This ocean-front restaurant offers indoor and outdoor seating. Go for a basket of fresh fish and chips on the old Crystal pier that serves as the patio, but make sure you begin with the hot crab dip, a favorite among the regulars. The appetizer is made from local crabmeat broiled with threecheeses, a secret blend of seasonings, and garlic bread for dipping. Entrees include seafood, chicken, and beef dishes. Leave room for the key lime pie. $$–$$$.

South Beach Grill. 100 S. Lumina Ave.; (910) 256-4646; southbeachgrillwb.com. Outdoor seating at South Beach grants a view of the sun setting over the banks channel. Get a good burger or nicely done fish dish at this restaurant where locals gather in the evening. $$–$$$.

where to stay

Blockade Runner Beach Resort. 275 Waynick Blvd.; (910) 256-2254; blockade-runner .com. Built in the 1970s, this 150-room beachfront property has been thoroughly renovated over the years. Beautifully landscaped with tropical plants, the hotel's grass lawn and gardens serve as a buffer between the beach and the hotel. Truly a paradise for young and old, kids' programs are offered during summer months. $$–$$$.

The Harbor Inn. 701 Causeway Dr.; (888) 507-9402; wharborinnwb.com. Although it's not on the beach, this is a nice place with a pool, access to the beach, and a short dock for fishing or watching the boats come in. Rooms have been remodeled in a contemporary style. $$$.

One South Lumina. 1 S. Lumina Ave.; (800) 421-3255; onesouthlumina.info. This beachfront hotel is within walking distance to stores and other amenities and offers large rooms and suites. The rooms' decor is simple but sufficient. $$$.

day trip 10

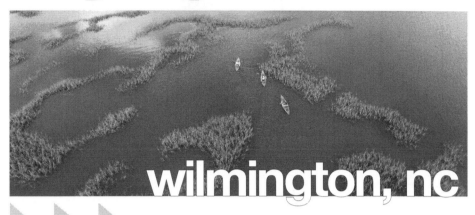

wilmington, nc

crystal island:
morehead city, nc; atlantic beach, nc

Linked most closely by their proximity, Morehead City is a mature stop with outstanding culinary delights and opportunities for shopping or enjoying other cultural rewards, while Atlantic Beach is a popular post to ride waves and explore coastal ecology. Beachgoers have been coming to Atlantic Beach since 1887, when a small, one-story pavilion was all that was here—well, that and the beach itself. Back then, visitors stayed in Morehead City and traveled by sailboat to the beach. It wasn't until the1930s that the first permanent residents began to move here. Today a high-rise bridge provides access to this part of the Crystal Coast where excited vacationers set up housekeeping in one of the many fine properties along the beachfront. Only 1,700 residents make their home in Atlantic Beach year-round, but the population swells to accommodate the 35,000 visitors who come here during the summer months. Morehead City is less transient. Sure, it's still a summertime resort, but its population of 9,000 blends more seamlessly with those who choose to visit here.

morehead city, nc

Incorporated in 1861 and named for prominent Governor John Motley Morehead, who helped establish the city on the site formerly known as Shepherd's Point, Morehead City is located on a peninsula flanked by Bogue Sound and the Newport River. A summer resort, Morehead City is also the state's only deepwater port north of Wilmington. On the downtown waterfront, seafood reigns supreme and art galleries come together along this beautiful

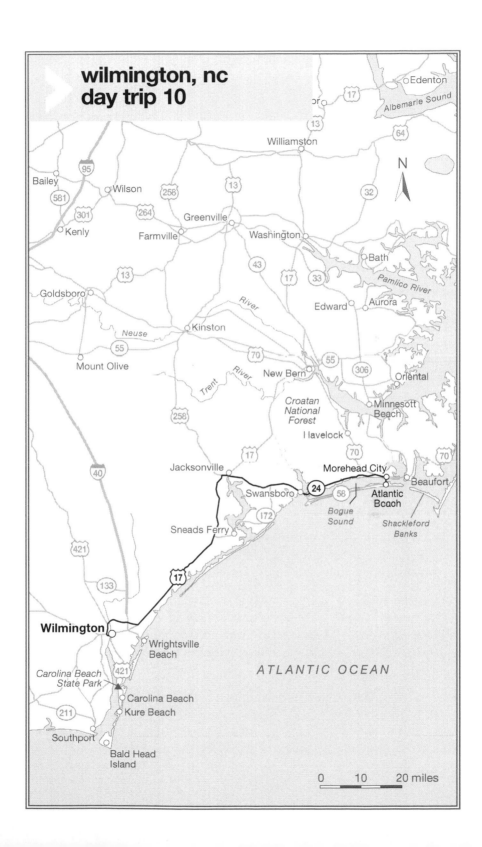

wilmington, nc
day trip 10

stretch where the smell of hush puppies mixes with the excitement of Gulf Stream sportfishing. Fishing charter companies aren't hard to come by if you want to take advantage of a guided fishing expedition. Train tracks cross Arendell Street, Morehead's main drag, a sort of dividing line between old and new parts of the city, creating an atmosphere of distinct architectural character.

getting there

From Wilmington, Morehead City is about a 90-minute drive north via US 17 through Jacksonville. From there, take SR 24 north until it merges with US 70.

where to go

History Museum of Carteret County. 1008 Arendell St.; (252) 247-7533; carterethistory .org. Home of the Carteret County Historical Society and Museum of History and Art, the museum collection includes artifacts of Native American inhabitants of this coastal region, costumes of the 18th and 19th centuries, furnishings, medical displays, and Civil War artifacts. The research library contains a notable genealogy collection, publications, archival manuscript material, and an extensive photography file. Free. Tours are offered Tues through Fri and the first Sat of each month, 10 a.m. to 4 p.m.

Morehead City Ferry Service. 709 Shepard St.; (252) 504-2488; moreheadferryservice .com. Find a real sand dollar or seek out dolphins aboard the Miss Morehead City. The Ferry service offers a number of trips throughout the year and provides service to several cities in the area. Prices start at $20 per person.

where to shop

Arts Council of Carteret County. 812 Evans St.; (252) 726-9156; artscouncilcarteret.org. More than a dozen galleries located here feature the work of local artisans. Available for purchase are paintings, hand-carved decoys, photography, and more.

Carolina Artist's Gallery. 800 Evans St.; (252) 726-7550; carolinaartistgallery.com. A cooperative representing 30 or more regional and local artists offers displays in the sunny gallery rooms of original paintings, pottery, batiks, photography, and other art forms. From classically trained artists to self-taught painters, the variety is outstanding. Open daily except Tues 11 a.m. to 5 p.m.

Dee Gee's Gifts and Books. 508 Evans St.; (252) 726-3314; deegees.com. A landmark on the Morehead City waterfront where, in addition to best sellers, greeting cards, and specialty gifts, you will find the complete collection of local nautical charts and possibly every book that has ever been written about the Crystal Coast area. Dee Gee's schedules frequent book signings with state and local writers. Open daily year-round.

where to eat

The Banks Grill. 2900 Arendell St.; (252) 499-9044; thebanksgrill.com. Start your day with homemade jelly on a fresh-baked biscuit at this popular breakfast and lunch spot. Breakfast features everything from a quick bite to eggs Benedict. Burgers and barbecue top the lunch menu. Open Mon through Fri 7 a.m. to 2 p.m., Sat and Sun 7:30 a.m. to 2 p.m. $–$$.

Circa 81. 4650 Arendell St.; (252) 648-8300; circa-81.com. Tapas plates that focus on farm and sea to table are the features here. Hot crab dip, shrimp and grits, and crab cakes top the list of selections. The Circa 81 martini also comes highly recommended. Open Mon, Wed, and Thurs 11:30 a.m. to 9 p.m., Fri and Sat 11:30 a.m. to 9:30 p.m., Sun 10:30 a.m. to 9:30 p.m. $$$.

Ruddy Duck Tavern, 509 Evans St.; (252) 726-7500; ruddyducktavern.com. Located on the water, the Ruddy Duck has a wide range of solid choices on its menu from soups and salads to burgers and flatbread pizza made from organic and locally-sourced ingredients wherever possible. Landlubber dishes are served alongside seafood. Open Thurs through Sun. 11 a.m. to 9 p.m. $$.

where to stay

The Lighthouse Inn. 2300 Bridges St.; (252) 247-3133. If you would prefer to avoid the national chains, try this small inn. Located near the Atlantic Beach Bridge and all area attractions, the Lighthouse Inn has 5 guest rooms with bath and 2 condo units that accommodate 6. $$.

atlantic beach, nc

Atlantic Beach was developed as a vacation destination beginning in the 1870s. Its first bathing pavilion was built in 1887, attracting beachgoers from across Bogue Sound. Later it became known as Money Island Beach, and in 1922 a second bathing area known as Asbury Beach was opened. Realizing its financial potential, a group of investors from Morehead City and Beaufort bought the property, built a bridge over Bogue Sound, and created a resort area around "The Circle" that still exists today. The state would later purchase that bridge and a vacation destination was born.

getting there

From Morehead City, Atlantic Beach is a short hop over Money Bay via the Atlantic Beach Bridge off US 70.

where to go

Fort Macon State Park. (252) 726-3775; ncparks.gov. Located on the east end of the island at MP 0 on Highway 58, Fort Macon is a popular destination for the variety of activities available. The Civil War fort is an interesting site hiding in the dunes to protect Beaufort Inlet. From the fort walls, you can see the wreck site of Blackbeard's flagship, *Queen Anne's Revenge*, which lies in 20 feet of water just off the inlet and is being recovered by the state. Rangers offer guided tours and the Coast Education Center has exhibits about the natural history of the park. A 1-mile nature walk from the fort leads to frequently good bird watching. At the mouth of Beaufort Inlet, the rock jetty is a reliable destination for lucky surf fishing. Open year-round with interpretive programs offered daily, there are picnicking facilities, a bathhouse, and lifeguard services. The swimming area is open in summer 10 a.m. to 5:45 p.m. The fort is open year-round daily except for Christmas Day 9 a.m. to 5:30 p.m.

North Carolina Aquarium. Roosevelt Drive at MP 7, Hwy. 58; (252) 247-4003; ncaquariums.com. The aquarium is perfectly situated in the Roosevelt Natural Area at Pine Knoll Shores. An interpreted trail through an ancient maritime forest begins at the aquarium parking lot. Another trail along a saltwater marsh begins inside the aquarium. The aquarium itself takes guests on an aquatic journey through 5 galleries "from the mountains to the sea." You'll view creatures in aquatic ecosystems from the mountains, the Piedmont, the coastal plain, the tidal waters, and the open ocean. You can watch—and talk to—divers in the "Living Shipwreck" exhibit with more than 300,000 gallons or meet an alligator face to face, pet a stingray, or see a rare white sea turtle. It also has a snack bar and a gift shop. The aquarium offers select programs and experiences throughout the area. Some programs require preregistration, so consult the aquarium's calendar. Admission is $12.95 for adults, $11.95 for seniors, and $9.95 for children ages 3 through 12. Open daily 9 a.m. to 5 p.m.

Roosevelt Natural Area. (252) 726-3775. At MP 7 on Highway 58, this rare and undisturbed ancient maritime forest surrounds the North Carolina Aquarium, land preserved by the children of the 26th US president, who inherited the part of the island that is now Pine Knoll Shores. There are 2 trails and nearly 300 acres to explore here: The **Theodore Roosevelt Trail** is a 30-minute walk among natural vegetation—especially the live oaks—and freshwater lakes (the trailhead is on the south side of the aquarium parking lot); the **Alice Hoffman Trail,** accessible from inside the aquarium, tours a salt marsh habitat with views of fiddler crabs and shorebirds. A reptile exhibit includes live animals that are at home in a salt marsh habitat and a maritime forest.

where to shop

Atlantic Station Shopping Center. W. Fort Macon Road. With convenient park-and-walk shopping in Atlantic Beach, shops include Trillium, a bright and colorful stop for home accessories and women's sportswear (252-247-7210), and Boaters World (252-240-0055) with marine equipment and accessories from tools and outboards to hooks, lines, and sinkers.

Capt. Stacy Fishing Center. 416 Atlantic Beach Causeway; (252) 247-7501 or (800) 533-9417; captstacy.com. Located right on the dock, this gift shop has more than you might expect at first glance. Jewelry, flags with nautical or beach themes, etched glass, crystal, and a variety of holiday decorations are offered. Of course, you'll find standard beach wares including T-shirts, beach bags, hats, sunglasses, and the like. The shop is open year-round, although winter hours are limited.

Kites Unlimited. 1010 W. Fort Macon Rd.; (252) 247-7011. Located at Atlantic Station Shopping Center, this kite shop offers hundreds of styles of kites for fun on the beach and banners for beauty at home. You'll also find windsocks, windwheels, puzzles, and games for all ages.

where to eat

Amos Mosquito's Restaurant & Bar. 703 E. Fort Macon Rd.; (252) 247-6222; amos mosquitos.com. The odd name of this restaurant came from a knock-knock joke, but what it has done for the culinary scene since opening in Atlantic Beach is serious business for the foodie. An eclectic menu features fillet and fried oysters, meat loaf, and more. Thursday is sushi and karaoke night. Open Tues 5 to 8:45 p.m., Wed 5 to 9 p.m., Thurs through Sat 5 to 9:30 p.m. $$$

The Crab's Claw. 201 W. Atlantic Blvd.; (252) 726-8222; crabsclaw.com. This restaurant on the beach is a popular lunch destination. Have a burger on the second-story deck, or try the salads and hot sauces. The Crab's Claw once billed itself as an oyster bar, but now focuses on dishes with a Caribbean twist. Open daily except Wed. 11:30 a.m. to 9 p.m. with reduced hours in the off-season. $–$$.

Island Grille. 401 Money Island Dr.; (252) 240-0000. This cozy beach restaurant is located at the parking lot of Sportsman's Pier. There's no view, but the food is spectacular and the regulars are regular. One popular dish: fillet stuffed with feta and served with garlic mashed potatoes. Choices always include a fish fillet (such as mahimahi) and a shellfish and pasta dish. Make reservations if you want to be seated on Mon or Tues night, even in Jan. Open daily 5 to 9 p.m. and Sun for brunch at 11 a.m. $$–$$$.

where to stay

Atlantis Lodge. 123 Salter Path Rd., MP 5 on Hwy. 58; (252) 726-5168 or (800) 682-7057; atlantislodge.com. One of the oldest lodging properties on the Crystal Coast, this 42-room oceanfront lodge saw very little natural vegetation removed during its construction. Thus natural barriers, wildlife, and vegetation remain very much a priority. It's difficult to get a reservation here unless you've been a regular guest, but don't let that stop you from trying. The private pool is arguably the island's most invitingly cool place, the definition of "having it made in the shade." All rooms are efficiencies. $$–$$$.

Bogue Shores Suites. 1918 W. Fort Macon Rd.; (800) 613-5043 or (252) 726-7071. Located on the sound across the street from the beach, this is an all-suite facility. Guests have access to fishing piers and a large pool. Reservations can be made by calling the number above, but suites are also managed by a number of local realtors. $$.

day trip 11

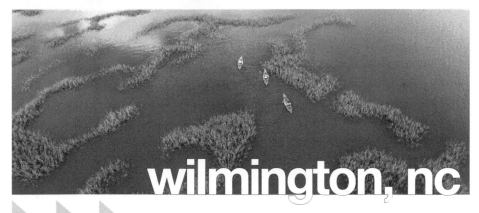

wilmington, nc

>>> **pleasure island:**
carolina beach, nc; kure beach, nc.

Closely associated with the Wilmington community to the north, Carolina vacationers are reconnecting with their namesake beach town that offers some tasty doughnuts that you can eat while walking the old-fashioned boardwalk—after you ride the Tilt-a-whirl. That's only the beginning of what day-trippers find on these beaches. Welcome to Pleasure Island, the site of Carolina and Kure Beaches. Reminiscent of classic beach towns of the early and mid-20th century, now-bustling boardwalks that were once overshadowed by more popular beach communities—Myrtle Beach to the south and the Outer Banks to the north. Today vacationers come here to enjoy the family atmosphere, a boardwalk amusement park, free concerts, and fireworks offered by the town at Carolina Lake Park, and events in their respective town centers. Carolina Beach is also home to one of the state's most ecologically unique state parks, while Kure Beach boasts historic attractions and one of North Carolina's three state-operated aquariums.

carolina beach, nc

Carolina Beach was the site of an engagement between Union and Confederate forces following the fall of Fort Fisher south of here on January 15, 1865. Once called Sugar Loaf, Carolina Beach was incorporated in 1925 and became known throughout the state for its boardwalk. The boardwalk fell into disrepair over the years, but it has slowly recovered. Storefronts that were boarded up a a couple of decades ago have reopened as colorful

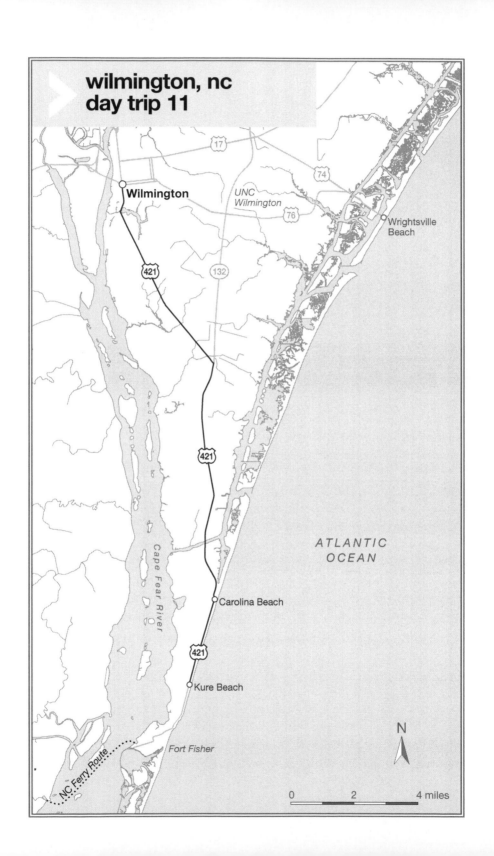

wilmington, nc
day trip 11

Wilmington

UNC Wilmington

17

74

76

132

421

Wrightsville Beach

Cape Fear River

421

ATLANTIC OCEAN

Carolina Beach

421

Kure Beach

NC Ferry Route

Fort Fisher

N

0   2   4 miles

new restaurants, ice-cream parlors, and retail establishments. An incredible doughnut shop called Brits has been one of a few mainstays. Carolina Beach State Park is home to a variety of natural areas that make it one of the most biologically diverse parks in North Carolina. This area is part of a small region of the world where the Venus flytrap grows naturally.

getting there

Take US 421 south from Wilmington to reach Carolina Beach in about 15 minutes. The only way off the island on the south end is via the NC Ferry System.

where to go

Carolina Beach State Park. 1010 State Park Rd.; (910) 458-8206; ncparks.gov. This state park offers fishing, camping, and miles of hiking trails that traverse a variety of distinct habitats, including the Venus flytrap trail, a half-mile loop through pocosin, longleaf pine, and turkey oak, and savanna communities. Learn more about the Venus flytrap and other indigenous species at the park's visitor center. It is also an excellent location for bird watching and is on the NC Birding Trial. Brown pelicans thrive in the coastal environment, and warblers, finches, and woodpeckers fill the woods. In summer, painted buntings, yellowthroats, and prairie warblers can be seen in the forest. The marina located here offers kayak and standup paddle board rentals. Visiting the park is free but there are fees for camping and other facilities. The park is typically open during daylight hours, and the visitor center is open daily 9 a.m. to 5 p.m. except Christmas Day.

Kayak Carolina. 103 Winner Ave.; (910) 707-0361; kayakcarolina.com. Join Angela and John Pagenstecher for a 2-hour guided ecotour of the coastal marshlands on extremely stable and comfortable touring kayaks, great for the uninitiated, plus day trips and skill building for experienced kayakers. Kids Kayak Camp is offered during the summer. Rental rates start at $40; guided tours start at $55 per person.

where to shop

Carolina Surf Brand. 11 Pavilion Ave. S. ; (910) 707-0125; carolnasurfbrand.com. In 2014 a group of surfers got together and began promoting surf films and the sport Itself. When they began producing film festivals it spawned the Carolina Surf Brand sports apparel for men, women, and children. This Is their flagship store but it can be found at other retailers on the North and South Carolina Coast.

Seaside Gifts and Treasures. 11 Boardwalk Ave.; (919) 665-1029; Set among the shops, food stands and amusements of the boardwalk, this retailer offers traditional beachwear and souvenirs alongside handcrafted items.

where to eat

Havana's Fresh Island Seafood. 1 N. Lake Park Blvd.; (910) 458-2822; havanasrestaurant.com. The pretty Caribbean-inspired decor matches the well-done Caribbean-inspired dishes. You can get a simple steak or blackened salmon topped with a citrus salsa. Open Mon through Thurs 5 to 9:30 p.m., Fri and Sat 5 to 10 p.m., Sun 10 a.m. to 2 p.m. $$–$$$.

The Ocean Grill. 1211 S. Lake Park Blvd.; (910) 458-2000; oceangrilltiki.com. Burgers and sandwiches at lunch give way to steaks and seafood for dinner, as enjoyable in the dining room as it is on the oceanfront patio. Savor shrimp and grits, New Orleans-style French toast with flambe bananas, or a breakfast burrito during Sun brunch. Stick around on select evenings for live music at the tiki bar located on the old town pier beyond the patio. It's like a concert on the ocean. Open Mon through Wed 11:30 a.m. to 10:30 p.m., Thurs through Sat 11:30 a.m. to midnight, Sun 10:30 a.m. to 10:30 p.m. $$.

Shuckin' Shack. 5 N. Lake Park Blvd.; (910) 458-7380; the shuckinshack.com. This local favorite may pride itself on being an oyster bar, but the shrimp isn't bad either. Although you will find a chicken finger sandwich on the menu, the Shack stays true to its mission, serving all things that can be shucked. Shuckin' Shacks can be found in a dozen or so other locations in the south, but this Is the original. $$.

kure beach, nc

Named for the Kure family, who first came here in 1867, Kure Beach today is a small, family-oriented shorefront located at the southern extreme of Pleasure Island. Kure Beach features large, uncrowded beaches, good seafood, and historic Fort Fisher, where you can tour the museum or take a hike around the Civil War earthworks. Less than 2 miles away is the North Carolina Aquarium, where you can view marine life and participate in special aquatic programs.

getting there

Access Kure Beach via Carolina Beach and continue south on US 421.

where to go

Fort Fisher State Historic Site. 1610 Fort Fisher Blvd.; (910) 251-7340; historicsites.nc .gov. Billed as "the last major stronghold of the Confederacy," this historic site includes interpretive exhibits and audiovisual presentations depicting two major battles fought here. Union forces overran the earthen fort in January 1865 and, in subsequent days, Wilmington. Today the site includes a gun battery with examples of cannons used in the Civil War, and a trail with markers and monuments. A museum traces the fort's history, the life of the soldiers who called it home, and technology used in interactive and audiovisual displays. Open Tues through Sat 9 a.m. to 5 p.m., Sun 1 to 5 p.m. Memorial Day through Labor Day. Free.

North Carolina Aquarium at Fort Fisher. 900 Loggerhead Rd.; (910) 458-8257; ncaquariums.com. Here day-trippers get more than a glimpse of the waters of the Cape Fear. Six galleries lead guests from nearby swamps to the ocean. The aquarium, one of 3 in the state, features a centerpiece 200,000-gallon ocean aquarium that includes a 2-story multilevel viewing of large sharks, groupers, barracudas, and loggerhead turtles swimming around re-created Cape Fear rock ledges. A touch pool, a variety of live demonstrations by staff, and other programs provide several hours of fun. Admission is $12.95 for adults, $11.95 for seniors and active military, and $10.95 for children ages 6 to 17. Open daily 9 a.m. to 5 p.m. except for Thanksgiving, Christmas, and New Year's Day.

North Carolina Underwater Archaeology Center. 1528 S. Fort Fisher Blvd.; (910) 458-9042; archaeology.ncdcr.gov/underwater-archaeology-branch. The state operates this small museum dedicated to all the archaeological discoveries that have been made in this region from prehistoric Native American finds to times when pirates sailed the seas to the Civil War. Admission is free. Hours vary seasonally.

where to eat

Jack Mackerel's Island Grill. 113 K Ave.; (910) 458-7668; jackmackerels.rcom. You'll find fun island food and decor on the bold side here. Dishes range from a typical club sandwich to more extravagant fish and shrimp dishes. Dining tables surround a tiki bar, and the sound system pours out Jimmy Buffett and Jack Johnson tunes. $$.

day trip 12

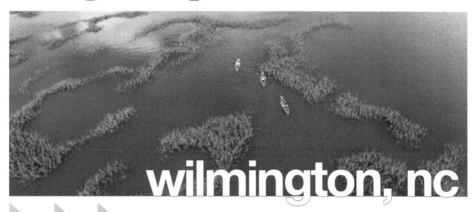

wilmington, nc

>>> **sea oats & southern charm:**
southport, nc; bald head island, nc

The graceful live oaks lining the streets of beautiful historic Southport give way to the sandcastles and sea oats of Bald Head Island where tourists find, instead of cars, beautiful beaches and the best in vacation amenities. Southport, one of the most charming towns in the state, garners praise as one of the best places to retire. It oozes coastal charm and boasts a rich maritime history detailed in one of the state-operated maritime museums. The town's protected harbor makes for popular water activities, as transoceanic vessels ferry within 100 feet of town. Historic homes, boutique shops, art galleries, and local restaurants now occupy a live oak forest, cultivated as shade trees here and in other coastal regions of the southern US.

A short ferry trip from Southport takes day-trippers to Bald Head Island. Once a preferred destination of pirates Blackbeard and Stede Bonnet, the island is now a refuge for those who truly enjoy getting away from it all. No gasoline engines are permitted here. Instead vacationers piddle about in electric golf carts. For a day it makes a good refuge amid unspoiled beaches, a maritime forest, and a preserved historic lighthouse.

southport, nc

The town that would become Southport was established around Fort Johnston, constructed in 1748 to protect the Cape Fear settlements from raids by Spanish pirates and privateers. Several decades later in 1792, the town of Smithville was founded, named after North

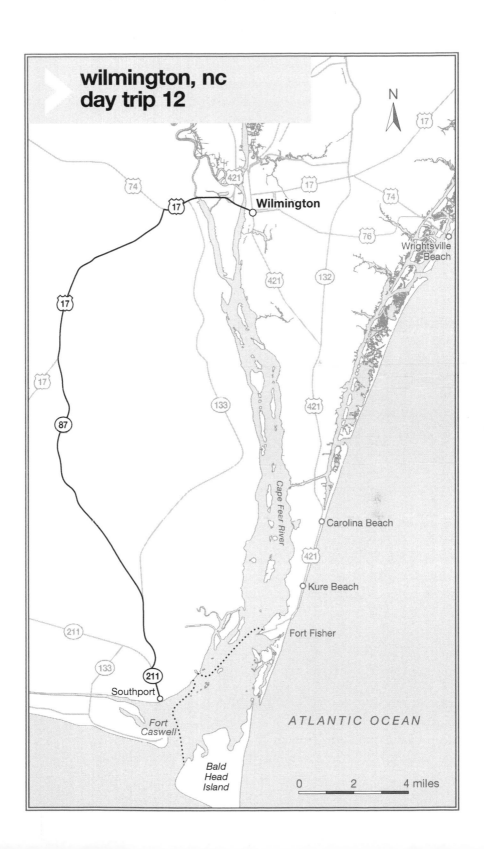

quirky carolina

While walking the historic downtown, listen for the "Seneca Drums," mysterious, low-pitched offshore booms that locals attribute to chunks of the continental shelf dropping off cliffs in the Atlantic Ocean. Truth is, no one knows what causes the low rumbles.

Carolina's colonial Governor Benjamin Smith. Located at the confluence of the mouth of the Cape Fear River, the Intracoastal Waterway, and the Atlantic Ocean, Southport became the town's adopted name in 1887, when town fathers sought to attract a state port to the region. Although the port was later located up the Cape Fear River in Wilmington, the river still plays a major part in Southport's economy. The films *Nights in Rodanthe* and *A Walk to Remember*, among others, were filmed here with nearby studios in Wilmington providing support. The fine folks at the Fort Johnson Southport Museum and Visitors Center (203 E. Bay St.; 910-457-7927; cityofsouthport.com) are glad to point you in the right direction.

getting there

Southport isn't accessible from Pleasure Island by car. To get here you have to take the ferry or make your way back to Wilmington and from there take US 17 to SR 87. The drive from Wilmington is 30 miles and will take about 40 minutes. The ferry ride, depending on your wait, will likely take the same amount of time.

where to go

North Carolina Maritime Museum at Southport. 204 E. Moore St.; (910) 477-5151; ncmaritimemuseums.com. One of three maritime museums on the North Carolina coast, this collection of memorabilia illustrates the vast nautical history of Southport, the Lower Cape Fear, and southeastern North Carolina. The museum's self-guided tour begins with a 2,000-year-old fragment of a canoe used by the Cape Fear Indians. The visitor then makes his way through stories of pirates and river pilots and learns about Civil War blockade runners. In addition to an on-site research library, films and programs are offered year-round. Admission is free. Open Tues through Sat 10 a.m. to 4 p.m.

Southport Walking Tours. 113 W. Moore St.; (910) 457-7927; downtownsouthport.org. Begin the mile-long, self-guided walking tour by printing out a map from Downtown Southport's website. This relaxed walk takes you through charming Historic Southport, packed with opportunities to pick a piece of art and to learn more about Southport's history. Your first stop, the Indian Trail Tree, is adjacent to the center. Cape Fear Indians bent the live oak sapling to point the way to tribal fishing grounds. That was 800 years ago. Today in the spring and the fall, you can see clusters of fishing boats on a line on either side of the tree. The Indian Trail Tree still points the way to the best spot to hook dinner.

where to shop

Franklin Square Gallery. 130 E. West St.; (910) 457-5450; franklinsquaregallery.com. This association of local artisans showcases works in varying media, including painting and pottery, all displayed in a beautiful historic building. Open Mon through Sat 10 a.m. to 5 p.m., and during June, July, and Aug, Sun 1 to 4 p.m.

Lantanas Gallery and Fine Gifts. 113 S. Howe St.; (910) 457-0957; lantanasgallery.com. Several dozen regional and national artists offer their works in metal, wood, ceramics, fiber arts, and other media here. You will also find a variety of home decor and collectibles. Open Mon through Sat 10 a.m. to 5 p.m., Sun noon to 5 p.m.

The Ricky Evans Gallery. 211 N. Howe St.; (910) 457-1129; rickyevansgallery.com. This self-taught artist specializes in lighthouse illustrations along the Eastern Seaboard. In addition to a lighthouse series, he has produced various works of waterfronts in North Carolina.

Uncorked by the Sea. 602 N. Howe St.; (910) 454-0633; uncorkedbythesea.com. This unique wine shop offers everyday and special-occasion wines as well as home decor and artwork. Tastings and other special events are also conducted here periodically. Open Tues through Sat 10 a.m. to 6 p.m.

where to eat

Dry Street Pub and Pizza. 101 E. Brown St.; (910) 457-5994; drystreetpubandpizza .com. Locals say this is the town's best-kept secret for lunch. Located in an old cottage just beneath the water tower, this cozy restaurant offers a range of freshly made sandwiches, salads, and pizza, with indoor and outdoor dining. Open Tues through Sat. $$.

Fishy, Fishy Cafe. 106 Yacht Basin Dr.; (910) 457-1881; fishyfishycafe.com. The deck, the dining room, or the raw bar—you decide where to dine. Regardless of the selection, diners get a great view. The fun decor is reminiscent of Key West, and the food goes a little further. Not only can you enjoy fresh local catches, Fishy Fishy tacos, or the taste of Key West, you can also get Maryland crab cakes and steaks. Open daily 11 a.m. to 8:00 p.m. until 9 Fri and Sat. $$–$$$.

Mr. P's Bistro. 309 N. Howe St.; (910) 457-0801; mrpsbistro.com. Mr. P's house specialty is the Oysters Bienville appetizer. Chef Stephen Phipps adds a few touches of his own to this classic New Orleans recipe, topping fresh oysters with a white sauce made from chopped shrimp, mushrooms, and sherry. Other low-country favorites are also on the menu here and the fried green tomatoes are just waiting to be devoured. Open Mon through Sat 5 to 9 p.m. $$$.

Oliver's on the Cape Fear. 101 W. Bay St.; (910) 477-9299; oliversonthecapefear.menu. Amazing sunset views are just the beginning of what makes this such a popular spot for dinner. Located on the water, Oliver's offers a sophisticated menu with a southern twist. Open daily 11 a.m. to 9 p.m.;

The Provision Company. 130 Yacht Basin Dr.; (910) 457-0654; provisioncompany.com. The Provision Company runs on the honor system with no hostesses. After you place your order, grab a seat where you can find one. But don't forget to grab a cool one from the cooler. The specialty is steamed shrimp. If you're really hungry, order the special, popular among the locals: crab cake, a half pound of shrimp, and cucumber salad. For lighter fare, you can get smaller portions of shrimp alone or the popular grouper salad. When it's time to settle up, you check out with the cashier. Leave a tip in the jar if you like. $$.

where to stay

Brunswick Inn Bed and Breakfast. 301 E. Bay St.; (910) 457-5278; brunswickinn.com. The romantic, 7,000-square-foot, 16-room, Federal-style mansion overlooks the Cape Fear. Dating back to the 1800s, accommodations include spacious bedrooms with fireplaces, period furniture, and views of the waterway. $$$.

Lois Jane's Riverview Inn. 106 W. Bay St.; (910) 457-6701; loisjanes.com. The rocking chair veranda of this turn-of-the-19th-century home affords views of the Cape Fear River. Inside, cozy rooms are appointed with period furniture. A full southern-style breakfast is served at 8:30 a.m., and a wine and cheese reception is offered at 5 p.m. $$$.

Robert Ruark Inn. 119 N. Lord St.; (910) 363-4169; robertruarkinn.com. Named for the mid-century newspaperman and best-selling author who lived in Southport as a boy, this inn is reflective of the Hemingway-like lifestyle Ruark lived. Four handsome, well-appointed rooms make up this extravagant inn. Ruark's book *The Old Man and the Boy* is an account of his boyhood years in Southport and is recommended reading for those making the trip here. Breakfast is served daily from 8 to 10 a.m. in the Victorian dining room. $$$.

worth more time

Brunswick Town and Fort Anderson State Historic Site. 8884 St. Phillips Rd. Southeast, Winnabow; (910) 371-6613; historicsites.nc.gov. Brunswick Town was the first capital of the colony of North Carolina, a leading seaport during most of the 18th century, and location of the Stamp Act Rebellion. Europeans established it here in 1726 to serve as a naval port. The museum at the site allows you the opportunity to examine various artifacts and exhibits excavated from the remains of the original buildings, which were burned to the ground by the British in 1776. Still evident are remnants of the massive earthworks of Fort Anderson, built to help keep the Cape Fear River open for Civil War blockade runners, who shipped supplies to Confederate forces. It fell in 1865 during a fierce battle that also destroyed several other area forts. Markers have been erected to explain the history of the area. Admission is free. Open 9 a.m. to 5 p.m. Tues through Sat. To get here, take SR 133 north out of Southport. It's about a 20-minute drive.

bald head island, nc

It is likely, scientists say, that Bald Head Island was formed from a seasonally emerging sandbar, stabilized by a succession of plant life that would become the maritime forest that stands here today. Such sandbars still emerge offshore here and almost as quickly melt back into the sea. More than 10,000 of the island's 12,000 acres are preserved and protected from development, thus Bald Head has 14 miles of pristine beaches. A meandering creek cuts through acres of salt marsh that border an expanse of maritime forest. On the developed land, the world-class Bald Head Island resort offers the vacationer a championship golf course, clubhouse facilities, croquet, a marina, tennis courts, swimming pools, restaurants, snack bars, a full-service grocery store, and hours of peaceful relaxation. Day-trippers can enjoy much of this, too.

getting there

There is no automobile access to Bald Head Island; visitors, short- and long-term, must take the Bald Head Island Ferry from Deep Point Marina. It's located at 1301 Ferry Rd.; (910) 457-5003. The ferry departs Southport for Bald Head Island daily every hour on the hour from 8 a.m. until 6 p.m., except at noon. The ferry returns on the half hour. Days and times vary by season; please call for information. The cost is $23 per adult round-trip, $12 for children 3 to 12.

where to go

Bald Head Island Historic Tours. (910) 448-1472. Guided tours via golf cart of the island include a visit to Smith Island Museum of History and tales of piracy, colonization and life on the island. Reservations are required. Cost for adults, $30; children 3 to 12, $20. Tours depart at 10:30 a.m. Tues, Fri, and Sat.

Old Baldy Lighthouse and Smith Island Museum. (910) 457-7481; oldbaldy.org. North Carolina's lighthouses are one of our state's greatest treasures and the oldest still standing is "Old Baldy," built in 1818. Visitors can now climb the 108 steps to the top of the lighthouse, retired in 1935. The history of the lighthouse and area is told through exhibits at the small museum. Admission is $8 for adults and $5 for children ages 3 to 12. Old Baldy is open to the public Mon through Sat 9 a.m. to 5 p.m., Sun 11 a.m. to 5 p.m.

Shoals Club. 100 Station House Way; (910) 454-4888; shoalsclub.com. The Shoals Club on Bald Head Island will remind you of old-time beach pavilions. It serves as a place for families and friends to gather just off the beach, out of the hot, summer sun. The Shoals

Club, with its oceanfront clubhouse, dining areas, lounge, fitness room, locker-room facilities, swimming pools, and direct beach access, is the perfect complement to the Bald Head Island Club. Many of the island's organized activities originate from here.

where to eat

Bald Head Island Club. (910) 457-7300. A private club for members and accompanying guests or for temporary members staying on the island. Open for lunch (lounge only) and dinner, except on Mon and Tues. Offers a prix-fixe menu and dinner buffets during the summer months and holidays. $$$

Jules' Salty Grub and Island Pub. 10 Marina Wynd; (910) 457-7217; julessaltygrubbhi .com. Soup, salads, and even brick chicken (a chicken cooked under a brick) can be enjoyed here. Scallops and other more traditional offerings are available, too. $$.

Delphina Cantina. 10 Marina Wynd; (910) 457-7390. Located in the harbor, this spot was once known as the River Pilot Cafe. The Latin menu features Baja chicken, fish tacos, and a range of other similar options. Open daily for breakfast and lunch; Mon through Sat for dinner. The early-bird special offers 20 percent off dinner from 5:30 to 6:15 p.m. $$$.

where to stay

Marsh Harbour Inn. (800) 680-8322; marshharbourinn.com. Located in Harbour Village, this New England–style inn's Cape Cod rockers, Shaker beds, and antique wood floors lend each room a simple appeal. All rooms offer television, a DVD player, telephone, and private bath. Many of the inn's 15 rooms have private decks overlooking Bald Head Creek or the Cape Fear River. Included with your stay: breakfast in the dining room, afternoon hors d'oeuvres, use of an electric golf cart, and temporary membership in the Bald Head Island Club. $$$.

day trip 13

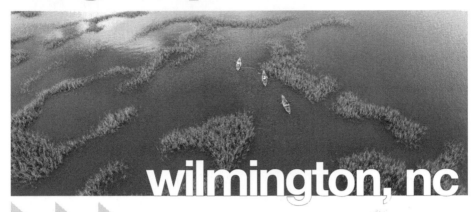

wilmington, nc

southern shores:
ocean isle beach, nc; sunset beach, nc

The south-facing beaches with calm surfs and spectacular sunsets of this small stretch of islands have become a perennial favorite for vacationers. In addition to long days of sun and surf, however, vacationers find the occasional diversion. Known as the South Brunswick Islands, there are a handful of similar communities here, each providing somewhat distinct offerings. The communities of Oak Island and Holden Beach are vacation residential areas that offer little other than some public beach access to the day-tripper. Two others—Ocean Isle and Sunset Beach—offer a small set of fun things to see and do.

ocean isle beach, nc

Ocean Isle Beach provides surf, sand, and sunshine—7 miles of beaches where you can swim and fish from the surf or pier. Get out on the ocean and try your fishing luck in deeper water, or if you prefer, try your hand at crabbing. This island's amenities include restaurants, specialty shops, and a miniature golf course.

getting there

Directly from Wilmington, you can reach Ocean Isle via US 17 in a little over an hour.

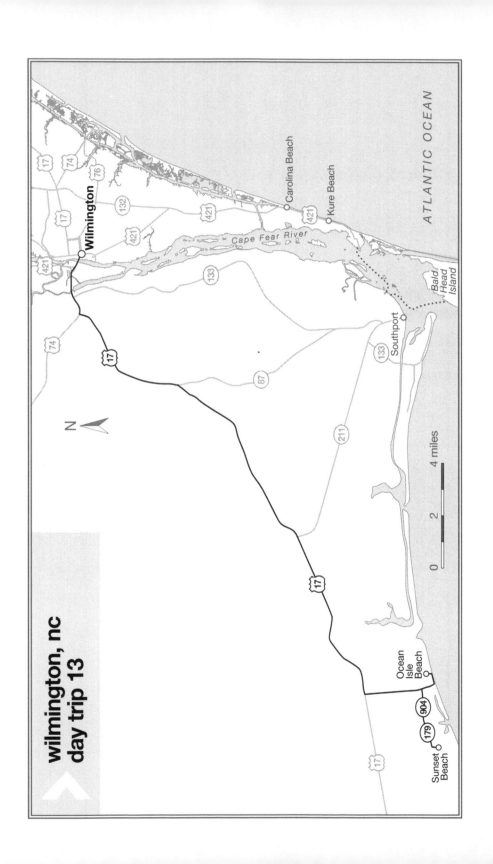

wilmington, nc
day trip 13

where to go

Museum of Coastal Carolina. 21 E. 2nd St.; (910) 579-1016; museumplanetarium.org. This small but well-done museum offers deep sea adventure without getting wet. Wall and floor murals and hand-carved specimens from the sea in the reef room give visitors a feeling of actually being in the water. The museum includes shark jaws, a huge seashell collection, dioramas of coastal animal life, and Civil War artifacts. In all, 7 specific galleries take the visitor from the Coastal Plain to the deep blue sea in just an hour or two. Open Mon through Thurs 10 a.m. to 8 p.m., Fri 10 a.m. to 5 p.m., Sat 10 a.m. to 1:30 p.m. Hours are limited in winter. Admission is $9.50 for adults, $8.50 for seniors, and $7.50 for children 3 to 12.

Ocean Isle Fishing Center on the Causeway. 65 Causeway Dr.; (910) 575-3474; oifc .com. This fishing center rents jet skis and other equipment. It also offers dinner cruises, charters, and a fishing school.

where to eat

Sharky's Restaurant. 61 Causeway Dr.; (910) 579-9177; sharkysoceanisle.com. This is the oldest restaurant on the island and a local favorite. It's also the only restaurant open year-round. Burgers, shrimp, salads, and entertainment come together to create a fun place to eat. Hours vary seasonally. $$.

Sugar Shack. 1609 Hale Beach Rd. Southwest; (910) 579-3844; sugarshackolb.com. A taste of Jamaica is served up inside the bright little yellow building just across the Intercoastal Waterway. Coconut shrimp and jerk dishes, along with tasty ribs, are served here. Finish up with a raspberry mango cheesecake. Open daily. $$.

where to stay

Islander Inn. 57 W. 1st St.; (888) 325-4753; islanderinn.com. The Islander Inn offers oceanfront accommodations, featuring a heated indoor pool, Jacuzzi, and an outdoor pool with a tiki bar overlooking the beach. A complimentary continental breakfast is included. $$$.

Four Mile Bed and Breakfast. 216 Ocean Isle Beach Rd; (910) 579-1776; fourmilebnb .com. Russell and Loretta Brown operate this accommodating inn on the mainland, where you can avoid the typical tourist crowds. Five modern rooms are offered on a nightly basis, which isn't permitted in many beach towns. $$.

The Winds Resort and Beach Club. 310 E. 1st St.; (800) 334-3581; thewinds.com. This resort hotel with a lovely subtropical garden of palm trees and hibiscus is the nicest of Ocean Isle's oceanfront accommodations. It offers rooms, suites, cottages, and a host of amenities, including a pool, hot tub, tiki bar, and restaurant serving light meals—wings, burgers, and the like by day, and full fish dishes by night. $$$.

sunset beach, nc

You'll quickly learn where this laid-back island just off the mainland got its name. Until recent years it was only accessible by a unique one-lane pontoon bridge. A feeling of seclusion will quickly descend upon you as you move into one of the large cottages situated behind the tall sand dunes on Sunset Beach. This little island, only 3 miles long, is the southernmost of the three communities.

getting there

Take SR 179 south from Ocean Isle and reach Sunset Beach in 15 minutes.

where to go

Ingram Planetarium. 7625 High Market St. in The Village at Sunset Resort; (910) 575-0031; museumplanetarium.org. Ingram Planetarium opened in summer 2002 as part of a collaboration with the nearby Museum of Coastal Carolina. It shows traditional planetarium programs on a 40-foot dome in its 90-seat theater as well a rocking laser shows from Pink Floyd, Michael Jackson, and others. The center also includes a few science-related exhibits, brainteasers, puzzles, and other hands-on activities. Open Mon, Wed, and Sat 11 a.m. to 5 p.m., Thurs and Fri 11 a.m. to 8 p.m. Admission is $9.50 for adults, $8.50 for seniors, and $7.50 for children 3 to 12.

where to stay

Sea Trail Plantation & Golf Resort. 211 Clubhouse Rd.; (888) 229-5747; seatrail.com. This is the largest resort on Sunset Beach, offering everything from efficiencies to villas, many overlooking the resort's championship golf course. The resort has a restaurant on a site that sports gardens, water features, and pristine fairways. The beach is only a few minutes' drive away. $$$.

charlotte, nc

day trip 14

charlotte, nc

charlotte, nc

Known as the Queen City and named in honor of Queen Charlotte of Mecklenburg-Strelitz, consort of King George III, Charlotte is the seat of Mecklenburg County and North Carolina's largest city. With a population of nearly 850,000 inside the city limits and 2.6 million in the metropolitan area, Charlotte is a bustling burg of cultural and business opportunity that grew exponentially in the latter part of the 20th century, thanks in part to a booming financial community led by Bank of America. The successful corporate community was in turn quick to support Charlotte sports and cultural assets; and even as the economy began to turn southward in the new century, public-private ventures to open new cultural facilities at the Levine Center for the Arts and to renovate or to move others continued.

The downtown area, known as uptown or Center City, includes Spectrum Arena, the 22,000-seat home of the Charlotte Hornets; Bank of America Stadium, the home of the Carolina Panthers; Truist Field, home to the Chicago White Sox AAA affiliate Charlotte Knights; and a host of museums, performance venues, restaurants, and other attractions. Shopping and other creature comforts are still developing in Charlotte's Center City, but for a day there is plenty to amuse. A light-rail system runs from downtown to the extreme southern side of the city. More is in development. In South Charlotte the day-tripper will find a plethora of upscale entertainment opportunities, shopping, and dining. North Charlotte is known as the University Area, the home of the University of North Carolina at Charlotte.

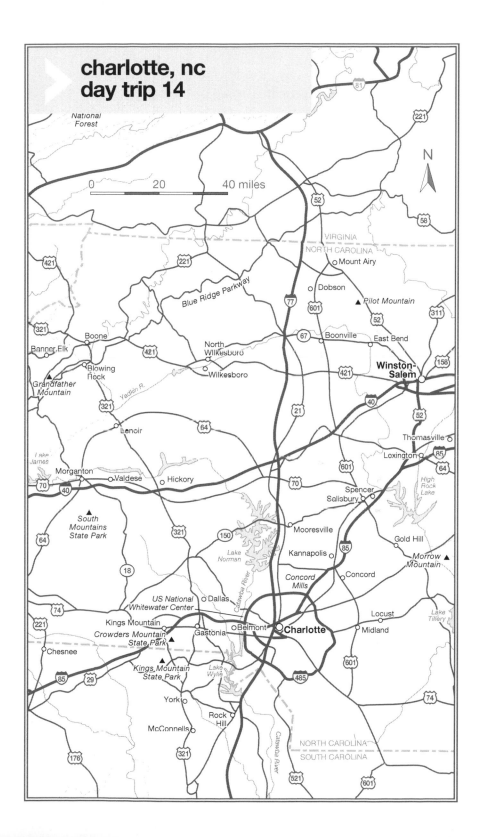

charlotte, nc
day trip 14

While there is much to do here, it's also a gateway for nearby day trips just outside the city proper. For more information visit charlottesgotalot.org.

getting there

Because of its size and central location, it's hard to miss Charlotte. From the Virginia state line, Charlotte is about 96 miles south on I-77 on the South Carolina border. From points west or southwest, take US 74, I-85, I-77, or US 21. US 74 comes out the other side, so take it if heading west from coastal communities. I-277 is the inner loop and tightly surrounds Center City. I-485 encircles the city 10 to 12 miles out.

onstage

Charlotte has no shortage of places to enjoy music, theater, and other performing arts. In addition to the football stadium and uptown arena, which both hold occasional events other than their respective sports, the **Knight Theater at the Levine Center for the Arts** *(430 S. Tryon St.; 704-379-1257; knighttheater.org) is a performance venue primarily playing host to the NC Dance Theater, the Charlotte Symphony, and Opera Carolina.* **The Blumenthal Performing Arts Center** *(130 N. Tryon St., 704-372-1000; blumenthalarts.org), a slightly older but stylish facility in the heart of uptown, has three theaters for larger productions including the Broadway lights series and smaller local productions.* **Spirit Square** *(345 N. College St.; 704-333-4686) was Charlotte's original cultural center. Located in a renovated church, it hosts small musical acts and other performances. The mid-20th-century but renovated* **Ovens Auditorium** *(2700 E. Independence Blvd.; 704-372-3600; ovensauditorium.com) hosts small concerts as well as some traveling Broadway plays. Next door is the original Charlotte Coliseum, built in the 1950s and now known as* **Bojangles Coliseum** *(2700 E. Independence Blvd.; 704-372-3600; bojanglescoliseum.com). The 11,000-seat arena hosts a variety of events including ice shows, benefit concerts, and regional performers. An even wider variety of shows is presented at the outdoor amphitheater at the* **NC Music Factory** *(935 N. Graham St.; 704-987-0612; ncmusicfactory.com), a burgeoning collection of indoor and outdoor venues, bars, and restaurants. Big-name acts appear at the larger arenas and at* **PNC Amphitheater** *(707 Pavilion Blvd.; 704-549-5555; livenation.com).* **Neighborhood Theater** *(511 E. 36th St.; 704-358-9298; neighborhoodtheater.com) is located in the artsy Noda area (short for North Davidson Street) and hosts small folk rock and indie rock shows as does the Evening Muse (3227 N. Davidson; (704-376-3737; eveningmuse.com.)*

where to go

Bechtler Museum of Modern Art. 420 S. Tryon St.; (704) 353-9200; bechtler.org. Among Charlotte's newest cultural facilities, this modern art museum is located on the campus known as the Levine Center for the Arts. The works in the collection were donated by Swiss artist Andreas Bechtler and include his pieces as well as an extensive collection that he inherited from his parents and art he accumulated himself. Works include those of Niki de Saint Phalle, Andy Warhol, and other mid- to late-20th-century artists. Admission is $9 for adults, $7 for seniors, $5 for ages 11 to 18, and free for children under age 11. Open Mon and Wed through Sat 10 a.m. to 5 p.m., Sun noon to 5 p.m.

Billy Graham Library. 4330 Westmont Dr.; (704) 401-3200; billygrahamlibrary.org. Almost like a presidential library, this impressive display tells the story of perhaps America's best-known modern-day religious leader. Billy Graham, who grew up on a farm near the library, would go on to preach to stadiums of people around the world and counsel US presidents and kings, queens, and other heads of state. The library includes audiovisual exhibits of the moving journey of his life story and the impact it has had on a wide variety of people. A collection of memorabilia is also displayed throughout the library. Also on the tour is his restored home place and a prayer garden. Free. Open Mon through Sat 9.30 a.m. to 5 p.m.

Carowinds. 14523 Carowinds Blvd.; (800) 588-2600; carowinds.com. This is the state's largest theme park, packed with a day full of fun and adventure for everyone in the family. Rides and attractions for younger guests include the Carolina Gold-rusher, a wooden mine train roller coaster; Woodstock Express, a kids roller coaster; Carolina Skytower, an air-conditioned cabin that travels up a 320-foot tower; and Ricochet, which takes riders through continuous twists and turns. Rip Roarin' Rapids, a soggy whitewater rafting expedition, and Boo Blasters on Boo Hill are fun for the older set, too. The truly adventurous will want to experience Vortex, a stand-up roller coaster; Nighthawk; Drop Zone, which drops visitors 174 feet at more than 50 miles per hour; or even the Intimidator, a super-fast, tall roller coaster named in honor of NASCAR racing legend Dale Earnhardt. Carowinds introduced an even faster and taller coaster, the Fury, in 2015. Cool off at Carolina Harbor , which includes several great waterslides and more. A county fair section has games and rides for all ages, including bumper cars, a carousel, and more. For a break in the action, you'll want to catch some of the shows at the park, including popular and Christian music concerts in the palladium. Tickets at the gate are $69.99 for those over 48 inches tall and $51.99 for those under 48 inches tall, but less expensive tickets are available through various Charlotte area promotions and on the Internet. Open Sat and Sun 10 a.m. to 8 p.m. mid-Mar, Apr, May, Sept, and through mid-Oct; open daily 10 a.m. to 8 p.m. June through late Aug. The park features a Halloween festival called Scarowinds some evenings in October.

Charlotte Museum of History/Hezekiah Alexander Homesite. 3500 Shamrock Dr.; (704) 568-1774; charlottemuseum.org. Built in 1774, the Alexander home is the oldest

festival in the park

*Adjacent to the Charlotte Nature Museum and Little Sugar Creek is **Freedom Park** (1900 East Blvd.; 704-336-2663), one of the city's oldest parks and location of one of the city's biggest and oldest annual events. Festival in the Park (festivalinthepark.org) is a 3-day fall event that has been held here since 1964. It includes arts and crafts, music, magic shows, rides, and, of course, plenty of food.*

dwelling in Mecklenburg County. The 5,000-square-foot stone house includes a museum with exhibits that concentrate on the history of the city. Docents in 18th-century costumes lead tours of the home, grounds, and outbuildings daily at noon and 2 p.m. A 36,000-square-foot museum building includes an extensive exhibits program that tells the story of Charlotte-Mecklenburg from the 18th to the 20th century. A changing exhibit space is located on the second floor. The American Freedom Bell, a 7-ton, ground-level bell guests can ring themselves in honor of those who fight for the freedom of America, is also on display. It acts as a permanent reminder that Charlotte was the location of the first official declaration of freedom from British rule. Admission is $10 for adults, $7 for students and seniors, free for children under age 6. Open Tues through Sat 10 a.m. to 5 p.m.

Charlotte Nature Museum. 1658 Sterling Rd.; (800) 935-0553; charlottenaturemuseum .org. Especially well-suited for younger children, this Charlotte landmark has a number of hands-on exhibits, audiovisual components, and push-button displays that help explain natural history. It features a puppet theater; a nature pavilion; an exhibit called Insect Alley; a live animal room that includes owls, snakes, and other nocturnal creatures; and a nature trail. Daily live presentations, storytime and puppet shows help explain some of nature's wonders. Admission is $8 per person. Open Tues through Fri 10 a.m. to 5 p.m., Sat 10 a.m. to 5 p.m., Sun noon to 5 p.m.

Discovery Place. 301 N. Tryon St.; (800) 935-0553; discoveryplace.org. Discovery Place is a sprawling, hands-on science and technology center, covering 2 stories over a city block that opened here in 1981 and received a big overhaul in 2010. The complex also includes the Charlotte Observer IMAX Dome Theatre. Younger children can tinker and play in Kid-Science, while everyone can conduct experiments in the Life Lab or dive into the aquariums at World Alive. Lie on a bed of nails; push, pull, and lift all in an exploration of scientific phenomena, simple machines, and more. A great 3D theater features a variety of shows while events at the IMAX range from *National Geographic*–style education presentations to a few Hollywood blockbusters and are scheduled throughout the year at this domed version of the technology. A variety of traveling exhibits that explore everything from dinosaurs to mummies to space are also scheduled throughout the year. Admission to the museum is $19 for adults, $15 for children and seniors. Admission to the IMAX is $10 for adults, $9 for children and seniors. Open Mon through Fri 9 a.m. to 4 p.m., Sat 10 a.m. to 6 p.m., Sun noon to 5 p.m. IMAX shows are held during operating hours, and during evening hours on weekends.

Harvey B. Gantt Center for African American Arts and Culture. 551 S. Tryon St.; (704) 547-3700; ganttcenter.org. Exhibition and performance spaces make up this center named for Charlotte's first African-American mayor. It hosts various traveling exhibitions that honor African-American art. Its most significant permanent collection comes from a retired librarian and her husband, a freelance writer who held works by Romare Bearden, Henry Ossawa Tanner, and Jacob Lawrence. The John and Vivian Hewitt Collection was purchased by Bank of America and toured the country before coming back to Charlotte, where it is housed permanently. Admission is $9 for adults, $7 for seniors and children age 6 and older. Open Tues through Sat 10 a.m. to 5 p.m., Sun 1 to 5 p.m.

Levine Museum of the New South. 200 E. 7th St.; (704) 333-1887; museumofthenew south.org. Nestled on the corner of 7th and College Streets is this bright, open history museum that focuses on post–Civil War history. The Levine's centerpiece exhibit is "From Cotton Fields to Skyscrapers," which illustrates the area's history and how it grew from a primarily farming area to a banking center. Visitors get this story from audio, video, and artifacts from the people who actually lived the history from 1865. It also hosts a variety of traveling exhibits and stages regular lectures and presentations. Admission is $10 for adults, $8 for seniors and children age 6 and older. Open Mon through Sat 10 a.m. to 5 p.m., Sun noon to 5 p.m.

The Light Factory. 1817 Central Ave.; (704) 333-9755; lightfactory.org. This unique museum is dedicated solely to photography and film. They organize exhibitions and film festivals, classes, camps, competitions, and other activities related to those media.

Mint Museum of Art. 2730 Randolph Rd.; (704) 337-2000; mintmuseum.org. The Mint Museum of Art opened in 1936 in what was the first branch of the US Mint. Housed and on display are a complete set of gold coins minted there, American and European paintings, pre-Columbian art, historic costumes, and ancient Chinese ceramics. It holds more than 27,000 items in its collection, among the largest in the state. You'll also see life-size paint-ings of King George III and his queen, Charlotte, for whom the city was named. Seeing the queen's carriage will round out your trip to the museum. Admission is $15 for adults, $10 for seniors, and $6 for ages 5 to 17. Admission tickets are good for 2 days from date of purchase and are valid for both branches of the museum, the other being located in at the Levine Center of the Arts in the Center City. Open Tues 10 a.m. to 9 p.m., Wed through Sat 10 a.m. to 6 p.m., Sun 1 to 5 p.m.

Mint Museum at Levine Center for the Arts. 500 S. Tryon St.; (704) 337-2000; mint museum.org. The Mint Museum is the uptown sister facility of the original Mint Museum located on Randolph Road. It was established here in 2010, moving into a new, much-heralded cultural campus. At the uptown facility is the Museum of Craft and Design, which includes pieces by Chihuly and other renowned artists who work in glass, clay, fiber, metal, and other media. A variety of American, contemporary, and European art is also on display. Admission is $15 for adults, $10 for seniors, $6 for ages 5 to 17. Admission tickets are good for 2 days from date of purchase and are valid for both branches of the museum. Open Tues 10 a.m. to 9 p.m., Wed through Sat 10 a.m. to 6 p.m., Sun 1 to 5 p.m.

NASCAR Hall of Fame. 400 E. Martin Luther King Blvd.; (704) 654-4400; nascarhall.com. The Hall of Fame opened in 2010 in Charlotte, which was selected over other US racing cities, including Daytona. It's not a typical hall of fame but engages visitors with simulators, interactive touch-screen displays, and dramatic video productions, all in addition to the hall of honor and archives associated with the sport's rich history. Don headphones and listen to pit crew communication, repair simulated engines, take the pit crew challenge, and experience the thrill of driving in a stock car in a simulator drivers say is as close to the real thing as they have ever experienced. NASCAR fans can trace the sport's history from Junior Johnson's days of running moonshine to the life and tragic death of the hall's first inductee, Dale Earnhardt. Each January a new class of inductees is featured at the hall. Admission is $25 for adults, $22 for seniors, and $18 for children ages 5 to 12. Open daily 10 a.m. to 6 p.m.

US National Whitewater Center. 820 Hawfield Rd.; (704) 391-3900; usnwc.org. The US National Whitewater Center is a sprawling, man-made rafting facility off I-85 just outside Charlotte. Integrated with miles of biking and hiking trails, the US Olympic Committee has designated the center as an official training site. The centerpiece is the world's largest man-made recirculating river, which forms a 2-hour Class III/IV rafting adventure for ages 12 and above. There's whitewater kayaking for ages 8 and above and flatwater kayaking for all ages. In addition, there's a climbing center for everyone over age 4 and a zip line that spans the facility. A restaurant provides a panoramic view of the whitewater in addition to selections that range from soup to salmon to steak. World Cup, Olympic Trials, and other competitions

quirky carolina

The 19th-century streets of Charlotte were literally paved with gold. When a gold nugget was discovered in nearby Midland in the early 1800s, it started a gold rush. The mines that sprang up in the area provided paving material to the city that actually contained low-grade gold.

art & architecture

The City of Charlotte and its arts community conduct a visible and well-promoted public art program with new pieces appearing on the landscape regularly. Some of the mainstays, however, include frescoes by Ben Long, the renowned North Carolina–born artist, at Bank of America Corporate Center and at TransAmerica Square, both on Tryon Street. The Green, which runs between Tryon and College Streets near the Wells Fargo Atrium and the Charlotte Convention Center, is a unique park with a literary theme. Bronze works depicting characters from literature, poems on bronze placards written by local schoolchildren, fountains, and hidden speakers that spill out whimsical sounds adorn the park. Bricks also contain fun word puzzles. In 2013 the city opened the 5-acre Romare Bearden Park in honor of the artist, who was born in the city. The city's architectural high points include Founders Hall, with a 10,000-square-foot glass atrium accessible from College Street or through Bank of America Corporate Center on Tryon Street, as well as the Wells Fargo building and Hearst Tower, which is larger on top than on the bottom. The Duke Energy Center includes several interesting artistic components including colorful, changing lights that line the building's facade.

are held here and may limit availability to the public, but events such as concerts and seasonal festivals provide regular fun. A fee is charged for various attractions. Generally open during daylight hours.

where to shop

The Bag Lady. 1710 Kenilworth Ave.; (704) 338-9778; the-bag-lady.biz. A book and gift store for "wild and wonderful women" (not this author's words), The Bag Lady carries jewelry, arts, gifts, and meditation supplies. Mon through Sat 10 a.m. to 7 p.m., Sun noon to 4 p.m.

Camp North End. 300 Camp Rd.; (980) 337-4600; camp.nc. Before the Great Depression Ford made cars here. During WWII, the Army used the location for a quartermaster depot then for missile production during the cold war. In the 1970s Eckerd Pharmaceuticals used the site for its factories. Today it's a popular destination for shopping, dining, and entertainment. The massive site is a still developing location for creatives, entrepreneurs, and day-trippers.

Charlotte Premium Outlets. 5404 New Fashion Way; (704) 523-8865; premiumoutlets .com. Outlet stores range from Adidas shoes to Zumiez clothing. When the Simon Property

Group opened this shopping center in 2014, they tried to put as much in it as they could. There are more than 50 clothing stores alone. Add a few retailers with other items, a handful of restaurants, and this mall becomes an all-day shopping delight. Open Mon through Sat 10 a.m. to 9 p.m., Sun 10 a.m. to 7 p.m.

Noda Arts District. Located on several blocks centered at North Davidson and 36th Streets; noda.org. Buy a piece of art that would suit a collector or get a tattoo in this funky and eclectic arts district that once served the area residents of this mill village. While most shops are open 7 days a week, a gallery crawl is conducted the first and third Fridays of each month from 6 to 9:30 p.m.

Paper Skyscraper. 330 East Blvd.; (704) 333-7130; paperskyscraper.com. This is one of Charlotte's best gift stores and carries cards, books, home decor, and a wide range of fun selections. It's located in Charlotte's Dilworth neighborhood, so venture out to discover other stylish boutiques. Open Mon through Fri 10 a.m. to 7 p.m., Sat 10 a.m. to 6 p.m., Sun noon to 5 p.m.

SouthPark Mall. 4400 Sharon Rd.; (704) 364-4411; simon.com. Located in South Charlotte, SouthPark is a Charlotte landmark with expected anchors such as Belk, Macy's, and Dillard's, but also includes Nordstrom, Neiman Marcus, and a wide selection of independently owned and chain stores, including Crate & Barrel and Tommy Bahama. In addition to a food court, shoppers will find 5 full-service restaurants, including a Cheesecake Factory. Open Mon through Sat 10 a.m. to 9 p.m., Sun 12:30 to 6 p.m.

where to eat

Alexander Michael's. 401 W. 9th St.; (704) 332-6789; almikestavern.com. A longtime local hangout near downtown, Al Mike's used to be a general store. It has a good selection of beer and fresh selections of salads, burgers, quesadillas, and pasta dishes. Open Mon through Thurs 11 a.m. to 10 p.m. and Fri and Sat 11 a.m. to 11 p.m. $$.

Cabo Fish Taco. 3201 N. Davidson St.; (704) 332-8868; cabofishtaco.com. The tasty honey wasabi sauce served on several of Cabo's dishes was enough to get the Food Network's Guy Fieri to Charlotte. Tacos, burritos, and other dishes fuse Mexican and California styles. Cabo also has a nice selection of beers and outdoor seating in this trendy Charlotte neighborhood of Noda. $$.

Diamond Restaurant. 1901 Commonwealth Ave.; (704) 375-8985. Set in a typical 1950s-style diner, the food, including burgers, chicken, and comfort food, is anything but typical. The modern-day Diamond menu is the result of a rift in ownership by the Penguin Restaurant that operated nearby at 1921 Commonwealth Ave. until it closed in 2014. The Penguin's longtime chef now works at the Diamond. $–$$.

Lupie's Cafe. 2718 Monroe Rd.; (704) 374-1232; lupiescafe.net. The unkempt building with a neon sign on top doesn't look like much from the road, but Lupie's has great burgers and home-style meals such as chicken and dumplings. You can also get chili—Cincinnati style, Texas style, or vegetarian style. Open Mon through Fri 11 a.m. to 10 p.m., Sat. noon to 10 p.m. $$.

Mert's Heart & Soul. 214 N. College St.; (704) 342-4222; mertscharlotte.com. Comfort food is served here in an atmosphere of southern blues. Dishes include collard greens, shrimp and grits, black-eyed peas, and other soul food. Sit at the counter to get a live cooking show in this almost always bustling downtown establishment. Open Mon through Thurs 11 a.m. to 9:30 p.m., Fri 11:30 a.m. to 11:30 p.m., Sun 9 a.m. to 9:30 p.m. $$.

Mimosa Grill. 327 S. Tryon St.; (704) 343-0700; mimosagrill.com. This is one of the upscale restaurants owned by a local group that operates several of Charlotte's more sophisticated dining options. The chef creates dishes with foods more typically associated with southern fare with an international flair. The menu varies with what's seasonally and locally available. Simple short ribs become something special when combined with leeks and risotto, for example. Open Mon through Thurs 11 a.m. to 10 p.m., Fri 11 a.m. to 10 p.m., Sat noon to 10 p.m., Sun 11 a.m. to 9 p.m. $$$.

Pike's Soda Shop. 1930 Camden Rd.; (704) 372-0092; pikessodashop.net. Old-fashioned soda shop fare is served at Pike's. It's where meat loaf meets milk shakes. It's where brunch is as good as the burgers. Or try some reliable comfort food like sweet potato casserole. Open Mon through Thurs 11 a.m. to 9 p.m., Fri and Sat 11 a.m. to 10 p.m., Sun 8 a.m. to 2 p.m. $–$$.

Pinky's Westside Grill. 1600 W. Morehead; (704) 332-0402; eatatpinkys.com. Why settle for hush puppies when you can have crab puppies? Why just shrimp when you can have corn dog shrimp? Don't settle for a cheeseburger when you can have a pterodactyl burger. Pinky's is among the funkiest, most fabulous eateries in the city. $$

where to stay

Ballantyne Resort. 10000 Ballantyne Commons Pkwy.; (704) 248-4000; theballantyne hotel.com. Ballantyne is a luxury resort located in South Charlotte. A spa, tennis courts, golf, and indoor and outdoor pools in addition to impeccable service are all at the guests' disposal. Rooms in the traditional hotel and adjacent lodge are available. $$$.

The Dunhill Hotel. 237 N. Tryon St.; (704) 332-4141; dunhillhotel.com. Listed on the National Register of Historic Places, this uptown hotel offers first-class treatment and is within walking distance to many attractions. Rooms have been updated but are still distinctly historic. $$$.

Morehead Inn. 1122 E. Morehead St.; (704) 376-3357; moreheadinn.com. Located just outside of uptown, this is a historic bed-and-breakfast with a sophisticated, grand flair. Built in 1917, it's decorated with antiques, and the rooms are extremely well appointed. $$$.

worth more time
beyond the borders

The northern areas of Mecklenburg County include Lake Norman, the university area, and the bordering Cabarrus County, all of which offer opportunities worth your time. **Lake Norman,** part of Duke Energy's system of power-generating lakes along the Catawba River, provides many recreational opportunities in the bedroom communities of Huntersville, Cornelius, and Historic Davidson, and hence more dining and shopping opportunities. **UNC–Charlotte** hosts speakers, exhibitions, festivals, and sporting events. Cabarrus County's city of **Concord** works closely with Charlotte in promoting the area as a NASCAR mecca. Racing is covered in themed day trip 50, but take a while to discover everything this area has to offer. Shopping is king at **Concord Mills Mall,** one of the biggest in North Carolina. It includes stores, dining, a NASCAR speed park, a mega movie theater, and more. Wolves are king at **The Great Wolf Lodge,** a fun north woods–themed hotel and water park. Both are located just off I-85 at the northern Charlotte city limits.

day trip 15

charlotte, nc

>>> **train keeps rollin':**
salisbury, nc; spencer, nc

The city of Salisbury does history right, boasting a 30-block area on the National Register of Historic Places. Just to the north is the outstanding North Carolina Transportation Museum that evolved out of the enormous locomotive repair shop created by Southern Railway, helping mold this area into what it is today.

salisbury, nc

Dozens of restored historic homes dot the city of Salisbury. This was the location of one of the Civil War's largest Confederate prisons, and more than 5,000 Union troops are buried here. Daniel Boone once roamed the Salisbury region, and Andrew Jackson practiced law here. Do you get the idea that Salisbury takes its history seriously? It does; but it has other claims to fame, too. It is the hometown of Elizabeth Dole, who served as director of the American Red Cross, secretary of transportation, secretary of labor, the state's US senator for 6 years, and the late presidential nominee Bob Dole's wife for more than 35 years. Cheerwine, the sweet, bubbly North Carolina soda, was invented here in 1917 in the basement of L. D. Peeler's wholesale grocery store.

getting there

Salisbury is less than an hour north of Charlotte on I-85. Take the Jake Alexander Boulevard (US 601) exit to Old Concord Road. Take a left, and it leads into Salisbury.

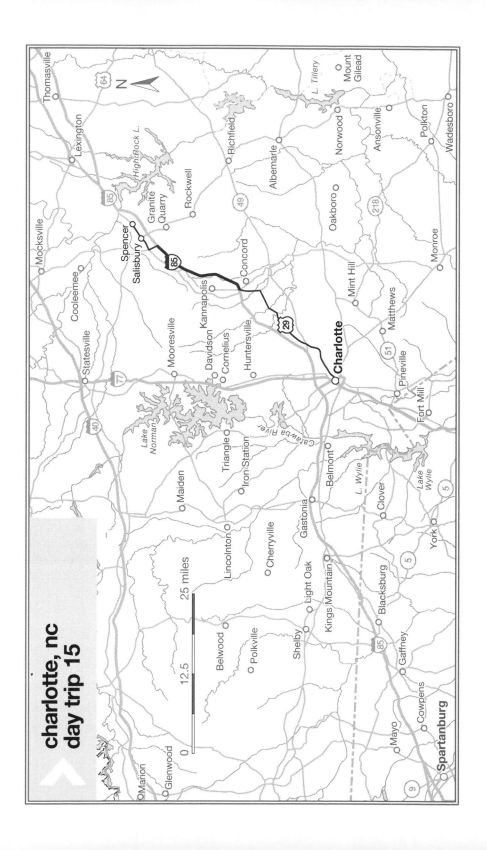

charlotte, nc
day trip 15

where to go

Dan Nicholas Park & Campground. 6800 Bringle Ferry Rd.; (704) 216-7800; dannicholas .net. This park's massive variety of activities makes it a popular stop for schools and families alike. Anglers head to the 10-acre lake where they can cast a line and others can rent a paddleboat. A small water park, a miniature golf course, a carousel, a gem-mining operation, and a small nature center with native species are all offered at this sprawling 330-acre park. The nature center, Rowan Wildlife Adventures, allows visitors to view bears, bald eagles, and other animals native to the region. A petting barn gives visitors the opportunity to get up close and personal with goats, donkeys, sheep, and even a belted Galloway cow. Admission is free, but various attractions require a fee. The park is typically open during daylight hours, but attraction hours vary.

Dr. Josephus Hall House. 226 S. Jackson St.; (704) 636-0103; historicsalisbury.org. Dr. Josephus Hall was chief surgeon at the Salisbury Confederate Prison during the Civil War, and his impressive Federal-style home has been preserved as a window into that era. Built in 1820 as an academy for girls, the house became a residence in 1825, and was renovated significantly in 1859 when Hall bought it and again in 1900 with Greek Revival and Victorian features. The interior has painted ceilings and original fixtures, and is filled with an impressive collection of mid-Victorian furnishings and other items that belonged to the Hall family. Docents in period dress conduct guided tours of this home that sits in what is now almost a parklike setting. Admission is $5 for adults and $3 for children ages 6 to 12. Open Sat and Sun 1 to 4 p.m.

Historic National Cemetery & Confederate Prison Site. 202 Government Rd.; (800) 332-2343 or (704) 638-3100; visitsalisburync.com. Nothing remains of the Salisbury prison but 3 monuments erected by the State of Maine, the Commonwealth of Pennsylvania, and the US government. Find those at the National Cemetery, a tribute to the Union soldiers who died while at the prison. Union General George Stoneman and his men burned the prison, which had already been abandoned, in April 1865 just before the war ended. More than 11,000 Union soldiers who died here are buried in 18 trench graves with stone markers offering a poignant reminder of the toll of the Civil War. A nearby log house, the former garrison for the prison, remains and holds various antiques and artifacts. CDs to accompany the driving tour are available from the visitor center on Innes Street for $5 each. Learn more about North Carolina Civil War sites in day trips 53 and 54.

Historic Salisbury. Located northwest of Main Street or either side of Innes Street; (704) 638-3100; visitsalisburync.com or historicsalisbury.org. The 30-square-block historic district consists of downtown Salisbury and the West Square residential district spanning out from the intersection on Main and Innes Streets. Listed on the National Register of Historic Places, this area includes the Dr. Josephus Hall House. Built in 1820 as the Salisbury Female Academy, it later became the home of physician Josephus Hall. Also in the historic district is

crossroads

A mural on the building at the intersection of Main and Fisher Streets by Salisbury native Cynvia Arthur Rankin, titled Crossroad: Past and Present, *features downtown Salisbury at the turn of the 20th century. It depicts more than 100 local residents—children playing and couples walking arm in arm—in period dress.*

the Utzman-Chambers House, an 1819 Federal town house constructed by master builder Jacob Stirewalt.

Meroney Theatre. 213 S. Main St.; (704) 633-5471; piedmontplayers.com. The Piedmont Players present their work in this renovated 361-seat theater, built in 1906. The Meroney's history is impressive, to say the least. Sarah Bernhardt, Lillian Russell, John Philip Sousa, William Howard Taft, Cary Nation, and the New York Symphony Orchestra have all made appearances here. In the early days it was able to attract big names and big shows because of Salisbury's location on the railroad. But that would not last long. In 1915 it changed ownership and was converted to a movie house for the next 75 years. The Piedmont Players bought it 10 years later and began to return it to its former glory.

Old Stone House. Old Stone House Road, Granite Quarry; (704) 633-5946; rowanmuseum .org. German immigrant Michael Braun, one of the area's largest landowners, built this 2-story, Georgian-style house in 1766, making it the oldest structure in Rowan County. Merchant, wheelwright, and farmer, Braun erected a veritable mansion in what was then a virtual wilderness. Openings on the second floor appear to be gun ports used to fight off Indians. Historians argue, however, that they are just ventilation ports. Today Braun's house is operated by the Rowan Museum. Free. Open Sat and Sun 1 to 4 p.m.

If you want more information on the historic district, visit the **Rowan County Convention & Visitor Bureau** at 204 E. Innes St. in person, call (800) 332-2343 or (704) 638-3100, or visit virtually at visitsalisburync.com. Get walking maps on the visitor bureau website or at the visitor center. Trolley tours also originate from here on Sat at 11 a.m. Apr through Oct.

Rowan Museum. 202 N. Main St.; (704) 633-5946; rowanmuseum.org. The 1854 courthouse, which survived Gen. George Stoneman's 1865 raid on the town, is one of the finest examples of pre–Civil War architecture in the state. The massive columns of the museum's facade are impressive. The well-curated artifacts and displays inside depict the life and history of Rowan County, including artifacts from the Civil War and documents and material culture that trace the community's commerce. Among the displays are tools and modes of transportation from the 19th century. Free. Open Fri through Sun 1 to 4 p.m.

Salisbury Railway Passenger Station. 215 Depot St.; (704) 636-0103; historicsalisbury
.org. Built in 1908 in a Spanish mission style, this train station when it first opened was one
of the busiest between Washington and Atlanta. The foundation restored it in the 1990s, and
it is now office and event rental space. Cathedral ceilings with arched wooden beams as well
as the original mosaic tile floor remain. Tours are available by appointment.

Utzman-Chambers House. 116 S. Jackson St.; (704) 633-5946. Constructed by Jacob
Stirewalt, this 1819 Federal town house is maintained as a museum that reflects the lifestyle
of the more affluent citizens of the early 1800s. That lavish way of living is evident in the
Chippendale and Hepplewhite furniture that is still part of the home. With an unusual curved
staircase and intricate interior moldings and details, it is one of the few surviving Federal
period town houses in the Piedmont. Free. Open Sat 1 to 4 p.m.

Waterworks Visual Arts Center. 123 E. Liberty St.; (704) 638-1882; waterworks.org.
Originally located in the city's first waterworks building, the center is now across the street
from the police station in another refurbished building. The center offers regional and national
gallery exhibitions, studio classes, workshops, and lectures. The sculpture gallery invites
visitors to participate in the art experience through touch, sound, fragrance, and sight. Free.
Open Mon through Fri 10 a.m. to 4 p.m. and Sat 10 a.m. to 2 p.m.

where to shop

Eagle's Farm. 2924 Old Mocksville Rd.; (704) 647-0063. Visitors can pick their own strawberries, cucumbers, squash, or tomatoes depending on the season. Those more interested
in eating than gathering can just stop at the roadside market. Open Mon through Sat 8 a.m.
to 6 p.m.

The Salisbury Emporium. 230 E. Kerr St.; (704) 642-0039. The Salisbury Emporium is a
collection of 85 shops and galleries in a renovated sawmill adjacent to the Salisbury train station. The emporium contains more than 15,000 square feet of gifts, antiques, home accessories, Christmas items, fine art, handcrafts, military relics, and more. Open Tues through
Sat 10 a.m. to 6 p.m. and Sun 1 to 5 p.m.

The Stitchin' Post & Gifts. 104 S. Main St.; (704) 637-0708; spgifts.com. This historic
1879 shop has high ceilings, original wood floors, and exposed brick walls. The renovated
storefront casts the warm feeling of walking into history. Unusual gifts for every season can
be found here in the heart of downtown Salisbury just off the square. Open Mon through
Sat 10 a.m. to 5:30 p.m. Also open Sun afternoons between Thanksgiving and Christmas.

where to eat

Haps Grill. 116½ N. Main St.; (704) 633-5872. This lunch counter restaurant offers some of
the best hot dogs and burgers for miles around. They come most often topped with homemade chili and a local offering of Cheerwine in a glass bottle. A plaque on the wall bears the

names of people who have met the Haps challenge by eating a random (but always large) number of hot dogs or hamburgers. There's not much seating, so plan to enjoy your dog elsewhere if you see a line outside the door. $.

La Cava. 329 S. Church St.; (704) 637-7174; lacavarestaurant.com. Located in an 1897 church, where the original altar now serves as wine alcove, La Cava specializes in Italian and continental cuisine with many fish and veal dishes. Open Mon through Sat 5:30 to 10 p.m. $$$.

Sweet Meadow Cafe. 105 E. Fisher St.; (704) 637-8715. This quaint cafe with a tearoom feel serves contemporary cuisine with a twist. An eclectic menu includes crab cakes, red beans and rice, and other items. Fresh breads are made daily. Works by local artists are on display. Open Sun through Thurs 11 a.m. to 2 p.m., Fri 11 a.m. to 2 p.m., and 5:30 to 8:30 p.m. $–$$.

where to stay

Turn of the Century Victorian Bed & Breakfast. 529 S. Fulton St.; (704) 642-1660; turnofthecenturybb.com. This B&B mixes historical elegance with contemporary comfort. The home was built in 1905 and offers 3 bedrooms and 1 suite for longer stays. Like many area homes, it has an inviting wraparound front porch and a comfortable parlor for relaxing. $$$.

spencer, nc

Spencer is 350 miles from Washington, DC, and 300 miles from Atlanta, so Southern Railway selected it in 1896 as a site for a major repair facility. It was later named for Southern Railway's first president, Samuel Spencer, who coincidentally died in a train accident. What the towns of Spencer and Salisbury have become is thanks in large part to Southern Railway. It opened Spencer up as an early cultural center and tourist attraction of sorts with easy access and a stable economy. The main draw now in this town of fewer than 3,500 people is the North Carolina Transportation Museum, on the site of the repair facility, where kids and railroad enthusiasts can get their fill of life on the rails.

getting there

Spencer is 2 miles north of Salisbury on Salisbury Avenue, an extension of Salisbury's Main Street. From Charlotte, you can skip over Salisbury and reach Spencer via I-85 at exit 79.

where to go

North Carolina Transportation Museum. 411 S. Salisbury Ave.; (704) 636-2889 or (877) 628-6386; nctrans.org. This massive facility defies the typical connotation of a museum. No puny dioramas here. It's a big, bold trip through the history of modern-day transportation.

Located on the site of what was once Southern Railway's largest steam locomotive repair facility, it includes 13 buildings and a restored roundhouse, on 57 acres. While the highlights of the museum are related to trains and the dozens of cars on display, exhibits include other modes of early transportation such as the automobiles at the Bumper to Bumper exhibit and the Conestoga wagon of the Wagons, Wheels & Wings display. The highlight is the restored 1924 Robert Julian roundhouse, an innovative working railroad repair shop. Visitors actually get an opportunity to ride on the turntable that once dealt out cars needing repair work to the roundhouse. But a trip to this museum would not be complete without a train ride around the facility. Admission is $6 for adults, $5 for seniors, and $4 for children ages 3 to 12. With the train ride the price is double. Open Mon through Sat 9 a.m. to 5 p.m. and Sun 1 to 5 p.m. May 1 through Oct 31; Tues through Sat 9 a.m. to 5 p.m. and Sun 1 to 5 p.m. Nov 1 through Apr 30.

Spencer Historic District. (704) 633-2231; ci.spencer.nc.us. Adjacent to the North Carolina Transportation Museum, the Spencer National Historic Register District was built between 1905 and 1920 as housing for the families of those who operated the repair facility. With 322 residential and commercial buildings, it is the largest contiguous historic district in North Carolina.

where to shop

The Little Choo Choo Shop. 500 S. Salisbury Ave.; (704) 637-8717; littlechoochooshop .com. Across the street from the North Carolina Transportation Museum, this well-stocked model-railroad shop is for serious model railroaders, but it is a must-see for any train enthusiast. Open Tues through Sat 10 a.m. to 5:30 p.m.

where to eat

Pinocchio's. 518 S. Salisbury Ave.; (704) 636-8891; pinocchiosofspencer.com. Home-style southern Italian fare, made to order from scratch, includes seafood, pasta, pizza, and homemade gelato. Live music is scheduled periodically. Open for lunch Mon through Fri and dinner Tues through Sat. $$.

day trip 16

charlotte, nc

>>>> **arts & sciences:**
winston-salem, nc

winston-salem, nc

Winston-Salem's notoriety as a cigarette giant has gone up in smoke in the 21st century, but the city can credit its development as a center for arts and culture to that heritage and the contributions of its corporate community, which included cigarette manufacturers. Richard Joshua Reynolds established his famous cigarette factory here in 1874, but more than a century before that, it was settled by German-speaking Moravians, members of the persecuted Protestant sect that came from Germany by way of Pennsylvania. They called the area Die Wachau, derived from the Latin Wachovia, the former name of Winston-Salem's second economic bastion, Wachovia Bank, which moved its headquarters to Charlotte in 2001 and was purchased by Wells Fargo in 2009. While the Winston-Salem economy would change, the historical mark left by those Moravians would remain at Bethabara and Bethania and at Old Salem, founded as a town and backcountry trading center in 1766. Old Salem has long been heralded as one of the most authentic restorations of its kind, but there are other good reasons to visit North Carolina's fifth-largest city of a quarter million residents. Since the 1960s the city has billed itself as the "City of the Arts." Community leaders here formed the nation's first arts council, used as a model in much larger cities. But even today Winston-Salem ranks first nationally in per capita contributions to the arts and boasts impressive art galleries, museums, and performance centers. The renowned North Carolina School of the Arts, now part of the state university system, is here. So is one of the nation's

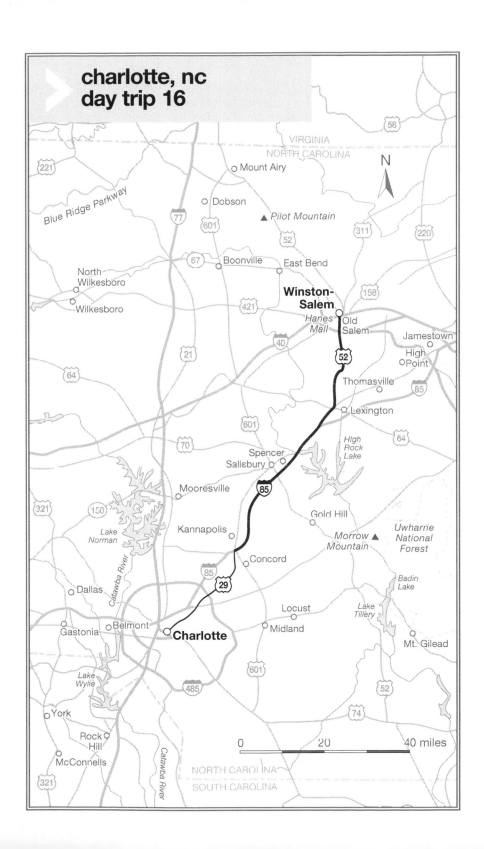

finest collections of American art at Reynolda House, as well as a fine symphony and an opera company. For more information, contact the **Winston-Salem Visitor Center,** 200 Brookstown Ave; visitwinstonsalem.com.

getting there

While Winston-Salem can be accessed from Charlotte via I-77 to I-40, a speedier route is I-85 north to US 52. The drive is an easy 80 miles that can be traversed in a little more than an hour.

where to go

Delta Arts Center. 2611 New Walkertown Rd.; (336) 722-2625; deltafartscenter.org. Exhibits, events, and activities held here emphasize the contributions of minorities, mainly African Americans, to the arts and humanities. Once located in a small house in a depressed area of the city, the Delta purchased a former ABC store and upfitted it for exhibition space. The center presents regularly changing exhibits by Hispanic as well as black artists. Open Tues through Fri 10 a.m. to 5 p.m.

Historic Bethabara. 2163 Bethabara Rd.; (336) 924-9148; bethabarapark.org. Part historic park, part wildlife preserve, Bethabara was the first colonial town site established in the Carolina Piedmont. At the beautiful 175-acre park is the only "house of passage" built by the Moravians at any of their colonial settlements in the New World. A National Historic Landmark, this 1753 site of the first Moravian settlement in North Carolina was the area's frontier trade and religious center until 1772. Guests can tour the 1788 congregation house known as the Gemeinhaus, view the archaeological remains in the reconstructed palisade fort, and stroll through the historic gardens. A visitor center offers exhibits and an introductory film. Exhibit buildings are open for guided tours Apr 1 through Dec 15, except for Thanksgiving Day, Tues through Fri 10:30 a.m. to 4:30 p.m. and Sat and Sun 1:30 to 4:30 p.m. Admission is $4 for adults and $1 for children. Grounds, gardens, and trails are open free of charge, all day, all year.

Old Salem Museums and Gardens. 601 Old Salem Rd.; (336) 721-7350; oldsalem.org. Founded in 1766 as a Moravian church town and backcountry trading center, Old Salem is frequently praised as one of America's most authentic and well-documented colonial sites. Costumed interpreters demonstrate daily activities and trades that were part of the lives of European-American and African-American residents of Salem in the late 18th and early 19th centuries. The cobblestone streets of Old Salem are lined with homes, shops, gardens, and other examples of how these missionaries lived and worshipped. St. Philips Moravian Church, the state's oldest standing African-American church, is also located here along with several museum shops, Salem Tavern restaurant, and the famous Winkler Bakery, where shoppers can still get Moravian cookies and other goodies. In all, this self-guided tour features about 100 restored and reconstructed buildings where costumed staff demonstrate various tasks or give abbreviated tours of specific buildings. Among them are the T. Vogler Gunsmith Shop, Shultz Shoemaker Shop, Single Brothers' House, and Salem Tavern.

Visitors are welcome to roam the streets of Old Salem as in any other small town and view a number of structures, but admission is required for the formal tours that include the Museum of Early Southern Decorative Arts, with an option to purchase tickets to attractions separately or a 2-day ticket is $27 for adults and $13 for children ages 6 to 16. Jan through Oct, Old Salem is open Tues through Sun plus Memorial Day and Labor Day. It is open 7 days a week in Nov and Dec. Hours of individual buildings and shops may vary slightly. Staff may close tour buildings periodically for maintenance. The Visitor Center, 900 Old Salem Rd., is open Tues through Sat (and Mon in Nov and Dec) 9 a.m. to 5 p.m. and Sun 12:30 to 5 p.m. Old Salem Interpretive Buildings are open Tues through Sat 9:30 a.m. to 4:30 p.m. and Sun 1 to 4:30 p.m.

Museum of Early Southern Decorative Arts (MESDA). 924 S. Main St.; (888) 348-5420; oldsalem.org. Located at Old Salem, MESDA is the only museum dedicated to exhibiting and researching the regional decorative arts of the early South, dating back to the late 17th century. With 12 gallery rooms, MESDA showcases the furniture, paintings, textiles, ceramics, silver, and other metalware made and used in Maryland, Virginia, the Carolinas, Georgia, Kentucky, and Tennessee through 1820. Admission for a self-guided tour is $10 for adults. Admission to MESDA is included in the Old Salem 2-day tickets. Guided tours begin on the hour and half hour, and last about an hour and cost $20. Open Tues through Sat 10 a.m. to 5 p.m. and Sun 1 to 5 p.m. The last tour is at 4 p.m. each day.

Reynolda House, Museum of American Art. 2250 Reynolda Rd.; (888) 663-1149; reynoldahouse.org. Reynolda House is at the center of this elegant historic district in what is still one of the city's most prestigious neighborhoods near Wake Forest University. An impressive collection of American masterpieces lines the walls throughout the gracious 64-room estate of R. J. and Katherine Reynolds, which is much like it was when they lived here beginning in 1917. The architecture, furnishings, costume collection of some 700 pieces, and artwork reflect their elegant and extravagant tastes. Visitors can view 3 centuries of major American paintings, prints, and sculptures by the likes of Jacob Lawrence, Jasper Johns, Stuart Davis, and Georgia O'Keeffe, one of the finest collections of American art in North America. A National Historic Property, Reynolda House also offers tours of the formal gardens and the estate's 28 support buildings, now converted to specialty shops, offices, and restaurants. Admission is $18, free for anyone age 18 or under. Open Tues through Sat 9:30 a.m. to 4:30 p.m., Sun 1:30 to 4:30 p.m. Closed Thanksgiving, Christmas, and New Year's Day.

Kaladium North. 400 Hanes Mill Rd.; (336) 767-6730; north.kaladium.org. Formerly Sci-Works, which opened here in 1974, this science center has been a national leader among science museums, and its hands-on exhibits continue to engage visitors of all ages. Kala-dium features permanent and traveling exhibitions on a variety of physical, natural, and life sciences. Exhibits take visitors from the Mountains to the Sea and teach about how sound works, how physics works, and how health works. The Coastal Encounters lab tank allows guests to touch horseshoe crabs and other coastal species while chemicals fizz, pop, and react in dazzling science shows, and models of dinosaurs open a window to the world as it was millions of years ago. A 120-seat planetarium allows audiences to tour the constellations and learn about the night sky over the Carolinas. Outdoor exhibits with live animals and other hands-on displays on 15 acres blend seamlessly with picnic areas and nature trails. Admis-sion is $10 for adults, $9 for seniors and students ages 3 to 19, and free for children ages 2 and under. Open Tues through Fri 10 a.m. to 4 p.m., Sat 10 a.m. to 5 p.m., and Sun noon to 5 p.m. The park and barnyard close 30 minutes before the museum.

Southeastern Center for Contemporary Art (SECCA). 750 Marguerite Dr.; (336) 725-1904; secca.org. Located in the 1929 English hunting lodge and home of the late industrial-ist James G. Hanes, SECCA has put together an impressive collection of works under the direction of the North Carolina Museum of Art. The lodge has been enhanced with 20,000 square feet of open-air exhibit space, where temporary exhibits change several times a year and represent the finest contemporary art both regionally and nationally. Shoppers can buy handcrafted jewelry, home decor, toys, and other items at the Centershop. Admission is free. Open Tues through Sat 10 a.m. to 5 p.m. (until 8 p.m. on Thurs), Sun 1 to 5 p.m.; closed national holidays.

Stevens Center. 405 W. 4th St.; (336) 721-1945; uncsa.edu/stevenscenter. This restored 1929 silent movie theater in downtown Winston-Salem is part of the acclaimed University of North Carolina School of the Arts and regularly showcases student and faculty work, as well as playing host to feature performances that include chamber music, jazz, ballet, the symphony, Piedmont Opera, and films. A series of renovations in 1983 have given the 1,400-seat facility great sight lines and outstanding acoustics.

where to shop

Downtown Arts District. Visitors can stroll along Trade and 6th Streets near the Marriott Hotel to visit a series of eclectic shops and galleries that make up the resurgent arts district. Some highlights include:

Artworks Gallery. 564 N. Trade St.; (336) 723-5890; artworks-gallery.org. Estab-lished in 1984, the artist-run cooperative exhibits members' works. Open Tues through Fri 10 a.m. to 5 p.m., Sat 10 a.m. to 4 p.m.

Fiber Company. 600 N. Trade St.; (336) 725-5277. This collective of fiber artists and designers was established in 1987 in this working studio, shop, and gallery. Open Tues through Fri 10 a.m. to 5 p.m., Sat 11 a.m. to 3 p.m.

Piedmont Craftsmen Gallery. 601 N. Trade St.; (336) 725-1516; piedmont craftsmen.org. The gallery showcases the works of more than 300 of the Southeast's finest craft artists who work in glass, fiber, clay, metal, and more. Open Tues through Fri 10:30 a.m. to 5 p.m. and Sat 11 a.m. to 4 p.m.

Hanes Mall. 3320 Silas Creek Pkwy.; (336) 765-8321; shophanesmall.com. One of the largest malls between Washington, DC, and Atlanta, Hanes Mall has more than 200 stores. Anchors include the typical Belk, Sears, and Macy's, but there is also an upper-level Venetian carousel. Open Mon through Sat 10 a.m. to 9 p.m., Sun noon to 6 p.m.

Historic Reynolda Village. 2201 Reynolda Rd.; (336) 758-5584. On the former estate of R. J. Reynolds, this shopping plaza has more than 30 upscale shops, including restaurants, art galleries, and offerings of jewelry and antiques, fine gifts, and specialty items. Open Mon through Sat 10 a.m. to 5 p.m.

where to eat

Muddy Creek Café at Old Salem. 626 South Main St.; (336) 201-5182; oldsalem.org. Located in the T. Bagge Merchant Building, the café offers sandwiches, soups, salads and other lite fare. Live music is also occasionally scheduled here. $$

Old Fourth Street Filling Station. 871 W. 4th St.; (336) 724-7600; theoldfourthstreetfill ingstation.com. This was indeed once a gas station, but now the restaurant offers the best patio dining in town. Menu choices range from salads and sandwiches to filet mignon. Try popular broiled mahimahi with a crab stuffing or the shrimp and grits. Open Mon and Tues 11 a.m. to 9 p.m., Wed and Thurs 11 a.m. to 10 p.m., Fri and Sat 11 a.m. to 11 p.m., Sun 10 a.m. to 9 p.m. $$–$$$.

Sweet Potatoes. 529 N. Trade St., (336) 727-4844; sweetpotatoes.ws. Forged in the great southern tradition, this downtown restaurant serves classics like fried okra, fried green tomatoes, and sweet potatoes—fried, baked, or just about any other way you would like. Sure you can get a good burger or spectacular meat loaf here, but the fried bologna sandwich

an original carolina treat

Now found across the US and in Canada, **Krispy Kreme** *doughnuts were first made at 259 S. Stratford Rd. in Winston-Salem, which is still home to this doughnut giant. Its famous neon hot now signs alert passersby that soft sugary delights are coming off the conveyor.*

comes highly recommended. Open Tues through Sat 11 a.m. to 3 p.m. and 5 to 10 p.m.; 10:30 a.m. to 3 p.m. Sun. $–$$.

Village Tavern. 221 Reynolda Village; (336) 748-0221. Enjoy delicious entrees in a warm, casual atmosphere. Treat yourself to a meal on the outdoor patio. Try the hot crab dip appetizer, which was created by the owner and hasn't changed in years. The Carolina burger, with homemade chili, is also another popular menu item. Open 11 a.m. to 11 p.m. Mon through Thurs, to midnight Fri and Sat, and 9 a.m. to 10 p.m. Sun. $$–$$$.

WestEnd Cafe. 926 W. 4th St.; (336) 723-4774; westendcafe.com. This trendy local favorite serves salads, grinders, Reubens, and other sandwiches. Open Mon through Fri 11 a.m. to 10 p.m., Sat noon to 10 p.m. $.

where to stay

The Augustus T. Zevely Inn. 803 S. Main St.; (800) 928-9299; zevelynn.com. The Zevely Inn is the only lodging in the Old Salem district. This 12-room bed-and-breakfast has been meticulously and accurately restored to its mid-19th-century glory and includes authentic reproduction furniture from the period. A continental breakfast of Moravian baked goods is served during the week, and a full buffet breakfast is offered on weekends. $$–$$$.

Brookstown Inn. 200 Brookstown Ave.; (800) 845-4262; brookstowninn.com. Built in 1837 and on the National Register of Historic Places, the inn was once one of the city's largest textile mills. The Brookstown has retained its old-world charm by keeping many of its architectural features inside and out. Guest rooms typically have exposed bricks and original beams. Rates include a complimentary wine and cheese reception every evening from 5 to 7 p.m., milk and cookies before bed, and a complimentary continental breakfast each morning. $$$.

Henry F. Shaffner House. 150 S. Marshall St.; (800) 952-2256; theshaffner.com. Built in 1907 by one of the cofounders of Wachovia Bank (now part of Wells Fargo), this Victorian-style mansion is now a restaurant and bed-and-breakfast just blocks from historic Old Salem and downtown Winston-Salem. Rooms, named for local attractions, are spacious and modern but maintain old-world charm. $$–$$$.

day trip 17

charlotte, nc

> all andy, all the time:
> mount airy, nc; pilot mountain, nc

Even though it's been a half a century since *The Andy Griffith Show* first appeared on CBS, local folks still say Mount Airy wouldn't be the town it is today without its Andy Griffith. Mount Airy is located just short of the Virginia state line, and the entire area figures prominently in the show that originally ran through much of the 1960s and is still popular in syndication today. Griffith, who went on to star as TV's Matlock and other film and TV characters, grew up here, and the fictional towns of Mayberry and Mount Pilot were based on the real-life towns. Today tourists snap shots of the squad cars that carry visitors who are getting a glimpse of that much-heralded history including Snappy Lunch, Floyd's Barbershop, a museum, and other attractions that pay homage to the show.

But it's not really all about Andy. Other well-known celebrities, including country music singer Donna Fargo and bluegrass legend Tommy Jarrell, are natives of Mount Airy. The original Siamese twins, Eng and Chang Bunker, lived in the nearby White Plains community. For more information, contact the Mount Airy Visitor Center (200 N. Main St.; 800-948-0949 or 336-786-6116; visitmayberry.com).

mount airy, nc

Most agree this town contributed more than anything else to the creation of the popular 1960s TV sitcom *The Andy Griffith Show.* Day-trippers can become part of the show and the tourist attraction by taking a squad car tour. They can visit places featured in the show and

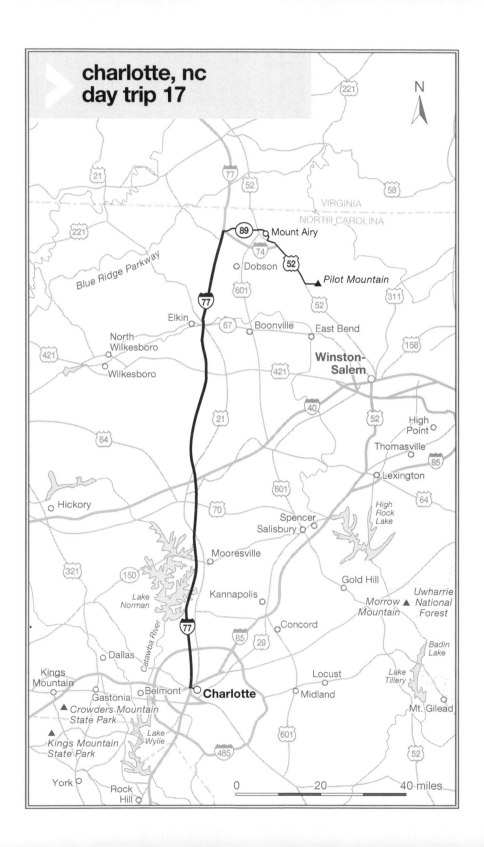

N

221

77

52

58

VIRGINIA
NORTH CAROLINA

221

89 Mount Airy

74

Blue Ridge Parkway

○ Dobson

52

Pilot Mountain ▲

601

77

311

52

Elkin ○

67

Boonville ○

East Bend ○

158

North
Wilkesboro ○

421

Wilkesboro

Winston-
Salem

421

40

52

High
Point ○

21

Thomasville

85

64

○ Lexington

64

Hickory ○

601

High
Rock
Lake

70

Spencer ○
Salisbury ○

Mooresville ○

321

150

Lake
Norman

Kannapolis ○

Gold Hill ○

Morrow ▲
Mountain

Uwharrie
National
Forest

Catawba River

77

Concord ○

85

29

Badin
Lake

Dallas ○

Kings
Mountain ○

Belmont ○

Gastonia ○

Charlotte

Locust ○

Lake
Tillery

▲ Crowders Mountain
State Park

Midland ○

Mt. Gilead ○

▲
Kings Mountain
State Park

Lake
Wylie

485

601

52

York ○

Rock
Hill ○

0   20   40 miles

places created because of the popularity of the show. Settled in the 1750s as a stagecoach stop, Mount Airy was incorporated in 1885.

getting there

Mount Airy is a straight shot out of Charlotte north on I-77, almost exactly 100 miles and just more than 90 minutes away. SR 89 at exit 100 leads to this TV town.

where to go

Andy Griffith Playhouse & Museum. 218 Rockford St.; (336) 786-7998 or (800) 286-6193; andygriffithmuseum.org. The first stop for any Andy Griffith fan should be this museum, home of the world's largest collection of Andy Griffith memorabilia, located on the lower level of Mount Airy Arts Center. Griffith's childhood friend and Mount Airy resident Emmett Forrest assembled the display with contributions from Andy and actors from the show, including Betty Lynn, who lived in Mount Airy and made regular appearances at the museum until she died in 2021. The collection contains everything from the chair Andy was rocked in as a baby to the seersucker suit he wore on *Matlock*. The museum includes the Justice of the Peace and Sheriff signs that were prominently featured on the doors of the TV courthouse and jail. The adjacent Andy Griffith Playhouse was built in 1920 as the first known site of a public school in Mount Airy. This is where Griffith attended elementary school and first performed onstage. Named for Griffith in the early 1970s, it now houses the Surry Arts Council's exhibits and performance venue. Admission is $8 for adults, $6 for children age 12 and under. Open Mon through Sat 9 a.m. to 5 p.m., and Sun 1 to 5 p.m.

Earle Theatre. 142 North Main St.; (336) 786-7998; surrycountymusic.com. The intense, driving sound of banjo and fiddle make up the heart and soul of old-time music, a predecessor of bluegrass and perhaps older than any kind of American music other than that played by Native Americans. Its history is traced at the Old-Time Heritage Hall located in the Earle, built in 1938. Local AM radio station WPAQ broadcasts its *Live Merry Go Round* show from here each Sat at 11 a.m. Admission to the show is $8. Admission to the Heritage Hall is $5 and its open Mon through Fri 11 a.m. to 3 p.m., Sat 9 a.m. to 4 p.m., and Sun 1 to 3:30 p.m.

Mount Airy Museum of Regional History. 301 N. Main St.; (336) 786-4478; northcarolina museum.org. The 4-story building includes a wall-size mural of the surrounding mountains, and displays and exhibitions on the natural history of the area, the Saura Indians, and Siamese twins Eng and Chang Bunker. The story of the area's culture, of the settlers who came to the area, and of the history of the world's largest open-face granite quarry are revealed here. Included is an authentic reproduction of a log cabin, a turn-of-the-20th-century general store, a train room with a 70-foot scale model train exhibit, and a gallery on firefighters that features 1916, 1926, and 1946 fire trucks. Rotating exhibits on the second floor focus on the early 1900s. Admission is $6. Open Tues through Sat 10 a.m. to 5 p.m.

quirky carolina

Eng and Chang Bunker, born in Siam (what is now Thailand) in 1811, became circus performers who fathered 22 children. Known as "the original Siamese twins," they are buried outside the Mount Airy city limits in the White Plains Church community. Many of their some 1,500 descendants still live the Mount Airy area. To get to the grave site, take SR 601 south from Mount Airy past a Wal-Mart on the left. Turn left onto Old Highway 601, then travel 2 miles to pass over I-74 to White Plains Baptist Church on the right. The cemetery is behind the church.

Wally's Service Station and Mayberry Courthouse. 625 South Main St.; (336) 786-6066. This re-creation of the jailhouse and courthouse seen in episodes of *The Andy Griffith Show*, including the jail cells and Andy's desk make a great photo op for fans. Next door at Wally's Service Station, renovated from a 1937 Gulf Station, you can grab a bottle of pop or a souvenir or hop on a tour in a refurbished 1962 squad car. Open Mon through Sat 9 a.m. to 5 p.m. Free.

Squad Car Tours. 625 S. Main St.; (336) 786-6066; tourmayberry.com. Departing with a sound of sirens from this 1937 service station that was restored in 2007 are 30-minute tours around town in replicas of the Ford Galaxy driven by the sheriff and deputy on *The Andy Griffith Show*. It's named for the filling station on the show, and a store with Mayberry souvenirs, collectibles, apparel, coffee, and more is also on-site. The cost is $40 for up to four people. Call for reservations.

where to eat

Snappy Lunch. 125 N. Main St.; (336) 786-4931; thesnappylunch.com. While tiny bits and pieces of *The Andy Griffith Show* are evident in Mount Airy, the Snappy Lunch is the most prominent. In one episode, Andy suggested to Barney that they go to the Snappy Lunch to get a bite to eat. In a television interview with *Biography*, Griffith talked about getting a hot dog and a bottle of pop for 15 cents at the Snappy Lunch when he was a boy. Mount Airy's oldest restaurant, ca. 1923, is famous for the pork chop sandwich. $.

where to stay

Andy's Homeplace. 711 E. Haymore St.; (336) 789-5999. Spend the night in the home where Andy lived with his mother and father until he graduated from high school. Furnished with all the comforts of home, it has 2 bedrooms, a kitchen, a living room, and 1 bath. Andy's Homeplace is located near the Andy Griffith Playhouse and Historic Downtown Mount Airy. $$.

Heart and Soul Bed & Breakfast. 618 N. Main St.; (336) 789-0126; heartnsoulbb.com. Located in Historic Downtown Mount Airy, this 3-story, brick, Victorian-style home has a towerlike front and an inviting wraparound porch. Rates include a complimentary homemade breakfast and an afternoon or evening refreshment. $$–$$$.

The Mayberry Motor Inn. 501 Andy Griffith Pkwy. North; (336) 786-4109; mayberry motorinn.com. A gazebo off Fife Street (named for the famed TV deputy Barney Fife) gives a great view of Pilot Mountain. Guests can walk along Thelma Lou's trail or check out the Andy Griffith and Donna Fargo memorabilia that adorns the inn's office. A 1963 Ford squad car and Emmet's fix-it truck sit in the driveway of the inn. $.

pilot mountain, nc

Twelve miles south of Mount Airy and 26 miles north of Winston-Salem on US 52, Pilot Mountain offers views of the Winston-Salem skyline and the Blue Ridge Mountains. Stop here on the way to or from Mount Airy to get a feel for the High Country. At an elevation of just over 2,400 feet, the area was occupied by the Saura Indians until they were forced off it by the Cherokee.

getting there

Pilot Mountain is a 20-minute drive south from Mount Airy east on US 52. From Charlotte, take I-77 to exit 85. From there, SR 268 East will carry you to Pilot Mountain.

where to go

Pilot Mountain State Park. 1792 Pilot Knob Park Rd., Pinnacle; (336) 325-2355; ncparks .gov. Pilot Mountain's solitary peak, a giant mound rising more than 1,400 feet above the rolling countryside of the upper Piedmont plateau, is the centerpiece of the state park. The park is divided into 2 sections with 1,000 acres on the Yadkin River and offers hiking trails, scenic overlooks, picnicking, family and group camping, and a climbing area. Though at a lower elevation the flora closely resembles that of the Blue Ridge and includes a lot of rho-dodendron and mountain laurel, it's an excellent place to observe wildlife, including the fall migration of raptors. Pilot Mountain was named a National Natural Landmark in 1976. Free. Typically open during daylight hours.

where to stay

Pilot Knob Inn Bed & Breakfast. 361 New Pilot Knob Ln.; (336) 325-2502; pilotknobinn .com. Three suites in the main lodge and rustic cabins converted from tobacco barns with lavish interiors offer a peaceful, private retreat at Pilot Mountain. Most have whirlpools and fireplaces. $$–$$$.

day trip 18

charlotte, nc

>>> the high country:
blowing rock, nc; boone, nc

Elevations of around 3,500 feet keep this area blustery in winter, and winter sports enthusiasts take advantage of a climate that can bring 100 inches of natural snow to area peaks and their corresponding ski areas each year. But an average high summertime temperature of less than 80 degrees creates the same enthusiasm for fair-weather outdoor activities.

Boone was incorporated in 1872, while Blowing Rock followed with incorporation in 1889 as the region was becoming a tourist destination with the opening of several hotels. Even as far back as the Civil War, soldiers would join their families here, and the wealthy from southern cities found their way to this locale to beat the heat of summer. Today it's a busy area with vacation homes, shopping, restaurants, and other amenities. For more information, visit one of the many information clearinghouses in the area including High Country Host, 6370 Hwy. 321, Blowing Rock (800-438-7500; highcountryhost.com). Both Boone and Blowing Rock have visitor centers, too: Boone Convention & Visitor Bureau, 331 Queen St. St., Ste. 10, Boone (828-266-1345; exploreboone.com); and Blowing Rock Tourism Development Authority, 132 Park Ave., Blowing Rock (877-750-4636; visitblowingrock.com).

blowing rock, nc

Blowing Rock is named from a Cherokee legend that says a warrior was blown back up into the arms of his maiden from the strong winds rising out of the Johns River Gorge below. The Blowing Rock is an outcropping that juts more than 1,000 feet from the surrounding

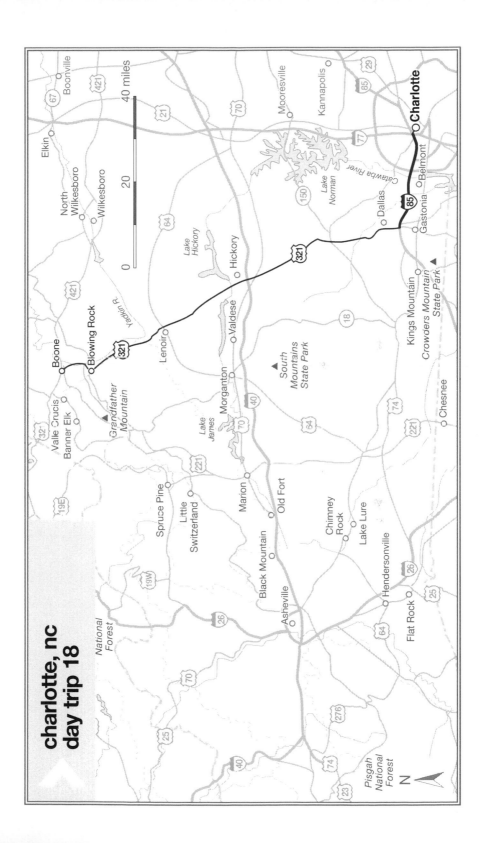

charlotte, nc
day trip 18

landscape. Indeed, strong winds coming out of the gorge 1,500 feet below will blow items back up. It's surrounded by a small town with a winter population of 1,400 and a summer population of 10,000 that depends heavily on tourism. Easy access to the Blue Ridge Parkway helps in that respect.

getting there

From Charlotte, travel south on I-85 to northbound US 321. Blowing Rock is less than 2 hours away.

where to go

The Blowing Rock. 432 Rock Rd.; (828) 295-7111; theblowingrock.com. Learn the legend of the Blowing Rock as you take in the views of Grandfather Mountain and Table Rock, all while breathing the fresh mountain air. Walking the entire trail at the Blowing Rock won't take 30 minutes, but it has been a tourist attraction since 1933. The scenic walk includes a waterfall and trout pond, a garden, and an observation tower. Admission is $9 for adults, $7 for seniors, and $3 for children ages 4 to 11. Open Apr through Oct daily 9 a.m. to 7 p.m., Nov and Dec daily 9 a.m. to 5 p.m., and Jan through Mar Thurs through Mon 9 a.m. to 5 p.m.

Mystery Hill. 129 Mystery Hill Ln.; (828) 263-0507; mysteryhill.com. Balls appear to roll uphill, water flows differently than it does at your house, and walking down a sloped floor is a struggle akin to walking uphill. This small, non-traditional science center features a gravity-related phenomenon apparently related to its location on a hill. Other exhibits allow guests to enclose themselves in bubbles and experiment with other phenomena. An American Heritage Museum, an historic home and native artifact display are also located at the same site. Admission starts at $12.95 for the museums, but there are various add-ons offered from ax throwing, a mechanical bull ride and more. Open daily 9 a.m. to 5 p.m. with extended hours in summer.

Tweetsie Railroad. 300 Tweetsie Railroad Ln.; (800) 526-5740; tweetsie.com. Since 1957 area families have been coming to this Wild West theme park to take a ride on ol' Number 12, a steam-powered train that takes a 3-mile jaunt around the park's wooded acreage. Careful . . . Indians or pesky robbers are likely to hop aboard at any time. Other traditional theme park rides have a county fair feel and include a carousel, Ferris wheel, and boat and plane rides that are especially good for younger children. Shopping, restaurants, a saloon, and live entertainment populate the western boardwalk town. Tickets are $52 for adults and $33 for children ages 3 to 12. Open 9 a.m. to 6 p.m. Fri through Sun in May, daily Memorial Day weekend through mid-Aug, and Fri to Sun mid-Aug through Oct. A Ghost Train Halloween Festival runs weekend evenings in Oct. Thomas the Tank Engine typically visits in summer.

where to shop

Historic Downtown Blowing Rock. Main Street; (877) 750-4696. A stroll through the walkable and shady streets of the village of Blowing Rock offers a dozen or so shops interspersed with restaurants and inns. A Bob Timberlake Gallery, handcrafted jewelry, dulcimer makers, and other artists represent the range of offerings.

Tanger Outlet. 278 Shoppes on the Parkway Rd.; (828) 295-4444; tangeroutlet.com. Located just off the parkway, this outlet offers 30 retailers. It has less personality than shopping districts in downtown Boone and Blowing Rock, but its location and layout are convenient. Offerings include outlets from the Gap to Ralph Lauren. Open Mon through Sat 10 a.m. to 9 p.m., Sun 11 a.m. to 6 p.m. Mar through Dec; Mon through Sat 10 a.m. to 7 p.m., Sun 11 a.m. to 6 p.m. the rest of the year.

where to eat

Bistro Roca. 143 Wonderland Trail; (828) 295-4008; bistroroca.com. Bistro Roca boasts a substantial wine list. Mussels and roasted figs come highly recommended to start, and the mac and cheese is a special treat. Other selections include wood-fired flatbread pizza and a Cuban crepe—slow-braised pork and prosciutto. Open daily 11 a.m. to 3 p.m. and 5 to 10 p.m. $$.

Blowing Rock Brewery. 152 Sunset Dr.; (828) 414-9600; blowingrockbrewery.com. One of the most popular craft breweries in western North Carolina operates the Ale House Restaurant in downtown Blowing Rock. Salads, bison burgers and a few other items are noteworthy.

The Woodlands Barbecue Restaurant. 8304 Valley Blvd.; (828) 295-3651; woodlands bbq.com. Live, local entertainment plays nightly at this restaurant that serves a good plate of barbecue. Plates with hush puppies and slaw are served in a rustic atmosphere that includes picnic tables indoors. Open Sun through Thurs 11 a.m. to 9 p.m., Fri and Sat 11 a.m. to 10 p.m. $–$$.

where to stay

Chetola Resort. 500 Main St.; (800) 243-8652; chetola.com. This spectacular resort, whose name in Cherokee means "Haven to Rest," was first developed as an estate after the Civil War. Its 87 acres include accommodations in the form of the lodge, condos, and resort rooms. Recreational activities feature a spa, fishing, boating, hiking, swimming, a fitness center, and tennis. It's close enough to downtown to walk and is adjacent to the national park. $$$.

Green Park Inn. 9239 Valley Blvd.; (828) 414-9230; greenparkinn.com. Since 1882 the Green Park's distinct green roof and shutters have given it a stately profile in the landscape.

Known as the Grand Dame of the High Country, it was among the first area hotels and is the second-oldest operating hotel in the state, listed on the National Register of Historic Places. Its storied history includes guests such as Eleanor Roosevelt, John Rockefeller, Annie Oakley, and Henry Fonda. Its 88 guest rooms are small but have all modern amenities. $$$.

Hemlock Inn. 134 Morris St.; (828) 295-7987; hemlockinn.net. Located in the bustling heart of the village, the Hemlock is the perfect location for the day-tripper who wants to turn an outing into an overnight. Rooms in the main building offer a rustic, mountain setting with hardwood floors and antique decor. A building that opened in 1999 has a more contemporary feel with vaulted ceilings and carpet. $$.

boone, nc

Boone gets its name from the legendary Daniel Boone, who is believed to have camped in the area. Appalachian State University was founded here as a teaching school in 1899 and became part of the state university system in 1967. Concurrently, clever entrepreneurs discovered they could draw skiers to the region, and the first of the region's three ski areas opened.

getting there

US 321 North turns seamlessly from Blowing Rock to Boone during the 15-minute drive, almost as if they were one.

where to go

Daniel Boone Native Gardens. 651 Horn in the West Dr.; (828) 264-6390; danielboone nativegardens.org. Native trees, shrubs, and wildflowers fill the distinctive informal landscape at these small gardens just outside downtown Boone. A driving force at this 3-acre facility is preserving native species—many of them rare or endangered—and educating visitors about them. The gardens encompass a bog garden, a fern garden, a rhododendron grove, a rock garden, a rock wishing well, a vine-covered arbor, and a pond alongside the historic Squire Boone Cabin. Admission is $2 for ages 16 and up. Open daily 9 a.m. to 6 p.m. May 1 through Oct.

Hickory Ridge Living History Museum. 591 Horn in the West Dr.; (828) 264-2120; horn inthewest.com. Several original log cabins, one dating to the last quarter of the 1700s, afford an opportunity to observe antique dwellings, tools, and lifestyles. Docents in authentic 18th-century dress demonstrate various trades and tasks like weaving and hearthside cooking. Free. The museum is located at the site of *Horn in the West* and is open 5:30 to 8 p.m. on the evenings of the show, Tues through Fri 10 a.m. to 4 p.m. and until 2 p.m. Sat mornings May through Mid-Nov. Tours are $8 for adults and $5 for children.

Horn in the West. 591 Horn in the West Dr.; (828) 264-2120; horninthewest.com. Written by Kermit Hunter, this is a Revolutionary War period story of the families that settled the Blue Ridge in an effort to escape the British. Since 1952 a cast of 50 has presented the outdoor drama on a natural stage. Tickets are $24 for adults, $16 for students ages 13 and up, and $12 for children ages 3 to 12. Shows nightly 8 p.m. late June to mid-Aug.

River & Earth Adventures Inc. 1655 SR 105 South; (828) 963-5491; raftcavehike.com. Guided whitewater rafting, spelunking in hidden caves, hiking, rock climbing, and canoeing trips start from this base in Boone or across the Tennessee state line near Asheville. Lunches and snacks are typically included on longer adventures. Offerings are seasonal, and costs vary widely.

where to shop

Mast General Store. SR 194, Valle Crucis; (828) 963-6511; mastgeneralstore.com. Although the Mast General Store in downtown Boone has spread to other areas through the Carolinas and Tennessee, this is the original store. Mast was founded in 1883 as the Taylor Store between Boone and Banner Elk. Candy, outdoor clothing, crafts, and specialty packaged food are for sale. This location offers an opportunity to warm up by the potbellied stove and see an era gone by that includes antique mailboxes in a corner of the store. Using one of those mailboxes is the only way to have a Valle Crucis address. Open Mon through Sat 7 a.m. to 6:30 p.m., Sun noon to 6 p.m.

where to eat

Coyote Kitchen. 200 Southgate Dr.; (828) 265-4041; coyotekitchen.com. Coyote, with a Caribbean to Mexican theme, has become one of the most popular restaurants in Boone. Its funky atmosphere features local art and the menu features burritos, tacos, and salads. open daily 11 a.m. to 9 p.m. $$.

Dan'l Boone Inn Restaurant. 130 Hardin St.; (828) 264-8657; danlbooneinn.com. Long lines are expected in front of this popular tourist spot, but people generally agree it's worth the wait. Big, filling, home-cooked meals are served family style in this restaurant. Mon through Fri. 11:30 a.m. to 9 p.m., Sat and Sun 8 a.m. to 9 p.m. $$.

The Gamekeeper. 3005 Shull's Mill Rd.; (828) 963-7400; gamekeeper-nc.com. Buffalo, ostrich, and pheasant are on the menu, but adventurous diners can bring more conservative companions, who will find more traditional fine-dining options, too. Vegetarians will even come away satisfied. Dinner is served beginning at 5 p.m. Days of operation vary seasonally. $$$.

where to stay

Lovill House Inn. 404 Old Bristol Rd.; (800) 849-9466; lovillhouseinn.com. This inn received a 4-diamond rating from AAA for its 7 spectacular rooms and 11 well-appointed, landscaped acres. Rockers stand ready on the wraparound porch, and a hammock beneath maple trees beckons. Inside, natural woodwork and impeccable hardwood floors cast a warm glow along with the numerous fireplaces. $$$.

worth more time
the jeffersons

Christmas tree farms fill the landscape east of Boone en route to **the Jeffersons.** Not only will this detour reveal a wide selection of Fraser firs, travelers will also find New River State Park and the confluence of what some geologists believe is one of the world's oldest rivers. **New River State Park** is accessible via US 221 North about 4 miles outside the town of Jefferson.

Before leaving the area make plans to view the frescoes of renowned artist Ben Long in two area churches. Long grew up in Statesville, not far from here, and discovered his remarkable talent for painting on wet plaster as he studied in Italy. His first frescoes were *Mary Great with Child*, *John the Baptist*, and *The Mystery of Faith* at **Saint Mary's Episcopal Church** in West Jefferson. A few years later he painted a life-size depiction of *The Last Supper* at **Holy Trinity Episcopal Church** in Glendale Springs. He now has more than 10 other murals in North Carolina, including in office buildings in downtown Charlotte.

day trip 19

charlotte, nc

>>> **textiles & tomahawks:**
belmont, nc; gastonia, nc

Just south of Charlotte across the Catawba River, visitors begin to learn a story about the area's first inhabitants—the Catawba Indians—first making a quick stop in the friendly town of Belmont before a natural diversion at a great state park. Though the county of Gaston is only a dozen miles or so from the hustle and bustle of downtown Charlotte, it seems many more miles away. Here day-trippers find an abundance of natural adventures, extending from a world-class botanical garden in the east to a rather unusual geographic formation on its western edge some 100 miles from the Blue Ridge.

The Catawbas inhabited this area until 1772, when they began to move to the reservation near Fort Mill as Scotch-Irish, Pennsylvania Dutch, and English began to settle the region. Though the Catawbas first settled this fertile land, utilizing the river for its agricultural benefit, Europeans would use it to join the industrial revolution with the construction of cotton mills. They were established throughout the county but particularly in the eastern part near the Catawba and South Fork Rivers. Both the Indian history and textile heritage would prove important in the cultural life of the area.

belmont, nc

Belmont was settled in the 1750s with the establishment of the Fort at the Point near the junction of the South Fork and Catawba Rivers. It would be nearly 100 years before Jasper Stowe opened one of the area's first textile plants to help establish the city, providing an

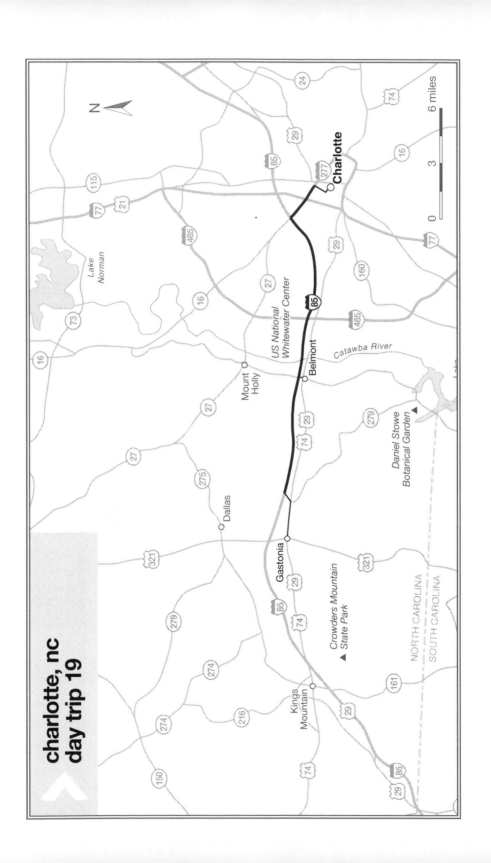

charlotte, nc
day trip 19

anchor to its economic stability for more than 100 years and giving way to the creation of a major botanical garden. In 1872 a Roman Catholic priest, Father Jeremiah O'Connell, purchased a small tract of land on which the Benedictine monks established a religious community and school. That property is now Belmont Abbey College, and the monks are among the area's largest landholders.

getting there

Although this day trip is west of Charlotte, travel south on I-85 and take exit 26 as the interstate bisects the area. Belmont is about 30 minutes from Charlotte.

where to go

Belmont Abbey Basilica. 100 Belmont–Mount Holly Rd.; (888) 222-0110; belmontabbey .org. Founded in 1876 Belmont Abbey is a monastery of about 20 men who operate Belmont Abbey College, a Roman Catholic undergraduate liberal arts school. Central to the 700-acre campus is the Abbey Basilica of Mary Help of Christians (its original and formal name). The striking German Gothic-Revival building was the largest Catholic church in the state at the time of its construction, and the Benedictine monks of Belmont did much of the actual work themselves. Notable is the ceiling crafted in the style of a sailing vessel and windows painted and heat-fused instead of stained, allowing for greater, magnificent detail. The spectacular clock tower was added in 1909. The interior of the church, then classified as a cathedral, was completely renovated in 1964–65. The Vatican elevated the cathedral to the rank of a minor basilica in 1998, and it is on the National Register of Historic Places. A brochure on the basilica provides information for a self-guided tour and is available inside the entrance to the Abbey Basilica or on request by calling (704) 461-6891. Masses and prayer services are held daily throughout the day from 6 a.m. to 7 p.m.

Belmont Historical Society & Heritage Learning Center. 40 Catawba St.; (704) 825-4848. Built originally as a log structure in 1899, the historical society collects, preserves, and restores artifacts from the area. Exhibits include Native American arrowheads and tools, an old-time spinning wheel, and other artifacts from the textile industry as well as the Belmont Sports Hall of Fame. Free. Open Fri through Sun 1 to 5 p.m.

Daniel Stowe Botanical Garden. 6500 S. New Hope Rd.; (704) 825-4490; dsbg.org. Textile magnate Daniel J. Stowe established this garden of 400 acres on the banks of Lake Wylie in 1991. Its main facility, 12 acres of manicured gardens and a large visitor center, opened in 1999. Among those gardens is a southern cottage garden, a subtropical garden, and beautifully designed perennial gardens that draw thousands of birds, bees, and butterflies. The Orchid Conservatory, which features orchids among other tropical plants, opened in 2008. The young garden, noted for its sparkling fountains, has received accolades nationally from the horticultural world and the media, including HGTV. It's constantly expanding with recently opened trails leading to the lakefront, a fun medieval-themed children's garden, and promises for botanical attractions to open over the next several decades. Admission is $14.95 for adults, $12.95 for seniors, and $7.95 for children 2 to 12. Open Wed-Sun 10 a.m. to 4 p.m. with additional hours in summer.

Stowe Park. 24 S. Main St.; (704) 825-8191; belmontparksandrec.com. Located in the middle of downtown, the oak trees are taller today, but this shady park still looks much as it did when it was established in the 1950s. Opened by and now a city park named for Robert Lee Stowe Jr., brother of Daniel Stowe, it is still a gathering spot for locals, whose children take advantage of the playground or get ice cream at the snack bar. A bandstand at the bottom of a grassy amphitheater provides space for bands during frequent seasonal events.

where to shop

Catawba River Antique Mall. 406 Catawba St.; (704) 825-2383; catawbariverantiquemall .com. The Shoney's Big Boy in red and white checkered overalls that used to greet diners now greets shoppers at this massive mall. More than 300 booths fill more than 67,000 square feet of vintiques shopping bliss.

Piccolo Antique Mall. 36 N. Main St.; (704) 825-5656; piccoloantiquemall.com. This great treasure trove of antiques features more than 70 dealers in collectibles, furniture, garden accessories, and funky finds of all types. It is one of a handful of secondhand shops to open in the downtown area in recent years. Open Mon through Sat 10 a.m. to 6 p.m., Sun 1 to 5 p.m.

where to eat

Old Stone Steakhouse. 23 S. Main St.; (704) 825-9995; oldstonesteakhouse.com. A popular after-five hangout, Old Stone provides outdoor seating in warmer weather as well as a handsome wood-paneled interior dining room. The steaks are good, but you can also get well-prepared crab cakes and crab legs. Open for lunch Mon through Fri 11:30 a.m. to 2:30 p.m. and Sat 11:30 to 4:30 p.m. and for dinner Mon through Thurs 5 to 9:30 p.m., Fri and Sat 5 to 10:30 p.m. $$$.

Sammy's Deli & Pub. 24 S. Main St.; (704) 825-4266; sammyspub.com. Sammy's most unusual offering is an odd-sounding but tasty barbecue salad. Typical pub food like burgers, wings, and fish and chips go well with a huge bar selection. Open Sun through Thurs 11 a.m. to 10 p.m., Fri and Sat 11 a.m. to 11 p.m. $-$$.

String Bean Fresh Market & Deli. 106 N. Main St.; (704) 825-3636; stringbeanmarket .com. When Chad Hutchinson opened his restaurant, he called it the String Bean because he wanted to create a place where people could gather just as his family did while stringing beans. The cafe serves hot sandwiches and flatbread pizza, but it also functions as a deli and fine wine and craft beer market. Pick a steak from the market and they will grill it to your taste. $-$$.

gastonia, nc

For more than a century, Gastonia has been a manufacturing hub serving as host to corporate headquarters for textile companies including the world's largest spun yarn manufacturer, Parkdale Mills. This was how an industrial America used the river the Catawba Indians had reserved for agriculture. As textile jobs have receded, the city has begun to transform with attempts to revitalize downtown, but it seems more natural mainstays beckon the day-tripper.

getting there

Take I-85 from downtown Belmont or SR 279 (New Hope Road) from Daniel Stowe Botanical Garden to reach Gastonia. Gastonia is 10 minutes from Belmont.

where to go

Crowders Mountain State Park. 522 Park Office Ln.; (704) 853-5375; ncparks.gov. A popular spot for Boy Scouts and more adventurous rock climbers, Crowders Mountain rises 800 feet above the surrounding terrain and 1,625 feet above sea level. Its 150-foot sheer vertical cliffs and the adjacent Pinnacle's Peak, at 1,705 feet, are remnants of an ancient mountain range from which the Appalachian range was formed. It's still about 70 miles to the Blue Ridge from this point, but it looks like that's where you are. Hiking trails vary from easy to strenuous and feature mountain laurel, wildflowers, and an extensive number of birds. Fishing is permitted at the small lake near the park office, where visitors can rent a canoe for a modest fee. The office also houses a small nature center on the mountain's history and ecology. The park is typically open during daylight hours. It Is Incredibly busy on weekends with rangers often closing the parking lot by mid-morning.

Schiele Museum of Natural History & Planetarium. 1500 E. Garrison Blvd.; (704) 866-6900; schielemuseum.org. The quality of this natural history museum, maintained by the city, rivals state museums and offerings from much larger cities. The collections, animals big and small amassed primarily by Boy Scout executive Bud Schiele, include birds, bear, buffalo, alligators, and other animals from around the world but with a focus on North America. They are presented in dioramas throughout the museum. Most significantly it presents the history of the American Indian in indoor exhibits and at an outdoor re-creation of a Catawba Indian Village. You'll find it on a Nature Trail that also includes an 18th-century backcountry farm complete with pigs, sheep, chickens, and other animals. Farther down the trail visitors can discover a Stone Age site that attempts to explain the area's aboriginal inhabitants. The James H. Lynn Planetarium presents seasonal shows about the nighttime sky, combining traditional projections on the dome with images captured by the Hubble Space Telescope. Regular demonstrations are held at each of the sites. Admission is $7 for adults, $6 for children ages 4 to 18 and for seniors Planetarium shows are $5 per person. Open Mon through Sat 9 a.m. to 5 p.m. and Sun 1 to 5 p.m.

where to eat

RO's Barbecue. 1318 Gaston Ave.; (704) 866-8143; rosbbq.com. RO's serves barbecue that's a little different than most barbecue restaurants around the Carolinas. First, it still offers carhop service (or eat inside if you prefer). Then you'll find the filling RO's sandwich is piled high with roasted pork (get it sliced) and topped with a zesty slaw that is now packaged and distributed regionally as a dip. Try it with a Cherry-Lemon Sundrop, a locally produced soft drink. $.

Tony's Ice Cream. 604 E. Franklin Blvd.; (704) 867-7085; tonysicecream.com. Tony's has been serving up homemade ice cream from this location since 1947. Standards like chocolate, strawberry, and vanilla are in the freezers here, but you can also branch out with nearly 30 other flavors that include lemon and banana. Lunchtime favorites include hot dogs, burgers (chili, slaw, and onions is "all the way"), fried bologna, and liver mush sandwiches. $.

day trip 20

charlotte, nc

>>> come see me:
rock hill, sc; york, sc

The story of the Catawba Indians continues to be told in Rock Hill, and nearby a spectacular re-creation of revolutionary and antebellum life is taking shape. Much like Gaston County, this area has depended on the textile industry in its modern industrial era. The presence of the Catawba Indians holds perhaps even greater significance here than it does for that neighbor to the north. Rock Hill is also a center of vigorous emerging cultural activity that has manifested itself in the developing Culture and Heritage Museums of York County. If those institutions don't hold enough history, the traveler need only look a little deeper to find part of the story of America's revolution at nearby Kings Mountain Battleground and the Southern Revolutionary War Institute.

rock hill, sc

With a population of just more than 70,000, Rock Hill is the fourth-largest city in South Carolina. With a dwindling dependence on textiles, city leaders have looked at ways to redevelop this manufacturing center with cultural opportunities through the support and establishment of a family of museums. These include Historic Brattonsville, McCelvey Center, Museum of York County, and Main Street Children's Museum. Old Town, which encompasses the historic downtown area, Winthrop University, parks, and the city's original neighborhoods, is becoming an entertainment and shopping hub.

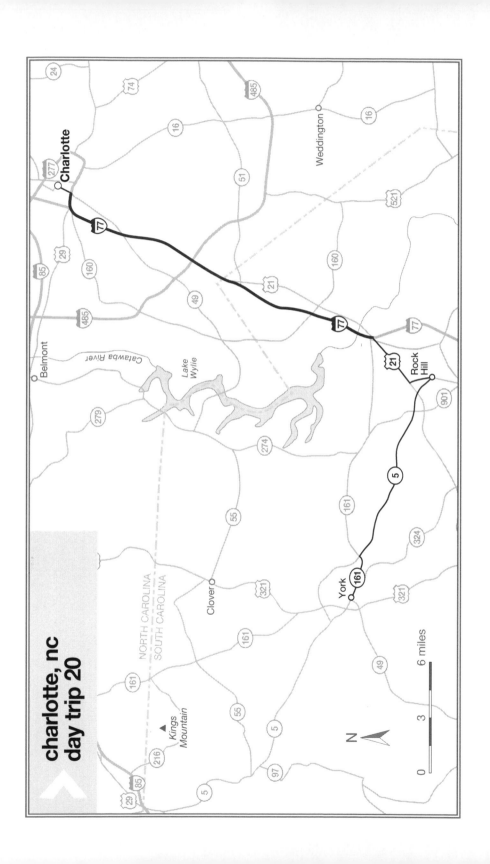

charlotte, nc
day trip 20

Charlotte

Weddington

Belmont

Catawba River

Lake Wylie

Rock Hill

Clover

York

NORTH CAROLINA
SOUTH CAROLINA

Kings Mountain

N

0   3   6 miles

getting there

Rock Hill is straight south of Charlotte on I-77 for about 30 minutes.

where to go

Catawba Cultural Center. 1536 Tom Steven Rd.; (803) 328-2427; catawbaindiancrafts .com. The story of the Catawba Indians is one of the oldest in American history. Some written accounts place the Catawbas in this area around the middle of the 16th century. The famous explorer John Lawson, who was first to survey the Carolinas, wrote extensively about the "people of the river" in his accounts early in the 1700s. The federal government carved out a reservation of several hundred acres here in the 1840s, but that reservation of the Catawba Indian Nation was terminated in 1960. It would take 30 years before that nation was again recognized by the federal government, but now members of the Catawbas have reestablished it through this center, where the story of their struggle is more fully told. Among the exhibits here are a dugout canoe, two replicas of a bark house, a replica of an old Catawba Indian garden, and walking trails. The most resilient aspect of the Catawbas has been their production of pottery. It is available for purchase here. Admission is free. Open Mon through Sat 9 a.m. to 5 p.m.

Ebenezer Park. 4490 Boatshore Rd.; (803) 366-6554; yorkcountygov.com. Joggers, bikers, and boaters turn out in droves at this tidy waterfront park. Picnicking, swimming, and fishing are also popular pastimes here. The park has campsites for RVs and tents. An entrance fee of $8 is charged for out-of-county visitors. A fee of $20 is charged for campsites. The park is typically open during daylight hours.

Glencairn Garden. 725 Crest St.; (803) 329-5620; cityofrockhill.com.com. Some 11 acres of dogwoods, camellia, wisteria, and other traditional southern plants are open for touring in the center of Rock Hill. Once the home of David and Hazel Bigger, the gardens surround their bungalow-style residence built in 1928. When Bigger, a local doctor, died in 1958, his widow donated their home to the city. Admission is free. Typically open during daylight hours.

Main Street Children's Museum. 133 E. Main St.; (803) 327-6400; chmuseums.org. This unique children's museum is inspired by Vernon Grant, the Rock Hill artist who created Kellogg's famous Rice Krispies characters Snap, Crackle, and Pop. It is part of the Cultural and Heritage Museums of York County. The museum is an abstract world that includes a pumpkin house, a tree house, a train, a sailing ship, and other colorful interactive components for preschool-age children. Admission is $6 for ages 1 and over. Open 10 a.m. to 5 p.m. Tues through Sat, noon to 5 p.m. Sun.

Museum of York County. 4621 Mount Gallant Rd.; (803) 329-2121; chmuseums.org. Impressive, realistic dioramas are at the heart of this natural history museum that takes visitors from the South Carolina Piedmont to the African Serengeti. Opened in 1950 as a museum on the Catawba Indians, it now houses a substantial collection of some of the world's largest animals on display. A Naturalist Center allows guests to learn about natural history hands-on with animal skins, skulls, and rocks and minerals curated especially for that purpose. Other exhibits include the Carolina Piedmont Hall's Landscapes and Lifeways: The Carolina Piedmont 600 Years Ago and Today. Settlemyre Planetarium takes visitors out of this world. The museum also pays tribute to Vernon Grant, the creator of Kellogg's Rice Krispies characters Snap, Crackle, and Pop, in an exhibit about his life growing up in York County. Admission is $8 for adults, $7 for seniors, and $5 for youth ages 4 to 17. Open Mon through Sat 10 a.m. to 5 p.m., Sun 1 to 5 p.m.

The White Home. 258 E. White St.; historicrockhill.com. The White Home, ca. 1840, evolved over 40 years from humble beginnings as a small 1-room farmhouse to the distinct home and outbuildings that guests see today. It is named for the White family, who lived in the house until the historical society bought it in 2005. It's a window into the lives of this family, who were leaders in the community, and into the city's development. Among the exhibits are photographs, china, furniture, documents, and other artifacts in the home and outbuildings on this elegant piece of property. It now serves largely as event space but is open to the public. Admission is $8 for adults, $7 for seniors, $5 for children ages 5 to 17. Hours are Mon through Fri 10 a.m. to 4:30 p.m. and by appointment.

where to shop

Bobbie's Place Toy Store. 133 E. Main St.; (803) 327-6400; chmuseums.org. Located at the Main Street Children's Museum, this is not the typical museum store. It focuses on low-tech gifts and toys for children. While some of the items reflect the experience in the children's museum, others come out of the cultural experiences in Rock Hill. Hours are 10 a.m. to 5 p.m. Tues through Sat, noon to 5 p.m. Sun.

Gettys Art Center. 201 E. Main St.; (803) 328-2787; yorkcountyarts.org. This art center, managed by the Arts Council of York County, includes the Rock Hill Pottery Studio and Gallery, Grace with Fire pottery studio, the South Carolina Arts Alliance headquarters, Social Design House, artist studios, and Gallery Up, a fine arts retail store, gallery, and custom frame shop. The artist-run gallery sells jewelry, sculpture, paintings, photos, woodwork, and scarves, all by local artists. Open Mon through Fri 10 a.m. to 5 p.m.

The Shoppes at River's Edge. 951 Celriver Rd.; (803) 324-2300; shoppesatriversedge .com. A variety of merchants selling just as wide a variety of merchandise offer their wares at this unique shopping mall. Antiques, handmade items, collectibles, and more are available here. Open Tues through Fri 10 a.m. to 6 p.m. and Sat 10 a.m. to 5 p.m.

where to eat

Legal Remedy Brewing. 129 Oakland Ave.; (803) 324-2337; legalremedybrewing.com. The original brewery is located here in this restored car dealership in what Is known as Old Towne. In addition to beer, cured and smoked meats are the specialty of the house. Try the smoked turkey for a slight deviation from the typical pork. Open Thurs 4 to 8 p.m., Fri and Sat, noon to 8 p.m. and Sun. noon to 6 p.m. $$.

The Pump House. 575 Herrons Ferry Rd.; (803) 329-8888; rockhillpumphouse.com. Located In the actual pump house that supplied water to the Celanese Factory on the Catawba River, this restaurant serves interesting southern cuisine with locally sourced Ingredients. Start with lump crab cake or a salad and finish with filet mignon or drunken lamb chops. Open daily 11 a.m. to 10 p.m. $$$

where to stay

East Main Guest House. 600 E. Main St.; (803) 366-1161; eastmainguesthouse.com. Located near Old Town this Craftsman Bungalow has 3 queen guest rooms. $$

worth more time
historic brattonsville

There's not much more to McConnells than **Historic Brattonsville** (1444 Brattonsville Rd.; 803-684-2327; chmuseums.org). The 700-acre site is dedicated to the Scotch-Irish Bratton family, and thus to the many families who settled the South Carolina upstate. To get there, take SR 322 to the west of Rock Hill, which is also known as McConnells Highway, and it heads straight into McConnells. The sprawling Historic Brattonsville, part of the family of museums in York County, is a Revolutionary War living history site and the plantation home of the Bratton family. It provides a glimpse of how the people of the Carolinas lived from the middle of the 18th century to the period just before the Civil War. The restoration is an ambitious undertaking that includes the meticulous renovation or replication of more than 30 structures, whose many stories are told by costumed guides. Hightower Hall, featured in the Mel Gibson film *The Patriot*, is the Italianate villa mansion where the Brattons lived. Part of the heritage farm exhibit includes animals not often seen, such as Gulf Coast sheep, Devon cattle, and Ossabaw Island hogs, cared for here just as they were hundreds of years ago. Other restorations and replicas are also part of the tour. The Walt Schrader Trails are an 8.5-mile network of backcountry paths. Admission is $6 for adults, $5 for seniors, and $3 for youth ages 4 to 17. Open Mon though Sat 10 a.m. to 5 p.m., Sun 1 to 5 p.m.

york, sc

The town of Yorkville was the town closest to the middle of the county, so in 1785 it became the county seat of York. It also became York in 1915 when citizens voted to shorten the name. About 180 buildings in downtown are listed on the National Register of Historic Places, preserving forever the remarkable architectural features and character of the small-town South.

getting there

From Rock Hill, take SR 5 west to the town of York. It is about a 25-minute drive. Starting in Charlotte, I-77 to SR 161 west is a direct route and will also take less than 30 minutes. Take exit 85 to Fort Mill.

where to go

McCelvey Center. 212 E. Jefferson St.; (803) 684-3948; chmuseums.org. In addition to fulfilling its mission as the home of the Southern Revolutionary War Institute, the McCelvey Center houses the 500-seat Lowry Family Theater, which hosts an annual performing arts series. As a historical center, it is a must-see for the history buff, providing opportunities for genealogical and historical research through extensive collections of documents, photographs, York County court records, microfilm reels, rare books, maps, church and cemetery indexes, and family genealogical books. The building, historic itself, opened in 1852 as the Yorkville Female Academy, one of the state's leading schools for women. It later became part of the public school system, which turned it over to the McCelvey Center in 1987. Admission is free except for performances. Open Mon through Fri and the second Sat of the month, 10 a.m. to 4 p.m.

Sylvia Theater. 27 N. Congress St.; (803) 684-5590; sylviatheater.com. Just like old times (almost), the Sylvia Theater shows first-run family flicks in this 100-year-old space. It also provides an opportunity where unknown, newly discovered, and popular singers and songwriters can gather to play. Regional performers such as Edwin McCain and older groups such as The Drifters and comedians like James Gregory perform here.

where to shop

The Peach Tree. 2077 Filbert Hwy.; (803) 684-9996. Get your peaches here. This stand also serves great ice cream in peach and other flavors. Other seasonal fruits and vegetables are available for purchase, and kids can make their way through the straw-bale maze or pick out a pumpkin in the fall. Open Mon through Sat 9 a.m. to 6 p.m., Sun 1 to 6 p.m.

Windy Hill Orchard & Cider Mill. 1860 Black Hwy.; (803) 684-0690; windyhillorchard .com. This has become a York County traveler's tradition, and it must be because of the cider doughnuts in addition to traditional favorites such as pies, cider, peaches, pumpkins, and strawberry butter. In the fall enjoy apple slushes. Tours, hayrides, and other fun events, including hard cider tastings, are scheduled seasonally throughout the year. Open Aug through Dec.

worth more time
kings mountain battleground

There are two parks (a South Carolina state park and a national military park) and one North Carolina city named for Kings Mountain, and the Charlotte day-tripper could actually visit any one of the three during any number of these day trips. So why all the Kings Mountains? Many historians believe that the Battle of Kings Mountain on October 7, 1780, was the turning point in the Revolution. It was the first patriot victory since the British took Charleston 5 months earlier. A ragtag but determined bunch of militia known as the Overmountain Men, who marched from Tennessee, fought for only an hour before beating back more than 1,000 redcoats at Kings Mountain. A film on the battle is shown at the National Park Visitor Center, located on SR 216 near Blacksburg. A 1.5-mile loop trail features monuments and highlights important parts of the battle. The adjacent **Kings Mountain State Park** (803-222-3209; southcarolinaparks.com) is located on SR 161 near Blacksburg, South Carolina, and features a living history farm and camping facilities. Notably the city of Kings Mountain is home to North Carolina's second casino—Two Kings, opened by the Catawba Indians in 2021.

asheville, nc

day trip 21

asheville, nc

asheville, nc

Bohemian, refined, adventurous represent the diversity of words that may be used to describe people who find appeal in this mountain town. Asheville boasts the largest private residence in America, the largest concentration of B&Bs in the state, and one of the coolest vibes any city in the Carolinas has to offer. It's a good place to branch out, to test your courage, and to live life to the fullest.

In the shadow of the Black Mountains of the Blue Ridge, this region was once inhabited by Cherokee Indians, but today it is inhabited by artists, musicians, and those who appreciate the outdoors the most. Culture is close at hand in Asheville's art district, at Biltmore Estate, Biltmore Village, and the city's museums. The food is great. The beer is better, and opportunities to hike, raft, camp, fish, and simply breathe the cool mountain air are even better.

Sited on a massive plateau, the area that is now Asheville was Cherokee hunting ground until late in the 18th century when it was settled by the Davidson family at the mouth of Bee Tree Creek. Lawmakers established its county of Buncombe in 1792 and founded Morristown, where two Indian trails crossed, a year later. Morristown was renamed Asheville after North Carolina Governor Samuel Ashe in 1797. Fast-forward 100 years. The Western North Carolina Railroad from Salisbury to Asheville is complete, and the city begins to prosper with the establishment of textile mills and plants producing products from the area's

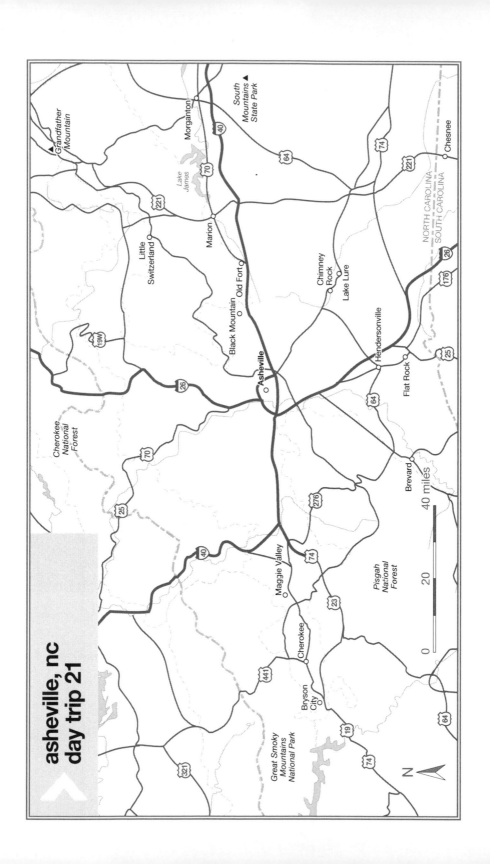

asheville, nc
day trip 21

Grandfather
Mountain

Morganton

South
Mountains
State Park

Chesnee

40

64

74

221

70

Lake
James

221

Marion

26

176

Little
Switzerland

NORTH CAROLINA
SOUTH CAROLINA

Black Mountain

Old Fort

Chimney
Rock

Lake Lure

Hendersonville

25

19W

Asheville

Flat Rock

26

64

70

25

Brevard

Cherokee
National
Forest

276

40 miles

40

Maggie Valley

74

20

25

23

Pisgah
National
Forest

Cherokee

441

Bryson
City

84

Great Smoky
Mountains
National Park

19

321

74

N

rich stone and wood resources. George Vanderbilt bought 120,000 acres here and in 1895 completed the famed Biltmore Estate. By the beginning of the 20th century, Asheville was also recognized as a tourist destination. E. W. Grove established a golf course here in 1899 and a decade later built the luxurious Grove Park Inn. Day-trippers will find pieces of all this history in their adventures high in the mountains of Asheville.

getting there

Asheville is accessible via I-40 (from the east or west), passing south of the city and completing a loop with I-240 arcing north of the city. Some choose to reach Asheville from the east by taking US 74 west, which merges with I-26 near Flat Rock. This might prove confusing for the unfamiliar driver because farther southeast US 74 splits off at Forest City and merges with US 64. This leg of 74 also leads to Asheville. The Blue Ridge Parkway runs north to south east of Ashville and clips the city's southeastern corner. From points north, take US 19/70/25 (a portion of I-26).

where to go

Asheville Area Arts Council. 1 Page Ave.; (828) 222-0436; ashevillearts.com. Begin exploring the deep arts community in Asheville at the Asheville Area Arts Council. Located in the Grove Arcade downtown, it has exhibition space for dozens of local and emerging artists. Admission is free. Open Mon through Sat 10 a.m. to 6 p.m.

Asheville Art Museum. 2 S. Pack Sq.; (828) 253 3227; ashevilleart.org. Featuring exhibitions primarily of 20th- and 21st-century American art, the museum focuses on works of the Southeast, including those artists who have a connection to the Asheville area. While some of the work can be classified as contemporary and some as regional craft, the collection is more diverse than at some of the art museums in the state. Admission is $15 for adults, $10 for students and $13 for seniors. The Holden Community Gallery on the first floor of the museum is free. Open daily except Tues11 a.m. to 6 p.m. with extended hours on Thurs. Tues through Sat 10 a.m. to 5 p.m., Sun 1 to 5 p.m.

asheville urban trail

Part of the city's park system, this tour of bronze sculptures related to its history and the notable people who have lived in the city includes authors O. Henry and Thomas Wolfe. The tour begins at Pack Place, and in about 2 hours at a comfortable walking pace leads to 30 stations marked by pink granite stones. Download a map and podcasts for the self-guided tour at romanticasheville.com.

Asheville Outdoor Center. 521 Amboy Rd.; (828) 232-1970; ashevilleoutdoorcenter.com. Regardless of the flavor of outdoor adventure you favor, the Asheville Outdoor Center is likely to have a big helping of it for you. It hosts a variety of services that include flatwater float trips on the French Broad River and canoe, kayak, tube, and bike rentals from its riverside location. It also operates a public gem-mining operation. Hours are seasonal.

Basilica of St. Lawrence. 97 Haywood St.; (828) 252-6042; saintlawrencebasilica.org. This spectacular architectural gem dating to 1909 was designed by the same architects who worked on Biltmore Estate, including nationally renowned architect Rafael Guastavino, designer of Grant's Tomb, Grand Central Station, and Carnegie Hall. The Catholic church was built in a Spanish Renaissance style with no beams in the entire building, making its dome the largest freestanding dome in the country. Intricate details and artwork fill the basilica from the vestibule to the altar and windows. Download a guide from the website or pick one up in the vestibule. Open daily 9 a.m. to 6 p.m.

Biltmore. 1 Approach Rd.; (828) 225-1333; biltmore.com. An astonishing 250-plus rooms, extensive gardens, a winery, and more make up the largest private home in America. On the grounds visitors can hike, ride horses, raft, and sling mud in a 4-wheel-drive vehicle. Experiencing all that Biltmore has to offer simply cannot be done in a day or even two, so make plans to return often.

Built in 1895 by George Vanderbilt, the grandson of a railroad tycoon, who originally bought more than 120,000 acres of land in this area, Biltmore is still known as the largest residence in America. Vanderbilt would leave a legacy by selling through his bequest to the federal government for a token price what is now Pisgah National Forest. He is known for having led an effort to manage forestry but is better known for the lavish home that includes more than 50,000 works of art, furnishings, and antiques, which Vanderbilt and his wife, Edith, spent years collecting in Europe and Asia. Among the works at the home are pieces by Renoir and Whistler, in addition to a chess table once owned by Napoleon Bonaparte. The home was constructed over a 5-year period and took a total of one million hours of labor. In addition to the 22 rooms in which the Vanderbilt family lived, the home also includes an indoor swimming pool, a bowling alley, and servants' quarters, all of which are open for tours.

The home is especially beautiful during the evening candlelight tours during the Christmas holidays. **Antler Hill,** the newest part of the estate, was developed in the winery area to add space for concerts, a vintage car exhibit, shopping, and dining. It also includes an outdoor adventure center that is a base for carriage rides, biking, Segway tours, and even off-road Land Rover experiences. **The Inn on Biltmore Estate** provides a gracious environment and outstanding views. A carriage ride or meal in one of Biltmore's restaurants tops off a day trip nicely. Frederick Law Olmsted, known as perhaps the country's foremost landscape architect, designed the seemingly endless gardens on the 8,000-acre property. An azalea garden, English walled garden, and rose garden are just the beginning. The estate's trees and gardens highlight Vanderbilt's interest in horticulture. Adult tickets to tour the home and grounds start at $76. Additional fees are charged for a variety of other attractions and activities. Biltmore is open 365 days a year, and hours of various attractions vary by activity and by season. Things typically open by 9 a.m. and close by 5 p.m., except during the holidays when a candlelight tour is offered.

Botanical Gardens at Asheville. 151 W. T. Weaver Blvd.; (828) 252-5190; ashevillebotani calgardens.org. Located on the campus of the University of North Carolina, an unaffiliated nonprofit organization maintains the 10 acres of native plantings of southern Appalachia. A half-mile trail along a stream, meadow, and woodland holds some expected and unexpected treasures in the form of trees, grasses, sedges, wildflowers, and shrubs. The garden's collection includes rare and endangered species such as broad-leaved coreopsis and pale yellow trillium. Free. Generally open during daylight hours. Closed from early Dec through Feb.

Asheville Museum of Science. 2 S. Pack Sq; (828) 254-7162; asheveillscience.org Sparkling gemstones, ancient fossils, and common Carolina minerals make up most of the exhibits at this well-done earth science museum that makes rocks and plate tectonics engaging. Once known as the Colburn Science Earth Science Museum, it includes those standard collections of rocks and minerals, but other hands-on exhibits make weather, volcanoes, and earthquakes more fun and, more important, understandable. Admission is $8.50 for adults, $7.50 for students and seniors. Open Mon 10 a.m. to 5 p.m., Wed 10 a.m. to 3 p.m., Thurs 11 a.m. to 5 p.m., Fri and Sat, 10 a.m. to 5 p.m. and Sun 1 to 5 p.m.

Diana Wortham Theatre. 2 S. Pack Sq.; (828) 257-4530; worthamarts.org. This theater is another of Asheville's intimate presentation spaces, with 500 seats. Productions run the gamut from bluegrass concerts to Shakespeare. It hosts a variety of musicals, dramas, and dance theater presentations from professional touring groups and some of the city's own cultural groups.

Grovewood Gallery. 111 Grovewood Rd.; (828) 253-7651; grovewood.com. Located adjacent to the Grove Park Inn, the Grovewood property includes the Estes-Winn Memorial Automobile Museum, the North Carolina Homespun Museum, a small sculpture display garden, and a working artist studio. The automobile museum holds horse-drawn carriages as well as vintage automobiles, and the city's 1922 American La France fire engine is on display. The Homespun Museum tells the story of the Biltmore Industries wool-weaving business at the early part of the 20th century. The studios have a dozen or so artists in residence producing fiber art, ceramics, and more. Free. Open Wed through Sun 10 a.m. to 5 p.m.

Hazel Robinson Amphitheatre. 100 Gay St.; (828) 254-5146; montfordparkplayers.org. Hazel Robinson Amphitheatre is home to the Montford Park Players, which produces North Carolina's longest-running and most acclaimed Shakespeare festival. The free productions are staged in the outdoor theater throughout the summer, Fri, Sat, and Sun 7:30 p.m.

Orange Peel Social Aid & Pleasure Club. 101 Biltmore Ave.; (828) 398-1837; theorange peel.net. Nothing characterizes the funky appeal of the Asheville music scene better than this venue. Originally a skating rink in the 1950s and '60s, it operated as the Original Orange Peel in the 1970s, but closed for a period, serving as an auto parts warehouse. In 2002 it reopened to national acclaim, listed as one of *Rolling Stone*'s top 5 rock clubs in the country and getting coverage from everyone from *Cosmopolitan* to *GQ*. Accommodating only 1,100 people even for national acts such as Bob Dylan, Smashing Pumpkins, and Ziggy Marley, this venue is intimate by comparison to others. When major acts aren't in town, the club caters to regional and indie artists.

Pinball Museum. 1 Battle Sq.; (828) 776-5671; ashevillepinball.com. If these flashing, dinging, tilting, bell-ringing machines were part of your past, you absolutely have to play the Adams Family Game. One of Asheville's newest museums doesn't have anything to do with art, history, science, or any of that—it's just for fun. The pinball museum has more than 30 machines at any given time, from the 1960s through the '90s. Admission is $15 for adults and $13 for children under age 10. Play all you like for one low price. Open Wed through Fri 2 to 9 p.m., Sat noon to 9 p.m., and Sun 1 to 6 p.m.

Smith-McDowell House Museum. 283 Victoria Rd.; (828) 253-9231; wnchistory.org. This stunning brick Victorian home, ca. 1840, is meticulously maintained by the Western North Carolina Historical Association. It was built by James McConnell Smith, the son of a Revolutionary War colonel who acquired great wealth, became mayor of Asheville for a period, and owned a number of businesses. Two other families and the Catholic diocese would own the home during its history. Today the house and exhibits trace that history through period rooms, clothing, and other items. Admission is $10 for adults, $5 for ages 5 to 18. Open Wed through Sat 10 a.m. to 4 p.m., Sun noon to 4 p.m.

Thomas Wolfe Memorial State Historic Site. 52 N. Market St.; (828) 253-8304; wolfe memorial.com. This home is the basis of Thomas Wolfe's novel *Look Homeward, Angel*.

quirky carolina

Only in Asheville will you find this fun, impromptu drum circle that's not so impromptu anymore. Each Friday in warm weather, a group of bongo players, dundun beaters, cowbell shakers, and other percussionists show up at downtown Asheville's Pritchard Park (Patton Avenue at College Street) for the Drum Circle. They are sometimes joined by hundreds of dancers and others who want to play some sort of rhythmic instrument. Things are usually well underway by 6 p.m. and last as late as 10 p.m.

Known in the novel as "old Kentucky Home," it is the boyhood home of one of America's great 20th-century novelists. The home was tragically and significantly damaged by arson in 1998, and although restoration took 6 years, it reopened with artifacts that give a glimpse of life in this boardinghouse operated by Wolfe's mother. A visitor center presents slick audiovisual exhibits and other artifacts from Wolfe's short life (he died at 37) and stoic work. Admission is $5 for adults and $2 for students. Guided house tours are offered daily beginning at the bottom of each hour. Open Tues through Sat 9 a.m. to 5 p.m.

Whitewater Sportsman. Various locations around the Asheville area; (828) 216-1336; whitewatersportsman.com. Whitewater Sportsman offers guided raft fishing trips on the French Broad River, one of the state's best for smallmouth bass, even for anglers with little or no experience. Full-day trips take 7 to 8 hours, while half-day trips take 4 to 5 hours. Lunch is provided on full-day trips. Rates start at $275 and include everything needed for the trip, including a personal guide.

WNC Nature Center. 75 Gashes Creek Rd.; (828) 298-5600; wildwnc.org. This small, well-done zoo is located in a wooded area between downtown and the Blue Ridge Parkway. Gray wolves, bobcats, cougars, and coyotes are among the species represented along a hilly but navigable trail. It also has a farm exhibit with a petting zoo as well as indoor exhibits of spiders, snakes, and other small critters. The center is also engaged in the reintroduction of elk to the Smoky Mountains of North Carolina and the Red Wolf Species Survival Program. Admission is $8 for adults, $7 for seniors, and $4 for children ages 3 to 15. Open daily 10 a.m. to 5 p.m., with reduced hours in winter.

where to shop

Downtown Asheville Arts District. (828) 505-8341; downtownarts.com. This association was developed to help promote the 25 or more art galleries in downtown Asheville. Among them are **The Bender Gallery** (29 Biltmore Ave.; 828-505-8341; thebendergallery .com) with a large selection of glass works; the **Haen Gallery** (52 Biltmore Ave.; 828-254-8577; thehaengallery.com) with rotating group exhibitions; and **Woolworth Walk** (25 Haywood St.; 828-254-9234; woolworthwalk.com), located in the old five-and-dime, which is the only area gallery to exclusively feature local artists. A complete guide can be downloaded at the website or pick one up at the Chamber of Commerce or any of the participating galleries.

Asheville Gallery of Art. 82 Patton Ave.; (828) 251-5796; ashevillegallery-of-art.com. Located in Pritchard Park, this is a partnership of 28 professional, regional artists offering original two-dimensional works from representational to abstract. The collector as well as the homeowner will likely find something to take away from here. Open daily 11 a.m. to 6 p.m.

Grove Arcade. 1 Page Ave.; (828) 252-7799; grovearcade.com. The Grove building, opened in 1929 by E. W. Grove, was a thriving public market until World War II, when the federal government took it over as part of the war effort. The government maintained control of the building until the 1980s, when an effort began to renovate it for its original use. Today it includes dozens of fun, boutique stores with everything from gifts to clothing to bed and bath. The south end features a portico market with local artisans selling their wares. Open Mon through Sat 10 a.m. to 8 p.m.; Sun hours vary by store.

Historic Biltmore Village. 7 All Souls Crescent; (828) 274-8788; historicbiltmorevillage .com. The Historic Village was developed as part of George Vanderbilt's estate but now includes several dozen shops, galleries, and restaurants located in historic homes on tree-lined streets. Toy stores, antiques shops, craft galleries, hobby shops, and others make up this area. A handful of B&Bs are also located among the retailers. Hours vary by merchant.

River Arts District. Clingman Avenue at Lyman Street; (828) 252-9122; riverartsdistrict .com. Located along the French Broad River and the railroad, dozens of artists studios are open in one of Asheville's coolest neighborhoods. An old depot, warehouses, and once-deteriorating buildings are vibrant works of art themselves.

Western North Carolina Farmers' Market. 570 Brevard Rd.; (828) 253-1691; ncagr.gov. Fresh fruits and vegetables, jams, cheese, bakery items, honey, homemade fudge, hand-made crafts, flowers, and plants are all offered. A deli, full-service restaurant, and complete garden center are also on the site. Open daily 8 a.m. to 5 p.m.

where to eat

French Broad Chocolate Lounge. 10 S. Lexington Ave.; (828) 252-4181; frenchbroad chocolates.com. The Liquid Truffle is the specialty of the house at this sweet spot in down-town Asheville. The handcrafted chocolates and other desserts are made largely from local and organic ingredients. Staff will even help pair chocolate desserts with the perfect wine. Open daily 11 a.m. to 10 p.m.t. $.

Green Sage Cafe. 5 Broadway St., 1800 Hendersonville Rd., 70 Westgate Pkwy.; (828) 252-4450; greensagecafe.com. The 3 locations of the Green Sage Cafe epitomize the cul-ture of Asheville. The small chain is as committed to sustainability as any restaurant around. And the food—all organic—is good. From biscuits or omelet sandwiches in the morning to sandwiches and wraps in the afternoon, Green Sage makes for a great stop for the day-tripper. Open daily 8 a.m. to 7 p.m. $$.

Table. 48 College St.; (828) 254-8980; tableasheville.com. Table is regarded as one of Asheville's best fine dining experiences. Local meats and produce are used to prepare exotic dishes. Pork chops are combined with creamed hominy, curry, and chowchow, and brussels sprouts make it to the table combined with lobster or scallops. The decor is con-temporary, slick, and simple. Open daily for lunch 11:30 a.m. to 2:30 p.m., dinner 5:30 to 10 p.m., Sun brunch 10:30 a.m. to 2:30 p.m. $$$.

Tupelo Honey Cafe. 12 College St.; (828) 255-4863; and 1829 Hendersonville Rd.; (828) 505-7676; tupelohoneycafe.com. The cooks at Tupelo twist southern traditional favorites such as fried chicken with custom creations that come largely from local ingredients and become menu items like sweet potato pancakes and fried green tomatoes with goat cheese grits. The wait could be as long as 2 hours at the downtown location. $$.

12 Bones. 5 Riverside Dr.; (828) 253-4499; 12bones.com. This barbecue restaurant that attracted Barack Obama is so cool, so trendy, and so popular you have to work with their schedule: it's only open for lunch on weekdays. That makes taking the day off for a day trip totally worth it. Unlike many barbecue joints in North Carolina, 12 Bones specializes in slow-smoked ribs, though traditional pulled pork is available along with other southern selections, too. Open Mon through Fri 11 a.m. to 4 p.m. $$.

where to stay

Biltmore Village Inn. 119 Dodge St.; (828) 274-8707; biltmorevillageinn.com. This luxury inn is close to the estate but is run independently. The 1892 Queen Anne Victorian is located on Reed Hill, named for George Vanderbilt's attorney, overlooking the village and Swan-nanoa Valley. Unusually large rooms are located in the inn's 2 buildings. The baths, some with fireplaces, are luxurious. $$$.

Grove Park Inn. 290 Macon Ave.; (800) 438-5800; groveparkinn.com. This is the hotel that E. W. Grove built, and he didn't spare comfort or convenience. It offers restaurants, a spa, golf, great views, a spectacular lobby known as the Great Hall with a massive stone fireplace, and more. The St. Louis entrepreneur erected the inn between 1912 and 1913 in less than 12 months, using local stone. $$$.

Sourwood Inn. 810 Elk Mountain Scenic Hwy.; (828) 255-0690; sourwoodinn.com. Located outside Asheville near the parkway, this rustic cedar and stone structure sits at an elevation overlooking Reams Creek. A private balcony offers great views in warm months, while a wood-burning fireplace in each room offers a cozy atmosphere in cooler months. Rockers and quiet places scattered about the property beg for a little reading. $$$.

day trip 22

asheville, nc

>>> **qualla boundary:**
cherokee, nc

cherokee, nc

For decades families have made their way here to learn about the tragedy of the Trail of Tears and to get the real scoop on how Native Americans have shaped this part of the country. They also find a fair share of tourism glitz. Other than the state lottery, Harrah's Casino on the Cherokee Indian Reservation is the only one of two opportunities in North Carolina for legal gambling, so it's a big draw. The Cherokee, a federally recognized Native American tribe, preserve a portion of this land's heritage prior to European settlement. It is the sole town located in the 56,000-acre Qualla Boundary, home to roughly 8,500 members of the Eastern Band of the Cherokee. Nestled between Great Smoky Mountains National Park and the western end of the Blue Ridge Parkway, the town is a full-fledged tourist attraction with museums, historical sites, family attractions, and outdoor opportunities galore.

Some historians say archaeological evidence suggests the Cherokee have inhabited this area for more than 10,000 years. As the Europeans began to settle the area, the Cherokee remained in control of most of southern Appalachia through eight states. Largely through the end of the Revolutionary War, the Cherokee were left alone to the west of the Great Continental Divide. But as the new country expanded, conflict with the Indian nation arose with land speculators claiming areas for establishing plantations and for mining gold. In 1838 Andrew Jackson ordered the removal of the Cherokee to Oklahoma. The Cherokee in North Carolina today are the descendants of those who hid in the hills in defiance

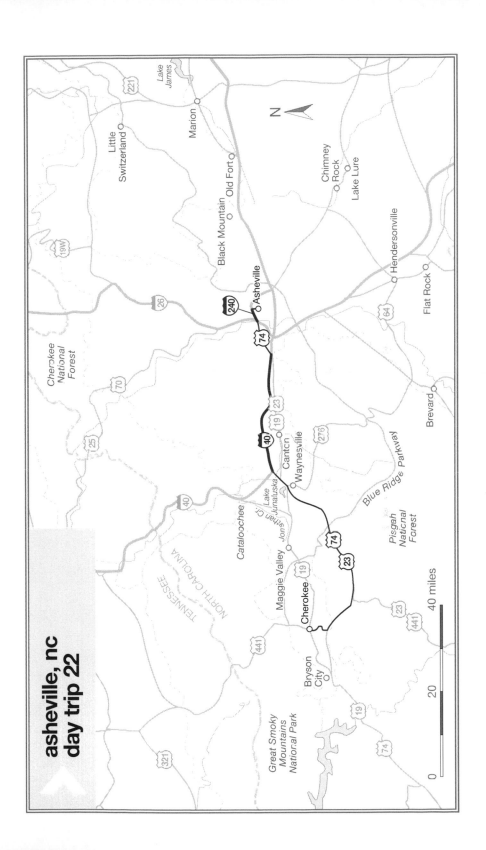

asheville, nc
day trip 22

of Jackson's order. In the 1840s and '50s, a white man named Will Thomas, who had been adopted by the tribe that remained on the small reservations in North Carolina, won legal battles to keep the Cherokee in their mountain homes. His assistance was enough to establish them on that land until the federal government would recognize the Cherokee as a sovereign nation in the 1970s.

getting there

From Asheville, take US 74/23 west. At exit 81, Highway 23 peels off to the south while 74 merges with US 441 and takes drivers into Cherokee. The drive should take about an hour.

where to go

Harrah's Cherokee. 777 Casino Dr.; (828) 497-7777; harrahscherokee.com. This massive casino, hotel, and entertainment center is a huge revenue and job producer for the Eastern Band of the Cherokee. More than 4 million people visit the resort annually. Although by law the casino originally could offer only games of skill, statute changes have permitted live gaming in craps, blackjack, and roulette. A 3,000-seat entertainment center offers nationally known acts and Vegas-style shows while restaurants from Johnny Rockets to Ruth's Chris offers a variety of culinary delights from burgers to steaks.

Museum of the Cherokee Indian. 589 Tsali Blvd.; (828) 497-3481; mci.org. This museum offers a primer on Cherokee heritage, history, and culture. Visitors are greeted by a 20-foot California redwood statue of Sequoyah, who invented the Cherokee alphabet, which visitors can hear spoken through special phones. In addition to a massive collection of clothes, crafts, weapons, and artifacts—some of which are more than 10,000 years old—the museum also has an art gallery and theaters that feature the culture's history through innovative audiovisual shows and computer-generated graphics combined with traditional museum collections. An exhibit of striking contemporary photos taken along the Trail of Tears details the removal of the Cherokee from the Appalachian Mountains to Oklahoma, a journey that cost the lives of 4,000 Cherokee. Admission is $12 for adults, $7 for ages 6 to 13, and free for children under 6. Open 9 a.m. to 5 p.m. daily, with hours extended to 7 p.m. Mon through Sat in summer.

Oconaluftee Indian Village. 218 Drama Rd.; (828) 497-2315; cherokeehistorical.org. This village remains one of the most authentic and enlightening places to visit in the Cherokee area, where the story of the 18th-century past is told in remarkable living detail. The village is an authentic re-creation of a Cherokee Indian community. Here costumed guides lead tours of the village, where local people work at the ancient arts of basket making and pottery, and demonstrate blowguns, canoe hulling, and finger weaving. Tours include a visit to the 7-sided council house—a simple wood and dirt structure—to learn how the Cherokee tribes functioned. Admission is $16 for adults and $10 for children 6 to 12. Open May through Oct, Mon through Sat, 10 a.m. to 5 p.m.

Oconaluftee Islands Park. US 441, near downtown; (800) 438-1601. Wade in the water, float on an inner tube, or just relax at this grassy island park with the Oconaluftee River running through it as children build dams and hunt for salamanders under a canopy of oak and sycamore trees. Two local retailers offer a daylong rental of an inner tube for about $10: **Cherokee Rapids River Tubing** (1681 Acquoni Rd.; 828-736-3535) and **Indian Summer Gifts & Tube Rentals** (833 Tsali Blvd.; 866-317-2975). There is no admission fee for the park. Typically open during daylight hours.

Santa's Land Family Fun Park and Zoo. 571 Wolftown Rd.; (828) 497-9191; santaslandnc.net. Especially well-suited for families with young children is this fun theme park that allows day-trippers to celebrate Christmas in spring, summer, and fall a few minutes' drive east of Cherokee. The kids get an early order to Santa and his elves and visit the animals in the petting zoo, where they will see dozens of domestic and exotic creatures. Also found in this temperate wonderland are paddleboats, train rides, and the Rudi-Coaster. Admission is $23.25 per person. Open 10 a.m. to 6 p.m. daily, May through Oct, and on weekends in Nov.

Unto These Hills. 688 Drama Rd.; (828) 497-2111; cherokeehistorical.org. Near the village is the Cherokees' Mountainside Theater, where *Unto These Hills* is performed during the summer. The outdoor drama, written by Kermit Hunter, is an inspirational piece that captures the history of the Cherokee Indians from the mid-1500s to the tragedy of the Trail of Tears in the late 1830s. The Cherokee people originally settled much of this land, but many were forced off it by the US government and made to march to Arkansas and Oklahoma. During these marches more than 4,000 of the 15,000 Native Americans involved died of disease or exposure. Others, whose descendants still live here, managed to escape into the mountains. The play, produced by more than 130 performers and technicians, runs about 2 hours. Tickets are $20 for adults and $10 for children 12 and under. They are available by phone and at the box office across the street from the Museum of the Cherokee Indian. Shows are presented at 7:30 p.m. Mon through Sat, mid-June through late Aug.

cherokee fishing

Trout fishing on the Cherokee Indian Reservation is excellent with dozens of miles of streams and several ponds in the area. Two North Carolina trout-fishing records have been established on the reservation in recent years. A special reservation fishing license, available at local tackle shops, costs $10 per day, and children younger than 12 can fish on a parent's license.

where to shop

Bearmeats Indian Den. 4210 Wolftown Rd.; (828) 497-4052; bearmeats-indian-den.com. This unique shop features original and traditional Native American artwork. From oil paintings to ceremonial masks to baskets, the work is exquisite. Open daily 10 a.m. to 6 p.m.

Qualla Arts Showroom. 645 Tsali Blvd.; (828) 497-3103; quallaartsandcrafts.com. Founded in 1946, this cooperative of Cherokee craftspeople features remarkable pottery, wood carvings, baskets, and other traditional works. Their themes and techniques have been passed down through the generations. Open 8:30 a.m. to 4:30 p.m. Mon through Sat with hours extended to 7 p.m. in summer, and Sun 9 a.m. to 5 p.m. Closed Sun in Jan and Feb.

where to eat

The Chestnut Tree. 37 Tsali Blvd.; (828) 497-9181. Part of the hotel of the same name, this restaurant offers a nice prime rib buffet and salad bar with enough options for everyone in the family. Diners will also find a full selection of cooked-to-order menu items if the buffet won't work. Art by local artists fills the dining room. $$$.

Granny's Kitchen. 1098 Painttown Rd.; (828) 497-5010; grannyskitchencherokee.com. Roast beef, fried chicken, and other country-kitchen favorites are waiting on the buffet at Granny's. Each day it has a featured favorite for breakfast, lunch, and dinner. Open 11 a.m. to 8 p.m. Apr through Nov. Breakfast served 7 to 11 a.m. June through Oct. $$$.

where to stay

Pink Motel. 1306 Tsali Blvd.; (828) 497-3530. With its neon sign, this cute hotel puts out a distinctive 1960s vibe. It's probably been around since then, but is well-kept. Located on the Oconaluftee River, it is also within walking distance to shops and restaurants. $$

Pioneer Motel and Cottages. US 441 near US 19; (828) 497-2435. This motel offers rooms as well as riverside cabins. Lots of extras, such as horseshoes and basketball courts, are offered in this moderately priced resort. $$.

Rivers Edge Motel. 1026 US 441; (828) 497-7995; riversedgecherokee.com. Hanging out over the water is this small hotel with private balconies outside all 21 large rooms. The river runs right next to the lower-level rooms. $$.

Riverside Motel and Campground. US 441 South; (828) 497-9311; riversidemotelnc .com. This small motel features all riverfront rooms and a covered area with picnic tables and grill. The campground has 30 sites for your camper, RV, or tent on the river, of course. $–$$.

day trip 23

asheville, nc

>>> **where deer, elk & people play:**
maggie valley, nc

maggie valley, nc

More than two centuries ago, massive elk roamed the valleys and hills of this great valley of the Smoky Mountains. But it was a hunting ground for Cherokee Indians and later Europeans, who expanded and settled here. Today after a decades-long program by the US Department of Fish and Wildlife, the elk have been successfully reintroduced. Nearly 200 elk live here now in a more harmonious relationship with man. Visitors can see the elk, mainly in the evenings and mainly during mating season in the open fields of Cataloochee Valley.

Though the area depends on tourism—skiing in winter; hiking, biking, horseback riding, and the like in summer—it thrives on being a friendly, old-time town. Only about 1,000 people call Maggie Valley home, and many of them work in the service industry spurred by an unparalleled location: Blue Ridge Parkway to the south and the Great Smoky Mountains National Park to the north. For decades beginning in the 1960s, families flocked here to the western theme park Ghost Town in the Sky, but it didn't reopen after the 2009 season. While this cost hundreds of seasonal jobs, the town has refocused on other attractions and shopping opportunities that line Jonathan Creek. In 2012 Alaska Pressley, one of Ghost Town's original investors, purchased the property and began to reopen one piece at a time, but she sold the property in 2020, once again thwarting effort to reopen the the park.

The area originally known as Cataloochee was slow to develop, but by 1825 the population of farmers and loggers was sufficient to require the construction of the Cataloochee

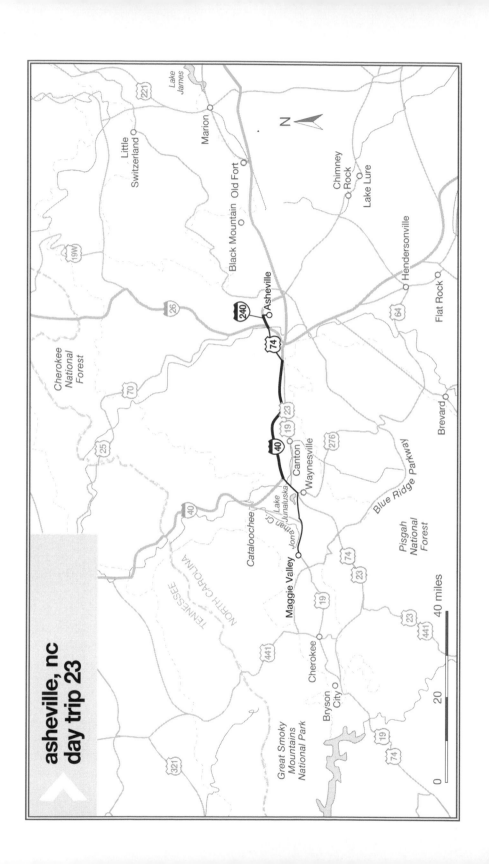

Turnpike, completed in the 1856. Because it was still remote, the area was relatively untouched by the Civil War, and not much reconstruction was required. Maggie Valley was named for the 14-year-old daughter of Jack Setzer—a pretty girl with blonde hair and blue eyes. The US Post Office picked her name among her sisters to establish a post office at the Setzer home in 1904. For more information, contact the **Maggie Valley Area Convention and Visitors Bureau,** (800) 785-8259 or (828) 926-1686; maggievalley.org.

getting there

Maggie Valley is 45 minutes west of Asheville. Take I-40/US 74 west, then take exit 103 for US 19. It leads straight to Maggie Valley.

where to go

Cataloochee Guest Ranch. 119 Ranch Dr.; (800) 868-1401; cataloocheeranch.com. Cataloochee Ranch has operated as a sheep and cattle ranch north of Maggie Valley for more than 75 years. The ranch, one of only three private entrances to Great Smoky Mountains National Park, offers more than 1,000 acres of rolling landscapes, massive ancient hardwood forests, quiet trails, and all the amenities of a luxury vacation. In fair weather, lodge packages come with horseback riding, wagon rides, bird watching, and mountain hikes. The winter season brings skiing and snowboarding for ranch guests and day-trippers. Accommodations include cozy and fully furnished cabins with chestnut paneling at the heart of the ranch, or more private facilities on a ridge overlooking the property. The Silverbell Lodge and the ranch house offer simpler accommodations. Throughout the year, staff harvests vegetables from its garden to produce a great variety of food that makes its way to the dinner table in a hearty family-style setting. If that's simply not enough, the lodge offers tennis, hiking, trout fishing, horseshoes, table tennis, badminton, and croquet. Relax by the swimming pool, take a hayride, or walk through the ranch's glorious meadows, where wildflowers abound in spring and summer. Bonfires, complete with storytelling and roasted marshmallows, round out the day.

The Stompin' Ground. 3116 Soco Rd.; (828) 926-1288. Located in a big barnlike building in the middle of town is this Maggie Valley staple. The Stompin' Ground offers a glimpse of the mountain's Scotch-Irish heritage that includes clogging, square dancing, line dancing, and other traditional mountain dances that have been passed down from generation to generation. Musical acts include bluegrass, gospel, and traditional country performances. You'll be moved to stomp your feet yourself during the shows that are presented nightly. Shows begin at 8 p.m. nightly Apr through Oct.

Wheels Through Time Museum. Soco Road; (828) 926-6266; wheelsthroughtime.com. If the Stompin' Ground gets your toes a tappin', this museum will get your engines revving. It features more than 300 commercial, police, and military motorcycles that date back to 1908 when motorcycles began to emerge as a reliable form of transportation. More than

30 rare and vintage machines, artwork, photos, and other memorabilia create a sort of time line in motorcycle transportation. If you don't believe some of these things still run, they'll crank them up for you. From classic Harleys, to one-off production models that just didn't catch on, the museum takes guests right up to the machines that thrill today's riders. Wheels Through Time founder Dale Walksler has gained national prominence as an authority on the history of motorcycles. He and the museum have appeared regularly on national television shows, from the History Channel's *American Pickers* to Velocity Channel's *What's in the Barn*. Admission is $15 for adults, $12 for seniors, $7 for children. Open Thurs through Mon 9 a.m. to 5 p.m.

where to shop

Jelly Bellies Mountain Gift Shop. Market Square; (828) 926-9069; jellybelliesmaggievalley .com. The friendly folks at this candy and gift shop say they can supply a different candy for every day of the year. Those selections include everything from the popular Jelly Belly brand jelly beans to old-fashioned candy to 24 different kinds of fresh homemade fudges. There is also a healthy selection of mountain souvenirs, T-shirts, and similar wares.

Maggie Mountaineer Crafts. 2394 Soco Rd.; (828) 926-3129; maggiemountaineercrafts .com. One might need to be at a certain point in one's life to remember Raggedy Ann and Andy, but those who do would be thrilled to stop in at this store where they still sell hand-made versions of the dolls that were popular in the early and middle of the 20th century. In addition to other mountain craft items such as pottery, the store also specializes in collectible Fenton glass. Hours vary by season.

where to eat

J Arthur's. 2843 Soco Rd.; (828) 926-1817; jarthurs.com. Steak and prime rib are the specialties of the house, but the unusual and rich Gorgonzola cheese salad is what made J Arthur's famous in these parts. In warmer months live music is presented on the porch of the wood-frame building. Open noon to 2 p.m. and for dinner daily beginning at 4:30 p.m. $$$.

Maggie Valley Restaurant. 2804 Soco Rd.; (828) 926-0425; maggievalleyrestaurant.net. The Carver family has run this southern-style diner since the 1950s. Located in a small low-profile building in the middle of town, this restaurant's menu is dominated by meat and potato–type meals, greens, and pintos. The Carvers also serve breakfast, including omelets, country-style eggs and sausage, pancakes, and more, anytime. Open daily 7 a.m. to 9 p.m. May through Oct. $$.

where to stay

Jonathan Creek Inn and Villas. 4324 Soco Rd.; (800) 577-7812; jonathancreekinn.com. This handsome inn with 42 rooms plus several suites and a cottage is family oriented, with an indoor pool, a playground, and children's programs. All the rooms have homey, country touches such as handmade wreaths. It is appropriately located on Jonathan Creek, which runs parallel with the main road through Maggie Valley. $$–$$$.

Laurel Park Inn. 257 Soco Rd.; (800) 451-4424; laurelparkinn.com. Large rosebushes stand in front of each of the rooms of this small, affordable inn. Rooms have minimal amenities but the property has an outdoor pool, covered gazebo, and charcoal grill that guests are welcome to use. $$.

Smoky Falls Lodge. 2550 Soco Rd.; (877) 926-7440; smokyfallslodge.com. Wooden construction, rustic furnishings, and fireplaces make this a comfortable, desirable place to stay for a night or more. Suites and rooms with lots of amenities are offered in cabin-like settings. $$.

The Swag. 2300 Swag Rd., Waynesville; (800) 789-7672; theswag.com. This sprawling and romantic mountaintop resort has a Waynesville address but is accessible to Maggie Valley. The lodge and restaurant here are rustic but luxurious, with split-rail fences outside and big hearth fireplaces inside. Hiking trails and recreation like croquet rejuvenate by day, and handmade quilts comfort by night. $$$.

day trip 24

asheville, nc

>>> **a day on the tracks:**
bryson city, nc

bryson city, nc

In the years following the establishment of a railroad at Asheville in 1880, the Western North Carolina Railroad worked feverishly to extend the line to the remote western reaches of North Carolina. It was complete all the way to Murphy by the turn of the 20th century, and at the time the railway at the top of the Balsam Mountain (elevation 3,100 feet) was deemed the highest in the country. The railroad remained critical for shipping through the two world wars, and it was used as a passenger line as well. As automobile ownership grew, however, use of the railroad as a passenger line diminished and finally stopped. Changing hands from the Western North Carolina Railroad to Southern Railroad to Norfolk-Southern, the line closed altogether in the 1980s. The state purchased the line in 1985 and three years later managed the establishment of Great Smoky Mountain Railway. The heritage railway is now a major tourist attraction for the area, but day-trippers are just as likely to come here for the outstanding outdoor opportunities with whitewater rafting at the top of their list of things to do.

Bryson City is surrounded by sweeping vistas of mountains on all sides: the Great Smoky Mountains to the north, Cherokee's Qualla Boundary to the east, and Nantahala National Forest to the south. The Cherokee believe their oldest village, which would become the village of Kituwa, existed in the area that is now Bryson City some 14,000 years ago. That village was burned by American soldiers in 1776. In the early 1800s the area at the confluence of Deep Creek and Tuckaseegee River became the Cherokee Indian Reservation

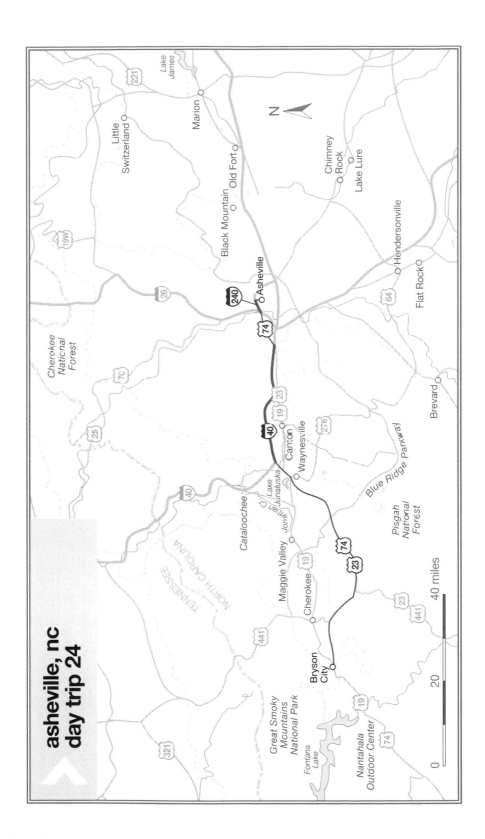

asheville, nc
day trip 24

of Chief Big Bear, who would sell the property that would become known as Bear Springs. Long disputed in legal proceedings, much of the property would be purchased by Col. Thaddeus Bryson. In 1871 when Swain County was formed, the area was named Charleston and became the county seat with a courthouse and jail. Then in 1889 citizens decided to change the name to avoid confusion with the South Carolina city of Charleston, renaming it in honor of Bryson. Today it is the center of much outdoor activity, a great campground, and the Great Smoky Mountain Railroad.

getting there

From Waynesville, take US 74 west and arrive in Bryson City in 40 minutes or so.

where to go

Carolina Outfitters Rafting Company. 12121 Hwy. 19 West; (828) 488-6345; carolina outfitters.com. Carolina Outfitters is one of nearly a dozen groups that offer guided whitewater rafting trips and other outdoor adventures. In addition they offer rentals of a variety of equipment, including inflatable kayaks. Rafting trips are combined with gemstone mining, horseback riding, and trips in conjunction with the Great Smoky Mountain Railroad.

Deep Creek Tubing. It might take those who have never gone tubing a little while to get their head around this soft adventure, but Bryson City's Deep Creek might be the best place in the state to participate in it. Campers and day-trippers alike can rent tire inner tubes from a handful of area retailers at the entrance of the Great Smoky Mountain National Park on West Deep Creek Road. Tubers haul the inflated tube just like those used at water parks up a short trail and ride the rapids downstream for a little more than a mile. Companies that provide tube rentals for tubing on Deep Creek include **J. J. Tubes** (828-736-3651), **Deep Creek Lodge/Creekside Tubing** (828-488-2587), and **Deep Creek Tube Center** (828-488-6055). All are easy to find on your way to Deep Creek by vehicle and by tube as you finish your day.

quirky carolina

In 1948 the federal government began construction of a new highway west out of Bryson City. After nearly 25 years, only 7 miles were completed. Eventually environmental and financial issues halted the project, now known as "The Road to Nowhere." You can drive on it; it's a pretty drive, but it still won't get you any farther than 7 miles.

Endless River Adventures. 14157 Hwy. 19 West; (828) 488-6199; endlessriveradventures
.com. Endless River, like most area outfitters, offers trips on the Nantahala River, but also
schedules trips on the Cheoah and Ocoee Rivers that include transportation over the Tennessee state line. The rapids of these two rivers tend to be a higher class than the more
family-friendly rapids of the Nantahala. Endless River also offers kayak and fly-fishing lessons
with guided trips for each sport. Hours are seasonal, and rates are determined by activity.

Fly Fishing the Smokies. (828) 488-7665; flyfishingthesmokies.net. The forest is the physical address of this group that specializes in teaching beginners the graceful art of fly fishing.
In addition they offer full and half-day wading trips, float trips, and backcountry camping
and fishing expeditions throughout the Bryson City area. Rates start at $120 for 1 person
and $150 for 2.

Great Smoky Mountain Railroad. 226 Everett St.; (800) 872-4681; gsmr.com. One of
the best ways to see the area is by taking a ride on the Great Smoky Mountain Railway.
The railway offers regularly scheduled trips originating in Bryson City on a train pulled by
a steam locomotive or 1 of 4 conventional diesel locomotives. While the railway offers a
number of different trips, the most popular is a 4-hour, 44-mile excursion along Fontana
Lake to the Nantahala Gorge and back. Beverages, snacks, and light meals are available on
the trains, but it also includes a 1-hour layover at Nantahala Outdoor Center. Ride in either
a comfortable, enclosed, first-class coach or an open-air car, providing breathtaking views
and excellent photo opportunities. Special excursions include a holiday Polar Express and
visits from Thomas the Train, among others. Trips run Mar through Dec. Reservations are
recommended.

Great Smoky Mountains National Park. (615) 436-1200; greatsmokies.com. Found in
Bryson City is one of two North Carolina entrances to Great Smoky Mountains National Park,
regarded as the country's most visited national park. Fontana Lake forms the southwestern
border of the park, which covers a total of 520,000 acres bisected by the North Carolina–
Tennessee state line. The mountains of the park are among the oldest in the world and rise
more than 6,000 feet. Plant and animal life is varied, with more than 140 species of trees
and 200 species of wildflowers. In the spring the park comes alive with color as azaleas,
rhododendron, and wildflowers bloom. Among the animal life spied here are deer, wild turkey, ruffed grouse, and bear. More than 900 miles of horseback riding and hiking trails and
735 miles of fishing streams are close at hand. Many area campgrounds have organized
activities, including presentations by park rangers.

Nantahala Outdoor Center. 13077 Hwy. 19 West; (828) 488-6900; noc.com. The Nantahala Outdoor Center is the area's biggest and most popular outfitter and center for outdoor adventure. The center offers family-friendly adventures on 6 rivers in North Carolina,
South Carolina, Georgia and Tennessee. From a well-maintained and active center on the
banks of the Nantahala River here in Bryson City you can choose from a variety of options

from guided rafting tours to zip line tours. Dining, lodging, shopping, mountain bike rentals, lake kayaking, and a wide variety of activities originate from here.

Wildwater-Nantahala Gorge Adventure Center. 10345 Hwy. 19 South; (800) 451-9972; wildwaterrafting.com. Like most of its competitors, Wildwater runs trips on the Nantahala, but also on the Ocoee, Pigeon, and Chattooga Rivers. It also offers a zip line canopy tour, and half-day Jeep tours as well as a raft and rail tour. Need a place to stay? Try a yurt. These are octagonal structures that are part tent and part cabin originally used by nomadic people of Central Asia.

where to shop

The Cottage Craftsman. 44 Frye St.; (828) 488-6207. Located in a charming yellow cottage downtown, the shop features only regional, handcrafted items from area artisans. Unique finds here include baskets, pottery, wood pieces, art, and jewelry. The Cottage Craftsman also carries North Carolina wine and cheeses with Saturday wine tastings in season. Hours change seasonally.

Pincu Pottery. 80 Hwy. 28 South; (828) 488-0480; pincupottery.com. Artist Elise Willa Pincu Delfield takes the typical paint-your-own pottery shop to the next level by offering one-day pottery classes to a variety of ages and skill levels. Shoppers can purchase Pincu pottery that is handmade and often functional. Hours change seasonally.

where to eat

Everett Street Diner. 126 Everett St.; (828) 488-0123; brysoncityrestaurant.com. Probably the area's best country breakfast can be eaten at Everett Street Diner. At lunchtime the menu turns to a variety of sandwiches, homemade soups, salads, and desserts. Local artwork is also on display. Open daily 8 a.m. to 1 p.m. $$.

High Test Deli. 145 Everett St.; (828) 488-1919; thefillingstationdeli.com. This sub shop is the perfect place to go after a day of tubing on Deep Creek. Try the Cuban, piled high with meat and zesty spices. Look for auto-themed menu items, but simple hot dogs, salads, soups, and even chili have made their way onto the list of offerings. There is no indoor seating, but it's not hard to find a seat on the streets of Bryson City. Open Mon through Thurs 11 a.m. to 4 p.m., Fri 11 a.m. to 7 p.m., Sat 11 a.m. to 4 p.m. $.

Pasqualino's Italian Restaurant. 25 Everett St.; (828) 488-9555; pasqualinorestaurant .com. Good classic Italian cuisine comes out of the kitchen at this small, street-corner restaurant. It gets high marks for typical spaghetti, manicotti, lasagna, and chicken parmesan. Open daily at 11:30 a.m. $$.

Slow Joe's Cafe at Nantahala Outdoor Center. US 19/74 West; (828) 488-2176. If anyone stays behind on the rafting trip, they can grab a bite at Slow Joe's while enjoying the action on the river. It's also a good place to stop in during the layover on the Smoky Mountain Railroad. The menu is simple with hot dogs, sandwiches, and salads, but the riverside view is really special. $.

Soda Pops. 141 Everett St.; (828) 488-5379; sodapopsicecream.com. This old-time soda shop serves ice cream with special toppings, fountain sodas, malts, sundaes, and shakes. The shop is filled with Coke memorabilia including signs, clocks, and even antique drink machines and matching red checkered floor. Open Mon through Thurs noon to 8 p.m., Fri and Sat noon to 9 p.m., Sun 1:30 to 7 p.m. $.

where to stay

Deep Creek Campground. 1090 W. Deep Creek Rd., Bryson City; (828) 488-6055; deepcreekcamping.com. This great campground, located on the edge of Great Smoky Mountains National Park, is the place to be in Bryson City. Crowded creekside sites are the first to be claimed on weekends, but quieter sites typically remain open on the hill. The campground accommodates tents and RV sites and even offers a handful of rustic cabins for rent. $.

Fryemont Inn. 245 Fryemont St.; (828) 455-2159; fryemontinn.com. Listed on the National Register of Historic Places, the Fryemont was built in 1923. It now offers 32 cozy rooms, fireplace suites, and a cabin. Exposed beams and chestnut paneling throughout most of the lodge add warmth to the comfortable accommodations. The Fireside Bar and restaurant are also located here. $$.

Nantahala Village Resort and Spa. 9400 Hwy. 19 West; (800) 438-1507; nantahalavillage .com. The area's most spectacular resort includes a wide range of amenities such as the Village Restaurant with ribeye steak and salmon, a full-service spa, and a variety of organized activities. Take a hike, go horseback riding, or play in the game room. Accommodations here range from spa rooms to tree-house cabins and luxurious suites. $$$.

Two Rivers Lodge. 5280 Ela Rd.; (828) 488-2284; tworiverslodgenc.com. This natural wood and stone structure appears to be a luxury lodge but is really just a comfortable hotel. It offers a large lawn next to the river, a swimming pool, a horseshoe pit, and a volleyball court. Rooms are large with sitting areas and kitchenettes. $$.

day trip 25

asheville, nc

>>> **charleston of the mountains:**
hendersonville, nc; flat rock, nc

There's no beach here, but in the 1800s this area was so prominent as a vacation resort among the Charleston elite, that's what it seemed like. Today the state theater is here and preserved is the home of writer Carl Sandburg. Located on a plateau at 2,200 feet above sea level, the Hendersonville and Flat Rock area doesn't suffer from rugged winters like its neighbors to the north and west. It does have the benefit of cooler summertime weather than areas in the Carolina Piedmont and Coastal Plain. And those living at lower elevations discovered its remarkable qualities more than 200 years ago.

Famous now for its apples and apple festival held each Labor Day weekend, Hendersonville is the largest apple producer in North Carolina, which ranks seventh among all states in apple production. The city's architecture is reflective of the late 19th and early 20th centuries, and downtown's designation on the National Register of Historic Places in 1988 led to a renaissance of sorts through much of the 1990s. Storefronts that were unoccupied for years, in some cases, were reopened as stores, galleries, restaurants, or other businesses.

hendersonville, nc

Established as the seat of Henderson County in 1847, Hendersonville and her county were named for North Carolina Supreme Court Justice Leonard Henderson. Located in the heart of the Carolina Blue Ridge, it was known as the City of Four Seasons, to capitalize on its popularity as a midsummer resort town. Botanists have also noted its great diversity of plant

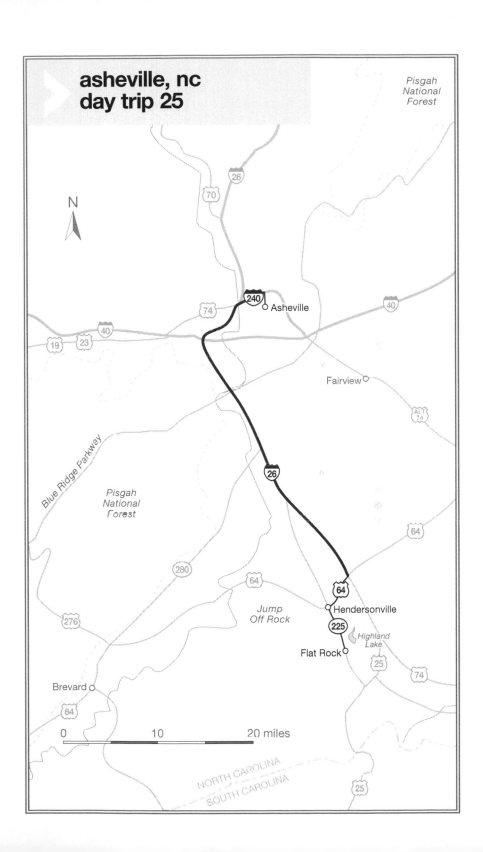

life derived from its mild but variable climate. The appealing serpentine main street and its buildings were entered into the National Register of Historic Places more than two decades ago. Just blocks from downtown is Oakdale Cemetery, where day-trippers will find Wolfe's Angel, which marks the plot of the Johnson family, who bought the Italian marble statue from author Thomas Wolfe's father. Wolfe references it several times in his novel *Look Homeward, Angel.*

getting there

Hendersonville is 30 minutes, or about 22 miles, south of Asheville on I-26/US 74.

where to go

The Bullington Gardens. 33 Upper Red Oak Trail; (828) 698-6104; bullingtongardens.org. This 12-acre facility was once the home of Bob Bullington, but is now an education center formed through a partnership with Hendersonville County Schools and Cooperative Extension Service. While its key mission is serving local schoolchildren, day-trippers can visit the grounds, a therapy garden, shade garden, and perennial gardens. It also includes a half-mile nature trail and butterfly habitat. Typically open weekdays 9 a.m. to 4 p.m., but there are frequent specials events at other times.

Elijah Mountain Gem Mine. 2120 Brevard Rd.; (828) 693-3123; elijahmountain.com. Emeralds, rubies, sapphire, quartz, and amethysts along with other stones are found on a daily basis at this tourist mining operation. Flumes are covered to make mining comfortable for patrons, who can pan for gold, too. Prices per bucket start at $12.99. Open daily 10 a.m. to 6 p.m.

Henderson County Heritage Museum. 1 Historic Courthouse Sq.; (828) 694-1619; hendersoncountymuseum.com. Visitors can learn about the area's history at this center, located in the county's restored courthouse, which also houses county offices. The museum's storyline begins with the Cherokee who once hunted here and the pioneers who made the area their home in the wilderness. Examine Civil War uniforms, and watch a video of Henderson area connections to American wars. The museum also houses documents, archives, artifacts, and other items. Free. Open Wed through Sat 10 a.m. to 5 p.m. Sun 1 to 5 p.m.

Hendersonville Depot. Maple Street off 7th Avenue East; (828) 890-8246; avmrc.com. In 1879 Southern Railway began running a steam engine on the Saluda Mountain Grade to Hendersonville, one of the steepest mainline railroads (600 feet in 3 miles) ever built in the US. The route opened up western North Carolina, and in 1902 the company had to build this second, larger depot. By 1911 it was a major stop on the route between Charleston and Cincinnati. Today it has been refurbished to help illustrate the importance of the railroad to the Eastern Seaboard in those early days of rail transportation. Exterior paint has been restored to its original mustard and green colors, and a Southern Railway caboose is on display. The depot's baggage room houses the Apple Valley Model Railroad Club and its meticulously produced HO-scale model railroad, a replica of Hendersonville, Asheville, Brevard, and Saluda. Free. Open Wed 1 to 3 p.m., Sat 10 a.m. to 2 p.m.

Holmes Educational State Forest. 1299 Crab Creek Rd.; (828) 692-0100; ncesf.org/HESF. Scenic trails, rock outcroppings, and a variety of plant and animal life create an interesting study in nature not far from downtown Hendersonville. This small park, a managed forest, offers a series of trails that are easy to navigate, making it an especially appealing stop for families. "Talking trees" inform visitors about the variety of species living in the forest. Also on the site is an exhibit on fire control, including a watchtower and helicopter. Free. Open during daylight hours Tues through Sun mid-Mar through late Nov.

Jump Off Rock. Laurel Park Highway. A Cherokee legend says that more than 300 years ago, an Indian maiden threw herself off this rock upon receiving news that her young chief had been killed in battle. According to the story, you can see the ghost of the maiden near here on moonlit nights. Jump Off Rock impressively juts out of the surrounding landscape to an elevation of 3,100 feet. In addition to providing a consistent reference point for drivers, the rock provides an excellent vantage point of the surrounding Blue Ridge. Free. Open during daylight hours.

The Mineral & Lapidary Museum of Henderson County. 400 N. Main St.; (828) 698-1977; mineralmuseum.org. A life-size replica of a *T. rex* skull in a small prehistoric display is the most impressive artifact of this small museum and work by the local gem and mineral society. Rows of lighted cases include exhibits that range from gems, geodes, fossils, and fluorescent minerals to Indian artifacts. Free. Open Mon through Fri 1 to 5 p.m., Sat 11 a.m. to 5 p.m.

Mountain Farm & Home Museum. 101 Brookside Camp Rd.; (828) 697-8846. A log corn crib and a modern metal storage building indicate the range of exhibits at this unusual museum. It showcases antique farm equipment, antique steam engines, children's toys, paint grinders, looms, threshers, washing machines, and more to provide a chronicle of the area farming industry. Among the exhibits are a restored hand-pump gasoline dispenser, cement mixer, tractors, and more. Free. Hours vary.

Western North Carolina Air Museum. 1340 Gilbert St.; (828) 698-2482; wncairmuseum.com. The Western North Carolina Air Museum is one of the oldest air museums in the state and now displays more than a dozen restored, replica, antique, and vintage airplanes that date mostly to the 1930s and 1940s. In 2 hangars at the Hendersonville Airport, visitors will discover a 1930 Curtiss Robin and several Pipers. Free. Open Wed and Sun noon to 6 p.m., Sat 10 a.m. to 5 p.m. Apr through Oct; Wed, Sat, and Sun noon to 5 p.m. Nov through Mar.

where to shop

Carolina Mountain Artists Guild. 444 N. Main St.; (828) 696-0707; carolinamountain-artists.com. A couple dozen or so artists came together to form this guild and open this shop dedicated to works done in the Hendersonville area. Corn husk dolls, old wooden toys, baskets, and pottery are often produced on-site. Open Mon through Sat 10 a.m. to 5 p.m., Sun 1 to 5 p.m.

Narnia Studios. 315 N. Main St.; (828) 697-6393; narniastudios.com. With a theme from the popular C. S. Lewis stories, this shop features flowers, fragrances, and fairies of all types. In addition to fresh flowers, shoppers find gifts and home decor. Open Mon through Sat 9:30 a.m. to 6:30 p.m.

Village Green Antique Mall. 424 N. Main St.; (828) 692-9057. This is the largest and old-est antiques store in Hendersonville. In addition to furniture, you'll find china, glass, silver, and jewelry. Open Mon through Sat 10 a.m. to 5 p.m., Sun 1 to 5 p.m.

where to eat

Hannah Flanagan's Pub and Eatery. 300 N. Main St.; (828) 696-1665; theoriginalhannah flanagans.com. This is a busy hangout for locals. A long list of beer matches up well with classic Irish dishes like corned beef and cabbage, fish and chips, and Reubens. You'll also find a selection of burgers, and the fried mushrooms on the appetizer menu are a must. $$.

Mike's on Main. 303 N. Main St.; (828) 698-1616; mikesonmain.com. This 1950s diner and soda shop even has occasional sock hops on Saturday nights. The patty melt might really take you back. Save room for a shake, malt, or banana split. Open Tues through Sat 8 a.m. too 4p.m. $.

where to stay

The Charleston Inn. 755 N. Main St.; (828) 693-6737; thecharleston.net. Among the larger bed-and-breakfasts in the area, The Charleston, once known as the Claddagh Inn and the Charleston Boarding House prior to that, is listed on the National Register of Historic Places. Its construction dates to the 1880s. Several of the 16 rooms have fireplaces and claw-foot tubs, but the wraparound porch can be enjoyed by all. $$.

Echo Mountain Inn. 2849 Laurel Park Hwy.; (828) 693-9626; echoinn.com. Comfortable and cozy, this inn overlooks Hendersonville and the surrounding area from one of the town's peaks. Constructed of local stone, the 2-story inn has a lot of personality, including 4-poster beds and other homey touches. Outside, guests will find a shuffleboard court and a pool. $$.

1898 Waverly Inn. 783 N. Main St.; (800) 537-8195; waverlyinn.com. The rocking-chair front porch beckons at this inn on Main Street. Built as the Anderson Boarding House, its name changed to Waverly Inn in 1915. The warm and friendly environment is accompanied by a host of amenities like a big DVD collection, board games, and sitting rooms. In addition to breakfast, the inn also offers fresh baked treats in the afternoon and wine and cheese at evening socials. $$$.

Inn on Church Street. 201 3rd Ave. West; (828) 696-2001; thehendersonnc.com. A red awning rolls out into the downtown location of this hotel, one of the few that remain from construction at the turn of the last century. The rooms are pretty and bright with immaculate attention to detail. The innkeepers also operate a gourmet restaurant here at Hendersonville's only downtown B&B. $$.

flat rock, nc

Once, this plateau was a meeting place for Cherokee, but Europeans began settling it in 1807. The wealthy of South Carolina's Low Country referred to the Village of Flat Rock as the Charleston of the Mountains—an affectionate way of referring to this North Carolina mountain town that had become their home away from home. Nearly 200 years ago, they came here to escape outbreaks of yellow fever and malaria. That and for a little vacation. Some built big summer homes and gave a boost to the early economy of the area. Still today it's a small village, lying wholly in an area on the National Register of Historic Places, with just about 3,000 local residents.

getting there

Flat Rock is minutes from Hendersonville on SR 225 (Greenville Highway). From Asheville you can save a minute or two by accessing it directly from I-26/US 74 South at exit 53.

where to go

Carl Sandburg Home National Historic Site. 81 Carl Sandburg Ln.; (828) 693-4178; nps .gov/carl. A prolific poet, historian, author, and lecturer, Carl Sandburg spent the final 22 years of his life, which ended in 1967, at this 1838 estate, known as Connemara. The "Poet of the People," Sandburg was Abraham Lincoln's biographer and wrote most extensively about the struggle of the American working class. Sandburg won two Pulitzer Prizes but only received an eighth-grade education. Today this national historic site preserves the dairy goat farm his wife, Lilian, operated and displays more than 65,000 artifacts from Sandburg's life and work. The site offers walking trails on 264 acres where visitors can stroll through gardens and explore nature. Admission to the site is free. Thirty-minute guided tours cost $10 for visitors ages 16 and over and are offered daily 9:30 a.m. to 4:30 p.m. The site is open daily 9 a.m. to 5 p.m. except Christmas Day.

Flat Rock Playhouse. 2661 Greenville Hwy.; (828) 693-0731; flatrockplayhouse.org. What started as a summer theater in the 1930s in an old gristmill has become the State Theatre of North Carolina and one of the state's most renowned venues. The current playhouse, founded in 1952, is in a barnlike structure and fits appropriately on the campus, which also includes the 1885 Lowndes House, where the administrative offices are located. Other structures house the theater's education programs, storage and production units, and rehearsal halls. The theater runs a 6-month season, presenting selections for every age and taste. Usually on the schedule are Broadway hits, classics, comedies, and even whodunits. It also offers holiday productions after the regular season concludes in October; matinees and evening performances are presented Wed through Sun mid-Apr through mid-Oct.

St. John in the Wilderness Episcopal Church. 1895 Greenville Hwy.; (828) 693-9783; stjohnflatrock.org. Charles Baring, a wealthy banker from England, built a mountain lodge for his wife, Susan, in 1833. As Baring continued to accumulate land in the area (as much as 3,000 acres at one point), he began to desire a house of worship, in the middle of this Baptist stronghold, that was loyal to the Church of England. So he built the private chapel and in 1836 deeded it to the bishop of North Carolina. The church's graveyard includes plots for signers of the Declaration of Independence, members of the Confederate government, and others significant to area history. Open Tues through Sun 9 a.m. to 4 p.m.

where to shop

Little Rainbow Row. Greenville Highway. Located in the geographic center of the Village of Flat Rock is this small shopping district that is a nod to the big Rainbow residential area of Charleston. It includes The Wrinkled Egg (800-736-3998; thewrinkledegg.com), where shoppers find necessities, art, and local crafts; Sweet Magnolia Gallery (828-697-2212); and Dogwood, which carries unique housewares and garden décor. A tailgate market is held here on Thurs from 3 to 6 p.m. May through Oct.

where to eat

Flat Rock Village Bakery. 2710 Greenville Hwy.; (828) 693-1313. Located inside the Wrinkled Egg, this bakery offers organic wood-fired breads and pizzas, salads, and sandwiches. If you stop in for lunch, save room for pastries, brownies, cookies, and a cup of joe from a local blend. Mon through Sat 7 a.m. to 5 p.m., Sun 8 am. to 5 p.m. $.

Hubba Hubba Smokehouse. 2724 Greenville Hwy.; (828) 694-3551; hubbahubbasmoke house.com. Usually it is all about barbecue at this food stand. Standard barbecue offerings are always available, but on Friday and Saturday nights, Hubba Hubba cranks out shrimp and fish. It's a cash-only operation, and there are only a few picnic tables outside to eat at. Open Mon through Wed 11 a.m. to 3 p.m., Thurs through Sat 11 a.m. to 7 p.m. Closed in winter. $.

where to stay

Highland Lake Inn. 86 Lily Pad Ln.; (800) 762-1376; hlinn.com. This elegant retreat with several buildings and room types is nestled in the woods on a 26-acre site. A lake on-site is just big enough for the complimentary canoes and paddleboats. Fancy hens, a peacock, and other animals rambling on the property add to the countryside atmosphere, complemented by a selection of games like badminton, croquet, and horseshoes. Season's Restaurant located here provides the most sophisticated dining in Flat Rock, with a menu that includes local trout, top cuts of steak, lamb, and more. The restaurant is open Mon through Sat 11:30 a.m. to 2:30 p.m. and 5 to 9 p.m. as well as for Sunday brunch 10:30 a.m. to 2 p.m. $$$.

Mansouri Mansion. 2905 Greenville Hwy.; (828) 693-6016; mansourimansion.com. Built in 1852 on 28 rolling acres and originally known as the Farmers Hotel, this inn served as the first stagecoach stop along the Old Indian Trail. During the Civil War, Confederate soldiers were garrisoned here, and it is rumored that they hid gold and jewelry from Union troops and renegades in a secret room that is still accessible from one of the 2nd-story rooms. Today the inn is on the National Register of Historic Places with unique expansive gardens and slate walkways. $$.

worth more time
chimney rock

One of North Carolina's most iconic attractions, **Chimney Rock,** towering 315 feet above the alluring Lake Lure, is just 24 miles east of Flat Rock on US 64. Now state-maintained, Chimney Rock Park (Highway 64/74A; 800-277-9611; chimneyrockpark.com) had been privately owned by the Lucius Morse family since 1902. The park includes more than 4,000 acres of hiking trails and other outdoor adventures. A preserved historic downtown offers a welcome variety of shops and restaurants. The nearby town of Lake Lure has become a retirement resort but also has a sandy beach and a marina that offers boat tours for day-trippers.

day trip 26

asheville, nc

white squirrels & waterfalls:
brevard, nc

brevard, nc

White squirrels scamper across the campus of Brevard College in this colorful Blue Ridge community at the edge of the Pisgah National Forest. Brevard provides easy access to many of the area's 250 waterfalls and a portion of the forest where there are outdoor activities aplenty. Found here are the famous Brevard Music Center and other opportunities to engage in the arts.

Once part of the state of Georgia and fought over by North and South Carolina, Brevard came under the control of the Old North State in 1811. It wasn't until 1861 that Transylvania County was formed, so named "the land of waterfalls" because literally translated, Transylvania means "across the woods (or land)." At the heart of this day trip is Sliding Rock, an interactive element to waterfall hunting.

getting there

Brevard is 45 minutes from Asheville. Travel south on I-26/US 74. Take exit 40 for SR 280, which leads to Brevard.

where to go

Brevard Music Center. 349 Andante Ln.; (888) 384-8682; brevardmusic.org. Since 1936 the renowned Brevard Music Center has offered study opportunities to some of the country's

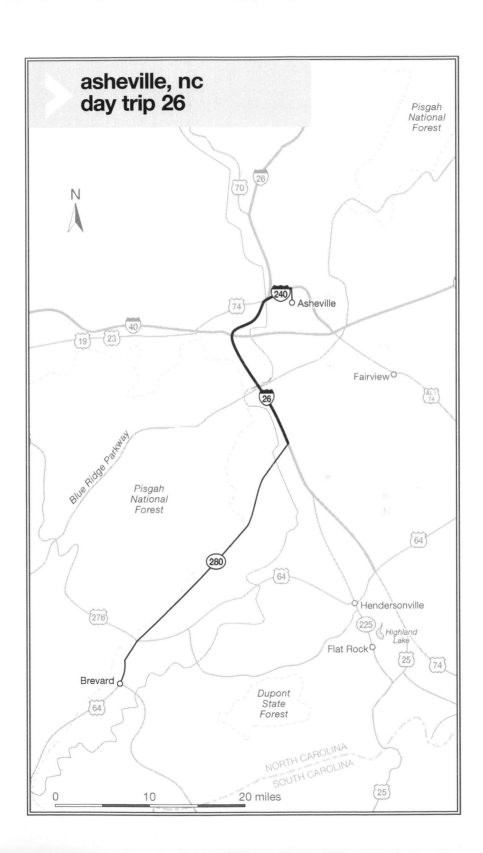

asheville, nc
day trip 26

most promising young musicians. Each summer 400 students from around the country live on the 180-acre campus and produce in conjunction with their instructors a 7-week festival that includes more than 80 productions. The center also works in conjunction with the Paul Porter Center at Brevard College, which produces shows throughout the rest of the year.

The Cradle of Forestry in America & Forest Discovery Center. 1001 Pisgah Hwy. (US 276); (828) 877-3130; cradleofforestry.com. Congress set aside this 6,500-acre site to commemorate the beginnings of a more conservation-minded forestry industry more than a century ago, when George Vanderbilt began buying land in this area. Located in the Pink Beds valley, which features spectacular mountain laurel, rhododendron, and azaleas that bloom in spring and summer, a visitor center features a short film about Vanderbilt and other pioneers in forestry conservation. An exhibit gives examples of how forestry conservation has advanced in the past century through touch-screen video and more. It features a fire-fighting helicopter simulator, and offers young children the Forest Fun exhibit with puppets, puzzles, and costumes in a well-done exhibit hall. It also exhibits a restored 1915 logging locomotive and a helicopter. Admission is $6 for ages 13 and older and $3 for ages 5 to 12. Open daily mid-Apr to mid-Nov 9 a.m. to 5 p.m.

Downtown Sculpture Tour. (828) 884-2787. Bear, bobcat, elk, and eagles fill 10 blocks of downtown Brevard in an art exhibit on area wildlife. The 16 works in steel, bronze, copper, marble, and stone are intended as a tribute to those creatures that make this region their home and to provide motivation to protect their habitats.

Pisgah Center for Wildlife Education. 1401 Fish Hatchery Rd.; (828) 877-4423. Located adjacent to the Bobby N. Setzer State Fish Hatchery is this center that features exhibits on life in mountain waters and on land. It provides a trail with interactive exhibits, including realistic models of animals typically found in the forest. A trout raceway where brook, rainbow, and brown trout are bred for stocking mountain waters helps visitors understand the breeding process. The trout hatchery, the largest in the state, consists of 16 indoor rearing tanks and 50 outdoor raceways, where the fish are grown until they are catchable size. They are then used to stock area waters. A nature center features exhibits on native wildlife and includes several habitats with fish, frogs, salamanders, and snakes. Free. Open Mon through Sat 8 a.m. to 4:45 p.m.

Pisgah Forest Riding Stables. 476 Pisgah Dr.; (828) 883-8258; pisgahstables.com. These stables offer 1- to 3-hour rides through the forest trails featuring waterfalls or mountain vistas. Riders must be at least 7 years old. Cost is $50 to $120 per person. Open Mon through Sat Apr through Oct 9 a.m. to 5 p.m.

Pisgah National Forest. (828) 877-3265; fa.usda.gov. George Vanderbilt sold this expansive national forest of a half-million acres to the federal government, creating some of the country's best outdoor activities. Opportunities for hiking, camping, picnicking, fishing, and horseback riding abound. The forest covers 12 North Carolina counties, but its best offerings

quirky carolina

The curious colony of white squirrels in the picturesque town of Brevard is growing, and in the 20 years the squirrels have been officially counted, their importance to the town has grown, too. Each fall the White Squirrel Institute, founded by retired Brevard College Professor Bob Gleesner, counts the town's population of white squirrels. Not albinos but likely a variation of the Eastern grey squirrels, the creatures now number about 1,000.

are accessible by entering on US 276 at the intersection of US 64/280 in Brevard. Start exploring at the ranger station on the right, 1.5 miles inside the forest entrance. Here you can pick up information about the forest and the surrounding area. A small nature center gives visitors an idea of the plant and wildlife species they will likely encounter. Davidson River cuts through the forest and typically runs along the forest road. Several stores and outfitters at the entrance of the forest rent inner tubes that allow for a lazy afternoon drifting down the river. A designated driver can drop off riders upstream and pick them up at a predetermined location. Roadside camping is permitted for free on a first-come, first-served basis, but private facilities are also available for a fee. Among the attractions are public access areas generally open during daylight hours.

Pure Vida Adventures. 152 Hendersonville Hwy.; (772) 579-0005; pvadventures.com. This outdoors group leads adventures in mountain biking, hiking, paddling, climbing, and canyoneering, also known as waterfall rappelling. You can also add a more laid-back brewery tour to your adventure.

Sliding Rock. Located on US 276 about 7 miles from the ranger station; (828) 877-3350. For decades this has been one of western North Carolina's most popular natural attractions; it's a rite of passage, some may say. Mother Nature has provided an exhilarating natural waterslide with 11,000 gallons of chilly 60-degree water rushing over the rock every minute. The 60-foot slide ends with a plunge into a deep pool. Lifeguards are on duty. Admission to the park is $4 for sliders and non-sliders. Open 10 a.m. to 5:30 p.m. Memorial Day to Labor Day.

Waterfall Trail. Traveling on Brevard's Waterfall Trail will likely yield some of the best views and vistas in the state. None has a physical address, but the most popular among them are downright crowded in the summer. Others are little more than a noticeable trickle, but still qualify as a waterfall. The following is a list of the most spectacular. A more complete interactive map and list can be found at visitwaterfalls.com.

Hooker Falls. This waterfall is located in Dupont State Forest on the Little River at the former gristmill near Cascade Lake. Travel south from Brevard on US 276, take a left on Cascade Lake Road, and travel 2.5 miles before taking a right on Staton Road.

Triple Falls. You can walk to Triple Falls from the Hooker Falls parking lot in Dupont State Park, too. Cross over Staton Road and hike upstream to find these 3 falls.

High Falls. At 150 feet this is the tallest of the Dupont State Park waterfalls. Continue upstream to High Falls Trail. Take a left, walk 2,000 feet, and take a right to stay on the well-marked trail. High Falls is accessible by either of the 2 trails near here.

Bridal Veil Falls. One of the area's favorite falls, Bridal Veil was featured in the movie *Last of the Mohicans*. You can actually walk under the waterfall. Find Bridal Veil in Dupont State Park off Conservation Road.

Looking Glass Falls. Located just off US 276 (Forest Road) about 5 miles into Pisgah National Forest, the 65-foot-high waterfall is easily accessible via stairs leading to the base. It's often crowded in summer.

Cove Creek Falls. The hike to Cove Creek is a little more challenging at 1 mile, but this waterfall is worth the walk. Take US 276 3.5 miles from the ranger station and turn left on Forest Road 475. Take this road to Cove Creek Group Campground just beyond the state fish hatchery and park there.

Falls at Graveyard Fields. There's not a real graveyard here. The waterfall derives its name from the tree stumps in the surrounding area. Get here by traveling 14 miles on US 276; take a right to access the Blue Ridge Parkway. Turn left and travel south on the parkway. Park at Graveyard Fields Overlook at MP 419 and take the short but moderately difficult hike from there.

Toxaway Falls. Take SR 215 to US 64 west. Travel 14 miles. At 125 feet this waterfall is one of the larger falls in the area. US 64 actually crosses over the top of it.

Whitewater Falls. At 411 feet this narrow waterfall is the tallest east of the Mississippi. It is located 18 miles west of Brevard on US 64 and is easily accessible down a short paved path.

Connestee Falls. This double, crisscrossing waterfall is one of the most interesting. Take US 276 south of Brevard 5.5 miles. A number of trails lead to Connestee Falls from the parking area.

where to shop

Art Galleries. A half-dozen art galleries are located along East and West Main Streets in downtown Brevard. Travelers will also find a 13-mile stretch of shops, studios, potters, and artists of all types on US 276 south of Brevard to the state line. For more information, contact the Transylvania County Arts Council, 349 S. Caldwell St.; (828) 884-2787 or check out explorebrevard.org.

D. D. Bullwinkel's. 60 E. Main St.; (828) 862-4700; ddbullwinkels.com. This general store was once more of a soda fountain and grill, now it has become the go-to place in Brevard for outdoor apparel. It seems you can find everything here, from blue jeans to backpacks to water bottles. There's also a bar with craft selections on tap in the map room. Open Mon through Sat 10 a.m. to 6 p.m., Sun 11 a.m. to 6 p.m.

O. P. Taylors. 6 S. Broad St., (828) 883-2309; optaylors.com. At more than 6,000 square feet, this independently owned toy store is part of a dying breed that offers just about any toy you could imagine. Owner John Taylor has established a store that does everything in a big, wacky fashion. Promotions include singing or tap dancing for a discount at the register. Taylor has now opened locations in Asheville and Greenville. Open Mon through Sat 10 a.m. to 6 p.m. and Sun noon to 5 p.m.

where to eat

Marco Trattoria. 230 W. Main St.; (828) 883-4841; marcotrattoria.com. Mediterranean Italian is served in this friendly restaurant that features fish much like you would find in northern Italy. Typical spaghetti and lasagna dishes are also included on the menu, as is wood-fired pizza. Open for lunch Mon through Fri 11 a.m. to 3 p.m., Sat 11:30 a.m. to 3 p.m., and Sun brunch 10 a.m. to 3 p.m. Dinner served daily 5 to 9 p.m. $$.

The Square Root. 33 Times Arcade Alley; (828) 884-6171; squarerootrestaurant.com. The old Brevard newspaper building is now home to this charming restaurant just inside a downtown alley. Selections on the menu include a wide variety of interesting fish from mountain trout to ahi tuna. While the more exotic Asian dishes are good, the restaurant is just as well known for its burgers. Open Tues through Sat 11 a.m. to 9 p.m. $$.

where to stay

The Inn at Brevard. 315 E. Main St.; (828) 884-2105; theinnatbrevard.com. Located on 100 spectacular acres, this inn is one of the nicest in Brevard. It is a European-style mansion with big white columns in front, but Howard and Faye Yager, who own the property, still provide plenty of southern charm. A collection of Renaissance art is on display in the home's public areas and rooms, decorated with period antiques. $$$.

Campbell House Inn. 243 W. Main St.; (800) 553-2853; campbellhousebrevard.com. Although this inn changed ownership in 2014 and got a complete makeover, it still retains its charm as a New Orleans–style French country inn. A courtyard patio that feels like it is on the streets of Paris is perfect for sipping lemonade or more potent potables. $$$.

Red House Inn. 266 W. Probart St.; (828) 884-9349; brevardbedandbreakfast.com. This bed-and-breakfast offers an experience with a traditional English feel. It once served as the county courthouse, a general store, a railroad station, and a schoolhouse. Today its rich red exterior makes it stand out in the landscape, and the accommodations make it stand out among guests. Big cozy beds fill the rooms, and a hot breakfast awaits guests in the morning. $$–$$$.

worth more time

Pisgah Astronomical Research Institute. 1 Pari Dr., Rosman; (828) 862-5554; pari.edu. Created by NASA in the early days of the US space program, this Rosman research station became the nation's primary East Coast tracking facility. It is now a not-for-profit education facility, which offers guided tours and the chance to view the cosmos through high-powered optical telescopes. Tours are generally for groups of 10 or more but there are other special events for the general public.

day trip 27

asheville, nc

>>> fine funiture:
hickory, nc

hickory, nc

Not long ago the city of Hickory traded in the jute webbing used to make furniture for fiber optics. Once a world leader in furniture manufacturing, names like Bernhardt, Thomasville, Kincaid, and Broyhill dominated the region. Now names like Google and Apple with major data centers here provide jobs for people in this area of the foothills known as the Unifour region.

Furniture is still made here. And twice each year an aftermarket sale is held after the High Point market for wholesalers is held some 90 miles to the east. Thrice named an All-American city, Hickory has managed to develop a substantial center of arts and culture.

Hickory Tavern (an actual tavern) was built of logs under a big hickory tree here in the 1850s. The name stuck, and Hickory Tavern (the city) was established in 1863, becoming simply Hickory in 1873. The city's proximity to wood resources and stable transportation led to the establishment of Hickory Manufacturing Company in 1902 and a host of others that would follow suit.

The massive Hickory Furniture Mart with more than 100 furniture and home decor retailers is the heart of the retail industry. The Salt Block is simply the city's offering of "Science, Art and Literature Together," but it has added much to the traveler's experience. It includes the city's science and art museum along the main branch of the county library that are all located in one place.

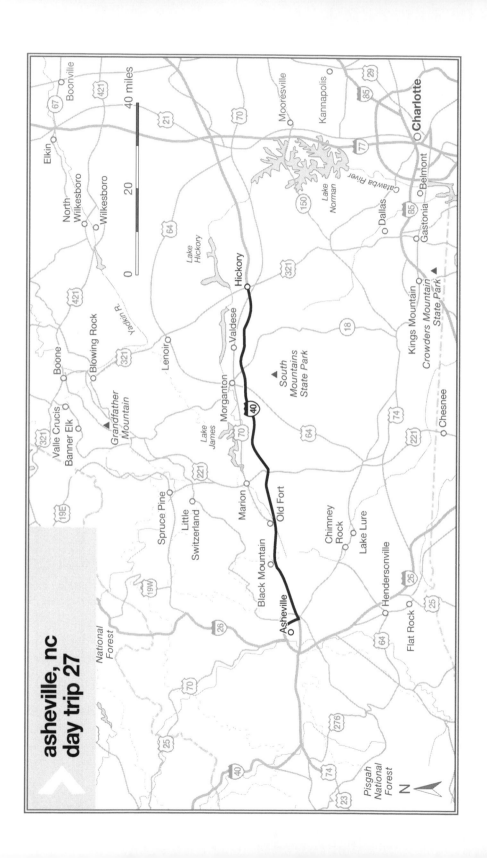

asheville, nc
day trip 27

The **Hickory Metro Convention & Visitor Bureau** is a great resource for things to see and do, and it can help guide you through what still appears to be a maze of furniture dealers—what they call 20 miles of furniture. Contact the fine folks at the bureau by calling (800) 509-2444, or visit them online at visithickorymetro.com.

getting there

From Asheville, Hickory is a straight shot east on I-40. Take exit 123B, US 321 north, into the city. Hickory is a bit of a maze when it comes to roads. Numerically named roads with directional qualifiers, such as 3rd Avenue Southwest, might give you pause. Your GPS will likely work, but you might want to confirm directions with a detailed printed map.

where to go

Bunker Hill Covered Bridge & Murrays Mill Historic District. Located at the intersection of SR 10 and US 70 east of Hickory; (828) 241-4299; catawbahistory.org. Operated by the historical society in the rolling countryside along the banks of Balls Creek outside Hickory's moderately busy streets is this example of a late 19th-century town. Water from a placid pond slips over a mill dam, and the 28 foot waterwheel and a porch swing await at the general store. Preserved intact are the 1913 mill, the 1880s wheat house, and the 1913 John Murray House. Admission is $7 per person. Open Fri and Sat 9 a.m. to 4 p.m., Sun 1:30 to 4:30 p.m.

Catawba Science Center. 243 3rd Ave. NE; (828) 322-8169; catawbascience.org. Families flock here to check out the aquarium of sharks, stingrays, frogs, and fish. And they push, pull, turn, and trip to learn about scientific phenomena, nature, and technology. They learn about the night sky in the astronomy exhibit or in the Millholland Planetarium and in the Hall of Astronomy. Admission is $8 for adults, $6 for seniors and for youth ages 3 to 18. Open Wed through Sat 10 a.m. to 4 p.m., Sun 1 to 4 p.m.

Harper House. 310 N. Center St.; (828) 465-0383; catawbahistory.org. The Hickory History Center and Catawba County Historical Society, which preserve and operate a number of area historical facilities, are based in this ca. 1887 Victorian home. Built by local banker Daniel Webster Shuler, the house passed to several owners until 1923, when the Harper family purchased it. The most notable features of the home are the ornate brasswork, the stained glass window in the foyer, and the silhouettes of the Harpers' friends on the walls of the attic, where they entertained during Prohibition. Moved to the same site in 2004, the Craftsman-style Lyerly House, ca. 1912, was built by E. Josephine Bonniwell Lyerly and her husband, Eubert Lyerly. A mayor of Hickory, Lyerly was owner and president of Elliott Knitting Mills, president of Clay Printing Company, and publisher of the *Hickory Daily Record* at its 1915 inception. Also architecturally significant, it houses an exhibit on area history. Tours of the Harper House are $10; admission to Bonniwell-Lyerly House is free. Open Fri and Sat 9 a.m. to 5 p.m.

Hickory Museum of Art. 243 3rd Ave. NE; (828) 327-8576; hickorymuseumofart.org. Founded in 1944, the Hickory Museum of Art is the second-oldest art museum in the state. Now located in what was Claremont High School, its permanent collection includes a wide range of American art in a number of media totaling more than 1,500 pieces. Significantly, it holds large collections of southern contemporary folk art and works by North Carolina artists. It also hosts temporary exhibits from other museums and private collections. Free. Open Tues through Sat 10 a.m. to 4 p.m., Sun 1 to 4 p.m.

Maple Grove Historical Museum. 542 2nd St. NE; (828) 322-4731; hickorylandmarks .org. The Hickory Landmarks Society is responsible for this and other architectural restorations in the community. Listed on the National Register of Historic Places, Maple Grove is a restored Italianate-style house completed in 1883, and one of the city's oldest remaining homes. This was the home of Adolphus Lafayette Shuford, one of Hickory Tavern's founding fathers. The 2-story frame house has a distinctive 2-tier front porch and simple but intricate interior and exterior detail. It's furnished with authentic Victorian furnishings. Free. Open Mon through Fri 9 a.m. to 4 p.m.

Propst House. 332 6th St. NW; (828) 322-4731; hickorylandmarks.org. This Second Empire–style cottage with French detail was competed in 1883 and is listed on the National Register of Historic Places. *House Beautiful* said it was a "Victorian gem," built by J. Summie Propst, a local carpenter. The historical society moved the house to its current location at Shuford Park from Main Avenue. Using his skills as a woodcarver, Propst included carved details throughout the home. It is topped with a cupola tower glazed on all 4 sides. Free. Docents offer guided tours Thurs and Sun 1:30 to 4:30 p.m., Mar 15 through Dec 15.

where to shop

Twenty Miles of Furniture. US 321, Hickory to Blowing Rock. The marketers with the Caldwell County Furniture Dealers Association found a way to direct shoppers to some of the best discounts on furniture and slapped this clever moniker on it. Most of the outlets are concentrated in the city limits of Lenoir and feature all the famous brands.

Hickory Antiques Mall. 348 US 70 SW; (828) 322-4004. If eclectic describes your home decor, stop by the Hickory Antiques Mall to add a touch of character. Eighty vendors offer furniture, collectible dolls, Depression glass, coins, china, and silver. Open Mon through Sat 10 a.m. to 6 p.m., Sun 1:30 to 6 p.m.

Hickory Furniture Mart. 2220 US 70 SE; (800) 462-6278; hickoryfurniture.com. More than 100 factory outlet stores populate this monstrous complex of 4 levels. Everything to decorate the home and even a design center are here. Shoppers find home furnishings, accessories, lighting, art, rugs, fabrics, and on and on. There's even a cafe and coffee bar complete with Wi-Fi. The best time to visit for good deals is following the High Point wholesale market in the fall. Open Mon through Sat 9 a.m. to 6 p.m.

where to eat

Bistro 127. 2039 N. Center St.; (828) 328-3432; hickorybistro.com. Located outside Hickory on SR 127, this bistro focuses on organic and all-natural foods. On the menu are gourmet pizzas, burgers, pastas, and entrees made from local meats and produce. Open for breakfast, lunch, and dinner Mon through Sat. $$.

Café Rule and Wine Bar. 242 11th Ave. NW; (828) 324-2005; caférule.com. Wood-fired pizzas, salad from local ingredients and farm-to-table entrées have made Café Rule a fast favorite in Hickory especially for its wine. The restaurant has won four Wine Spectator awards since 2017.

Olde Hickory Tap Room. 222 Union Sq.; (828) 322-2965; oldehickorytaproom.com. If you don't get your fill of craft beer while visiting Asheville, make the stop here for some of the state's best. The big cheese cheeseburger, fish and chips, and other similar offerings make fair accompaniments to the brews made just a couple blocks away. Open daily 11 a.m. to 2 p.m. $$.

where to stay

Sweet Tea Bed and Breakfast. 315 6th St., Conover; (704) 325-3736; sweetteabb.com. Hickory offers a few chain hotels, but If you are looking for something with a bit more character, try one of the four rooms at this Craftsman style bungalow located In the heart of nearby Conover. A special bonus of fresh made bakery goodies is proffered.

worth more time

A few miles west of Hickory in the Hildebran community, fans of the 2012 film *The Hunger Games* will find the Henry River Mill Village, which was used as District 12 and the home of Katniss in the film. Though that area is now posted as private property, it is still frequented by fans. Want to tour the site with permission? The Hunger Tours (949-610-5570; hunger gamesunofficialfantours.com) offers 2 distinct tours starting from this site or a tour that features arena scenes in the Brevard area, traveling to virtually all the western North Carolina filming locations.

columbia, sc

day trip 28

columbia, sc

southern capital:
columbia, sc

columbia, sc

South Carolina's capital city includes one of the best zoos in the Southeast and a burgeoning arts district known as the Congaree Vista. From here in practically any direction, the daytripper can find an astounding collection of recreational activities thanks to the convergence of the Saluda and Broad Rivers, which form the Congaree River. Columbia, centrally located in the Palmetto State, became the South Carolina capital in 1786 when the legislature voted to move itself from Charleston. It is now the state's largest city with a population of about 135,000 people.

In the 19th century the Columbia Midlands region became a leader in cotton exports, thus the state was quick to secede from the Union when the institution of slavery and state's rights came into question. During the Civil War, Gen. William Tecumseh Sherman nearly burned the city to the ground, destroying military holdings, homes, and reportedly bales of cotton in retaliation for the city's taking the lead in the state's secession from the Union. Today visitors can follow the path that Sherman and his men took and see the structures that survived.

In the years following Reconstruction, Columbia became a textile manufacturing center and, early in the 20th century, a retail distribution center, whose warehouses would eventually become a thriving arts district. Fort Jackson, built here as an artillery depot,

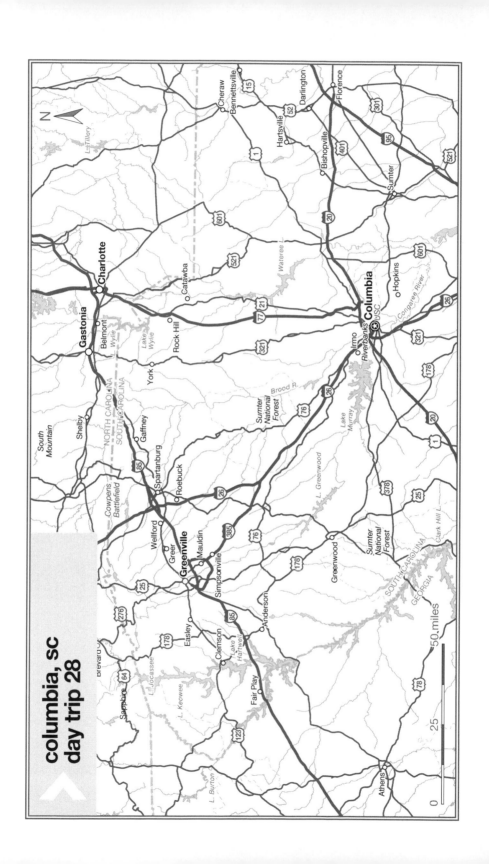

columbia, sc
day trip 28

quirky carolina

You may notice that the downtown streets of Columbia are wider than they are in most towns. Leaders made them that way with the mistaken belief that it would somehow control the mosquito population. Mosquitoes, they reasoned, could not fly more than 60 feet without starving to death.

was activated as a full military installation in 1940 and still provides a basis for much of the Columbia economy as the largest army training post in the country.

getting there

I-77 comes into Columbia from the north, looping east of the city and ending south of the city where it meets I-26, which trails off to the coast. I-26 then runs out of the northwest side of Columbia to Spartanburg and eventually the mountains of North Carolina. I-20 begins to the east at I-95 and helps form the northern part of the loop around the city.

where to go

Columbia Fire Museum. 1800 Laurel St.; (803) 545-3701; columbiasc.net. Located in the historic downtown building in the city's fire department headquarters, the Columbia Fire Museum displays artifacts of firefighting equipment from the mid-1800s. A photo history of firefighting in Columbia and a history of African-American firefighters in the department are also on exhibit. Free. Open Mon through Fri 8:30 a.m. to 5 p.m.

Columbia Museum of Art. 1515 Main St.; (803) 799-2810; columbiamuseum.org. European and American fine and decorative art, including one of the largest collections of Baroque and Renaissance art in the Southeast, make up the collections at this fine art museum. It is located in a renovated department store with an open design that leads through each of its 25 thematic galleries. Temporary programs and exhibitions also provide an artistic window into the community and its history with exhibits that feature local works about the area. The museum has also had a more recent focus on collection and curation of Asian art and antiquities. Also of particular interest are Sandro Botticelli's *Nativity*, Claude Monet's *The Seine at Giverny*, Canaletto's *View of the Molo*, and art glass by Louis Comfort Tiffany. Admission is $12 for adults, $5 for students, and $10 for seniors. Open Tues through Sun 10 a.m. to 5 p.m.

EdVenture Children's Museum. 211 Gervais St.; (803) 779-3100 edventure.org. Part science center, part children's museum, EdVenture was also part of Columbia's 21st-century revitalization plan. Visitors can climb through the stomach, head, and heart of Eddie, a

40-foot-tall playground pal. They can also visit the Little Pig Market, head down to the farm to get a little work done, get the family VW fixed at the auto repair shop, anchor the evening news, and more. Butterflies flutter seasonally in an outdoor exhibit while other outside exhibits explore solar power, recycling, and conservation. Admission is $11.95 for children and adults and $10.95 for seniors. Open Tues through Sat 9 a.m. to 5 p.m., Sun noon to 5 p.m.

Fort Jackson Museum. 4442 Fort Jackson Blvd.; (803) 751-7419. Camp Jackson was established here in 1917 as an artillery replacement depot for the First World War. Just before World War II, it was reactivated as Fort Jackson and now is the army's largest initial training center. Half of all new US soldiers will come through here. While there are few formal public attractions on the 52,000-acre site, the museum here displays more than 4,000 military weapons, uniforms, and other equipment to illustrate how American soldiers train, live, and work. Free. Open Mon through Fri 9 a.m. to 4 p.m.

Governor's Mansion. 800 Richland St.; (803) 737-1710. Spared by Union soldiers in the 1865 fire that nearly destroyed the city, the South Carolina Governor's Mansion became the official residence for state governors in 1868. The stately white mansion with black shutters was built in 1855 as a residence for officers of Arsenal Military Academy. Today its features include some of the most spectacular magnolia and crape myrtle trees in the state under which guests are welcome to picnic. Tours are offered mainly for school groups Tues and Wed mornings, so appointments are required. Gardens are open 9:30 a.m. to 4:30 p.m.

Hampton-Preston Mansion & Gardens. 1615 Blanding St.; (803) 252-1770; historic columbia.org. A wealthy and prominent local merchant, Wade Hampton integrated some Greek Revival influences into his 1818 Federal-style home. His daughter, Caroline, along with her husband, John Preston, expanded the home to twice its original size in the 1850s, and period rooms provide a time line of the house through its many occupants. Sherman spared the home for use by nuns as a temporary convent after their building was destroyed. Through its history the estate would serve as College for Women, Chicora College, Westerveldt Academy, and Columbia Bible College. On the basement level is an exhibit on the use of urban slaves, which had become prominent in Columbia and other large southern cities. Tours of the house begin at the top of the hour. Purchase tickets in the museum shop on the grounds of the Robert Mills House, 1616 Blanding St. Admission is $10 for adults and $7 for ages 6 to 17. A discount is offered for multiple historic home tours. Open Tues through Sat 10 a.m. to 4 p.m., Sun 1 to 5 p.m.

Mann-Simons Cottage. 1403 Richland St.; (803) 252-1770; historiccolumbia.org. On this site is a collection of commercial and residential buildings believed to have been owned by the same African-American family from about 1843. The historical society has narrowed construction of what they believe was a one-room house to the late 1820s, but it is unclear how Celia Mann, a slave in Charleston, later acquired the home. It is believed she arrived in Columbia on foot and earned a living as a midwife as early as 1843. She left the home to her youngest daughter, Agnes Jackson, who married Bill Simons and lived there until she died in 1907. "Ghost houses," frames of structures that once stood here, serve as interpretive pieces on the site. Purchase tickets in the museum shop on the grounds of the Robert Mills House, 1616 Blanding St. Admission is $10 for adults and $7 for ages 6 to 17. A discount is offered for multiple historic home tours. Open Tues through Sat 10 a.m. to 4 p.m., Sun 1 to 5 p.m.

Memorial Park. Corner of Gadsden and Hampton Streets; (803) 545-3100; columbiasc .net. This park, occupying about a city block, memorializes those South Carolinians who served in wars throughout American history. Monuments honor the USS *Columbia* warship and those that served with her during World War II, the China-Burma-India theater veterans of WWII, South Carolina casualties of the Pearl Harbor attack, South Carolina Holocaust survivors, and the state's Vietnam War veterans. The park was dedicated in November 1986 along with the unveiling of the South Carolina Vietnam Monument. In June 2000 the Korean War Memorial was dedicated at Memorial Park. Free. Typically open during daylight hours.

Nickelodeon Theatre. 1607 Main St.; (803) 254-3433; nickelodeon.org. With only 75 seats in this storefront theater near the university, it is hard to get a bad seat. Credited with helping revitalize downtown, the Nickelodeon shows independent and low-budget films and is the only nonprofit theater in the state. It also hosts regular film festivals, including a 10-day indie film event in spring. Ticket prices vary. Two screenings are typically held each evening with occasional matinees.

Riverbanks Zoo and Garden. 500 Wildlife Pkwy. (just off I-126 at Greystone Boulevard in Columbia); Botanical Garden, 1300 Botanical Pkwy. (off Highway 378 in West Columbia); (803) 779-8717; riverbanks.org. While the zoo and garden have different addresses that technically put them in different cities, they are adjacent and can be visited together. The zoo's bar-free exhibits benefit from the garden's horticulturalists who create lush naturalistic surroundings for the zoo's residents. Here colorful Australian lorikeets land on your shoulder (or head), visitors can feed giraffes on the African Plains, see penguins from the bottom of the world in the Birdhouse, or come within almost an arm's reach of Galapagos turtles. The zoo features a massive 20,000-square-foot aquarium and reptile complex, an island for lemurs, and a barnyard. Across the river in the Botanical Garden, native and exotic plants likewise provide a look at environments that are worlds away. Located on the peaceful Saluda River, the grounds includes a spectacular walled garden, a big rose garden, nature trails, and more. Fun, additional activities include a zip line and canopy tour, rock-climbing walls, and a ropes course. Admission is $21.99 for adults, $18.99 for children ages 3 to 12. Open daily 9 a.m. to 5 p.m. with additional hours to 6 p.m. weekends Apr through Sept.

Robert Mills House & Gardens. 1616 Blanding St.; (803) 252-1770; historiccolumbia.org. Designed by the same architect responsible for the Washington Monument, this home is one of only 5 National Historic Landmarks in Columbia. Robert Mills was the first architect born and trained within the US; he designed the home at the request of Englishman Ainsley Hall, who died before it was completed. His wife, Sarah, soon sold it to the Presbyterian

Synod of South Carolina and Georgia, which established a seminary there. It also served as Westerveldt Academy and later the Columbia Bible College. The house contains 19th-century furniture and decorative art. The English-style gardens were added in the 1960s. Purchase tickets in the museum shop on the grounds. Admission is $10 for adults and $7 for ages 6 to 17. A discount is offered for multiple historic home tours. Open Tues through Sat 10 a.m. to 4 p.m., Sun 1 to 5 p.m.

Sesquicentennial State Park. 9564 Two Notch Rd.; (803) 788-2706; southcarolinaparks .com. Located minutes from downtown Columbia, the focal point of this park is a 30-acre lake with meandering trails and beautiful spots to picnic under shady trees. Fish, camp, or rent canoes, kayaks, and pedal boats for a nominal fee. In 1969 the state moved here what is believed to be the oldest house in the county: a 2-story log house, dating back to the mid-18th century. Daytime admission is $6 for adults $3.50 for children ages 6-15. Generally open during daylight hours.

701 Center for Contemporary Art. 701 Whaley St.; (803) 779-4571; 701cca.org. Artists who become part of this program live and work in this innovative space converted from an old community center for up to 12 weeks. In addition to the artist-in-residence program, the center presents other contemporary art exhibits by area artists. The center also conducts concerts, workshops, and other programs for both children and adults. Free. Admission charged for various events. Open Wed 11 a.m. to 8 p.m., Thurs and Fri 11 a.m. to 5 p.m., Sat 9 a.m. to 5 p.m., Sun 1 to 5 p.m.

South Carolina Military Museum. 1225 Bluff Rd.; (803) 299-4440; scmilitarymuseum .com. At this museum, opened in 2007 and expanded to a second building in 2014, visitors can peruse big equipment used in wars beginning with the Civil War. The exhibit includes a Civil War cannon, an M-48 tank, and a self-propelled howitzer. A collection of equipment from Col. Melvin Purvis, who shot John Dillinger at the Biograph Theater, is on display here along with many military exhibits from the colonial period to current conflicts. Exhibits include the Hall of Heroes, a memorial to those South Carolinians who have received the Congressional Medal of Honor; an exhibit on "Carbine" Williams, who developed the smaller, lighter, more accurate Carbine rifle used in WWII; and more. Free. Open Mon through Sat 10 a.m. to 4 p.m.

South Carolina State House. 1100 Gervais St.; (803) 734-2430; sc.gov. Appropriately, palmettos line the entrance of the copper-capped statehouse, home to the state's collection of art, historical portraits, sculpture, and monuments. The massive Corinthian columns at 43 feet high are among the largest in the world. This building was under construction when Sherman invaded in 1865 and burned what was then the statehouse, where most of the drawings for the new legislative building were kept. After those delays and the passing of the jobs to several architects due to death and political jockeying, the building was completed in 1903 and renovated from 1995 to 1998. While most of those renovations were to bring the building up to contemporary code, the House and Senate Chambers both received serious face-lifts as did other public areas that included new marble floors and a refurbished dome—a false dome in the interior. The grounds of the statehouse include more than 30 historical markers and memorials. Open Mon through Fri 9 a.m. to 5 p.m.

South Carolina State Museum. 301 Gervais St.; (803) 898-4921; scmuseum.org. This massive, 4-story facility is the official state museum and stages major exhibitions of art, science, and history. The museum is located in what was the world's first totally electric 1894 textile mill. Giant sharks hang overhead and a large collection of fossils provides the basis of a dinosaur exhibit and for active research on prehistoric life. More than 14,000 years of artifacts note South Carolina's cultural heritage. Well-done dioramas take visitors from the foothills of the upstate to the state's coastal habitats. Dozens of interactive technology exhibits focus on advances and uses of laser technology, space science, and aviation. South Carolina's history is covered through a series of artifacts that include some of the oldest ever found in the state and tell the area's story that begins 14,000 years ago. The American Revolution, the state's role in the Civil War, and its black history are covered with exhibits of tools, weapons, modes of transportation, and other artifacts. The museum also houses the South Carolina Confederate Relic Room and Military Museum. The Lipscomb Art Gallery provides space for art exhibits staged here twice a year. A 4-D theater presents educational films and adapted featured films with the addition of special environmental effects. Even with all that, the museum has saved space for national touring exhibitions. Admission is $13.95 for adults, $12.95 for seniors, and $11.95 for children ages 3 to 12. Open Tues through Sat10 a.m. to 5 p.m., Sun noon to 5 p.m.

University of South Carolina. 816 Bull St.; (803) 777-2489; sc.edu. This 350-acre campus in downtown Columbia is home to Gamecock sports and more than 30,000 students who come here for education in a wide range of disciplines. Its undergraduate international business program consistently ranks at the top in *US News & World Report*, not bad for a public university, the flagship of South Carolina's university system. Founded in 1801, it began operating in 1805 with an enrollment of 9 students. The university libraries hold the largest collection of Robert Burns works outside of Scotland. The Koger Center for the Arts is the site of Broadway plays, performances by the city ballet, and other events. The center of university life, the Horseshoe, on the National Register of Historic Places, was the location of the campus's original Federal-style buildings. It is now spreading west toward the Congaree River.

McKissick Museum. 816 Bull St.; (803) 777-7251; artsandsciences.sc.edu. Located on the USC campus on the Horseshoe, McKissick Museum was founded as the university museum in 1976. It has become a sort of unofficial museum of the region with a focus on natural history exhibits that range from rocks, gems, and minerals to rare books and an unusual collection of 18th-century British silver. The museum, located in a beautiful 1839 building that was the university's first library, is a nice combination of natural science, art, and history. Free. Open Mon through Fri 8:30 a.m. to 5 p.m., Sat 11 a.m. to 3 p.m.

Melton Memorial Observatory. 1429 Greene St.; (803) 777-4180; physics.sc .edu/~melton. Stars, moons, planets, and other celestial objects come into focus thanks to the powerful telescopes and expert direction at the Melton Observatory on the USC campus. Tours of the facility are conducted along with night sky viewing on clear Monday nights throughout the year. Free. Hours are 8:30 to 10:30 p.m. Nov through Mar and 9:30 to 11 p.m. Apr through Oct.

Woodrow Wilson Family Home. 1705 Hampton St.; (803) 252-1770; historiccolumbia .org. In 2009 the Historic Columbia Foundation began restoring the childhood home of the nation's 28th president. With the painstaking, historically accurate restoration completed in 2014, visitors are now permitted to walk its halls as Wilson did when it was new. The Italian villa home was built in 1871 as the city began to rebuild from the Civil War. It includes an exhibit on the Reconstruction era, period vignettes, and virtual history lessons. Purchase tickets in the museum shop on the grounds. Admission is $10 for adults and $7 for ages 6 to 17. A discount is offered for multiple historic home tours. Open Tues through Sat 10 a.m. to 4 p.m., Sun 1 to 5 p.m.

where to shop

Adluh Flour Mills. 804½ Gervais St.; (803) 779-2460; adluh.com. A blinking neon sign attracts customers to this mill that's become famous for its flour and cornmeal over the past 100 years. It is so famous, in fact, the state department of agriculture declared it the official state flour. Though it is sold at grocers and restaurants throughout the Southeast, you can stop by the plant to make a purchase. Open Mon through Thurs 7:30 a.m. to 5 p.m., Fri 7:30 a.m. to noon.

The Congaree Vista. 701 Gervais St.; (803) 269-5946; vistacolumbia.com. Spanning north from the Congaree Riverwalk and concentrated on and near Gervais Street, the Congaree Vista is a massive shopping, dining, and entertainment district. It includes an extreme mix of residential property, art galleries, restaurants, and other entertainment.

Devine Street. Devinestreetcolumbiasc.com. This trendy neighborhood street east of downtown Columbia has two dozen shops and boutiques and almost as many restaurants. Bohemian and Bohemian Home sell their own style of home decor and women's clothing. At Cupcake, which we will sample again in Charleston, you can satisfy the taste of any sweet tooth.

where to eat

Cafe Strudel. 118 State St., West Columbia; (803) 794-6634; cafestrudel.com. Breakfast dishes like the breakfast burrito are mainstays at this eclectic restaurant. During lunch and dinner, Cafe Strudel offers Philly cheesesteaks, off-the-charts burgers, and similar fare. Open Mon through Wed 8:30 a.m. to 3:30 p.m., Thurs through Sat 8:30 a.m. to 10:30 p.m., and Sun 10 a.m. to 2:30 p.m. $.

Carolina Ale House—Vista. 708 Lady St.; (803) 407-6993; carolinaalehouse.com. Though branches of this sports bar are slowly popping up across the Carolinas, the rooftop dining and bar make this a special kind of sports bar that's good for families by day and evening, and partiers by night. Burgers, wings, and other hearty foods synonymous with sports bars are on the menu. $$.

The Gourmet Shop. 724 Saluda Ave.; (803) 799-3705; thegourmetshop.net. If you don't try anything else, check out the chicken salad at the Gourmet Shop. The cafe here offers shady outdoor seating and delectable food that comes out of a renowned bakery. After lunch, shop for gourmet cheeses, wines, and even gourmet kitchen gadgets. Open daily 9 a.m. to 4 p.m.

Motor Supply Bistro. 920 Gervais St.; (803) 256-6687; motorsupplycobistro.com. This high-end, farm-to-table restaurant, located in the Vista District, changes menus daily as evidenced by handwritten menus. Its contemporary selections blend American, French, Italian, and Asian cuisine. Open for lunch Tues through Fri 11 a.m. to 2 p.m., and for dinner Tues through Thurs 5 to 9 p.m., Fri and Sat 5 to 10 p.m., and Sun 5:30 to 9 p.m. It is also open for Sunday brunch, 10 a.m. to 2 p.m. $$$.

where to stay

The 1425 Inn. 1425 Richland St.; (803) 252-7225; 1425inn.com. The wraparound porch and notable red door invite guests into one of the luxurious rooms themed to honor the palmetto state. The Magnolia and Laurel rooms offer a botanical touch while Gervais and The Sumpter lend themselves to a historical significance, $$

The Graduate. 1619 Pendleton St.; (803) 779-7779; innatusc.com. Once the Inn at USC, this stately and elegant boutique hotel located on the campus of the University of South

quirky carolina

Lunch Island (aka Bomb Island; aka Doolittle Island) may well be the site of the largest purple martin roosts in the world. In late afternoons of July and August, what is estimated to be nearly a million purple martins arrive in a cloud-like form over Lake Murray as they settle to feed and roost. The daily phenomenon occurs until they head off to South America for winter hibernation.

Carolina has been converted into a Graduate Hotel, designed with Gamecocks and Game-cock colors. It's close to downtown attractions and withmarble floors and luxurious furnishings and bedding, this one of the most desirable places to stay in Columbia. $$$.

worth more time
lake murray

Located 30 minutes from Columbia via I-26 west, resorts, golf courses, marinas, and other recreational facilities dot the 650 miles of shoreline around **Lake Murray.** At the time it was built in the 1930s to accommodate production of hydroelectricity, it was the largest man-made reservoir in the world. Still, covering 50,000 acres, it is central South Carolina's premier recreational center. A visitor center is located on Highway 6, 2184 N. Lake Dr. in Columbia. For more information, visit lakemurraycountry.com or call (803) 781-5940. Keep in mind this is a big lake; it would take the better part of a day to travel over all of it. Target your destinations carefully.

Among the hot spots are **Dreher Island State Park** (3677 State Park Rd., Prosperity; 803-917-1808; southcarolinaparks.com) where 3 islands comprise a 342-acre recreation area. Hiking and fishing are the main pastimes here with a short nature trail along the shore and more strenuous trails up to 2 miles. Both RV and tent camping sites are available. **Lexington County Museum** (231 Fox St., Lexington; 803-359-8369; lexingtoncountymuseum .org) offers a tour by costumed guides at this large complex of 2 antebellum homes and 3 cabins. The 7-acre site actually includes a total of 36 structures that give a glimpse of life in the late 1700s through the Civil War. **Lorick Plantation House** (2184 N. Lake Dr., Irmo; 803-781-5940) is a ca. 1840 plantation house, called Green Acres from 1952 to 1995 when the owners donated it to the Tourism and Recreation Division. It offers exhibits and an aquarium with various species of fish from Lake Murray.

day trip 29

columbia, sc

>>> **hub city:**
spartanburg, sc

spartanburg, sc

Once a place where textiles were king and not much more than peaches had appeal, the city of Spartanburg has begun to capitalize on its Revolutionary War history and the growing interest in cultural opportunities. Found near here are more Revolutionary War battle sites than anywhere else in the country. Standing sentinel over downtown Spartanburg's revitalized Morgan Square is a statue of General Daniel Morgan, who led the American forces to victory at the Battle of Cowpens, frequently recognized as a tactical masterpiece. Also here are no fewer than eight institutions of higher learning, a new musical trail, and a wide variety of cultural opportunities.

The city and county of the same name were named for the Spartan Regiment of the South Carolina Militia that formed in this area. Later, construction of the railroads helped Spartanburg during the industrial revolution as it began to develop textile mills along the banks of its plentiful rivers. Spartanburg became known as the Hub City, partly because of its central location in the foothills of the Blue Ridge between Charlotte, Atlanta, Columbia, and Asheville, but initially and primarily because of the number and layout of rail lines in the city.

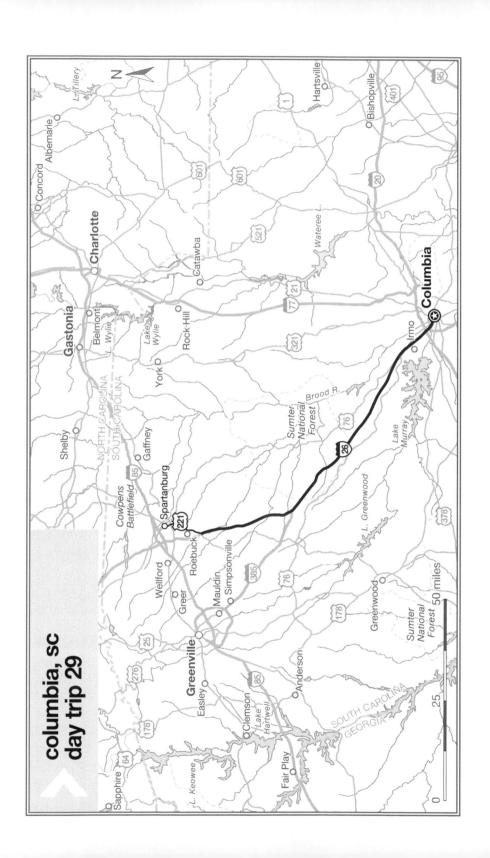

getting there

An hour and a half from Columbia, Spartanburg is located west on I-26, passing through the southwestern corner of Sumter National Forest along the way.

where to go

Chapman Cultural Center. 200 E. Saint John St.; (864) 542-2787; chapmancultural center.org. Science, history, and art exhibits and performances by local and national artists are offered here at this complex of 3 buildings opened in 2007. The Spartanburg Science Center, located here, includes 4 exhibit spaces on the human body, physics, life science, and earth science. Push-button exhibits allow guests to better understand the circulatory system, nutrition, and other aspects of the human body. Simple machines, principles of energy, and fiber optics also come to light. The corresponding Spartanburg Regional History Museum is also on the property and presents a time line from Spanish exploration to Spartanburg involvement in military activity to the area's rich manufacturing heritage. Also located here are 2 theaters: a beautiful traditional theater with seating for 500 and an intimate black box theater that is also used for instructional space. Admission to the science center is $5. In addition to evening performance times, the center is open Tues through Sat 10 a.m. to 5 p.m.

Croft State Natural Area. 450 Croft State Park Rd.; (864) 585-1283; southcarolinaparks .com. The 150-acre Lake Craig is the centerpiece of this park known for its equestrian facilities. Once this 7,000-acre property was an army training facility. Now horse shows are held here frequently, but the park also offers biking trails, camping, fishing, and other outdoor activities just a few minutes outside downtown Spartanburg. Admission is $2. Typically open during daylight hours.

Hollywild Animal Park. 2325 Hampton Rd., Wellford; (864) 472-2038; hollywild.com. The only working rhino in the country plus other television-commercial and film stars are residents of Hollywild, a small zoo featuring exotic animals, shows, feeding stations, and demonstrations. Many of its residents have appeared in movies and commercials, some living out retirement here; others still find occasional work in the industry. While there are typical zoo exhibits here, a safari ride takes visitors through about 70 acres where animals roam free. Admission is $9 per person for everyone over age 14, $7 for children 2 to 14. Open Mon through Fri 9 a.m. to 4 p.m., Sat 9 a.m. to 6 p.m., Sun 11 a.m. to 6 p.m. Open Sat and Sun only in Sept and Oct.

Hub-Bub. 149 S. Daniel Morgan Ave.; (864) 582-0056; hub-bub.com. This has been called one of the leading artist-in-residence programs in the nation. Living upstairs in the former Nash Rambler car dealership for 11 months are three visual artists and one creative writer who produce works based loosely on their experience in Spartanburg. Those works, along with the works of other artists, are exhibited in a gallery, and the performance hall provides space for a wide range of events. Staged here throughout the year are concerts, films, progressive art exhibits, poetry readings, experimental theater, workshops, and more artistic endeavors. The display gallery is open Mon through Fri 9 a.m. to 5 p.m.

Hub City Railroad Museum. 298 Magnolia St.; (864) 594-5050; hubcityrrmuseum.org. Southern Railway, Charleston and Western Carolina Railway, Piedmont & Northern Railway, Clinchfield, and a handful of other railroads and streetcars served this area through much of the 19th and 20th centuries. Railroad enthusiasts learn about the service by visiting the exhibit located in this train depot of the Southern Railway. The museum includes artifacts of the city's textile heritage and its continuing agricultural industry. Also included are artifacts from the Hayne Shops of Southern Railway, the area's only freight and passenger car repair shop. Free. Open Wed and Sat 8 a.m. to 2 p.m.

Walnut Grove Plantation. 1200 Otts Shoals Rd., Roebuck; (864) 596-3501; spartanburg history.org. Located in the unincorporated community of Roebuck, just south of Spartanburg near the intersection of I-26 and US 221, is this well-preserved, 18th-century plantation. Built by Charles Moore for his wife, Mary, and 8 children (2 more were born at Walnut Grove), the home amazingly stayed in the family until 1961. Several Patriot military units were formed on the property, including the Spartan Regiment, from which the county and city eventually took their names. The family donated the plantation to the Spartanburg County Historical Society, which restored the home and still operates it as a museum today. Admission is $7 for adults, $3 for ages 6 to 17. It's open Tues through Sat 11 a.m. to 5 p.m., Sun 2 to 5 p.m. Apr through Oct, and Sat 11 a.m. to 5 p.m. Nov and Mar. Guided tours begin hourly.

where to shop

Hub City Bookshop. 186 W. Main St.; (864) 577-9349; hubcity.org. This independent bookstore looks out on Morgan Square in downtown and specializes in new releases and regional authors, including its own Hub City Press titles. You are likely to find the Hub-Bub writer-in-residence working here. Little River Coffee Bar and Cakehead Bakery are also located in the building that was once the Masonic Temple. Open Mon through Thurs 10 a.m. to 7 p.m., Fri and Sat 10 a.m. to 9 p.m.

where to eat

Beacon Drive-In. 255 John B. White Sr. Blvd.; (864) 585-9387; beacondrivein.com. This local landmark, which once served Bill Clinton, offers tons of items but is best known for its iced tea, generous portions of fries, and big, sloppy burgers known as burger a-plenty. While it became famous for its sweet tea, people also came to see J. C. Strobel, who for decades welcomed guests, hollered out their orders to the cooks, and politely asked you to "move on down the line." Though Strobel died in 2013, diners still come for burgers. Open Mon through Sat 6:30 a.m. to 10 p.m. $.

Nu-Way Restaurant and Lounge. 373 E. Kennedy St., (864) 582-9685; nuwaylounge
.com. Nu-Way is one of several Spartanburg restaurants to receive national attention. In this
case for the redneck cheeseburger, topped with pimento cheese. Some might call it a dive.
Others can't resist stopping in. And that's why it has been in business since 1938 serving
up burgers, beer, and occasional entertainment. $.

Wades. 1000 N. Pine St.; (864) 582-3800; eatatwades.com. This little meat and potatoes
restaurant regularly wins accolades from the media and others. It has been operating in
Spartanburg since 1947, and although the menu and buildings have changed through those
years, the locals keep coming back for the quality and consistent food and service. Open
Mon through Sat 10:45 a.m. to 8:30 p.m., Sun 10:45 a.m. to 3 p.m. $$.

where to stay

The Inn on Main. 319 E. Main St.; (864) 585-5001; innonmainofspartanburg.com. This
nostalgic 1904 inn, with a grand facade with big columns, big porches, and a redbrick
exterior, has changed hands only 4 times. Inside, rooms are elegant and bright and repre-
sent some of the city's Revolutionary-era history. It has operated as a B&B since 2002, and
comes readily recommended. $$.

worth more time

Cowpens Battleground. 4001 Chesnee Hwy.; (864) 431-2828; nps.gov/cowp/index.htm.
Located in the town of Chesnee, this is the site of what historians say was the turning point
in the Revolutionary War. The battlefield was the location of the January 17, 1781, battle in
which a force of militia from Virginia, Georgia, and the Carolinas commanded by General
Daniel Morgan won a decisive Revolutionary War victory over the British. Afterward British
General Cornwallis abandoned South Carolina and marched north to his surrender at Yorktown. Considered a tactical masterpiece, this battle is a staple of many formal military edu-
cations. That strategy is interpreted well by park rangers, in a small museum located here,
and through signage on the park's trails. Events on this site each year include an anniversary
reenactment. Free. Open daily 9 a.m. to 5 p.m.

day trip 30

columbia, sc

>>> **bridge city:**
greenville, sc

greenville, sc

This South Carolina city hasn't always enjoyed the best reputation, but its time has come. It's become a unique city of arts that is enjoyed by day-trippers from all around. The Liberty Bridge, a much-talked-about design curiosity, opened in 2004, and now the 345-foot suspension bridge sweeps around the falls of Reedy River and through the tops of trees planted nearly 50 years ago. It has helped the city maintain its natural charm and encouraged its residents to value its historic treasures. The National Trust for Historic Preservation awarded Greenville the Great American Main Street Award in 2003 and 2009. Probably most important, the city has become known as a bastion of the arts and culinary delight. A busking program is a city effort to offer daily performances at several key locations. Main Street Gallery offers the same opportunity to visual artists to showcase their talents. In addition, the city commissioned original works of sculpture to honor Greenville's past as well as more contemporary whimsical works. Download a guided tour of downtown or get more information about the city at visitgreenvillesc.com.

Now the third-largest city in South Carolina, much of this city's history is inglorious at best. Little distinguishes its early history from other surrounding cities and foothill communities of the Upstate. It was established as a trading post in 1768. Founded originally as Pleasantburg, no one really knows for sure why its name changed in 1831 or even for whom it is named. In the middle of the 20th century, it struggled with a littered downtown, a polluted

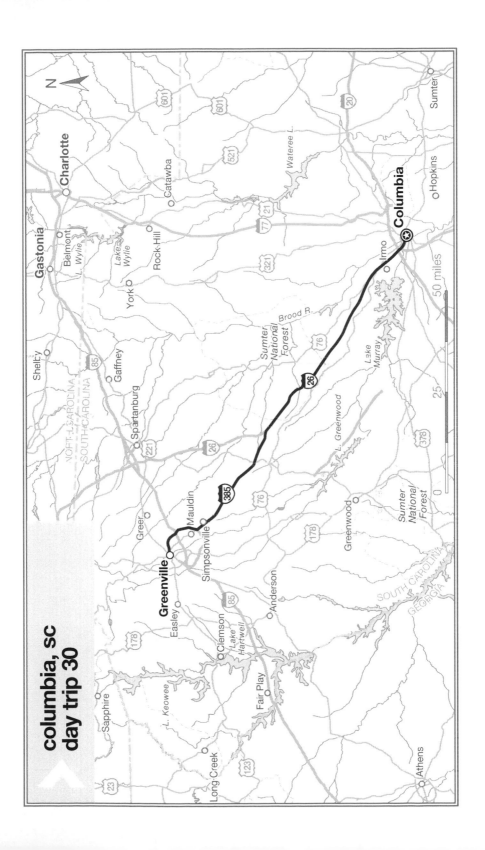

columbia, sc
day trip 30

Reedy River, and a less-than-positive image. This all began to change in the 1970s when the city began a revitalization effort that is unmatched in this region. Trees and decorative light fixtures were added to narrowed streets, creating friendly parks and plazas. In the 1980s the city began a project that would create a 20-acre park in downtown, highlighted by the completion of the bridge.

getting there

To Greenville, about an hour and 45 minutes from Columbia, take I-26 west. Once through Sumter National Forest, take I-385 north.

where to go

Bob Jones University. 1700 Wade Hampton Blvd.; (864) 242-5100; museumandgallery .org. South Carolina's largest private liberal arts university has created a host of cultural opportunities for the city. With 3,000 students, it is the largest fundamentalist Christian college in the world with a 200-acre campus. A museum and gallery with a significant collection of religious art that dates to 14th-century Europe is open to the public. Displayed here in 25 galleries are furniture, sculpture, and tapestries among more traditional baroque paintings and even Egyptian, Roman, and Hebrew antiquities. There is also a Bob Jones gallery at Heritage Green downtown, where the Greenville library and other cultural centers are located.

Centre Stage. 501 River St.; (864) 233-6733; centrestage.org. Centre Stage is Greenville's professional theater that brings to the city current Broadway and off-Broadway comedies, dramas, and musicals. The theater space with 285 seats is also used by local groups. It stages art shows, chamber music concerts, independent film screenings, and more.

Greenville Theatre. 444 College St.; (864) 233-6238; greenvilletheatre.org. The Greenville-Theatre Company has been in continuous operation since 1926 and produces professional-quality musicals, mysteries, comedies, and dramas. The theater actually operated for 75 years beginning in 1836 as the Theatrical Corps. It is proud to have had Joanne Woodward as one of its cast in 1946 and again in 1976 after her significant film career.

The Children's Museum of the Upstate. 300 College St.; (864) 233-7755; tcmupstate .org. This is one of the largest children's museums in the country with exhibit space that spans 80,000 square feet over 3 floors. Opened in a former library in 2009, it includes 18 galleries with typical children's museum interactive exhibits of workplaces, stores, a hospital, a supermarket, a television studio, a farm, and other environments, based largely on real Greenville places. A traveling exhibit hall provides space for national touring shows based on children's educational programs and literature. Admission is $12. Open Tues through Sat 9 a.m. to 5 p.m. and Sun 11 a.m. to 5 p.m.

Greenville County Museum of Art. 420 College St.; (864) 271-7570; greenvillemuseum .org. The popular contemporary work of Andrew Wyeth is among the most significant at the Greenville County Museum of Art, which holds 35 pieces of his work. The museum also collects a wide range of American art from Josef Albers, Jasper Johns, Andy Warhol, and Romare Bearden. Its "Southern Collection" traces the artistic fabric of the area from colonial times to the present. Free. Open Tues through Sat 11 a.m. to 5 p.m., Sun 1 to 5 p.m.

Greenville Zoo. 150 Cleveland Park Dr.; (864) 467-4300; greenvillezoo.com. This small zoo located within Cleveland Park, known as the "city park," on the banks of the Reedy River is operated by the city. Included are big animals like elephants and other African species as well as favorites like monkeys. A reptile house contains various slithery species. A picnic shelter and playground are also to be found here. Admission is $12 for adults, $9 for children ages 3 to 15. Open daily 9 a.m. to 5 p.m.

Paris Mountain State Park. 2401 State Park Rd.; (864) 244-5565; southcarolinaparks .com. Originally built by the Civilian Conservation Corps during the Great Depression, this state park is frequented by bicyclists, hikers, picnickers, and school groups. A renovated bathhouse, now called the Park Center, serves as the hub of activity at Paris Mountain and includes several natural history exhibits. Swimming and fishing are allowed in 15-acre Lake Placid. Admission is $6 for adults, $3.75 for seniors, and $3.50 for ages 6 to 15; free for ages 5 and younger. A nominal fee is charged for some activities. Generally open during daylight hours.

The Peace Center for the Performing Arts. 300 S. Main St.; (864) 467-3000; peacecenter.org. Built from 3 nearly dilapidated factory buildings, this performing arts center opened in 1990 in the heart of downtown and quickly became the core of the city's cultural community. It includes the Peace Center Hall, the Gunter Theatre, the Dow Brand Amphitheatre, and the Wyche Pavilion. The center hosts performances by the Greenville Symphony, Greenville Chorale, Carolina Ballet Theatre, South Carolina Children's Theatre, and Greenville's International Ballet. The center also presents intimate concerts by national acts and independent films in a state-of-the-art, high-def theater.

Shoeless Joe Jackson Museum & Baseball Library. 356 Field St.; (864) 235-6280; shoelessjoejackson.org. Shoeless Joe Jackson's trophy room now houses a collection of books on the impact of baseball on American culture. Jackson's home in Greenville was dismantled and moved in 2006 to its current location near Flour Field, home of the Greenville Drive baseball team, a Class A affiliate of the Boston Red Sox. Jackson, who is third on baseball's all-time batting average list, grew up here and returned to Greenville following his major league career. He is remembered, unfortunately, for being part of the shunned 1919 Chicago White Sox team accused (and later acquitted) of throwing the World Series, an episode that would lead to his and 7 other players' banishment from the game. In addition to personal effects, the museum includes records, artifacts, photographs, film, and other items associated with Jackson. Free. Open daily 11 a.m. to 7 p.m. and during and after all Drive games.

Upcountry History Museum. 540 Buncombe St.; (864) 467-3100; upcountryhistory.org. Audiovisual and interactive displays take visitors through 300 years of history on Upcountry South Carolina. The museum, operated in partnership with Furman University, tells the 15-county region's story from its agricultural heritage to the industrial revolution. Admission is $10 for adults, $9 for students and seniors, $8 for children ages 4 to 12. Open Tues through Sat 10 a.m. to 5 p.m., Sun 1 to 5 p.m. Also open 10 a.m. to 5 p.m. in summer.

where to shop

Art Crossing at River Place. 300 River St.; (864) 430-8924; artcrossing.org. An art colony has been forming on the west bank of the Reedy River, where 20 studios have been converted from parking garages. For sale are remarkable works in paint, ceramics, photographs, and colorful mosaics. Open Tues through Sat 11 a.m. to 6 p.m.

Haywood Mall. 700 Haywood Rd.; (864) 288-0512; simon.com. The largest mall in South Carolina is anchored by the predictable Belk, JCPenney, and Macy's, but because of its size it's a major regional draw. In addition, Haywood Mall houses more than 150 specialty shops from Aeropostale to Williams-Sonoma. Open Mon to Sat 10 a.m. to 9 p.m., Sun 12:30 to 6 p.m.

where to eat

Blue Ridge Brewing Company. 217 N. Main St.; (864) 232-4677; blueridgebrewing.com. One of the leaders on the craft brew front here was Bob Hiller, who opened this pub and tap house in 1995. It's now one of Greenville's most popular restaurants and nightspots. Meat and veggie plates come alongside dishes more palatable with beer such as fish and chips, steaks, and sliders. Open daily 11 a.m. to 2 a.m., closing Sun at midnight. $$.

Brick Street Cafe. 315 Augusta St.; (864) 421-0111; brickstreetcafe.net. Located in the historic district of the West End, Brick Street serves home cooking with a little something added in. You can get fried green tomatoes alongside halibut or shrimp and grits. It's also a pretty place to eat with fresh flowers and colorful decor. Save room for sweet potato cake or a Love Muffin! $$.

Larkin's on the River. 318 S. Main St.; (864) 467-9777; larkinsontheriver.com. Located at the Peace Center, Larkin's is a great place for dinner before a show or dessert afterward. Operated by Mark and Larkin Hammond, who also have restaurants in Lake Lure and Columbus, North Carolina, this restaurant focuses on aged beef and well-prepared fish dishes. Open Mon through Sat 11 a.m. to 3 p.m. and for dinner beginning at 5 p.m. Open for Sunday brunch 11 a.m. to 2 p.m. $$$.

The Lazy Goat. 170 River Place; (864) 679-5299; thelazygoat.com. A Mediterranean-themed menu features global influences from Spain, Morocco, Italy, France, Greece, Africa, and the Middle East at this restaurant in the Falls Park area. It offers both outdoor dining and communal tables. Open for lunch at 11 a.m. and for dinner at 5 p.m. $$.

Soby's. 207 S. Main St.; (864) 232-7007; sobys.com. This trendy restaurant in the West End is located in a 100-year-old cotton exchange. A loft dining area was installed to overlook the busy kitchen, but its architectural character is preserved with exposed brick and beams surrounding diners who sit on chairs and eat off tables from wood salvaged from the building. The food can be described as New South cuisine with familiar ingredients with a twist. Meat loaf, for example, is served with a maple Creole mustard glaze. Open Mon through Thurs 5:30 to 10 p.m., Fri and Sat 5:30 to 11 p.m., Sun brunch 10:30 a.m. to 1:30 p.m. and 5:30 to 9 p.m. $$$.

where to stay

Pettigru Place. 302 Pettigru St.; (864) 242-4529; pettigruplace.com. White Adirondack chairs provide a peaceful respite in an English garden on this shady, tree-lined street. The brick Georgian Federalist design home built in the 1920s is stately, yet comfortable with luxurious guest rooms that reflect various themes. Victorian decor fills one room while another is themed from the African rainforest. $$$.

The Phoenix. 246 N. Pleasantburg Dr.; (864) 233-4651; phoenixgreenvillesinn.com. The Phoenix is an upscale, full-service hotel with dining on-site. It is a handsome and comfortable independent hotel with southern-style charm. Plantation shutters and manicured gardens on the outside and mahogany 4-poster beds inside add to that style. $.

day trip 31

columbia, sc

>>> **home of the tigers:**
anderson, sc; fair play, sc; clemson, sc

The home of the Tigers—Clemson University forms the southern border of the city of Clemson in Pickens County. The university and its 20,000 students create most of the cultural opportunities in the area, including a great botanical garden and renowned geology museum. Lake Hartwell forms Clemson's western border, sweeping south past Anderson and into Georgia. Formed by the Corps of Engineers dam in Hartwell, Georgia, the 56,000-acre lake has 962 miles of shoreline along with vast and varied recreational opportunities. It's the southernmost of three lakes in western South Carolina. Lake Keowee and Lake Jocassee lie to the north of Lake Hartwell. Though they lie wholly in South Carolina, they are less accessible than the popular Lake Hartwell, offering a golf course, parks, boater access, fishing, and more.

anderson, sc

Anderson is the largest of a number of cities that provide access to the amenities offered by Lake Hartwell, formed by the Savannah, Tugaloo, and Seneca Rivers. The towns of Seneca, Fair Play, and a handful of other smaller communities offer addresses for these attractions but little more. The massive reservoir provides municipal water, power, and a hefty amount of recreational opportunities for the day-tripper. Its shoreline spans nearly 1,000 miles from north of Clemson south to the northeast Georgia mountains, bisecting I-85 near Anderson and providing dozens of boat launches, parks, and access areas. Anglers, both professional

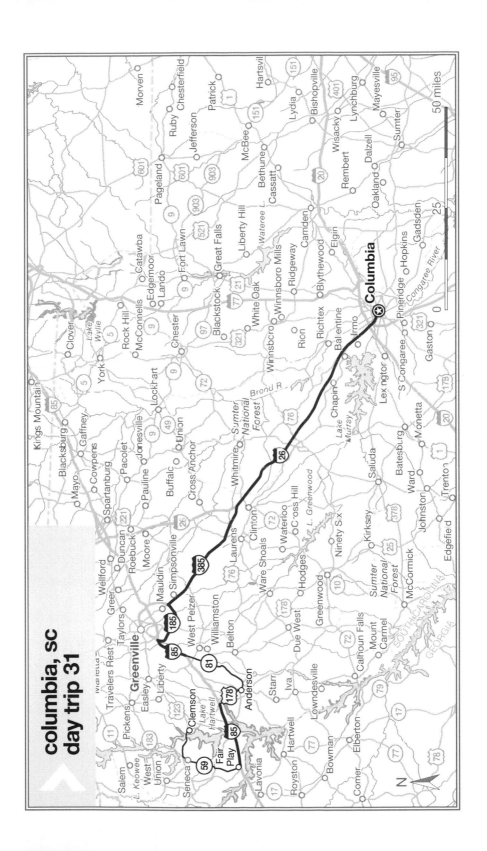

columbia, sc
day trip 31

turn up the radio

Actor Cuba Gooding Jr. made Anderson resident James Robert "Radio" Kennedy famous in the 2003 film Radio. The touching story details developmentally disabled Radio's relationship with a coach at T. L. High School where now stands a statue of Radio, a fixture in the school's football program since the 1960s. It is located at 2600 SR 81.

and amateur, come from miles around seeking one of the lake's whopping striped bass. Fresh produce stands, pick-your-own orchards and farms, flea markets, and antiques malls dot the landscape.

Anderson was the first city in the US to have continuously running electricity, supplied by a water mill on the Rocky River. In 1897 it operated the first cotton gin run on electricity, earning it the nickname "The Electric City." Walking-tour brochures for Anderson's Boulevard and Downtown historic districts are available at the visitor center at 110 Federal St.

getting there

The travel time from Columbia to Anderson is just over 2 hours. Take I-26 west from Columbia to northbound I-385. You could diverge and take country roads (SR 418 and US 25) into Anderson, but you'll spend a little less time traveling the longer route I-385 to the I-185 (a toll road) to I-85 south. From there, approach Anderson from the north via SR 81.

where to go

Anderson Arts Center and Arts Warehouse. 110 Federal St.; (864) 222-2787; anderson arts.org. Located in a renovated 100-year-old, 33,000-square-foot building in the heart of Anderson is the city's center for the arts. Here you'll find display galleries and retail space for art and design as well as classroom space. Open Tues through Fri 10 a.m. to 5 p.m.

Anderson County Museum. 202 E. Grenville St.; (864) 260-4737; andersoncounty museum.org. The Anderson County Museum has collected more than 20,000 objects with which it stages multiple exhibits throughout the year. Among them are artifacts that detail the area's history and culture as well as the Anderson County Hall of Fame. The museum often focuses on the region's development from an agricultural community to its dependence on textiles. Open Tues 10 a.m. to 7 p.m., Wed through Sat 10 a.m. to 4 p.m.

Sadlers Creek State Recreation Area. 940 Sadlers Creek Rd.; (864) 226-8950; south carolinaparks.com. This 395-acre park spans a peninsula on the eastern side of Lake Hartwell. Lots of shoreline means lakeside camping, fine fishing, and picturesque picnicking.

While swimming is permitted, there are no formal facilities or lifeguards on duty. Admission is $3 for adults, $1.50 for seniors and $1 for children. Typically open during daylight hours.

where to shop

Anderson Jockey Lot & Farmer's Market. 4530 Hwy. 29 North; (864) 224-2027; jockey lot.com. The marketing folks at the Anderson County tourism office say this is the South's biggest flea market. While that can't be confirmed, you will be unlikely to complain about this market's size and variety. An estimated 30,000 or more people attend each weekend to visit up to 1,500 vendors. Antiques, clothes, collectibles, sporting goods, and everything in between are offered. Open Sat 7 a.m. to 5 p.m. and Sun 8 a.m. to 5 p.m.

Grady's Great Outdoors. 3440 Clemson Blvd.; (864) 226-5283; gradysoutdoors.com. Before REI and Bass Pro Shops, there was Grady's Great Outdoors—or at least its predecessor, the Hobby and Sport Shop. While its inventory has varied over 50 years, it has become a great place for hunting, fishing, and other outdoor adventure equipment and supplies. Open Mon through Sat 9:30 a.m. to 8 p.m.

where to eat

McGee's Irish Pub. 116 W. Orr St.; (864) 261-6401; mcgeesirishpub.com. From British to Irish, shrimp po'boys, fish and chips, and other classic Celtic food are mainstays in this fun gathering spot. It's located in a rather shabby building in downtown, so unaware visitors may simply pass it by. Open Tues through Sat 11 a.m. to 10 p.m., Sun 11 a.m. to 3 p.m. $$.

where to stay

Bleckley Inn. 151 E. Church St.; (864) 255-7203; bleckleyinn.com. This boutique hotel with only 14 guest rooms offers great sophistication for a smaller city. Well-appointed rooms and technology upgrades are combined with wood floors and exposed brick to create an eclectic environment. $$$.

fair play, sc

The town of Fair Play isn't much more than a stop in the road. Located on I-85, a state welcome center is here, but not much else beyond the 600 or so residents. It is a day trip destination because it's a major access to Lake Hartwell.

getting there

Take US 178 north out of Anderson to I-85. Then take I-85 to exit 4, and reach Fair Play in about 30 minutes.

where to go

Lake Hartwell State Recreation Area. 19138-A Hwy. 11 South, Fair Play; (864) 972-3352; southcarolinaparks.com. The park's information center displays a wide variety of vintage fishing equipment, getting visitors ready to wet a line as they seek bass, largemouth, crappie, bream, and catfish. In addition to lake access, this park has a camp store and opportunities for hiking and camping. One-room camper cabins are available for rent. These are on the primitive side but feature bunk beds, a porch, and electricity, but no running water or bathrooms. Other campground facilities are located throughout the area. Admission to the park is $3 for adults, $1.50 for seniors, and $1 for children. It's typically open during daylight hours.

clemson, sc

This South Carolina town was known as Calhoun until 1943. With a population of 12,000, which pales by comparison to a student population of 20,000, the town is by and large defined by the university. It's a college town with a 2-block downtown north of the university. The university is well known for its colleges of agriculture and forestry and life sciences, and its engineering programs. It was founded through the bequest of Thomas Green Clemson, who married Anna Marie Calhoun, daughter of national political leader John Calhoun. It opened in 1893 as Clemson Agricultural College—an all-white military school. Former Charlotte Mayor Harvey Gantt was the first black student admitted here in 1963, and it was renamed Clemson University in 1964. Its biggest claim to fame may be Death Valley, the famed stadium where the Clemson Tigers, a perennial national championship contender and recent winner , play football games.

getting there

From Fair Play, take SR 59 north and US 76 east to complete the 30-minute trek to Clemson.

where to go

Bob Campbell Geology Museum. 140 Discovery Ln. on the university's garden property; (864) 656-4600; clemson.edu. An impressive collection of more than 10,000 rocks, minerals, fossils, and other objects tells a story beneath the earth's surface with a goal of delivering connections to today. It also houses a large collection of historical tools, including those of Native Americans, that help form a geological time line. Constructed in 1998, Bob Campbell Geology Museum at Clemson University, named for an area quarry owner, is as dynamic as a geology center can be. A skeleton of a saber-toothed tiger, meteorites, and other unusual holdings are on display. Admission is free. Open Mon through Sun 10 a.m. to 5 p.m.

Fort Hill/John C. Calhoun House Museum. 103 Tillman Hall; (864) 656-4789; clemson .edu. US Vice President John C. Calhoun lived at Fort Hill plantation until his death in 1850. Today it is the home of the John C. Calhoun Mansion and Library, a National Historic Landmark at the center of the university campus. Calhoun was considered one of South Carolina's leading statesmen in antebellum times. A proponent of slavery, he would go on to serve as vice president of the US. The home includes a presentation of antebellum furnishings and family artifacts that tell the story of how the home was passed down to the Clemson family through the marriage of Thomas Green Clemson to Calhoun's daughter.

South Carolina Botanical Garden. 102 Garden Trail; (864) 656-7697; clemson.edu/scbg. More than 295 acres of horticultural beauty span out along Lake Hartwell on the western side of the Clemson campus. The spectacular garden features thousands of varieties of ornamental plants in natural landscapes, display gardens, a 70-acre arboretum, and other horticultural gems. Visitors can hike miles of nature trails, along streams and through forests, while a butterfly garden and wildflower meadow offer additional opportunities to explore nature. More formal displays take care of an extensive collection of more than 400 camellias plus holly, magnolias, and hydrangea. The 1716 Hanover House was reconstructed on Clemson's campus in 1941 and moved here in 1994. The Fran Hanson Discovery Center, built as a Southern Living Idea house in 1998, is now the garden visitor center and hosts various events and exhibits. Free. Open daily dawn to dusk.

where to shop

'55 Exchange. Hendrix Student Center, Clemson University; (864) 656-2215. Clemson's class of 1955 established this student-run shop as a gift on its 50th anniversary. It had been known as the Agricultural Sales Center and still carries on the tradition of selling the acclaimed Clemson University ice cream, blue cheese, and other agricultural products. Open Mon through Fri 11:30 a.m. to 6 p.m. (until 8 p.m. in summer), Sat 1 to 6 p.m., Sun 1 to 6 p.m.

where to eat

Pixie & Bills. 1058 Tiger Blvd.; (864) 654-1210; tigergourmet.com. A Clemson tradition since 1971, Pixie & Bills serves prime rib and seafood in comfortable dining rooms with fireplaces and white linen. The restaurant changed owners after 20 years, but offerings have remained consistent. Open Mon through Fri 11:30 a.m. to 1:30 p.m. and 5 to 9:30 p.m.; also open Sat 5 to 9:30 p.m. $$.

Tiger Town Tavern. 368 College Ave.; (864) 654-5901; tigertowntavern.com. Two words describe this pub: college bar. Located in a 2-story, brick storefront, the top of the tavern is technically a private club for people age 21 and older, thus it requires the purchase of a $10 membership. Typical sandwich selections, BBQ chicken plates and a broad selection of wings are offered. The longest list on the beverage menu is the shooters, including the Tiger Balm made of orange vodka and orange juice. $$.

where to stay

Clemson Inn and Conference Center. 230 Madren Center Dr., Clemson University; (864) 654-9020; stayatclemson.com. This luxurious 4-story hotel is located at the conference center on campus, providing a great starting point for day trips. It affords views of gardens, the campus, and nearby Lake Hartwell. Amenities here are extensive and include a golf course. $$$.

day trip 32

columbia, sc

>>> **equine adventure:**
aiken, sc

aiken, sc

A stop sign at Powderhouse Road in Aiken says "Whoa" instead of "Stop." It's an indica-tion—along with unpaved roads and street names like Huntsman Drive, Roses Run, and Squire Street—of how deeply this city's appreciation of horses runs. There are more than 50 polo fields in the area, particularly along the famed Highway 302, and it is a training ground for Kentucky Derby competitors. It's the home of the Aiken Thoroughbred Racing Hall of Fame & Museum and a vacation spot for the rich and famous. Names of people who have vacationed or lived here include Goodyear, Astaire, and Churchill. Beautiful, majestic homes line the streets along with well-manicured gardens and hundreds of green spaces, a good match for the numerous public gardens and golf courses.

Once the plantation home of Captain William White Williams, Aiken grew out of a love story. Williams agreed to allow Andrew Dexter, an engineer working for Charleston railroad executive William Aiken, to have his daughter's hand in marriage if he convinced William Aiken to route the railroad to this area. Dexter succeeded, married Sarah Williams, and in 1835 Aiken was incorporated. It gained early prominence as a wintertime resort for the wealthy of the northeastern US. In 1950 the federal government selected a site on the Savannah River on which to build a plant to produce nuclear fuel, leading to suburban development southeast of the city. In town, however, the day-tripper will find preserved the past with a growing center for the arts and plenty of room to stroll, to shop, or to just sit.

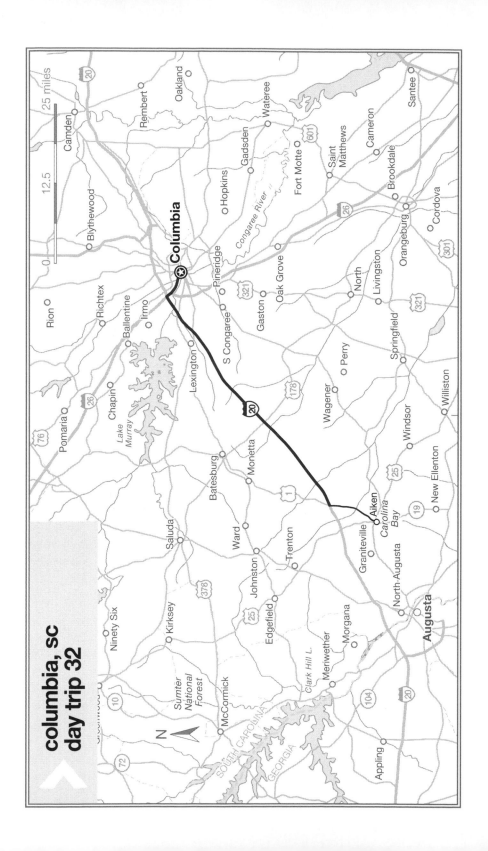

**columbia, sc
day trip 32**

thoroughly thoroughbred

*The Aiken Triple Crown reigns as this city's premier event. This is a homecoming as big and glorious as any found at a college. On these days out come the prettiest sundresses and the biggest, fanciest hats. Held on three consecutive Saturdays in March, the Aiken Triple Crown begins with the **Aiken Trials** (803-648-8955; aiken-trainingtrack.com), a series of six races held at the Aiken Training Track. The Trials have been held since 1942. Next up is the **Spring Steeplechase** (803-648-9641; aikensteeplechase.com), a time-honored tradition since 1966 held at Ford Conger Field. The final leg of the Triple Crown is a polo match at Powderhouse Field on the campus of the University of South Carolina at Aiken. It is a fund-raiser for the university athletic department. A Fall Steeplechase is also held at the end of October and benefits the Hitchcock Woods Foundation and the local rescue squad.*

getting there

Aiken is a straight, 1-hour shot west on I-20 from Columbia.

where to go

Aiken County Historical Museum. 433 Newberry St.; (803) 642-2015; aikencountysc .gov. Established in the white and black–shuttered colonial known as Banksia is the county-run historical museum. Named for the roses prominent in the gardens here, the "cottage" is 2 houses, combined to create a 32-room facility. The house and its furnishings provide a timeline for the city, and its various items on loan from residents are used to create 20 or more special exhibitions. Art exhibits, quilt shows, a lecture series, and other events with a unique local flair are regularly staged here. Free. Open Tues through Sat 10 a.m. to 5 p.m., Sun 2 to 5 p.m.

Aiken Thoroughbred Racing Hall of Fame. 135 Dupree Place; (803) 642-7631; aikenracing halloffame.com. Names such as Pleasant Colony and Swale, both of whom won two legs of racing's prestigious Triple Crown, are installed on the walls of this hall of fame. Pleasant Colony is the 1981 Kentucky Derby and Preakness Stakes winner, and Swale is the 1984 Kentucky Derby and Belmont Stakes winner. To be inducted, a horse, among other requirements, must have spent some part of its training in Aiken. Open since 1977, the hall of fame displays photos, trophies, silks, and other racing memorabilia. Free. Open Tues through Fri and Sun 2 to 5 p.m.; also Sat 10 a.m. to 5 p.m. Sept through May; Sat 10 a.m. to 5 p.m. June through Aug.

Aiken Visitors Center & Train Museum. 406 Park Ave.; (803) 293-7846; aikenrailroad depot.com. Reopened in 2010 this depot has been restored to appear much as it did in its heyday of the first part of the 20th century. Nine dioramas built with the HO-scale model railroads depict some of the towns along the railroad right-of-way between Charleston and Hamburg, southeast of Aiken. At the time this route formed the longest in the world. Make this an early stop, so you can pick up maps and chat with the friendly staff. Free. Open Tues through Fri 10 a.m. to 5 p.m., Sat 9 a.m. to 2 p.m. Two-hour trolley tours also depart from here daily at 10 a.m.

Dupont Planetarium. 471 University Pkwy.; (803) 641-3769; rpsec.usca.edu. Located at the Ruth Patrick Science Education Center at the University of South Carolina at Aiken, this planetarium includes a 30-foot dome with traditional planetarium star projectors as well as panoramic video. It also houses several telescopes in an observatory through which several programs for the school and the public are conducted. Tickets are $6.50 for adults, $5.50 for seniors, and $4.50 for ages 4 to 12. Shows are typically presented on Saturday nights on the hour.

Hitchcock Woods. 1700 Dibble Rd. with entrances surrounding the park; (803) 642-0528; hitchcockwoods.org. These 2,100 acres of urban forest were once owned by equestrians Thomas and Louise Hitchcock and are now overseen by a foundation that maintains the trails and ecologic diversity here. The Aiken Horse Show is held here each spring. Prohibiting vehicular traffic has enabled the foundation to preserve the longleaf pine forest in a natural state, and its historical character, too. Free. Typically open during daylight hours.

Hopelands Gardens. 135 Dupree Place; (803) 642-7631. A tall, white, serpentine brick wall holds back the flowers and shrubs bursting with color at this spectacular city-run garden. Magnolia and cedars, including the oldest and tallest in America, compete for light under 100-year-old oaks at this 14-acre estate garden. It was willed to the city and opened as a public garden in 1969. Free. Open daily 10 a.m. to sunset.

Whitney Field. Mead Avenue (look for the "Polo" sign); (803) 643-3611; aikenpolo.org. The Aiken Polo Club played its first match here in 1882, and they still play here every Sunday. This is the longest, continuously running polo series in the country, and some of the biggest names in the sport have played here. Tickets are $5 per person. Matches are Sun at 3 p.m. year-round.

where to shop

Aiken Center for the Arts. 122 Laurens St. Southwest; (803) 641-9094; aikencenter forthearts.org. Fine art works and craft pieces by local artists are on sale at the center. Five galleries have been established for rotating exhibitions, and a small gift shop offers a number of unique finds.

Aiken County Farmers Market. 115 Williamsburg St.; (803) 642-7761. The site of the current farmers' market was once a cotton exchange for local farmers, who began to struggle in the 1940s as larger manufacturers grew fatter. The city razed the old cotton exchange in 1952 and built the structure from which local farmers, descendants of the original farmers, still sell produce today. Open Tues and Sat 7:30 a.m. to 11:30 a.m.

where to eat

Dukes Barbecue. 4248 Whiskey Rd.; (803) 649-7675. Great barbecue, fried, and roasted chicken is on the menu at Dukes. There's also an excellent, all-you-can-eat buffet packed with down-home cooked food. Open Wed through Sat 10:30 a.m. to 8 p.m. and Sun 11:30 a.m. to 8 p.m. $$.

Malia's. 120 Laurens St. Southwest; (803) 643-3086; maliasrestaurant.com. One diner at Malia's recommended having the raspberry pie before the entree so you don't have to worry about saving room. If you prefer to do it like mother taught, refer to the menu for the daily chef's selection, a scrumptious steak salad, or popular sesame salmon. Open for lunch Tues through Sat 11:30 a.m. to 2:15 p.m. and for dinner Wed through Sat at 5:30 p.m. $$$.

Track Kitchen. 420 Mead Ave.; (803) 641-9628. This casual, family-style restaurant is hard to forget. Locals suggest stopping in for a big country breakfast and then walking around the nearby stables to get a sense of the area. Open 7 a.m. to 1 p.m. $.

where to stay

Carriage House Inn. 139 Laurens St. Northwest; (803) 644-5888; aikencarriagehouse .com. This beautifully restored B&B once served as Efrins Taxi Company. Now elegant accommodations are offered inside the stately yellow Victorian, set among the old oak trees of Aikens's Main Street. Common areas are as comfortable as the rooms, which have 4-poster beds and renovated baths. $$$.

quirky carolina

Since 1875 the ponies have raced at Churchill Downs. Since 1984 lobsters have raced on the track at Newberry Street Festival Center. Held each year the day before the Kentucky Derby, lobster race heats are held on the long, tiered water-filled track. No left turns in this race. Bands play and children enjoy games. Everyone enjoys food and fellowship. It's a homecoming of sorts. In the end, proceeds go to local organizations caring for physically and developmentally challenged children.

Rose Hill Estate. 221 Greenville St. Northwest; (803) 648-1181; rosehillaiken.com. Learn the definition of "Winter Colony" estate at this Shingle-style Dutch colonial that was a wintertime retreat for diplomats and industrialists. Listed on the National Register of Historic Places, the property occupying a city block is on the highest point in the city, 2 blocks from the center of town. Bedrooms, suites, and a furnished cottage are offered amid historic gardens and courtyards. $$$.

Willcox Inn. 100 Colleton Ave. Northwest; (803) 648-1898; thewillcox.com. This grand, white-pillared hotel is among the finest in Aiken. Rocking chairs on the front porch invite guests to sit with a mint julep in their hands, and the spa urges them to while away the day. Once visited by royalty, politicians, and captains of industry, the Willcox stands ready to create more modern special memories. $$$.

worth more time
the natural side of aiken

Located east of Aiken in the town of Windsor is **Aiken State Natural Area** (1145 State Park Rd.; 803-649-2857; southcarolinaparks.com), a spectacularly pristine site on the Edisto River. This black-water river is the longest in North America and brings with it great fishing and canoeing. Kayaks and canoes can be rented through the ranger station for $15 per day. A 3-mile trail also offers evidence of the park's early history. Built by an African-American division of the Civilian Conservation Corps, some of the original structures still remain.

Carolina Bay Nature Reserve, located just south of Palmetto Golf Club on Whiskey Road, is a city-maintained wetland around one of the famous Carolina Bays—unusual landlocked oval bodies of water whose origins remain unconfirmed. Since these bays, unique to the sandhills region of the Carolinas, are atypical, so are their surrounding ecosystems. Wood ducks, red-tail hawks, Mississippi kites, and other birds make their homes here along with flora and fauna not typically seen in an area so close to an urban setting.

day trip 33

columbia, sc

watermelon & other juicy tidbits:
bennettsville, sc; cheraw, sc

The Great Pee Dee River drops out of North Carolina's Yadkin Valley into South Carolina, where it flows freely, unobstructed by dams and loosely connecting the towns of northeastern South Carolina. Once the Pee Dee Indians hunted in this broad valley. Later, in colonial times, it was an important trade route, carrying pine lumber and later rice and cotton. Now sportsmen are more likely to use the river and the great natural resources surrounding it. Vast expanses of farmland, once so rich it was rumored they sold it by the pound instead of by the acre, separate farmhouses interrupted occasionally by a manufacturing plant or a warehouse. One-stoplight towns are even less frequent as travelers barrel down one of many country roads leading, just like the Great Pee Dee, to the Atlantic Ocean.

Many towns have multiple acres of property on the National Register of Historic Places and to the west is Pageland, known widely as the watermelon capital of the world. Running from southeast to northwest between this region and I-20 are acres of natural undisturbed areas that include the Carolina Sandhills Wildlife Refuge, state parks, and more locations for outdoor adventure.

bennettsville, sc

Founded in 1819 and named for Thomas Bennett, onetime governor of South Carolina, is the seat of Marlboro County. Antebellum and colonial homes line the streets of the historic district here. Union troops occupied it for much of the Civil War, and William T. Sherman

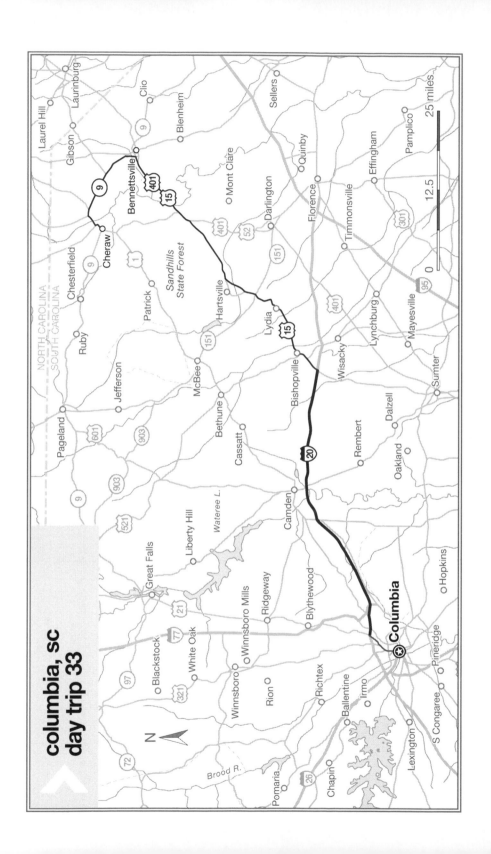

columbia, sc
day trip 33

used the county courthouse as a headquarters for a period, leaving intact (unlike in many southern towns) its historical records. Thereafter it would become one of the richest agricultural areas in the state.

getting there

Bennettsville is less than 2 hours from Columbia. Take I-20 east to US 15.

where to go

D. D. McColl House. 304 E. Main St.; (843) 479-3941; visitbennettsville.com. This Queen Anne–style home was built of yellow brick stained to resemble red brick. It was elaborate construction instigated by McColl, who established the first bank here, built the Bennettsville Textile Mill, and is credited with helping establish the railroad here. D. D. McColl was the great-grandfather of Hugh L. McColl Jr., who would become chairman and CEO of Bank of America. D. D. McColl first lived in the ca. 1826 home at 300 W. Main. In the ca. 1884 home now is located the Bennettsville Visitor Center. Self-guided tours of the historic district originate from here, which include McColl's 1886 Bank Building, several turn-of-the-century churches, and "the Gulf," the only place prior to integration where African Americans could congregate for entertainment and shopping.

Jennings-Brown House & Marlboro County Historical Museum. 123 S. Marlboro St.; (843) 479-5624. The 1826 Jennings-Brown House with its detached kitchen and period furnishings shares the grounds with the Marlboro County Historical Museum, where exhibits detail the county's history, Civil War military exhibits, farming methods, and early textile business. The house, built by Dr. E. W. Jones, was used as headquarters for Union troops in 1865 and features a stenciled ceiling (ca. 1830) discovered during the restoration. Also on the grounds is the Bennettsville Female Academy, moved to this location in 1977, and a one-room medical museum. Museum admission is free. A guided tour of the main house is $4. Open Mon through Fri 10 a.m. to 4 p.m.

Lake Paul Wallace. Jefferson Street, north of downtown; (843) 479-5600. This 600-acre lake is a center for summertime recreation in Bennettsville. It includes sunny grass terraces and sandy beaches. One area is set aside for swimmers, while another is stocked with fish for anglers. A 1-mile channel provides space for skiers. The lake is home to many migrating waterfowl. Free. Generally open during daylight hours.

Marlboro Civic Center. 106 Clyde St.; (843) 454-9496; marlborociviccenter.org. In vaudeville's heyday the Bennettsville Opera House, built in 1917, was a major stop on the circuit between Miami and New York. Known in its early days as the Garden Theatre and the Playhouse, it served as a silent theater and motion picture theater before being abandoned and falling into disrepair. In the 1990s town leaders united to restore it to the stunning architectural beauty it is today. The Marlboro Civic Center hosts hundreds of programs and events, including community theater productions, revivals, recitals, and concerts.

where to eat

Dairy Dream Drive-In. 400 Cheraw St.; (843) 479-9432. Burgers, footlong hotdogs and fried chicken are the dining staples and dipped Ice cream cones star for dessert. It Is, of course, the evening hangout of choice for local high school students. $

Magnolia on Main. 224 E. Main St.; (843) 479-9495. The unassuming downtown storefront location of Magnolia's offers a surprisingly good selection of southern-style dishes. Look for hearty meat and potato entrees, but remember to save room for the wide-ranging variety of desserts that come from the bakery located here. $–$$.

cheraw, sc

Located on the banks of the Great Pee Dee River, Cheraw was a trading post named for the Indians whose town center was also located near here, but they were virtually eliminated by disease by the middle of the 18th century. By 1766 Cheraw was well established with a town green that is now on the National Register of Historic Places. With elms lining the city streets, it was incorporated in 1820, boasting the biggest cotton market between Georgetown, South Carolina, and Wilmington, North Carolina. During both the Revolutionary War and the Civil War, it escaped destruction—used largely in both wars to treat the injured—although an accidental fire at the county courthouse has made it difficult to date many houses. Somewhere along the line it picked up the nickname "Prettiest Little Town in Dixie." More than anything, it is refuge for those seeking activities outdoors.

getting there

From Bennettsville, take the 20-minute drive on SR 9 to reach Cheraw.

bebop

Jazz great Dizzy Gillespie, the trumpet player credited with developing the bebop style of jazz, was born in Cheraw, South Carolina. A bronze statue of Gillespie, bulging cheeks and all, is located on the town green. A map of other places related to his life can be obtained at the Cheraw Chamber of Commerce, and fans can celebrate his life during the South Carolina Jazz Festival the third weekend of each October.

where to go

Carolina Sandhills National Wildlife Refuge. 23734 US 1, McBee; (843) 335-8401; fws .gov/carolinasandhills. Though this wildlife refuge has an address in McBee, it is accessible from Cheraw. Spanning 47,850 acres, it is one of the Carolinas' premier, although diminishing, longleaf pine and wiregrass ecosystems. Hiking and biking trails, wildlife-viewing platforms, bird blinds, and numerous ponds provide for a range of activities. Hunting and fishing are allowed during certain seasons. Birders can spot the endangered red-cockaded woodpecker and the southern bald eagle as well as more than 200 other species of birds.

Cheraw Fish Hatchery. 433 Fish Hatchery Ln.; (843) 537-7628; hatcheries.dnr.sc.gov. The South Carolina Wildlife Department breeds warm-water fish in 31 ponds at the Cheraw Hatchery. More than 2 million bass, bluegill, sunfish, crappie, and other species are raised and distributed each year. The hatchery is located south of Cheraw on US 1. Visitors are welcome to tour some of the ponds, and picnic facilities are available, but there are few formal exhibits here. Free. Open Mon through Fri 8 a.m. to 4 p.m.

The Cheraw Lyceum. Located on the town green on Market Street, the Lyceum was built as a chancery court for the judicial district in 1820. After the court moved to the Market Hall across the street in 1837, the building was used by the gentlemen of the Lyceum as a meeting place and library. It also housed Cheraw's first telegraph, the Confederate and Union quartermaster's office, and the Federal occupation headquarters. In the 20th century it was home to a private library. It now houses a small museum depicting Cheraw's history. Free. The Lyceum can be visited by picking up the keys at the Cheraw Chamber of Commerce (221 Market St.) or by calling the Cheraw Visitors Bureau at (843) 537-8425.

Cheraw State Park. 100 State Park Rd.; (843) 537-9656; southcarolinaparks.com. Cheraw's state park is the oldest in the South Carolina park system and with 7,361 acres is one of the largest, too. In addition to traditional state park amenities, it has a full public 18-hole golf course. The cypress trees of Lake Juniper provide an excellent opportunity for viewing nature while kayaking or canoeing. Rentals are available for $30 per day. Take a walk along the lake's boardwalk, camp by the water's edge, or stay for a week in one of the cozy cabins. Admission is free with fees for various activities. Typically open during daylight hours.

Sand Hills State Forest. US 1 south of Cheraw; (843) 498-6478; state.sc.us. The 46,000 acres of Sand Hills State Forest and Sugar Loaf Mountain provide even more recreational opportunities. Found here are 13 fish ponds, hiking trails, and mountain bike and equestrian trails, as well as camping and picnic sites. The forest is part of the Wildlife Management Area program, and hunting is allowed in season. Some of the rarer plants and animals in the area are the red-cockaded woodpecker, pixie moss, and the pine barren tree frog. The small Sugar Loaf Mountain has been a favorite family gathering place for generations. Free with fees charged for some activities. Typically open during daylight hours.

where to shop

Pee Dee Outfitters. 115 Chesterfield Hwy.; (843) 921-9900; peedeeoutfitters.com. Pee Dee Outfitters is well located with the plethora of outdoor activities available in the region. They offer clothing as well as fishing and camping equipment and supplies. Open Mon through Fri 9 a.m. to 6 p.m., Sat 10 a.m. to 6 p.m.

where to eat

El-Sherif's House of Pizza. 217 2nd St.; (843) 921-0066. The decor here, a blend of Italian and Middle Eastern, is a bit confusing, but the lasagna gets high marks. It is also a good place to stop in for pizza. Substantial American and Greek dishes are also on the menu. Maybe it's the definition of eclectic. $–$$.

The River's Edge Restaurant. 162 2nd St.; (843) 537-1109; theriversedgecheraw.com. Kids and adults are invited to write on the chalkboard that runs the length of the brick wall in this comfortable restaurant. The burgers and steaks on the lunch menu pale by comparison to the long list of desserts. Conveniently, a full bakery is located here, too. Open Mon through Fri 10:30 a.m. to 8:30 p.m. Bakery open 10 a.m. to 3 p.m. $$.

where to stay

Spears Guest House. 228 Huger St.; (888) 424-3729; spearsguesthouse.com. The front porch swing makes a definitive statement that southern charm awaits inside this cottage-style home. Art and antiques fill the 4 available guest rooms and common areas. Sleep in if you like; a continental breakfast is self-served at your leisure. $$.

worth more time
pageland

The Watermelon Capital of the World (though there are others who claim this fame) is only 30 minutes away from Cheraw. Pageland, located on Highway 9 west of Cheraw, hosts an annual Watermelon Festival each July, but it's a worthy detour all summer long. Originating in 1951, the Watermelon Festival now attracts up to 100,000 people annually. It includes melon races, watermelon-eating contests, seed-spitting contests, a parade, a rodeo, a beauty pageant, and more.

day trip 34

columbia, sc

>>>

high cotton:
bishopville, sc; hartsville, sc

The Pee Dee River continues to amble south into the land of cotton, large expanses of low-lying agricultural areas—cotton, tobacco, a little corn, soybean, and a little more cotton. Historically this area has been the state's leader in cotton production, and fittingly, the state established its cotton museum here. Because cotton is no longer king, the area is largely economically depressed with as much as 25 percent of the population living below the poverty level. But it's not without its jewels. A man name Pearl made this area famous with numerous television appearances and magazine articles for his topiary art.

bishopville, sc

The city of Bishopville's population doesn't even break the 3,000 mark, but it's still the seat of the county of Lee. It got its start as a tavern at the corner of Mecklenburg Road and McCallum Ferry Road—now Church and Main Streets. Stagecoaches would stop here en route from Georgetown to Charlotte. Largely wilderness, Bishopville was slow to develop, and even though it was declared the legal county seat in 1892, it would take 10 more years for the courthouse and jail to be built here.

getting there

Bishopville is less than an hour from Columbia, a straight shot on I-20 and just minutes on US 15.

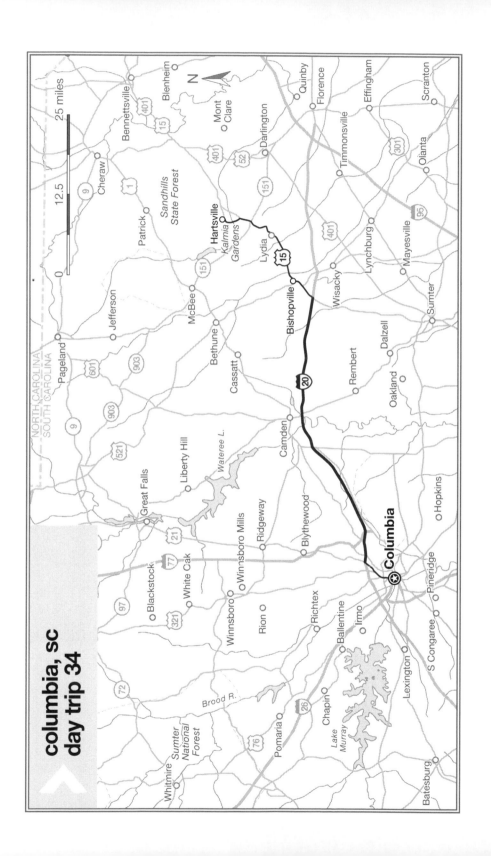

columbia, sc
day trip 34

N

25 miles

0   12.5   25

NORTH CAROLINA
SOUTH CAROLINA

Bennettsville

Blenheim

Mont
Clare

Darlington

Quinby

Florence

Effingham

Scranton

Cheraw

Sandhills
State Forest

Patrick

Jefferson

McBee

Bethune

Cassatt

Pageland

Hartsville

Kalmia
Gardens

Lydia

15

Bishopville

Wisacky

Lynchburg

Mayesville

Sumter

Timmonsville

Olanta

301

95

401

Dalzell

Rembert

Oakland

Hopkins

20

Camden

Wateree L.

Liberty Hill

Great Falls

Blackstock

White Oak

Winnsboro Mills

Ridgeway

Winnsboro

Rion

Richtex

Ballentine

Irmo

Blythewood

Columbia

Pineridge

S Congaree

Lexington

Chapin

Lake
Murray

Pomaria

Brood R.

Sumter
National
Forest

Whitmire

Batesburg

77

21

97

321

72

26

76

521

903

9

601

903

151

1

9

401

52

151

401

where to go

The Button Museum. 55 Joe Dority Rd.; (803) 428-3841; scbuttonking.com. The late Dalton Stevens, the self-proclaimed button king and founder of this roadside attraction, first made his way onto the national scene with an appearance on *The Tonight Show* with Johnny Carson three decades ago. His rise to fame was the result of insomniac behavior that led to the strange hobby of sewing buttons on just about everything he could think of. It started with sewing more than 16,000 buttons on his denim suit. Then he turned to glue and covered his guitar, his shoes, and later an outhouse, a coffin, and even a hearse. Stevens family friends now operate the Button Museum in a quonset hut adjacent to his home. All the items are on display as is a plethora of media coverage, including videos from those Carson shows and appearances on *Late Night with David Letterman*. Admission is free and hours are undetermined.

Fryar's Topiary Garden. 145 Broad Acres Rd.; (803) 484-6495 (the Lee County Chamber of Commerce). Since the 2006 release of the documentary *A Man Named Pearl*, that man, named Pearl Fryar, has been on the speakers' circuit, appearing at garden clubs from South Carolina to New England, at home expos, at schools. He's been on the *Martha Stewart Show*, on *Oprah*, in *Southern Living*. He has an agent. He's received dozens of awards and his work has provided inspiration to millions. Pearl's 2 acres of meticulously sculpted plants, including graceful arches, spirals, geometrics, abstract shapes, and fantasies, are open for touring. The gentle black man with salt-and-pepper hair and mustache has been shaping these topiaries (works of art, really) since the 1980s, pulling discarded items from the mulch piles at local nurseries. Interspersed are found pieces of art and messages of peace, love, and goodwill. If Pearl is in the yard, he's willing to share those messages with you, too. There are no public facilities here. Free. Open Tues through Sat 10 a.m. to 4 p.m.

quirky carolina

At one time a local resident offered a $1 million reward for information leading to the Lizard Man of Scape Ore Swamp. The Lizard Man reportedly destroyed cars and was repeatedly spotted in this area of Bishopville. Lizard Man stories have been told here from colonial times. He apparently took a break following Hurricane Hugo's rampage through here in 1989, not seen or heard from for more than a decade. Residents thought the 7-foot-tall creature had been killed, but unexplained damage near the swamp in recent years leaves them to wonder.

South Carolina Cotton Museum. 121 W. Cedar Ln.; (803) 484-4497; sccotton.org. The money you spend is made partially of cotton. Of course, we've worn cotton since the 1790s, but some cultures even eat cotton. These are among the facts learned when touring South Carolina's official cotton museum. Examine a plantation spinner, a 130-year-old loom, and a 3-foot-tall model of a boll weevil, blamed for wiping out 70 percent of South Carolina's cotton crop in the early part of the 20th century. Admission is $6 for adults, $4 for seniors, $3 for students 5 and older. Open Mon through Sat 10 a.m. to 4 p.m.

where to eat

Harry and Harry, Too. 719 Sumter Highway; (803) 428-4622. The culinary offerings In Bishopville are few and far between, but you can get a nice hamburger steak or a Lizard Man Hoagie here. $$

hartsville, sc

With a population of 8,000 people, Hartsville depends heavily on its largest employer, the Fortune 500 Sonoco Products Company, a worldwide supplier of packaging products. Settlement of the area dates to around 1760 by Captain Thomas E. Hart, who established a farm and mercantile here, and for whom the city is named. His son John Law Hart followed in his father's footsteps by helping establish a plantation in the area of the current downtown as well as a handful of other businesses in the middle of the 19th century.

getting there

Hartsville is accessible via US 15 from Bishopville.

where to go

Black Creek Arts Center. 116 W. College Ave.; (843) 332-6234; blackcreekarts.org. This 10,000-square-foot facility includes gallery space dedicated largely to regional artists. It displays rotating works for a month or 2 at a time and frequently features artists from the Cotton Trail, a group of about 30 who produce work based on the influence of cotton to this region. Other periodic and annual events are based at the arts center, including an artist's crawl that engages actors and musicians as well as visual artists. Open Tues through Thurs 10 a.m. to 5 p.m., Fri 10 a.m. to 2 p.m., and the second Sat of the month 10 a.m. to 1 p.m.

Coker Farm. 1257 S. 4th St.; (843) 383-3005. In 1903 David Coker opened Coker Experimental Farms, a part of the Pedigreed Seed Company, to develop a cotton-breeding program that would produce long staple cotton that could be grown throughout the South. Over time Coker broadened his work to include other field crops as well. By the 1960s more than half of all cotton, oats, tobacco, corn, and soybean could be traced to this research. Today the property has been recognized on the National Register of Historic Places and has been

> ## south carolina cotton trail

This driving tour connects many of the attractions and historic sites in Cheraw, Bishopville, Hartsville, Darlington, and more. It begins at I-20 in Bishopville and ends at I-95 near Dillon. It enables drivers to enjoy many of the historic homes, farms, and barns along the way. For more information, log on to schistorytrail.com.

designated a National Historic Landmark, one of only 14 representing agricultural industry in the country. Exhibits depicting the company's impact on southern agriculture are housed in a replica of the site's original dairy barn. Free. Open daily 9 a.m. to 6 p.m.

Hartsville Museum. 222 N. 5th St.; (843) 383-3005; hartsvillemuseum.org. Housed in a 1930s post office building, the Hartsville Museum includes a centerpiece exhibit, *Cotton, Field to Fabric*, as well as a collection of early 20th-century silver, and a number of other historic pieces related to Native American occupation of the area, and to the pride and joy of Hartsville, major-league pitcher Bobo Newsome. Free. Open Mon through Fri 10 a.m. to 5 p.m., Sat 10 a.m. to 3 p.m.

Kalmia Gardens. 1624 W. Carolina Ave.; (843) 383-8145; kalmiagardens.org. Now a part of Coker College, Kalmia was named for its many mountain laurel, the *Kalmia latifolia*. It was originally developed by May Roper Coker, who obtained the land from her brother-in-law Dr. William Chambers Coker, head of the Botany Department at UNC–Chapel Hill. The 56-acre garden began as Miss May's Folly, a run-down dump site that was turned into an immaculate setting. She deeded the gardens to Coker College in 1965 in memory of her husband, David Coker. Areas include an expanded boardwalk down to and along Black Creek, a sensory garden, an herb garden, and a memory garden. The gardens also border the 700-acre Segars-McKinnon Heritage Preserve. Free. Typically open during daylight hours.

where to eat

Bow Thai Kitchen. 150 E. Carolina Ave.; (843) 917-4026. From simple fried rice and pad thai to more complex dishes such as basil duck, this restaurant gets high marks across the board for authenticity. Located a block from campus, it's popular with the cost-conscious college crowd. Open Mon through Thurs 11 a.m. to 2:30 p.m. and 5 to 9 p.m., Fri 11 a.m. to 3 p.m. and 5 to 9:30 p.m., Sat noon to 2:30 p.m. and 5 to 9:30 p.m. $$.

The Rooster 136. 136 E. Carolina Ave.; (843) 383-0800; therooster136.com. This is Hartsville's go-to place for breakfast and brunch. Fresh coffee, cold brews, and espresso all make it onto the menu alongside blueberry pancake, spinach omelets, and many other selections. $$

where to stay

Oak Manor Inn. 314 E. Home Ave.; (843) 383-9553; oakmanorinn.com. Expansive lawns and manicured gardens beneath 100-year-old live oaks and cedar trees create a classic southern home atmosphere. The stately Federalist-style inn includes a backyard patio and well-appointed rooms—some with fireplaces. $$.

day trip 35

columbia, sc

> **a day at the races:**
> darlington, sc; florence, sc

Find the track that can't be tamed on this day trip. This is the home of Darlington Raceway and Stock Car Museum. The track is the oldest paved raceway in America, and it still holds two major NASCAR contests each year. While cotton still fills the roadside here well into fall, this is now tobacco country and boasts South Carolina's tobacco museum as well as the War Between the States Museum.

darlington, sc

In 1985 the city of Darlington unveiled a mural by Columbia artist Blue Sky, depicting a scene from the Public Square from the early part of the 20th century. The trees are a little taller now, but they still line the streets. The cars in the painting are a little different than they are today, but other than that, the Public Square in Darlington looks much like it did 100 years ago. Darlington has managed to maintain its timeless charm and unparalleled friendliness.

The city's origins date to the late 1700s when the state was being divided into districts. It is believed that the Public Square and courthouse are located here today because of an argument between Colonel Lamuel Benton and Captain Elias Dubose. One wanted the courthouse in Mechanicsville, the other wanted it in Cuffey Town. To settle the dispute, they agreed each to depart from his favored location and ride out on horseback until they met. Thus, they split the difference and had the courthouse built in the compromise location. Fire destroyed the original structure a few years later, but it was rebuilt with brick in 1825.

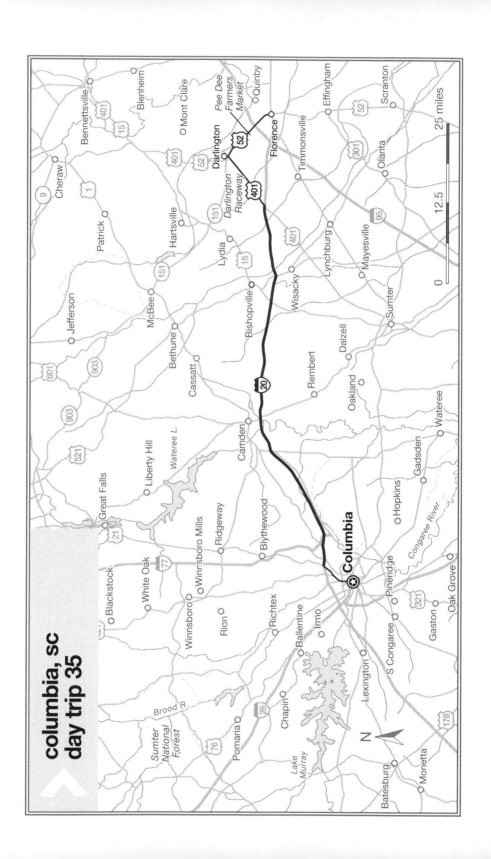

25 miles

12.5

0

N

Columbia

Quinby

*Pee Dee
Farmers
Market*

Florence

Scranton

Effingham

Blenheim

Mont Clare

Timmonsville

52

Olanta

Darlington

52

52

301

Bennettsville

401

15

*Darlington
Raceway*

401

95

Cheraw

1

401

151

Lynchburg

Mayesville

9

Patrick

Hartsville

151

Lydia

15

401

Wisacky

Sumter

Jefferson

McBee

Bishopville

Dalzell

601

903

Bethune

Rembert

Oakland

Wateree

903

Cassatt

20

Gadsden

521

Wateree L.

Liberty Hill

Camden

Hopkins

Congaree River

Great Falls

Winnsboro Mills

Ridgeway

Blythewood

21

77

White Oak

Pineridge

321

Oak Grove

Blackstock

Winnsboro

Rion

Richtex

Ballantine

Irmo

S Congaree

Gaston

Brood R.

Chapin

26

*Lake
Murray*

Lexington

178

*Sumter
National
Forest*

76

Pomaria

Batesburg

Monetta

getting there

From Columbia, Darlington is about 1 hour and 15 minutes away driving east on I-20. Take exit 131 for US 401 North.

where to go

Darlington Raceway. 1301 Harry Byrd Hwy.; (843) 395-8499; darlingtonraceway.com. The Southern 500 (as it is called now), part of the NASCAR Cup Series, is held at Darlington Raceway each year in the fall. Also at the track is the Darlington Stock Car Museum that takes fans down memory lane with classic cars and other memorabilia. The museum includes the National Motorsports Press Association Hall of Fame with photos and memorabilia of those who have covered the sport. Open Mon through Fri 10 a.m. to 5 p.m., Sat. 10 a.m. to 4 p.m., Sun 11 a.m. to 4 p.m. Museum admission is $5, free for ages 12 and under.

Edmund H. Deas House. 229 Avenue E; (888) 427-8720. Known as the Duke of Darlington, Edmund H. Deas was the African-American chairman of the Darlington County Republican Party from 1884 to 1888. He ran for Congress twice but was never elected. He was however a delegate to the Republican National Convention 4 times. Deas's house where he lived until his death is an excellent example of Victorian vernacular architecture. It is not open for tours, but can be visited on a walking tour of the historic district.

Williamson Park. Spring Street; williamsonpark.org. Located just a few blocks from downtown, this quiet respite is full of birds, trees, and other plants. A 3-mile-long boardwalk serpentines through the 60-acre park, and it, along with several other trails, offers an excellent opportunity to view nature in this cyprus swamp environment. There is also a great spot for picnicking. Free. Typically open during daylight hours.

where to eat

Carolina Lunch and Dairy Bar. 318 Pearl St.; (843) 393-4531. This local fast-food joint has been in Darlington about as long as anyone can remember. Stop in here for a hot dog and a big sloppy order of chili cheese fries. Open for breakfast and lunch. $.

Joe's Grill. 306 Russell St.; (843) 393-9140. Good solid traditional southern fare comes out of the kitchen at Joe's. The sign out front says that it's been in business since 1952. Although it's one of only a few independent restaurants in Darlington, you won't likely be disappointed with Joe's beef stew, roasted chicken, or any of the similar offerings. $$.

florence, sc

One of the original towns laid out by the Lord Proprietors in 1719, Florence wasn't well settled or well populated until the railroads set up here. That change was set in motion in

1850 when the Wilmington & Manchester and the Northeastern intersected here. Later the Cheraw and Darlington Railroad would run through town, too, making it a major hub. General W. W. Harley, president of the W&M, built a home here and named it after his daughter. During the Civil War it was the site of a stockade and brought prominence to Harry Timrod, the "Poet Laureate of the Civil War," who taught school here. Today its economy remains stronger than many of its neighbors: it's a major medical center and a financial hub with regional headquarters for J.P. Morgan Chase, BB&T, and Bank of America.

getting there

A 20-minute ride south on US 52 takes the driver from Darlington to Florence near the intersection with I-95.

where to go

Dooley Planetarium at Francis Marion University. 4822 E. Palmetto St.; (843) 661-1381; astro.fmarion.edu. Located in the Cauthen Education Media Center at Francis Marion University is this 33-foot planetarium dome and star projector. It was established largely for public schoolchildren, but shows open to all are presented on the second and fourth Sunday of each month at 3 p.m. Admission is free.

Florence County Museum. 111 W. Chevis St.; (843) 676-1200; florencemuseum.org. The Florence County Museum reopened in a sleek, contemporary, 2-story building in 2014 after a decade of planning and with 65 million years of history in hand. Its collection of art and historical objects include Cretaceous-period material and an ancient bald cyprus trunk. In addition to preserving the history of the county, the museum also stages temporary art exhibitions that have a link to the South and the city's history and culture. Open Tues through Sat 10 a.m. to 5 p.m. and Sun 2 to 5 p.m. Admission is free.

mars bluff

Located on and around the campus of Francis Marion University in an area known as Mars Bluff are several sites related to African Americans' impact on the city. Of particular interest are 2 hand-hewn timber cabins dating to about 1836. Built as slave cabins, they would become the homes of emancipated slaves, who could continue to work on area farms. Also here are a cemetery from the same period and an early 20th-century schoolhouse. Download a map to the sites at visitflo.com or call (843) 661-1311 to gain access to the insides of the cabins.

Francis Marion University Performing Arts Center. 201 S. Dargan St.; (843) 661-1720; fmupac.org. This spectacular performing arts center on the university campus is becoming the center of cultural life in Florence. In addition to providing office and practice space for students, it is a major, state-of-the-art facility for local organizations and national touring acts with its main stage with 849 seats and a smaller black box venue.

where to shop

Pee Dee State Farmers Market. US 52, 1 mile north of I-95; (843) 665-5154; agriculture .sc.gov. The official state farmers market offers the biggest and best selection of local fruits, produce, plants, and flowers. Because of its location, it's always busy, but friendly vendors seem to have time to pick out a good watermelon or bushel of peaches regardless. Open Mon through Sat 8 a.m. to 6 p.m.

Young Pecan Plantations. 2230 Baber Ln.; (843) 662-2452; youngplantations.com. You could order pecans from this producer off the Internet, but there is nothing quite like going there, trying some samples, and picking them out yourself. Find a variety of candies, gift baskets, and whole new ways to enjoy pecans. Open Mon through Sat 9 a.m. to 7 p.m., Sun noon to 6 p.m.

worth more time

South Carolina Tobacco Museum. 104 Northeast Front St., Mullins; (843) 464-8194; mullins.sc.us. Just a 30-minute drive east of Florence on US 301/76 is the official museum of tobacco for the state. It depicts life on a tobacco farm prior to 1950 with displays that illustrate the growing cycle and production cycle from field to auction. A short film explains the early importance of tobacco to the region and how auctions were conducted here. On exhibit is equipment such as wagons, a reconstructed pole barn, and tools. It is housed in a turn-of-the-century train depot. Free. Open Mon through Fri 9 a.m. to 5 p.m.

charleston, sc

day trip 36

charleston, sc

>>>

the low country:
charleston, sc

charleston, sc

The coast undoubtedly makes the greatest contribution to South Carolina's tourism economy, but it has many different alluring attributes. If each of its regions were to participate in
a beauty contest, Charleston would get high marks for beauty, grace, charm, congeniality,
and bonus points for its cooking. This port city is a historic and cultural gem, but some less
familiar travelers may miss the fact that it's not right on the coast. Many vacationers can
enjoy its offerings, however, by selecting one of the nearby islands for their annual vacation,
and day trip to Charleston's old-time market, its many restaurants, sprawling plantations,
and historical and cultural attractions. Those island communities are covered later; the day-
tripper can jump right in to Charleston.

Originally established as Charles Towne in honor of King Charles II in 1670, it would
be 100 years before this city became Charleston, then one of the largest cities in North
America. Its location at the confluence of the Ashley and Cooper Rivers, where locals jok-
ingly (or maybe seriously) claim the Atlantic Ocean begins, made it particularly defensible for
resistance against Native Americans and attacks by pirates as well as Spain and France,
who contested English rule of the New World. Though largely populated by the English, it
was ripe for settlement by all people coming from Europe. This created a melting pot of
cultures and religions, including the largest and wealthiest Jewish community in the country.

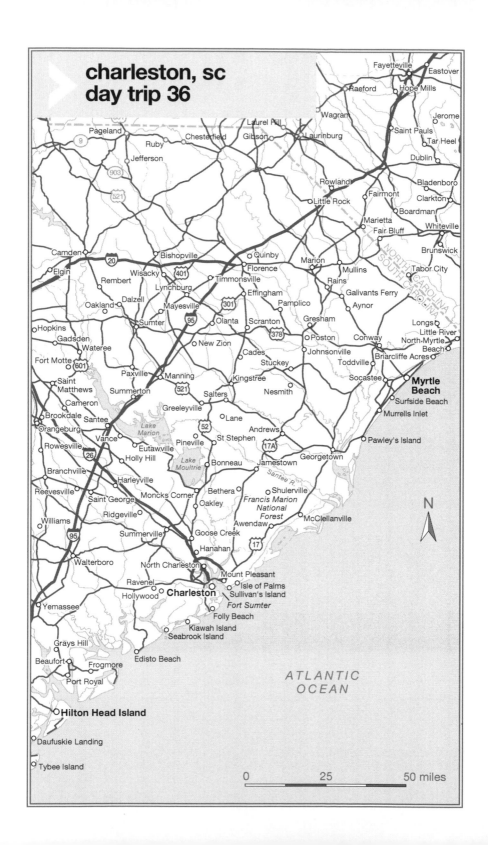

charleston, sc
day trip 36

Throughout the 18th century the port helped the city flourish with the development of the deerskin trade and growing rice plantations and their related exports.

Charleston became the site of the greatest defeat of the American Revolution when 5,260 American men were captured by 14,000 British in the Siege of Charleston in 1780. The British would occupy the city for two years, after which it became Charleston and cotton became king. Slaves were imported and sold here, as they became important throughout the New World to the cotton and other industries, and by 1820 more than half the city's population was black. Union-held Fort Sumter, which can be seen from downtown's Battery Park and visited by boat, became known as the site where the first shots of the Civil War were fired. The city was repeatedly bombarded by Union forces, which finally took control of the city in 1865, remaining there through much of Reconstruction. Thereafter, freed slaves lived in poverty, and the city's economy was nearly in ruins. In a cruel twist of fate, a major earthquake in 1886 nearly destroyed the city as it was struggling to recover from the bloody war.

Most of the first half of the 20th century brought tough economic times to the port city, too; nothing seemed to help, though a military presence propped it up throughout this period. Recommitted to a cultural and historical renaissance, the city began to blossom in the 1970s. Historical structures were restored, and city leaders embraced Charleston's cultural heritage and began to make investments in the tourism industry, which now boasts a major aquarium, a restored waterfront, that famous city market, and restaurants with chefs coming from the Johnson and Wales University located here. Today it's the state's second-largest city and simply a fun place to be.

getting there

I-26 cuts through the partial loop I-526 and runs into Charleston from the east. US 17, which runs the coast of the Carolinas, enters the city from the north and exits south before ending at I-95 between Charleston and Hilton Head.

where to go

Aiken-Rhett House. 48 Elizabeth St.; (843) 723-1159; historiccharleston.org. Occupied most prominently beginning in 1827 by William Aiken Jr., a former governor, one of South Carolina's wealthiest rice planters, and son of the canal and railroad pioneer, this home appears much the same today as it did then. Though it received updates for several decades, the Historic Charleston Foundation preserves it as it was when the Aikens lived here. It is now operated as a museum of art and history and houses many of the luxurious items the Aikens purchased during their travels to Europe. Admission is $15 for adults, $7 for children ages 6 to 16. Open daily 10 a.m. to 5 p.m.

Carriage Tours. Downtown Charleston. A handful of private companies operate carriage tours in downtown Charleston, and these are a great primer for exploring the city. Costumed guides are entertaining and knowledgeable in their presentation of historical references. Here are a few from which you can choose: **Classic Carriage Tours** (10 Guignard St.; 843-853-3747; classiccarriage.com); **Old South Carriage Company** (14 Anson St.; 843-723-9712; oldsouthcarriage.com); **Olde Towne Carriage Company** (20 Anson St.; 800-979-3370; oldetownecarriages.com); **Palmetto Carriage Works** (8 Guignard St.; 800-979-3370; palmettocarriage.com).

The Charleston Museum. 360 Meeting St.; (843) 722-2996; charlestonmuseum.org. Established in 1773, the Charleston Museum claims to be the oldest in America and now maintains 2 historic Charleston homes as well as this traditional history/natural history museum and a wildlife sanctuary on nearby James Island. At the museum facility, examine fossils, view a giant toothed whale skeleton, and explore a variety of prehistoric artifacts. The museum also preserves Civil War items and significant pieces of silver and clothing collections. Admission to the museum and each of the following homes is $12 for adults, $5 for children 3 to 12, and $10 for ages 13 to 17. Combination packages are also available. Open Mon through Sat 9 a.m. to 5 p.m., Sun noon to 5 p.m.

> **The Joseph Manigault House,** 350 Meeting St., is a National Historic Landmark built by the French Huguenot family that came to America to engage in the burgeoning rice business of the late 18th century.

> **Heyward-Washington House,** 87 Church St., was built in 1772 by rice planter Daniel Heyward as a town house for his son, Thomas Heyward Jr., who would solidify his own legacy as a signer of the Declaration of Independence and patriot leader. George Washington rented the home for a week in 1791, thus having his name attached to it.

Charleston Pirate Tours. Departing from the Powder Magazine, 79 Cumberland St.; (843) 442-7299; charlestonpiratetour.com. South Carolina native and swashbuckling pirate Eric Lavender, along with his macaw, Captain Bob, leads tours and storytelling events at various venues in Charleston. His most popular event is a 2-hour walking tour of Old Charles Towne. Eric tells stories of pirates and other characters from the town of old while providing an

angel oak

At 65 feet tall, the Angel Oak provides an estimated 17,000 square feet of shade under its massive, sprawling limbs. At 1,400 years old, this live oak tree appears to be a bit tired with some of its massive limbs resting on the ground. The tree is located at 3688 Angel Oak Rd. on John's Island southwest of Charleston.

overview of the city's history. Tours are also offered Wed, Fri, and Sat evening at 7:30 p.m. Tickets are $25 for adults and $15 for children.

Charles Towne Landing State Historic Site. 1500 Old Towne Rd.; (843) 852-4200; southcarolinaparks.com. In 1670 a group of English settlers landed near here to establish a new colony. Today the state historic site interprets their lives through a history trail with an audio tour, programs, and exhibits. Costumed guides lead visitors through the site that includes a replica of the 17th-century ship called the *Adventure.* A 12-room interactive museum is especially engaging for children with interactive exhibits that utilize video and technology. The property also houses a small natural-habitat zoo and historic gardens. The site is an active archaeological dig where visitors can view excavation projects in process. Admission is $12 for adults, $7 for ages 6 to 15. Open daily 9 a.m. to 5 p.m.

The Citadel. 171 Moultrie St., (843) 225-3294; citadel.edu. The famous Military College of South Carolina has operated with its Corps of Cadets since 1842. While there are few formal attractions on campus, visitors can venture into the Citadel Museum that includes a time line of the college's history, photos, uniforms, and archival documents. A cadet dress parade is held near the museum nearly every Friday at 3:45 p.m. The museum is open daily noon to 5 p.m.

Dock Street Theatre. 135 Church St.; (843) 577-7183; charlestonstage.com. Opened in 1736, Dock Street was the first building in the country constructed exclusively for theatrical productions. It was destroyed by fire 4 years later, then the Planters Hotel was built on the site in 1809. Following tough economic years after the Civil War, the hotel fell into disrepair, but was converted to the second Dock Street Theatre as a Depression-era Works Progress Administration project. Its second grand opening was held more than 100 years following the original one. Renovated in 2010 and now owned by the city, the theater is home to the renowned Spoleto Festival; Charleston Stage, the city's resident acting company; and dozens of productions each season.

Drayton Hall. 3380 Ashley River Rd.; (842) 769-2600; draytonhall.org. A National Trust Historic Site, Drayton Hall is a marvelous brick Georgian-Palladian structure that survived the American Revolution, the Civil War, the great earthquake of 1886, and even 1989's Hurricane Hugo. And it is impeccably preserved here to tell striking stories of slavery, of culture, and of sacrifice. John Drayton began construction of the home on the 630-acre site in 1738, and it would remain in the Drayton family until they sold it to the National Trust in 1974. It and the rice plantation the family operated here remain largely intact. In addition to detailing the Draytons' remarkable history, it also tells the story of 7 generations of the Bowen family, slaves who lived and worked here. Fine arts, decorative pieces, and other items also help docents put together this piece of American history. Admission is $24 for adults, $10 for ages 12 to 18, $6 for ages 6 to 11. Guided tours are offered Mon through Sat 9 a.m. to 3:20 p.m., Sun 11 a.m. to 3:20 p.m.

historic battery park

Despite its violent past, this historic site is a remarkably beautiful and peaceful location for an afternoon or evening stroll. It's located where Meeting Street ends just south of the Edmonston House. Affording stunning views of Charleston Harbor, Battery Park and White Point Gardens show off the drastic contrast of graceful oak trees and cannons used in the Civil War. It was here that Stede Bonnet and other 18th-century pirates were hanged at the town gallows. Now it provides access to boardwalks, paths, and fountains where children cool off in the summer.

Edmondston-Alston House. 21 E. Battery; (843) 722-7171; edmondstonalston.com. Located on Charleston's famous Battery, overlooking Charleston Harbor is this ca. 1825 home built by a Scottish shipping merchant. From here Gen. P. T. Beauregard would watch troops bombard Fort Sumter the night the Civil War began. Eight months later Robert E. Lee would be forced to take refuge here as Union troops burned his Charleston hotel. Built in the Federal style, the home was bought by Charles Alston of a prominent rice-planting family in 1827, who began adding Greek Revival features. Those distinctions are prominent during tours that also include an opportunity to view furniture, portraits, and other items that trace the home's history. Admission is $15 for adults, $10 for students and children. Open Mon 1 to 4 p.m. and Tues through Sat 10 a.m. to 4 p.m.

Gibbes Museum of Art. 135 Meeting St.; (843) 722-2706; gibbesmuseum.org. The Gibbes Museum collects colonial, local renaissance, and contemporary art and stages a variety of exhibitions from its own and loaned pieces. It owns an extensive collection of portraits as well as a body of work produced between 1915 and 1940. The museum describes that period as an artistic rebirth when many American artists, including those as well-known as Norman Rockwell, came to document the city's architecture and cultural heritage. Finally, the museum collects a wide variety of art from local artists in a variety of forms. Admission is $12 for adults, $10 for students and seniors, $6 for ages 6 to 12. Open Tues through Sat 10 a.m. to 5 p.m., Sun 1 to 5 p.m.

James Island County Park. 871 Riverland Dr.; (843) 795-7275; ccprc.com. Tidal creeks and lagoons create opportunities for fishing and crabbing at this 643-acre park located on James Island on the Folly Beach side of Charleston. Volleyball courts, horseshoe pits, and camping sites, as well as rental cottages, are located here. There is more contemporary fun on the slides and lazy river of the Splash Zone Water Park, open seasonally. The park is also the site of a summer reggae music festival, low-country Cajun festival, and other events throughout the year. The park is typically open during daylight hours. Gate admission is $2 per person, and other fees apply to various attractions.

Magnolia Plantation and Garden. 3550 Ashley River Rd.; (843) 571-1266; magnolia plantation.com. Classic Charleston with Spanish moss hanging from sprawling limbs of ancient oak trees is epitomized in this remarkable spot. Camellias and azaleas added by various generations of the Drayton family that have lived on the plantation for 300 years are spread throughout this spectacular piece of property. It's been a public garden (the oldest in America) since 1870, and has developed into one of Charleston's premier attractions. The experience now includes a tram ride and a boat ride through flooded rice fields. On either venture guests are likely to pass alligators and turtles lounging quietly on logs or to spy a great blue heron or egret among the other wildlife. Founded by the Drayton family in 1676, Magnolia became an important rice plantation as America was being colonized. In more recent years the plantation restored 5 slave cabins in an effort to tell the story of how

religious melting pot

Charleston's churches were important to the city's development throughout its history, and many of the original structures dating to the 18th century remain to help tell its story. While the earliest settlers primarily came from England, colonial Charleston was also home to French, Scottish, Irish, and Germans, representing numerous Protestant denominations, as well as Catholicism and Judaism. Sephardic Jews from Spain and Portugal migrated to the city in such numbers that Charleston became one of the largest Jewish communities in North America.

St. Michael's Episcopal (80 Meeting St.; 843-723-0603), Charleston's oldest church, was built on the city's square in 1752. The Jewish Coming Street Cemetery (189 Coming St.), owned by Kahal Kadosh Beth Elohim Synagogue (90 Hasell St.) first established in 1762, attests to their long-standing presence in the community. The first Anglican church, St. Philip's Episcopal, originally built in 1682, was destroyed by fire twice before relocated to its current location (146 Church St.). Free blacks and slaves helped establish the Old Bethel United Methodist Church (222 Calhoun St.) in 1797, and the congregation of the Emanuel A.M.E. Church (110 Calhoun St.), the site of a tragic massacre in June 2015, stems from a religious group organized solely by African Americans in 1791. The French Protestant Church of Charleston was founded in approximately 1681 by Huguenot refugees from the Protestant persecutions in France. The first two churches were destroyed, and a third was built at its current location (44 Queens St.) in 1845.

significant the Gullah people were to the Charleston culture. A swamp garden is located adjacent to Magnolia and a nature center and small zoo are housed on the garden site. Admission is $29 for adults, $15 for children 6 to 12. Additional fees are charged for the other tours and attractions. Open daily 10 a.m. to 5 p.m.

Middleton Place. 4300 Ashley River Rd.; (843) 556-6020; middletonplace.org. Sculpted terraced lawns, swans floating gracefully on a pond, and a stable yard overlooking the rice fields compose the portrait created on this hillside plantation that is now a living museum. A National Historic Landmark, the 65 acres of Middleton Place include immaculate gardens, a museum created at the birthplace of one the signers of the Declaration of Independence, and a stable yard inhabited by water buffalo and cashmere goats. Allowing the symmetry and geometry of the European style of the time to guide the design, Henry Middleton began to create this garden in 1741. It took almost a decade to create walkways, allées, and the artificial lake that extends beyond the plantings dominated by camellias blooming in winter and azaleas putting on their show in spring. About the same time Middleton began to build a 3-house complex here, but the structure known as the South Flanker (ca. 1755) is the only one still standing—two others burned during the Civil War. It's now a museum that includes artifacts from 3 centuries of the Middleton descendants, which includes Arthur Middleton, who signed the Declaration of Independence. Original portraits, silver, furniture, documents, and other items provide a chronicle of their lives and tell the story of the slaves who served them. Costumed guides demonstrate various trades of the late 18th and early 19th century at the stable yard. Here the most skilled of slaves cared for animals and made tools, pottery, and clothes. A casual restaurant and small, comfortable inn are also located on the property. Admission is $26 for adults, $15 for students age 14 and over, $10 for ages 6 to 13, and includes a guided tour of the gardens. The house tour is additional. Open daily 9 a.m. to 5 p.m.

North Charleston and American LaFrance Fire Museum. 4975 Centre Point Dr.; (843) 740-5550; legacyofheroes.org. More than a dozen shiny red trucks and a variety of historic firefighting equipment, dating back to the mid-1700s, fill this massive museum. It provides a time line for the firefighter and advances in equipment that made the firefighter's job safer. It includes interactive components allowing the visitor a great opportunity to experience what it is like to fight fires. The immersive Home Fire Hazard Theatre will give day-trippers a greater respect for firefighters and help them keep their homes safer, too. Admission is $6 for adults, free for children ages 12 and under. Open Mon through Sat 10 a.m. to 5 p.m., Sun 1 to 5 p.m.

North Charleston Wanamaker Park. 8888 University Blvd.; (843) 572-7275; ccprc.com. Part of the county system, this park spreads out over 1,000 acres of wetlands and woodlands. It provides a great place for a picnic, after which you can rent a bike, pedal boat, or kayak. Whirling Waters Adventure Water Park is also located here and includes a toddler play area, wave pool, 347-foot mat slide, lazy river, and more. Admission to the park is $1 per person with additional fees for other activities. The park is typically open during daylight hours with more limited seasonal hours for the water park.

Old Exchange and Provost Dungeon. 122 E. Bay St.; (843) 727-2165; oldexchange.org. Built by the British as a customs house in 1771, the architecturally significant building held captive American patriots and fierce pirates. Slaves were sold here, and George Washington delivered a speech from the steps. It is now owned by the South Carolina Daughters of the American Revolution, which offers tours through its 3 stories. Animated and knowledgeable docents lead groups through the creepy confines of the dungeon and give context to architectural details and artifacts. Admission is $10 for adults, $5 for students and ages 4 to 12. Open daily 9 a.m. to 5 p.m.

Old Slave Mart Museum. 6 Chalmers St.; (843) 958-6467; charleston-sc.gov. From 1808 to 1856 the Old Exchange building and other less significant locations served as auction sites for the slave trade, precipitated by the federal government's ban on participating in international slave trade and growth of southern plantations. In 1856 when the city of Charleston passed an ordinance prohibiting the public sale of slaves, traders opened the private Old Slave Mart on the site that is now a museum. Though several other sites opened, too, the Old Slave Mart is believed to be the only South Carolina auction site still in existence. It became a museum with African-American arts and crafts and other displays in 1964. The city purchased it in 1988. Admission is free. Open Mon through Sat 9 a.m. to 5 p.m.

Powder Magazine. 79 Cumberland St.; 843-722-9350; powdermag.org. The oldest public building in the Carolinas is the Powder Magazine, an extravagant structure with a pragmatic purpose. It was originally completed in 1713 and housed the public supply of gunpowder when a wall surrounded this city. Now it's a museum where day-trippers can explore Charleston's Colonial history. Admission is $6 for adults and $4 for children. Open Mon through Sat 10 a.m. to 4 p.m. and Sun 1 to 4 p.m.

South Carolina Aquarium. 100 Aquarium Wharf; (843) 577-3474; scaquarium.org. Pet a stingray, touch a shark, play alongside otters, marvel at endangered loggerhead turtles, and maybe even see a dolphin in the wild at this outstanding facility. The South Carolina Aquarium opened on Charleston Harbor in 2000 with dozens of exhibits that take the visitor from the aquatic habitats of Appalachia to the deep blue sea. A 3-story Ocean Gallery aquarium is home to more than 400 species including sharks and other massive forms of sea life. Smaller exhibits allow guests to explore jellyfish, crabs, moray eels, and other creatures. An outdoor terrace overlooking the harbor becomes a classroom on conservation, dolphins, and other life that inhabit shallow waters on the Carolina coast. A sea turtle hospital serves as the state's only respite for the sick and injured animals. Tours of that facility should be scheduled in advance and are an additional cost. General admission is $29.95 for adults, $22.95 for ages 2 to 11. Open daily 9 a.m. to 5 p.m.

rainbow row

Pastel pink, yellow, and blue colors coat the houses of this popular and oft-photographed Charleston landmark. Located on East Bay Street between Tradd and Elliot Streets, the homes were built as commercial buildings in the middle of the 18th century. Dorothy Porcher Legge purchased several of the homes in the early 1900s, painted them in the bright Caribbean colors, and started a trend. Other homeowners soon followed suit.

where to shop

Charleston Crafts Cooperative. 161 Church St.; (843) 723-2938; shopcharelestoncrafts .org. Featuring the work of 30 or more local craftspeople, this cooperative offers handmade baskets and works in clay, metal, paper, and more. To be permitted into the co-op, an artist must have made the items in South Carolina, and each month a different artist is given the opportunity for a feature exhibition in the gallery. Open daily 10 a.m. to 6 p.m.

Cupcake. 433 King St.; (433) 853-8181; freshcupcakes.com. Venture to the edge of downtown (you can walk) to this funky cupcake shop for its popular red velvet cupcake with cream cheese icing. Not a fan of red velvet? Then become a fan of the blueberry cobbler and cinnamon streusel cupcake or one of the other 50 flavors. The only drawback is that since everything is fresh and made from scratch, you only get to choose from about a dozen flavors each day. There's a second location in nearby Mount Pleasant. Open Mon through Wed 10 a.m. to 7 p.m., Thurs through Sat 10 a.m. to 10 p.m., Sun noon to 5 p.m.

French Quarter Art Galleries. 2 Queen St.; (843) 805-8052. Charleston's French Quarter is the city's epicenter of visual arts. With more than 30 galleries located within a 10-block area between South Market, Tradd, and Meeting Streets, it provides access to local arts, fine art, and a diverse selection of styles and media. The first Friday in March, May, October, and December at 8 p.m., the French Quarter Gallery Association sponsors a Gallery Walk. Hours of galleries vary.

Historic Charleston City Market. Located on Market Street between Meeting and Bay Streets. This famous open-air market has been in operation here since 1841 along a 3-block stretch led by a Greek Revival facade at Market Street. Here young boys, imitating Gullah women weaving sweetgrass baskets retailing for hundreds of dollars, hock simple woven roses for a few bucks. Through the market, shoppers discover fine art, souvenirs, spices for making low-country cuisine, home decor, clothing, and more. Vendors start business in the early morning hours and typically stay until 6 p.m.

The Shops and Belmond. Charleston Place Hotel. With entries on King Street, this Is a self-enclosed hotel of a couple dozen high-end shops. Here find Gucci, Louis Vuitton, and other luxury brands.

King Street Antique District. charlestonsfinest.com. This long stretch of shops is noted as one of the best antiques districts in the Carolinas. Upscale dealers and more typical vendors offer everything from estate jewelry to furniture. The bustling district is also full of clothing boutiques, restaurants, and other places to visit.

where to eat

Husk. 76 Queen St.; (843) 577-2500; huskrestaurant.com. One of Charleston's most popular restaurants, Husk Is unapologetically and consistently committed to providing food from the south, but the approach is uncommon. What arrives to your table are deviled eggs with pickled okra or pork lettuce wraps. The menu changes almost daily. Open for dinner at 5 p.m. daily and for brunch at 10 a.m. Sat and Sun.

Hyman's Seafood. 215 Meeting St.; (843) 723-6000; hymanseafood.com. A carriage driver recommended this seafood restaurant, saying, "It's not too expensive but it's good." He was right—good prices and great food. Small plaques with the names of the rich and famous who have dined here are tacked to the tables where they ate, many of them opting to order the famous and delectable whole flounder. Expect a bit of a wait outside this crowded store front of brick and oyster mortar. Find everything from oyster po'boys to shrimp and grits on the menu here. Open daily at 11 a.m. $–$$.

Magnolias. 185 E. Bay St.; (843) 577-7771; magnoliascharleston.com. Chef and cookbook author Donald Barickman developed a concept of uptown-downtown south cooking at his popular restaurant more than 20 years ago. It's southern cuisine with a twist. Simple shrimp and grits becomes a dish with shrimp, scallops, and lobster. A buttermilk fried chicken breast is served with sausage herb gravy. And daily, chefs prepare a changing vegetarian

gullah

Once spanning from the Cape Fear Coast in North Carolina to northern Florida, the population of African Americans known as Gullahs is now prominent only in the low country of South Carolina and Georgia. The Gullah people work to preserve their culture through crafts such as their sweet-smelling and high-quality sweetgrass baskets and are noted for their distinct lilting language. An English Creole hybrid, it is influenced by languages of the Caribbean.

dish with fresh selections. Regardless of the entree it all begins with a fried green tomato on cheesy grits. Open Mon through Sat 11:30 a.m. to 3:45 p.m. and Sun through Thurs 3:45 to 10 p.m., Fri and Sat 3:45 to 11 p.m., Sun 10 a.m. to 3:45 p.m. $$.

Poogan's Porch. 72 Queen St.; (843) 577-2337; poogansporch.com. Located in a brightly colored Victorian home with outside dining on 3 levels, Poogan's is one of Charleston's best-known restaurants. From biscuits to its extensive wine list, everything about it is elegant but down-home. Its shrimp and grits receives regular accolades. Open daily 9 a.m. to 9:30 p.m. $$$.

where to stay

Charleston Place Hotel. 205 Meeting St.; (843) 722-4900; charlestonplace.com. Charleston's premier hotel address, Charleston Place, is located in the historic district and offers first-class accommodations and amenities. The hotel includes a spa with a saltwater pool, Jacuzzi, and top-quality fitness center. Upscale shops and award-winning restaurants are also located here. $$$.

Francis Marion Hotel. 387 King St.; (843) 722-0600; francismarionhotel.com. Marble, crown molding, wrought iron, and other architectural details create an elegant atmosphere at this restored 1924 hotel. When it opened overlooking Charleston Harbor, it was the largest and grandest hotel in the Carolinas. Certainly there are larger hotels today, but not many are grander. Completely restored in 1996, a stay here includes extensive amenities—a doorman, bellhops, room service, valet parking, and more. $$$.

French Quarter. 166 Church St.; (843) 722-1900; fqicharleston.com. Wine and cheese in the afternoon and milk and cookies in the evening complement your stay at the French Quarter, a small luxury hotel in the Market area. The inn maintains a French chateau design with well-appointed rooms, rich fabrics, and fine furniture. $$$.

worth more time
mount pleasant

Mount Pleasant on the northeast side of Charleston Harbor is almost synonymous with Charleston. Though it's a separate and small town, there are a number of attractions here that are worth the 10-minute drive. **Patriots Point Naval and Maritime Museum** (40 Patriots Point Rd.; 843-884-2727; patriotspoint.org) offers a tour of the USS *Yorktown,* the USS *Clamagor*, the Medal of Honor Museum, the Cold War Submarine Memorial, and a Vietnam Support Base Camp. Traditional museum exhibits and hands-on experiences, especially good for families, make up the visit here. It's open daily 9 a.m. to 6 p.m.

    Boone Hall Plantation (1235 Long Point Rd.; 843-884-4371; boonehallplantation .com) will impress the day-tripper even after a visit to Magnolia or Drayton Hall. A visit here includes a walk down the famous Avenue of Oaks, a look at Gullah culture, 9 slave cabins, and the spectacular Boone Home. Open Mon through Sat 9 a.m. to 5 p.m., Sun noon to 5 p.m.

Charles Pinckney National Historic Site (1254 Long Point Rd.; 843-881-5516) is a National Historic Site on Snee Farm and the home of one of the framers of the US Constitution. Pinckney also served as governor, a senator, and a member of the House of Representatives.

Though many outdoor adventures here span the Charleston area as well as its beaches, the area's premier outfitter is based in Mount Pleasant. **Nature Adventure Outfitters** (483 W. Coleman Blvd.; 843-568-3222; kayakcharlestonsc.com) offers a wide range of trips including saltwater and black-water kayaking trips, island exploration, rentals, camps, and instruction.

day trip 37

charleston, sc

>>> it's folly:
folly beach, sc

folly beach, sc

A sign in the middle of the road near the only stoplight on Folly Beach reads "Slow down. It's Folly." Hit the brakes and park the car. Folly Beach is the only municipality located on this tiny barrier island where vacationers often give up cars in exchange for golf carts and hippies who survived the '60s found their place in the world. It's hard to find a bad meal here, but there are only a handful of places in which to enjoy such culinary delights.

The three beach resorts surrounding Charleston all share the same coastal waters, but each brings its own distinction. Folly Beach has a funky eclectic feel, while Sullivan's Island and Isle of Palms cater to families. Sullivan's and Isle of Palms are covered in the next day trip, but first is the beach community just south of Charleston. At Folly Beach it's mostly about the beach, but you need not look far for a place to get a good bite to eat or to wet a line if reeling in your dinner is more to your liking.

getting there

Folly Beach is convenient to the southwest side of Charleston—a 15-minute drive starting out on James Island Expressway out of downtown. Signs clearly indicate a left turn onto SR 171 (Folly Road).

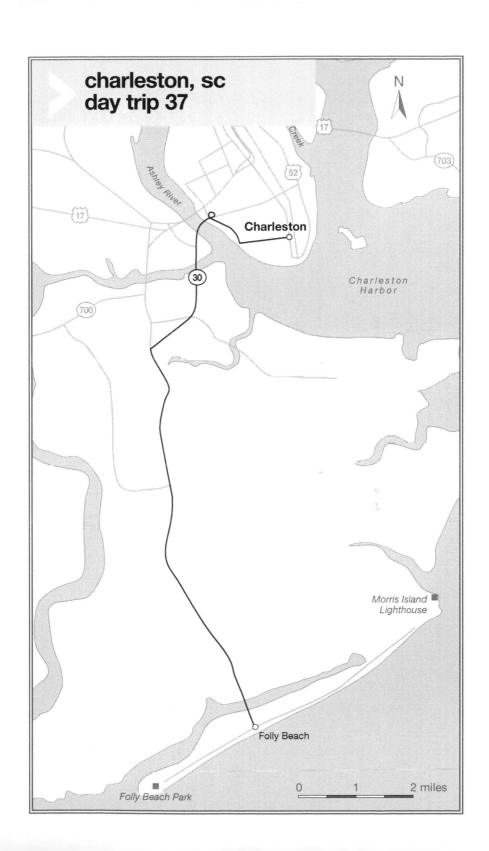

charleston, sc
day trip 37

N

Creek

17

52

703

Ashley River

17

Charleston

30

Charleston
Harbor

700

Morris Island
Lighthouse

Folly Beach

Folly Beach Park

0   1   2 miles

where to go

Folly Beach County Park. 1100 W. Ashley Ave.; (843) 588-2426; ccprc.com. Located on the west end of the beach at Folly River is a park that gives beach access to day-trippers and area residents. It includes dressing areas, restrooms, outdoor showers, picnic areas, and grills. Lifeguards are on duty seasonally, and you can even rent chairs and umbrellas here. Hours vary seasonally.

Folly Beach Fishing Pier. 101 E. Arctic Ave.; (843) 795-4386; ccprc.com. Operated by the Charleston County Parks and Recreation Department, the pier is a 1,000-foot center of activity for teens and anglers alike. It's the second-longest pier on the East Coast, offering rod and tackle rentals as well as a gift shop, a grill, and a separate full-service restaurant. Open daily 8 a.m. to 5 p.m. Dec, Jan, and Feb; 7 a.m. to 7 p.m. in Mar and Nov; 6 a.m. to 11 p.m. Apr through Oct.

Morris Island Lighthouse. Located at the northeast end of the island; savethelight.org. Standing sentinel over Folly Beach about 300 feet off the remote rocky shore is this lighthouse built in 1872. Since 1876 it has been leaning ever so slightly toward the northeast. Its function was replaced by the Sullivan's Island Lighthouse in 1962, but since then, a nonprofit organization called Save the Light is working to preserve it. Free.

Tideline Tours. 103 E. Cooper Ave.; (843) 813-5009; tidelinetours.com. Coastal geologist and amateur historian Captain Anton operates tours off the beaten path in salt marshes, sounds, and tidal creeks surrounding Folly Beach. He offers stories of the island while searching for dolphin, schools of fish, shrimp, and birds. Cost is $50. Trips are offered seasonally daily at 9:30 a.m. and 1:30 p.m.

where to shop

Center Street. Located at the center of Folly Beach on Center Street is a series of shops where day-trippers can find beachwear, souvenirs, gifts, a cup of coffee, or a cone of ice cream. They stretch out among the restaurants in the same area.

where to eat

Folly Beach Crab Shack. 26 Center St.; (843) 588-3080; crabshacks.com. In addition to the variety of crab dishes for which it is named, the Crab Shack also is one of the best raw bars around. A large thatch-covered deck allows diners to eat outside near this busy (well, busy by Folly standards) street. Hours change seasonally. $$.

Lost Dog Cafe. 1106 W. Huron St.; (843) 588-9669; lostdogfollybeach.com. A handwritten chalkboard in the Lost Dog Cafe reads, "Be the person your dog thinks you are." Dogs may be held in high esteem here, but so is a great breakfast. Omelets and eggs Benedict headline the morning menu but give way to items like mahimahi salad at lunch. If you have to wait for a table, take a stroll through the adjacent memory garden behind the community center. Open Mon through Sat 6:30 a.m. to 3 p.m., Sun 6:30 a.m. to 2 p.m. $$.

Taco Boy. 15 Center St.; (843) 588-9761; tacoboy.net. The masked Taco Boy logo hangs on a rusty corrugated metal facade where big sliding glass doors lead to streetside dining, setting up an unexpected delightful dinner. There is not much more on the menu here but tacos and street corn, but the cooks do them right. Choose from corn or flour tortillas and fish, shrimp, or meat tacos with various toppings. Open daily at 11 a.m. $$.

Woody's. 39 Center St.; (843) 588-0088; dowoodyspizza.com. There's thatch on Woody's roof, too, but instead of island fare he serves pizza, subs, and salads. Entertainment is presented occasionally on the front porch. Open daily at 5 p.m. $.

where to stay

The Tides. 1 Center St.; (843) 588-6464; thetidesfollybeach.com. Most of Folly Beach's accommodations are rental properties requiring multiple-night stays. The Tides is a hotel that doesn't have a minimum, and it's a full-service beachfront facility. It includes a pool, restaurant, and Juliet beachfront balconies. $$$.

day trip 38

charleston, sc

sun & sand:
sullivan's island, sc; isle of palms, sc

North of Charleston are the beaches of Sullivan's Island and Isle of Palms that provide a summertime haven for families from throughout the Carolinas and Georgia. Wild Dunes Resort on the northeast end of Isle of Palms provides the perfect weeklong getaway, but for the day-tripper there is laid-back dining, a beautiful oceanside park, quaint shops, and more. Just to the north, Cape Romain Wildlife Refuge holds some of the most pristine beaches on the East Coast. Hunt seashells, spy dolphins, and enjoy spectacular views of the Atlantic Ocean. The sprawling Francis Marion National Forest is just north of here, too.

sullivan's island, sc

It's estimated that half of all slaves—200,000 of those brought to America—came through Sullivan's Island. But today there is little evidence of that. The port here could not maintain its relevance as the port at Charleston on the opposite side of the harbor grew. Fort Sullivan (later Fort Moultrie) would stay relevant: it was the site of a major battle of the American Revolution and would be significant to the town's history until it closed in the 1940s. Today, with a full-time population of not much more than 2,000, Sullivan's Island is a quiet town, much of it on the National Register of Historic Places.

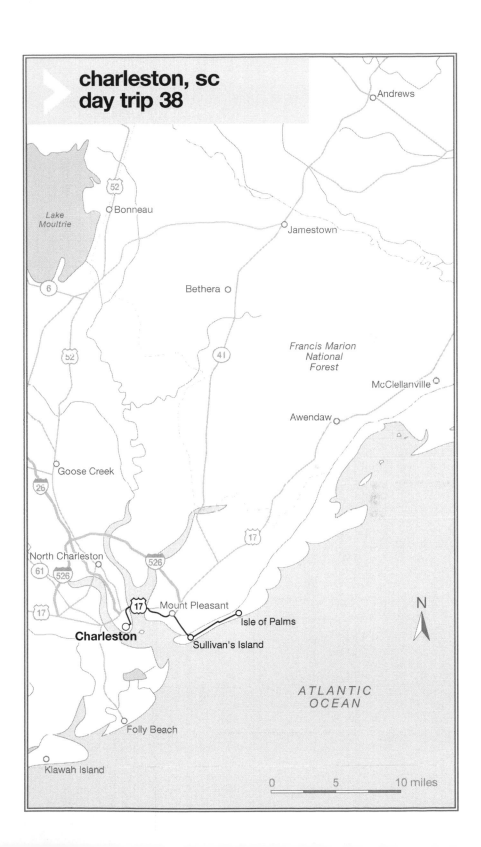

charleston, sc
day trip 38

getting there

Sullivan's Island is 15 minutes from downtown Charleston via Mount Pleasant. Take US 17 over the Cooper River Bridge and exit on SR 703.

where to go

Fort Moultrie. 1214 Middle St.; (843) 883-3123; nps.gov. Fort Sullivan wasn't even completed before stepping up to save Charleston from British occupation. Still under construction on June 28, 1776, it withstood a 9-hour attack from 9 warships. It was the first victory over the British navy. It held significance in other wars, too. Undergoing upgrades throughout its existence, the fort that stands today is actually a third structure, built in 1809. The National Park Service interprets 171 years of American seacoast defenses from 1776 to 1947. Now a national monument, a museum on the site includes items from all of those wars, a short film, and the stories of the men who were stationed here. Adults $10, Open daily 9 a.m. to 5 p.m.

where to shop

Adele's Pottery. 1659 Middle St.; (843) 883-9545. Wheel-thrown and hand-built, functional pottery comes from Adele Deas Tobin's studio. Most of her work is inspired by the sea and the beach that she has grown to love. Open seasonally.

Sandpiper Gallery. 2019 Middle St.; (843) 883-0200; sandpipergallery.net. Fine art including paintings and low-country crafts is featured in this large, comfortable gallery. Glass, pottery, prints, and other media are available for browsing and for purchase. Open seasonally with varying hours.

where to eat

High Thyme Cuisine and Cocktails. 2213-C Middle St.; (843) 883-3536; highthymecuisine.com. Located in a small, unassuming house on Sullivan Island's main street is a pleasant culinary discovery. Cozy and romantic, it serves tapas on Tuesdays and a full menu of steak, seafood, and dishes with a touch of Asia the rest of the week. Open for dinner Mon through Sat and for Sunday brunch. $$$.

Poe's Tavern. 2210 Middle St.; (843) 883-0083; poestavern.com. Edgar Allan Poe was stationed at Fort Moultrie for 14 months in 1827 and 1828, so this tavern stands in homage to him. Drink is more the focus than food here. It has a small wine list and wide-ranging offering of import beers. The menu also carries burgers and sandwiches named for the author's work. Open daily 11 a.m. to 2 a.m. $.

isle of palms, sc

This barrier island is twice the size of Sullivan's Island in population and acreage, and it's been a destination since the late 1800s when vacationers had to reach it by ferry. A small hotel was established here in 1906, and in 1912 a pavilion and an amusement park were added. Grace Memorial Bridge (now known as Cooper River Bridge) opened in 1929, giving access to automobile traffic, and the island developed rapidly. Today Wild Dunes Resort occupies much of the island, but vacation homes and a small town center offer a quiet retreat for the day-tripper.

getting there

Isle of Palms is mere minutes from Sullivan's Island via SR 703.

where to go

Aqua Safaris. Departing from Wild Dunes Yacht Harbor; (843) 886-8133; aqua-safaris .com. Aqua Safaris offers family daytime and sunset sails in and around Charleston Harbor aboard the sail sloop *Serena*, a comfortable, 50-foot vessel that accommodates up to 16 people. The trip takes guests past historic sites and spots that regularly produce dolphin sightings. Complimentary nonalcoholic beverages are provided, but guests can bring their own adult beverages. Cost is $40 for adults, $30 for children. Trips offered Mon, Tues, and Wed at 10 a.m. and 6 p.m.

Isle of Palms County Park. 1 14th Ave.; (843) 886-3863; ccprc.com. Located near the Isle of Palms Connector, this beachfront park provides easy access for visitors. Available are dressing rooms, restrooms, a picnic area with grills, and a sandy children's play area. Lifeguards are on duty, and you can rent chairs, umbrellas, and a selection of beach games to play. Hours vary seasonally.

Tidal Wave Watersports. 69 41st Ave.; (843) 886-8456; tidalwavewatersports.com. Go skiing or tubing with this adventurous water-sports outfit, which also rents wave runners and conducts charter trips. Skiing, wakeboarding, or tubing starts at $320 for 2 hours for up to 6 people. Open 8 a.m. to 7 p.m. Mar through Nov.

where to shop

Sand Dollar Gallery. 5 51st Ave.; (843) 886-4303. Whether you are looking for beachwear or for a gift for someone at home, you'll likely find It here at this boutique. Sand Dollar also carries nautical home décor.

where to eat

Acme Lowcountry Kitchen. 31 J.C. Long Blvd.; (843) 886-0024; acmelowcountrykitchen
.com. You can get shrimp and grits here, as you might expect, but the jerk shrimp comes
highly recommended, too. The Kitchen has a hefty breakfast menu, but you aren't likely to
leave this place hungry any time of day. Open daily 8 a.m. to 10 p.m. $$

Long Island Café. 1515 Palm Island Blvd.; (843) 886-8809; longislandcafesc.com. One of
the busiest restaurants in the area, reservations are highly recommended. Seafood is done
well here from the she crab soup to the sesame-crusted tuna. Open for lunch 11 a.m. to
2 p.m. and for dinner beginning at 5 p.m.

where to stay

The Palms Hotel. 1126 Ocean Blvd.; (843) 886-3003; palmscharleston.com. A poolside
lounge is only the first of the amenities offered at this oceanfront hotel, which has suites as
well as traditional rooms, some with private balconies. The pink stucco facade and palm
trees give it a South Beach feel. $$.

Seaside Inn. 1004 Ocean Blvd.; (843) 886-7000; seasideinniop.com. As indicative of its
name, this hotel is indeed seaside with all oceanfront rooms that reflect a tropical style.
It's an older hotel but went through a full renovation in 2014. The 3-story facility is festive
and convenient to restaurants as well as a boardwalk and a large sundeck. A continental
breakfast is included. $$.

worth more time

Explore the nature of the inland waterways, marine woodland, and coast of South Carolina
by visiting some of the state's most spectacular natural sites accessible from Isle of Palms
and Charleston. Spanning 250,000 acres to the northeast is **Francis Marion National
Forest,** about one-third of which was leveled by Hurricane Hugo in 1989. It is recovering,
however, with both old growth and new forestlands.

    Bulls Island State Park is a barrier island within the boundaries of Cape Romain
National Wildlife Refuge. To reach it, take the ferry from Garris Landing (843-881-4582;
bullsislandferry.com) about 16 miles north of Charleston off US 17 and Seewee Road. Once
on the undeveloped island, you can explore nature, hunt for seashells, and stroll uncluttered
beaches. Hundreds of sun-bleached oak trees, cedars, and pines span a 3-mile area called
the boneyard because of the trees' resemblance to skeletons. It's also home to American
alligators, foxes, sea turtles, bobcats, and more. Ferry fee is $40 per adult and $20 for
children age 12 and under. Ferries depart at 9 a.m. and 12:30 p.m. and return at noon and
4 p.m.

    At the **Center for Birds of Prey** (4872 Seewee Rd.; 843-971-7474; thecenterforbirds
ofprey.org), explore a 150-acre campus dedicated to the study and welfare of birds of prey

and their habitats. The center is an avian hospital for sick and injured birds and has on exhibit for educational purposes birds that cannot be returned to the wild. On a visit here, take a guided tour of the collection, see hawks, owls, eagles, and other birds in flight, and visit 40-some birds on a nature trail. Admission is $15 for adults and $10 for ages 6 to 18. Open Thurs through Sat 10 a.m. to 5 p.m.

The **Audubon Center at Francis Beidler Forest,** a 15,000-acre sanctuary for plant and animal life, is found in Four Holes Swamp and contains the largest remaining virgin stand of bald cypress and tupelo trees in the world. A 1.75-mile boardwalk begins at the visitor center and sweeps past portions of majestic swamp, where ancient trees, migrating birds, and colorful wildflowers can be quietly observed. The center is 35 miles northwest of Charleston, exit 187–SC 187 off I-26. Open 9 a.m. to 5 p.m., Tues through Sun. Closed Mon, Thanksgiving, Christmas Eve, Christmas, New Year's Eve, and New Year's Day. Adults pay $10, kids 6 to 18 years are $5, and children under 6 are free. Audubon members pay $7.

day trip 39

charleston, sc

>>> **the beach:**
myrtle beach, sc; north myrtle beach, sc

When people from North or South Carolina say they are going to "the beach," this is probably what they mean—Myrtle Beach, the most famous vacation area in the Carolinas. It spills out to the Ocean Drive and Cherry Grove in North Myrtle Beach and to the southern communities that include Garden City and Surfside, but it's all just "the beach"—the Grand Strand. For the day-tripper there is beach access throughout the area. Here you'll find a restaurant row, an amazing aquarium, a great garden, 250 golf courses, and much more. It's not necessarily for the sit-alongside-the-ocean-all-week vacation or even the leisurely day trip; there's too much to see and do. Major shopping and dining destinations are waiting to be discovered at each end of Myrtle Beach at Barefoot Landing and at Broadway on the Beach. The rich and famous are in town, too. Look for Dolly Parton's show and Alabama Theatre. Crass commercialism? Yes, granted, but it's still fun.

myrtle beach, sc

You are not alone. An estimated 15 million people come to the area known as the Grand Strand each year. The full-time population of 30,000 in Myrtle Beach is minuscule by comparison, but that population has built a substantial destination infrastructure. An island since the construction of the Intercoastal Waterway in 1936, Myrtle Beach was actually the last of the area communities to develop. Today city streets are separated from the beach, billed as the world's widest, by large, shifting sand dunes.

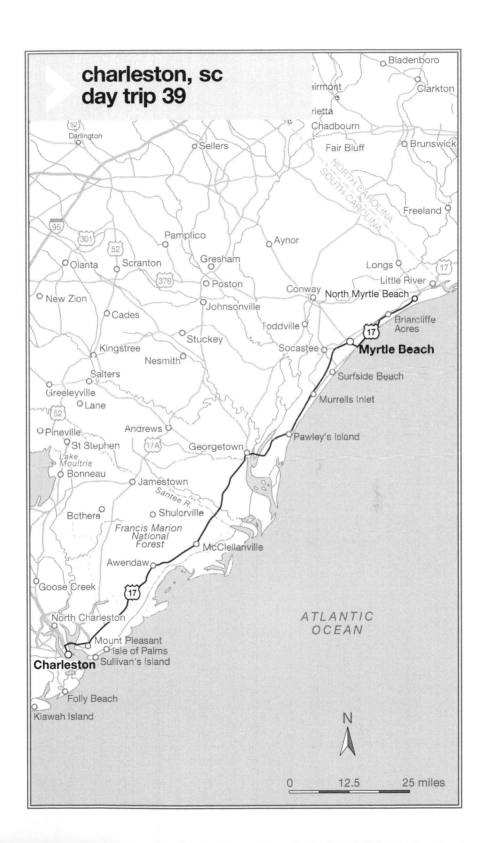

charleston, sc
day trip 39

Bladenboro
Fairmont
Clarkton
Marietta
Chadbourn
Darlington
Sellers
Fair Bluff
Brunswick

NORTH CAROLINA
SOUTH CAROLINA

Freeland

Pamplico
Aynor
Longs
Little River
Olanta
Scranton
Gresham
Conway
North Myrtle Beach
Poston
New Zion
Johnsonville
Briarcliffe
Acres
Cades
Toddville
Myrtle Beach
Stuckey
Kingstree
Socastee
Nesmith
Salters
Surfside Beach
Greeleyville
Murrells Inlet
Lane
Andrews
Pineville
Pawley's Island
St Stephen
Georgetown
Lake
Moultrie
Bonneau
Jamestown
Santee R.
Bethera
Shulerville
Francis Marion
National
Forest
McClellanville
Awendaw
Goose Creek
North Charleston
Mount Pleasant
Isle of Palms
Charleston
Sullivan's Island
Folly Beach
Kiawah Island

ATLANTIC
OCEAN

N

0   12.5   25 miles

The first tourists here were men working on the nearby Conway and Seashore Railroad, who would spend their weekends on the shore. Entrepreneur and railroad executive Franklin Burroughs at the turn of the 20th century was first to envision turning Myrtle Beach into a destination to rival Florida. He died before it would become a reality, but his sons completed the railroad and opened the Seaside Inn in 1901. In the decades that followed, investors built golf courses and resorts, and in 1949 the famed Myrtle Beach Pavilion opened.

getting there

Myrtle Beach is less than 2 hours from Charleston traveling north on US 17.

where to go

The Bowery. 110 9th Ave. North; (800) 826-9379; thebowery.com. This rowdy nightspot opened in 1944 and has become an entertainment legend of sorts. Country music hall of fame supergroup Alabama was the house band at the Bowery in the 1970s, giving the place a big boost in popularity. It still presents nightly entertainment from its new house band, the Bounty Hunters. Open daily at 11 a.m. Mar through Oct. Admission is free.

Carolina Opry. 8901 N. Kings Hwy.; (843) 913-1450; thecarolinaopry.com. This 2,200-seat theater's original show, called *Carolina Opry*, has been presented in Myrtle Beach since 1986. It's a country music variety act with singing, dancing, comedy, and tributes to big-name stars. A second offering, *Good Vibrations*, has a similar format with music and comedy from the '60s, '70s, and '80s. The shows, produced by the same cast, are presented on rotating days at 1 and 7 p.m. A laser light show, a Christmas show, and a clogging show occasionally substitute. Ticket prices start at $17 for children and $34.95 for adults.

Family Kingdom. 300 S. Ocean Blvd.; (843) 626-3447; familykingdomfun.com. Right in the middle of Myrtle Beach on the ocean, families play in the water park by day and hit the rides of the amusement park by night. This expansive amusement center features a wide-ranging array of attractions from bumper cars, to a log flume, to an old-fashioned wooden roller coaster. A lazy river and handful of different waterslides provide a fun way to beat the heat. Hours vary throughout the season. The amusement park is open early Apr through early Oct. Water park open late May through early Sept. Tickets are $27.95 for the water park and $32.95 for the amusement park. Combo passes and individual tickets are also available.

Legends in Concert. 2925 Hollywood Dr.; (843) 238-7827; legendsinconcert.com. A Las Vegas production company brought this show to Myrtle Beach in 1995 after successful shows in Branson and aboard numerous cruise ships. Remarkable look-alike/sound-alikes of popular performers such as Barbra Streisand, Aretha Franklin, Alan Jackson, Barry Manilow, Britney Spears, Katy Perry, and others perform nightly on a rotating basis. Tickets start at $19.95 for children and $45.95 for adults.

Medieval Times Dinner and Tournament. 2904 Fantasy Way; (866) 543-9637; medieval times.com. Jousting knights, sword fights, horses, and eating with your hands are on tap in an evening at this entertaining show. Audience members take sides as an epic battle from 11th-century Spain begins to unfold and they enjoy a selection of roast chicken and spare ribs. Cost is $28.95 for children and $55.95 for adults. Hours vary seasonally.

Myrtle Beach State Park. 4401 S. Kings Hwy.; (843) 238-5325; southcarolinaparks.com. South of downtown Myrtle Beach is the expanse of beach and maritime forest offering an opportunity to get out of sometimes stifling Myrtle Beach traffic. This state park offers hiking trails, campsites, a small selection of cabins, a fishing pier, and a chance to explore nature. In addition to the birds and other coastal animals that occur here naturally, a small nature center has aquariums, reptiles, and other exhibits. Admission is $8 for adults and $4 for ages 6 to 15. Open daily 6 a.m. to 10 p.m. Mar through Nov, 6 a.m. to 8 p.m. the rest of the year.

Palace Theatre. 1420 Celebrity Circle; (800) 905-4228; palacetheatremyrtlebeach.com. Located at Broadway at the Beach is the domed Middle East–themed palace building that hosts a handful of different variety shows throughout the year. A smaller knockoff version of the popular Cirque Du Soleil was the theater's staple for years, but it has also offered a Celtic show, a magic show, and a rock show. Tickets start at $29.95. Show times vary seasonally.

Pirate Voyage. 8901-B Hwy. 17 Business; (843) 497-9700; piratesvoyage.com. Country music legend Dolly Parton brought a country-and-western show to Myrtle Beach 20 years ago, but in 2011 traded in impressive horses for full-size pirate ships. Acrobatics, antics, mermaids, and a good sword fight or two make up this dinner theater presentation. Here, too, the audience picks a favorite and cheers for their swashbuckling heroes to claim the treasure. Tickets are $59.95 for adults and $29.99 for children. Hours vary seasonally.

myrtle beach fishing

Prime fishing locations aren't hard to find in the Myrtle Beach area. Charter operations are abundant, while more affordable options can be found by pier fishing or a group deep-sea fishing adventure. Find deep-sea fishing expeditions departing from Murrell's Inlet to the south and Little River near North Myrtle Beach. For deep-sea full- and half-day trips, call **Captain Dick's Deep Sea Fishing and Water Sports** *(843-651-3676;) departing from Murrell's Inlet or* **Little River Fishing Fleet** *(843-249-1100; littleriverfleet.com) departing from Little River. Fishing piers are located at* **Second Avenue** *(843-455-7437) and at* **Apache Family Campground** *(843-497-6486; apachefamilycampground.com).*

Ripley's Aquarium. 1110 Celebrity Circle; (843) 916-0888; ripleyaquariums.com. Ride on a conveyor belt beneath tanks full of sharks, rays, and colorful creatures of all kinds from the deep sea. The 340-foot path leads under arched glass tanks filled with crystal clear water and green sea turtles, tarpon, nurse sharks, and hundreds of other species. Other exhibits include piranha from the Amazon, octopi from the Pacific, and playful seahorses from around the world. Open tanks allow guests to pet a stingray or cradle a horseshoe crab. Open daily 9 a.m. to 8 Admission is $36.99 for adults, $24.99 for children 6 to 11, $12.99 for ages 2 to 5. Ripley's runs several other attractions in Myrtle Beach, including one of their famous Believe It or Not museums, and offers combo tickets in conjunction with them.

Wheels of Yesteryear. 413 Hospitality Ln.; (843) 903-4774; wheelsofyesteryearmb.com. Muscle cars, restored trucks, and other vehicles that are part of Paul Cummings's collection make up this exhibit. The collection totals more than 100 cars, but much like an art museum the collection is rotated—about 50 at a time. Admission is $10.92 for adults, $7.80 for children 9 to 15. Open daily 9:30 a.m. to 5:30 p.m.

Wonderworks. 1313 Celebrity Circle; (843) 626-9962; wonderworksonline.com. Wonderworks is a top-secret laboratory that was ostensibly cast in this location from Bermuda by a man-made tornado. Now the lab is "upside down," giving inverted guests a strange sensation. Just go with it, okay? Other science phenomena are presented in hands-on exhibits much like a typical science center. Lie on a bed of nails, play with bubbles, and visit the hurricane shack to experience winds of 84 miles per hour. An indoor ropes course takes you on a simulated spacewalk. Admission is $29.99 for adults, $23.99 for ages 4 to 12. Open daily at 10 a.m. Closing hours vary seasonally.

where to shop

Broadway at the Beach. US 17 at 21st Avenue North; (800) 386-4662; broadwayatthebeach.com. This massive complex built around a man-made water feature includes extensive shopping and dining opportunities. Major attractions, including the aquarium and Palace Theatre, as well as hotels, create a big draw while a large selection of small shops and entertainment venues create a potential daylong destination. Seafood restaurants and T-shirt shops reign and Jimmy Buffett has opened a popular Margaritaville restaurant here. Less famous places to go include Señor Frog's, a restaurant where there is always a party going on, and a retro store where you can buy Kiss T-shirts and Bob Marley merchandise. Open daily at 10 a.m. Closing hours vary seasonally.

where to eat

There are reportedly more than a mind-boggling, stomach-rumbling 1,700 eating establishments in the Myrtle Beach area. The heaviest concentration is along **Restaurant Row** on US 17 (also known as Kings Highway) on the northern end of Myrtle Beach. Fish, burgers,

quirky carolina

A sky wheel, 200 feet above sea level, is one of the the newest attractions in Myrtle Beach. The oversize Ferris wheel with enclosed gondolas, located at the Oceanfront Boardwalk and Promenade in downtown Myrtle Beach, opened in 2012.

salads, doughnuts, coffee . . . point your car, hang your head out the window, and sniff your way to your selection.

Bummz Beach Cafe. 2002 N. Ocean Blvd.; (843) 916-9111; bummzcafe.com. This is a family-friendly hangout with a beachfront patio. There are big-screen TVs, karaoke, and other fun offerings alongside a menu of casual fare that's pretty good for bar food Open daily 11 a.m. to 9 p.m. $–$$.

Original Benjamin's Calabash Seafood. 9593 N. Kings Hwy.; (843) 449-0821; original benjamins.com. The massive buffet at this seafood restaurant is legendary. It includes more than 150 items from local catches to crab legs. Benjamin's has been operating on the Grand Strand for 30 years, so it's a tradition for many vacationers. $$–$$$.

Pier 14. 1306 Ocean Blvd.; (843) 448-4314; pier14.com. A seaman with a yellow slicker stands sentinel on the corrugated metal roof over Pier 14. It's actually located at the Myrtle Beach Pier and offers some outside dining. Menu items are the expected seafood selections with some diversions. $$$.

Sea Captain's House. 3002 N. Ocean Blvd.; (843) 488-8082; seacaptains.com. Since 1972 this house has operated as one of the Grand Strand's best seafood restaurants. Crab cakes Benedict start off the breakfast menu, and the fresh catch of the day is offered for dinner. Open daily. $$$.

Villa Romana. 707 S. Kings Hwy.; (843) 488-4990; villaromanamyrtlebeach.com. If you've had your fill of Calabash seafood, hit this Italian restaurant for an evening meal. With red tablecloths and linen napkins, it's a more upscale dining experience. Dinners start with homemade soup and bruschetta. Open daily 4:30 to 10 p.m. $$$.

where to stay

From hotels to condos to rental houses and resorts, Myrtle Beach has literally hundreds of places in which to stay. Target central Myrtle Beach's high-rise hotels if your time is limited; you will avoid spending time in traffic. In addition, they are often the only facilities to permit shorter stays. Many hotels will require 3 or more nights in-season, but just about any place will rent a room for a night at the last minute if something is available.

Breakers Resort. 2006 N. Ocean Shore Blvd.; (855) 861-9550; breakers.com. Three separate high-rise buildings make up this prominent resort on the ocean in the heart of Myrtle Beach. Traditional hotel rooms, condos, and suites are offered along with a full slate of amenities including indoor and outdoor pools, a lazy river, hot tubs, and on-site bars and restaurants. $$–$$$.

Compass Cove Resort. 2311 S. Ocean Blvd.; (866) 515-5290; compasscove.com. The oceanfront facility is one of the largest oceanfront resorts in Myrtle Beach with 3 pools, a lazy river, and other amenities. Accommodations are located in 3 buildings. $$–$$$.

Dunes Oceanfront Village. 5200 N. Ocean Blvd.; (888) 465-5889; dunesvillage.com. With one of the largest parks at any area hotel, this is a great place for families. Accommodations include studios, condos, and suites. $$$.

worth more time

Murell's Inlet, located south of Myrtle Beach, is a less populated resort area. Once a fishing village, it's now more of a retirement community and center of activities on the eco-side of tourism. Located here is **Brookgreen Gardens** (1931 Brookgreen Dr.; 843-235-6000; brookgreen.org), dedicated largely to the sculpture of nearly 300 American artists. It includes thousands of acres preserved as manicured gardens and natural areas as well as a small zoo. Across the highway is **Huntington Beach State Park,** a 2,500-acre escape to nature. See alligators here in their natural habitats, along with some 300 species of birds. The park also features 3 miles of unpopulated and unspoiled beach. Within the park is the Spanish-style castle known as Atalaya, home of artist Anna Hyatt Huntington, whose extensive works appear at Brookgreen Gardens. Families will enjoy **Georgetown Pirate Adventure** (4123 Hwy. 17 Business; 843-651-3676; myrtlebeachpirates.com). It includes face painting, lessons in pirate lingo, sing-alongs, and a 1-hour voyage aboard the *Sea Gypsie*, complete with water cannons.

north myrtle beach, sc

In 1968 Windy Hill, Crescent Beach, Ocean Drive, and Cherry Grove merged to become North Myrtle Beach. Though you will see some distinction for each of these four communities, they have all blended into one. And while it is by no means secluded, traffic is a little lighter, the high-rise hotels are a little shorter, and the beach a little less crowded than in Myrtle Beach proper. For decades this has been the place to go for families who want to add a dash of neon and a pinch of nightlife to their otherwise quiet vacation.

getting there

From Myrtle Beach, continue on US 17 north.

where to go

Alabama Theatre. 4750 Hwy. 70 South; (843) 272-1111; alabama-theatre.com. Extensive costuming, sets, lighting, and a state-of-the-art sound system come together here for a well-done country music presentation. Located on the stretch of Kings Highway in front of Barefoot Landing, the theater produces several shows by the house cast each year and welcomes other performers who do tributes to country music legends. One matinee and one evening performance are typically presented each day throughout the year. Tickets start at $39.95.

Alligator Adventure. 4604 US 17 South; (843) 361-0789; alligatoradventure.com. Featuring gigantic alligators alongside birds, bears, tigers, and other animals, Alligator Adventure is a veritable zoo. Educational programming, including feeding and handling shows, makes this facility more than a roadside attraction. Admission is $29.99 for adults, $27.99 for seniors, $19.99 for ages 4 to 12. Hours vary seasonally.

Inlet Point Plantation Stables. 5800 Little River Neck Rd.; (843) 249-2989; inletpoint plantation.com. Located just outside North Myrtle Beach, wranglers at this stable lead riders on tours of secluded beaches and along inland trails. The ride provides a primer on area history and ecology as well as an opportunity to see sights you won't see from the highway or beach. The cost of the trail rides starts at $120 per person.

Ocean Drive Pavilion and Amusement Park. 90 S. Ocean Blvd.; (954) 841-4777; od-pavilion.com. Resembling a boardwalk amusement park of old, the OD Pavilion features go-karts, bumper cars, a carousel, a Ferris wheel overlooking the ocean, a hall of mirrors, and other attractions. Buy cotton candy or a candied apple, play video games in the arcade, or just hang out in this neon-lit center of activity. Tickets can be purchased for each activity or in a group at a discount. Open daily 4 to 11 p.m. in season.

put your money down

A single ship departing from Little River just outside North Myrtle Beach takes guests out twice daily for gambling sessions. Not legal on land, the floating casino becomes South Carolina's only option for gambling. **Big M Casino** *(4491 Waterfront Dr.; 877-250-5825; bigmcasino.com) includes Las Vegas–style craps, blackjack, roulette, other games, and a buffet. Cruises Tues through Sun at 10:45 a.m. and 6:45 p.m.*

where to shop

Barefoot Landing. 4898 US 17 South; (843) 272-8349; bflanding.com. The House of Blues, Alligator Adventure, and Alabama Theatre occupy prime real estate in front of this shopping center with boardwalks that connect shops, restaurants, and attractions over a 27-acre lake that is complete with alligators. Hats, T-shirts, sunglasses, and kites make their way into the specialty shops here, but there are also shops with more elaborate fashions and home decor. Grab a bite to eat at California Pizza or at Greg Norman's Australian Grill, among others. Hours vary seasonally.

where to eat

Hoskins Family Restaurant. 405 Main St.; (843) 249-2014; hoskinsrestaurant.com. The atmosphere at Hoskins makes it look as if this diner has been in business for more than 5 decades. It has, and there's not much on the menu but the best breakfast in Myrtle Beach. Dishes are simple bacon-and-eggs offerings, but friendly staff brings it to the table in a timely manner. Hours vary seasonally, but this restaurant is typically open for breakfast, lunch, and dinner. $.

Painters Homemade Ice Cream. 2408 S. Hwy. 17; (843) 272-6934. The Vanna Bannana, named for native Vanna White of *Wheel of Fortune* fame, is one of the many flavors of homemade ice cream people rave about. Also with a location at Garden City, south of Myrtle Beach, there's no inside service or seating at this busy stand. $.

where to stay

Avista Resort. 300 N. Ocean Blvd.; (855) 710-4941; avistaresort.com. Like many of the hotels and resorts in Myrtle Beach, Avista may require 2 or more nights minimum stay, depending on the season and when you ask. This is one of the larger resorts on this end of the Grand Strand with pools, a poolside cabana, a lazy river, and live entertainment. $$$.

day trip 40

charleston, sc

>>> **plantation resort:**
hilton head, sc

hilton head, sc

Arrive on Hilton Head Island, rent a bike, and ditch the car. One of the most luxurious vacation resorts on the East Coast, Hilton Head, rife with history, was named one of the Top 10 island resorts by readers of *Condé Nast*. On this day trip, spend hours at the Salty Dog, a sprawling dining and entertainment complex, or learn how European explorers discovered this beautiful island. The more than 250 restaurants and 24 golf courses blend seamlessly into the natural environment with tasteful signage and creature comforts like grocery stores that follow strict code enforcement designed to maintain the Hilton Head experience. Even the high-rise condos, the Hilton and the Marriott of Palmetto Dunes, in the center of the island blend in. More than 50 miles of bike and walking paths run throughout the island and under highways. Often paths, leading through maritime forests, are filled with deer and other wildlife and end at the beach, shops, and restaurants. All of Hilton Head's beaches are public, and there is ample access for the public at parks and other areas, though many accesses remain private property.

Twelve miles long and 5 miles wide, Hilton Head is composed of several plantation areas that are the focus of sites at which to stay for a week or to visit for a day. A nominal entry fee is often charged just to enter the grounds. Those plantation areas include Sea Pines Resort, Palmetto Dunes, Wexford, Port Royal, Shipyard, and Hilton Head Plantation.

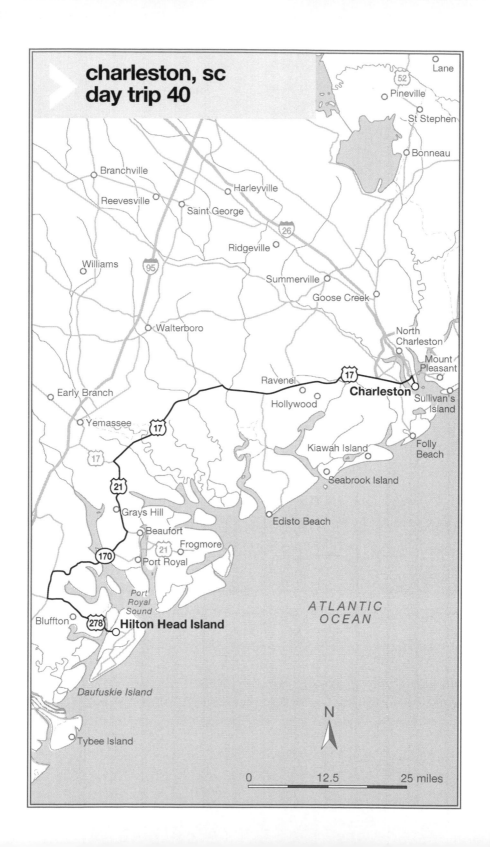

Lane

52

Pineville

St Stephen

Bonneau

Branchville

Harleyville

Reevesville

Saint George

26

Ridgeville

Williams

95

Summerville

Goose Creek

Walterboro

North
Charleston

Mount
Pleasant

Early Branch

Ravenel

17

Charleston

Yemassee

17

Hollywood

Sullivan's
Island

17

Kiawah Island

Folly
Beach

21

Seabrook Island

Grays Hill

Beaufort

Frogmore

Edisto Beach

170

21

Port Royal

Port
Royal
Sound

Bluffton

278

Hilton Head Island

ATLANTIC
OCEAN

Daufuskie Island

Tybee Island

N

0   12.5   25 miles

Hilton Head was named for Captain William Hilton, who founded it in 1663, but for a time it was known as Tench's Island after the first retail agent appointed by the Kingdom of Ireland. As the island was subsequently bought and sold, it was named John's Island and Jenkins Island. Significant during the Civil War, it was occupied by Union troops and served as a blockade and as a hospital for their injured. Hundreds of ex-slaves would flock here during this period, too. Their heritage is retained through the existence of descendants known as Gullah. Largely unoccupied until the James F. Byrnes Bridge was built in 1956, the island started to develop when Charles E. Fraser began work on the Sea Pines Resort and others followed. It would be 1983 before Hilton Head was incorporated. Fishing opportunities abound either using the canal system around Palmetto Dunes to fish from the banks (or even cast your lines from the beach) or for deep-sea fishing excursions from one of several marina areas.

getting there

A drive of just over 2 hours will take you from the heart of Charleston to Hilton Head. While you could opt to travel all the way to I-95, it might be slightly quicker to take US 17 south to US 21 and US 278, which leads directly to the island.

where to go

The Arts Center of Coastal Carolina. 14 Shelter Cove Ln.; (843) 842-2787; artshhi.com. This is the epicenter of the arts community in Hilton Head. The association presents a full slate of productions, exhibits, and festivals, including cultural events such as ballet but also family fun events that include outdoor concerts and fireworks from Shelter Cove Harbour. The facility here includes visual arts exhibit space, a 350-seat theater, and a black box theater. Galleries are open Mon through Fri 10 a.m. to 4 p.m. with later hours on performance days.

Audubon-Newhall Preserve. (651) 491-1851; hiltonheadaudubon.org. Located just off Palmetto Bay Road near Cross Island Parkway and Sea Pines Circle. One of 3 sanctuaries protected by the South Carolina Audubon Society, this nature preserve covers about 50 acres on the southern end of Hilton Head Island. Walking trails lead through a wide variety of trees and shrubs and a wetlands bog that is a common characteristic of low-country barrier islands. It's a great habitat for birds and other wildlife and a place for day-trippers to watch them. Free. Typically open during daylight hours. Free guided tours are offered Fri at 9:30 a.m. Mar through Nov.

Coastal Discovery Museum at Honey Horn. 70 Honey Horn Dr.; (843) 689-6767; coastaldiscovery.org. Located on an open 68 acres of historic property known as Honey Horn, the museum features several exhibits on the natural history of the area in a visitor center, a butterfly habitat, and a salt marsh and other ecosystems on the property. An active beehive produces Honey Horn Honey. A variety of family programs, including boat tours, nature tours, and cruises originate from here. The center also manages the island's sea turtle protection program. Free. Open Mon through Sat 9 a.m. to 4:30 p.m., Sun 11 a.m. to 3 p.m.

Coligny Beach Park. 1 Coligny Circle; hiltonheadislandsc.gov. Located in the busy heart of downtown Hilton Head among the shopping and restaurants of Coligny Plaza is this pretty park that provides beach access to the day-tripper. There are restrooms and showers and a place to rent beach equipment for the day. There is limited free parking in the area. You will find picnic facilities and a playground that includes a sprinkler park. Free. Open 6 a.m. to 9 p.m. with reduced hours in winter.

Driessen Beach Park. 64 Bradley Beach Rd.; hiltonheadislandsc.gov. A boardwalk leads through the maritime forest to the beach at this park on the northern end of the island. There are picnic facilities, outdoor showers, a playground, and lifeguards on duty in the summer. Free. Open 6 a.m. to 9 p.m. with reduced hours in winter.

Gullah Heritage Trail Tours. Departs from the Discovery Museum, 70 Honey Horn Ln.; (843) 681-7066; gullaheritage.com. These tours narrated by Gullah descendants travel through neighborhoods established before the Civil War and provide a look at the West African Gullah traditions, customs, beliefs, and art forms that survived centuries of slavery and modern development. Tours cost $42 for adults, $20 for children 12 and under, Tues through Sat at 10 a.m. and 2 p.m.

Harbour Town Lighthouse. 149 Lighthouse Rd.; (866) 305-9814; harbourtownlighthouse .com. The red-and-white lighthouse is the unmistakable centerpiece of the Sea Pines Plantation area. Completed in 1970, it was the first privately financed lighthouse to be built in the Carolinas in the 20th century. Not really built to guide ships, a climb to the top affords great views of the surrounding marsh and waterways as well as a unique collectibles shop. A small museum on the island's history is located here. Admission is $4.95, free for ages 5 and under. Open daily from 10 a.m. to 8:30 p.m.

ocean cruising

Several Hilton Head companies offer dolphin cruises, sightseeing, crabbing, and other seafaring adventures. Here are a few of them: **Adventure Cruises, Inc.** *(32 Indian Tr.; 843-785-4558;);* **Commander Zodiac, Inc.** *(232 Sea Pines Dr.; 843-671-3344; commanderzodiac.com);* **Dolphin and Nature Cruise** *(59 Marshland Rd.; 843-681-2522; hiltonheadtours.com);* **Drifter Excursions** *(11 Braddock Cove; 843-2900; hiltonheadboattours.com);* **Kayak Hilton Head** *(Simmons Road; 843-684-1910; kayakhiltonhead.com).*

biking

With 30 shops renting an estimated 15,000 bikes, it's not hard to find a place to rent a couple wheels. Here are a few choices in different locations: **Mike's Bikes** *(136 Beach City Rd.; 843-671-6453; mikesbikeshiltonhead.com.com);* **Hilton Head Bicycle Company** *(112 Arrow Rd., 843-686-6888; hiltonheadbicycle.com);* **Hilton Head Outfitters** *(80 Queens Folly Rd.; 843-785-2449; hiltonheadoutfitters.com).*

Lawton Stables. 190 Greenwood Dr.; (843) 671-2586; lawtonstables.com. This equestrian center offers everything from pony rides for the little ones, to trail rides through Sea Pine Forest Preserve, to boarding and training. A small petting zoo here includes potbellied pigs, a miniature pony, goats, rabbits, and other animals. Admission to the zoo is free. Pony rides are $15, and trail rides start at $75 per person. Call for reservations and times.

Pinckney Island National Wildlife Refuge. Lands End Drive, on the north mainland side of the island; (912) 652-4415; fws.gov. More than 4,000 acres of preserved islands, of which Pinckney Island is the largest, were once the plantation home of Major General Charles Cotesworth Pinckney and later managed as a game preserve. The salt marsh, forestland, and freshwater ponds support an amazing array of wildlife. Alligators and deer are abundant as are egrets, ibis, and herons. There is a parking area on Pinckney Island and 14 miles of trails beyond it, but cars aren't allowed any farther. You can bike or walk, but make sure you bring drinking water as none is available in the refuge.

Sea Pines Nature Preserve. 175 Greenwood Dr.; (843) 363-1872; seapines.com. More than 600 acres in the middle of Sea Pines Resort provide ample opportunity to explore the island's history and wildlife. At the southwest entrance of the park are what scientists believe to be the remnants of a 4,000-year-old Indian shell ring, 140 feet across and once 9 feet high. Since its demise the grounds have been used to grow cotton, indigo, and rice. It now includes bridle trails, fishing docks, observation decks, and boardwalks, but the natural beauty is preserved. Free. Typically open during daylight hours.

where to shop

Old Town Bluffton. Boundary and Calhoun Streets; oldtownbluffton.com. Located on the mainland just outside of Hilton Head is this historic shopping district with much of its patina intact filled with fine art galleries, antiques shops, and other fun places to visit. Potters work at the wheel, and colorful shops offer clothing items and home decor. Grab a cup of coffee, mead or cider or pick up some unusual jewelry finds. Hours vary by shop.

Shelter Cove Harbour Shops. Harbourside Lane; (842) 785-9100; sheltercovetowncentre .com. Among the many shops and boutiques that can be found throughout the island, the largest collection is at Shelter Cove, a part of Palmetto Dunes. Stroll along the marina boardwalks and watch the ships come in as you shop. Hours vary by vendor.

where to eat

Crazy Crab. 149 Lighthouse Rd.; (843) 363-2722; 104 William Hilton Pkwy.; (843) 681-5021; thecrazycrab.com. With one location overlooking the lighthouse in Harbourtown and another on Jarvis Creek, Crazy Crab has you covered on both ends of the island. Fresh, locally caught crab makes its way into low-country dishes, steam pots, and surf and turf offerings. $$.

Frosty Frog. 1 N. Forest Beach Dr.; (843) 686-3764; frostyfrog.com. This daiquiri bar in Caligny Plaza has more than 20 different daiquiris ready to pour. Enjoy them there or get a half gallon, 1 gallon, or 5 gallons to go. Hot wings, salads, wraps, and burgers all go with the wild and wacky flavors of daiquiris. $$.

Old Oyster Factory. 101 Marchland Rd.; (843) 681-6040; oldoysterfactory.com. Overlooking Broad Creek, the Oyster Factory location offers spectacular sunset views served with the area's best crab cakes and a monster shellfish sampler. Appropriately it has a full separate oyster menu. Open daily 11 a.m. to 9:30 p.m. $$$.

Salty Dog Cafe. 232 S. Sea Pines Dr.; (843) 671-2233; saltydog.com. The Salty Dog Cafe, Wreck of the Salty Dog, Lands End Tavern, Kiwi's Island Cookout, Jakes Pizza, and Salty Dog Ice Cream make up this complex of varied eateries on the water. The family-style atmosphere allows kids to play in open spaces while adults enjoy a beverage of their choice and everyone enjoys frequent musical entertainment. Hours vary. $–$$$.

where to stay

Many of the places to stay in Hilton Head are self-contained resorts or large, themed chain hotels, including a Disney Resort, a Hilton, and others requiring minimum night stays that vary by season. Many of the resorts and their accommodations are upscale, while independent hotels tend to be more affordable. If you are determined to stay at a resort but only for a night or two, booking close to your arrival date may be possible, especially in the off-season.

Here are a few other selections:

Inn at Harbour Town. 7 Lighthouse Ln.; (866) 561-8802; seapines.com. *Forbes* gives this luxury hotel 4 stars and so does AAA. Beautiful, open architecture reflective of the low country offer expansive windows with views of the harbor, pool, and golf course. A spa, restaurant, and just about anything you could ask for is available through the inn's spectacular service. $$$.

Palmera Inn and Suites. 12 Park Ln.; 843-686-5700; palmerainnandsuites.com. This all-suite hotel is affordable and dog friendly. While It Is about two miles from the beach, you'll have the benefit of small but fully-equipped kitchens and other amenities. $$.

worth more time
daufuskie

Daufuskie Island is a short ferry or Carolina skiff ride from the South Beach Marina and offers an opportunity to learn about this island community that is known for its Gullah history. No cars are allowed, but visitors can tour the island and visit its sites by a rental golf cart. End the trip by topping off your visit with a seafood dinner at **Daufuskie Crab Company** (256 Cooper River Landing Rd., 843-785-6652) before heading back to Hilton Head on the evening ferry.

food & drink

day trip 41

food & drink

>>>

microbrews:
asheville, nc

asheville, nc

While craft breweries, those beer-production facilities producing a limited quantity of barrels per year, are popping up across the country—including locations in the Carolinas—microbreweries with even more limited production have taken a strong hold in North Carolina. The state has more than 125 facilities qualifying as craft breweries, and the city of Asheville has bubbled to the top of the list of places where a beer drinker can soak up the best. With 30 craft breweries and a population of only 95,000 people, Asheville has more craft breweries per capita than any other city in the country. It has even been declared the beer capital of the country in online polls. It won the title of Beer City USA as judged by readers of Examiner.com four years in a row and in 2014 came in number 5. National brewers Sierra Nevada and New Belgium Brewing have now located near Asheville. The uncharacteristic bohemian charm of the mountain city provides the best place in the Carolinas to enjoy a pint.

getting there

Asheville's downtown is the unofficial center of the craft beer universe. Get there via I-40 from east or west; take I-26 from north or south. Signs will direct you to downtown, but look for US 74 or US 25.

where to go

Asheville Brewing Company. 77 Coxe Ave.; (828) 255-4077; ashevillebrewing.com. A big patio and full-service bar are to be found at Asheville Brewing Company. It also has available a selection of pizzas and burgers from its sister operation, **Asheville Pizza and Brewing** (675 Merrimon Ave.; 828-254-1281), and a third location at 1850 Hendersonville Rd. Sample the Shiva IPA or the Ninja Porter at either location. For something different, try the Fire Escape Ale, brewed with smoked jalapeños. Brewer-led guides are offered Fri 3 to 7 p.m. Open Mon through Thurs 11 a.m. to midnight, Sat noon to 2 a.m., Sun noon to midnight.

Brews Cruise. Most tours depart from Asheville Brewing Company, 77 Coxe Ave.; (828) 545-5181; ashevillebrewscruise.com. Walk among the stainless-steel brew kettles and fermenters. Smell the hops, the barley. Sample some of Asheville's best brews on these fun, innovative, and educational tours that take participants to 3 or 4 breweries on each trip. Led by personable and knowledgeable guides, tours—both mobile and walking—are scheduled Tues through Fri beginning at 4 p.m. and Sat and Sun beginning at 12:30 p.m. Cost is $62, which includes an ample number of samples and a snack. Participants can also order off the menu of the final destination.

French Broad Brewing Company. 101 Fairview Rd.; (828) 277-0222; frenchbroadbrewery.com. Located near Biltmore Village, this working brewery and tasting room regularly schedules live music, crammed into a small space with brewing kettles and a handful of tables. They focus on European-style beers, so try the Gateway Kolsh or 13 Rebels Extra Special Bitter. Open Mon through Sat 1 to 8 p.m.

Green Man Brewing. 23 Buxton Ave.; (828) 252-5502; greenmanbrewing.com. Known by locals as Dirty Jack's, Green Man, one of Asheville's original brewpubs, is a small bar with only a handful of tables and a big-screen TV that's likely to be playing a soccer match. Pale ales in the great British tradition reign supreme here. Enjoy them while munching on one of their signature pretzels. Open daily 3 to 9 p.m.

asheville cab companies

Remember to drink responsibly. If you don't stay within walking distance of Asheville's pub scene, call for a ride, from Uber, Lyft or one of the cab companies here:

A Red Cab Company. 194 Haywood Rd.; (828) 232-1112.

Beaver Lake Cab Co. 393 Haywood Rd.; (828) 252-1913.

brewing beginnings

Oscar Wong, a retired nuclear waste engineer, started all the Asheville beer madness when he opened Highland Brewing Company, Asheville's first and now largest brewery, in 1994 in the basement of Barley's Taproom. It's now located in a much larger facility east of downtown. Let's all raise a glass to nuclear engineering.

Highland Brewing. 12 Old Charlotte Hwy.; (828) 299-7223; highlandbrewing.com. Asheville's first and largest brewery is a bustling, working brewery and taproom, once a motion picture studio. Highland Brewing, well marketed and distributed throughout the state, is best known for its flagship Gaelic Ale (a malty amber brew) and its robust Oatmeal Porter. Tours are offered Mon through Fri beginning at 4:30, Sat at 2:30, and Sun at 2:14 p.m. at no charge. Tasting room open Mon through Fri 4 to 8 p.m., Sat 2 to 9 p.m., and Sun noon to 6 p.m.

Lexington Avenue Brewery. 39 N. Lexington Ave.; (828) 252-0212; lexavebrew.com. Lexington Avenue Brewery is also a full-service restaurant and bar. The beer lineup ranges from an American Pale Ale to an IPA. The food menu includes a varying selection of substantial and creative bar food. Open Mon through Sat 11:30 a.m. to 2 a.m., Sun noon to midnight.

Oyster House Brewing. 625 Haywood Rd.; (828) 575-9370; oysterhousebeers.com. Yep, brewers actually use oysters to brew their beer. Once located inside the Lobster Trap restaurant, the brewery moved to this location to increase production but it's still one of the city's best beers. It's also a seafood restaurant, so get something to eat with the Oyster Stout. Open Mon through Fri 3 to 11 p.m., Sat and Sun 11 a.m. to 11 p.m.

Pisgah Brewing Company. 2948 US 70 near Black Mountain; (828) 669-0190; pisgah brewing.com. Pisgah brews a large selection of certified organic brews. Pale and golden ales are their specialties. The working brewery has an art gallery, game room, backyard lawn, and occasional entertainment. Tours offered Sat at 2 and 3 p.m. Taproom open Mon, Tues, Wed 4 to 9 p.m.; Thurs, Fri, Sat 2 p.m. to midnight; Sun 2 to 9 p.m.

Wedge Brewing Company. 37 Paynes Way.; (828) 505-7292; wedgebrewing.com. Located in a warehouse converted into a brewery and art studio in Asheville's French Broad River Arts District, its brewing tanks are wedged into the space, but there is still room for a bar and tasting room. Or just hang out on the loading dock or patio while enjoying Paynes Pale or the Golem Belgian Ale and a movie in their outdoor theater. Open Mon through Thurs 4 to 10 p.m., Fri 3 to 10 p.m., Sat and Sun 2 to 10 p.m.

where to shop

Local 604 Bottle Shop. 604 Haywood Rd.; (828) 417-7002; local604avl.com. Find the best beers from Asheville's craft breweries as well as cider, wine an novelties.

where to eat

Many of Asheville's restaurants carry the local brews and import a wide variety of brews from around the world. Check out the music and culinary scene by pointing yourself in just about any direction, or take one of these suggestions.

Barley's Taproom. 42 Biltmore Ave.; (828) 255-0504; barleystaproom.com. This is where it all began; the basement of Barley's is where Highland Brewing was born. It's also one of the most popular places for locals to listen to music. Barley's Taproom is in a renovated 1920s appliance store, and it's been here since 1994. A restaurant that serves pizza and sandwiches is located on the main floor with a music stage. Open 11 a.m. until close. $.

Bier Garden. 46 Haywood St.; (828) 285-0002; ashevillebiergarden.com. With more than 200 beers from around the world, many on tap, this downtown restaurant may have the largest selection in town. They've got wine covered, too. The food menu ranges from typical pub items like wings, shrimp, and burgers to beef and pork tenderloin for dinner. Open daily 11 a.m. to 11 p.m. $$.

Jack of the Wood. 95 Patton Ave.; (828) 252-5445; jackofthewood.com. Play a game of darts, listen to music, drink a pint of ale, or get a plate of fish and chips at this warm and friendly Celtic pub downtown. Also try their specialties like shepherd's pie or Guinness stew along with burgers and salads. Green Man Brewing is located here. $$.

Thirsty Monk. 92 Patton Ave.; (828) 254-5470; monkpub.com. The Thirsty Monk's upstairs beer menu differs substantially from its downstairs menu. The upstairs bottle menu includes Arrogant Bastard, Epic Brainless on Cherries, and other colorful concoctions. Downstairs are more elaborate European beers largely from Belgium, Denmark, and the Netherlands. Pizza, baguettes, brats, and tacos fill the food menu. The Thirsty Monk's own brews are produced in the smallest of microbrew batches that result in unique beer offerings. $$.

where to stay

Haywood Park Hotel. 1 Battery Park Ave.; (828) 252-2522; haywoodpark.com. This luxurious, full-service hotel is conveniently located in downtown. Walk to many breweries, pubs, restaurants, shops, and galleries before returning to a well-appointed room. It's located in a historic, remodeled department store. $$$.

Hotel Indigo. 151 Haywood St.; (828) 239-0239. This boutique hotel is located near many of the places you will be going on this day trip. Many downtown shops and pubs are within walking distance. The hotel's sleek, contemporary design features hardwood floors, spy-type baths, and plush beds that make for a comfortable stay. A bar and restaurant located on-site offer a place for a nightcap or light meal. $$.

day trip 42

food & drink

yadkin valley wine:
dobson, nc; elkin, nc; boonville, nc;
east bend, nc; lexington, nc

North Carolina's roots in the wine business are deeply embedded in state history, going back to Sir Walter Raleigh's arrival in the 16th century on the Outer Banks; his men discovered the mother vine there and wine production began soon after. By 1840 the federal census listed the state as the country's top wine producer, but that came to a screeching halt in 1919 when Prohibition stopped its legal production and lightning struck—white lightning that is. It would be 50 years before wineries would begin to overcome moonshine stills, but now the state ranks seventh nationally in wine production and tenth in grape production. It's a billion-dollar industry when combining revenues from production and tourism at the state's 185 wineries and 525 vineyards.

Many of these wineries produce their potables with the sweet muscadine grape, the official state fruit also known as the scuppernong. Its sweet taste apparently pleases some southerners used to drinking sweet tea; others drink it for its benefits as an antioxidant. North Carolina's top-selling wine is a muscadine wine from **Duplin Winery** (800-774-9634; duplinwinery.com) located in Rose Hill near Jacksonville (outside Yadkin Valley). Other wineries produce their products from the more familiar European vinifera grapes. For the day-tripper wineries produce more than wine and inviting tasting rooms. Many have restaurants, intriguing histories, stunning rolling landscapes, and partner attractions. Begin near the Virginia state line in the town of Dobson, population 1,500, seat of Surry County. The state's largest family-owned vineyard, Shelton, is located here. Also here is Surry Community College, the only college campus in the Southeast with a working vineyard.

dobson, nc

getting there

Yadkin Valley's US 601 (running north to south) and US 421 (running east to west) offer scenic drives and other interesting places to visit. Yadkin Valley is the first of three American Viticultural Areas in the state and extends from the Virginia state line at I-77 hooking east and then south to Lexington to I-85. To get there from the Charlotte area, make your way to northbound I-77. Dobson is at exit 93.

where to go

Shelton Vineyards. 286 Cabernet Ln.; (336) 366-4724; sheltonvineyards.com. Sample wine as you tour the winery and learn the Shelton story at this beautiful vineyard on a rolling landscape. Have a picnic near the lake or eat at the Harvest Grill located here. Shelton offers a variety of European-style wines. Tours are $12. Open daily 10 a.m. to 5 p.m.

Stony Knoll Vineyards. 1143 Stony Knoll Rd.; (336) 374-5752; stonyknollvineyards.com. Two vineyards are located on this century-old farm that produces Cabernet Sauvignon, Chardonnay, Syrah, Cabernet Franc, and an American native called Niagara. A beautiful tasting room is located in a 2-story French chateau. Wine tasting costs $10. Open Mon and Thurs through Sat 10 a.m. to 6 p.m. with reduced hours in Jan and Feb.

where to shop

The Rockford General Store. 5174 Rockford Rd.; (336) 374-5317; rockfordgeneralstore .com. Jars of candy line several counters at the Rockford General Store, at the heart of the community since the 1920s. Grab a Grape Nehi or Orange Crush in the bottle before strolling back in time at this tiny village. Open Wed through Sat 10 a.m. to 5 p.m. and Sun noon to 5 p.m.

where to eat

The Depot at Cody Creek. 112 Old Depot Ln.; (336) 386-8222; codycreek.org. A functional water wheel, a display of stuffed game, and a waterfall decorate the entrance of the depot, an expansive rustic piece of property that's popular for weddings. Steaks, chops, and seafood are the stars of the menu served in a down-home atmosphere. After lunch, visit the old-time general store located here. Open Tues through Thurs 5 to 9 p.m., Fri 4 to 10 p.m., Sat 3:30 to 10 p.m., Sun 11:20 a.m. to 9 p.m. $$.

Harvest Grill. 286 Cabernet Ln.; (336) 366-3590; sheltonvineyards.com. Located at the base of Shelton's rolling vineyard is this bistro-style restaurant. A warm, wood-laden dining room adjoins an enclosed patio with fireplace. The menu features tasty blackened dishes, trout, and other local selections. Open Mon through Thurs 11 a.m. to 9 p.m., Fri and Sat 11 a.m. to 10 p.m., Sun 11 a.m. to 5 p.m. $$.

where to stay

The Rockford Inn Bed & Breakfast. 4872 Rockford Rd.; (336) 374-6644; rockfordbedandbreakfast.com. The historic Rockford community dates to the 18th century, and this inn has been here for most of that time, too. With big trees on 6 acres, this antebellum house with stone steps leading to it provides incredible country charm. $$.

elkin, nc

getting there

Elkin is about 20 minutes south of Dobson at exit 82 of I-77 on the banks of the Yadkin River.

where to go

Brushy Mountain Winery. 125 W. Main St.; (336) 835-1313; brushymountainwine.com. What once housed the Elkin Canning Company and the Harris Electric Company now is home to this popular downtown winery. A wide range of wines including familiar Chardonnay and blended reds are marketed alongside blueberry and raspberry wines. Open Thurs 1 to 5 p.m., Fri and Sat noon to 8 p.m., Sun 1 to 5 p.m.

Carolina Heritage Vineyard and Winery. 170 Heritage Vines Way; (336) 366-3301; carolinaheritagevineyards.com. Organic, gluten-free, and handpicked grapes including muscadines and American-French hybrids are used to produce distinct types of wine. Open Sat and Sun 1 to 6 p.m. for tours and tastings except for the month of January.

Elkin Creek Vineyard and Winery. 318 Elkin Creek Mill Rd.; (336) 526-5119; elkin creekvineyard.com. Perched on a knoll overlooking a babbling brook is this rustic timber-crafted winery located at a century-old mill. Six acres produce Merlot, Sangiovese, Pinot Grigio, Cabernet Sauvignon, and Viognier. Open Thurs through Sun 11 a.m. to 5 p.m.

Slightly Askew Winery. 913 N. Bridge St.; (336) 835-2700; slightlyaskewwines.com. This winery is slightly askew because of its incredibly long list of small-batch wines made from apples, strawberries, and peaches. Here you can even buy the supplies to make your own. Varieties are typically dry or semi-dry. Open Thurs through Sat Fri 1 to 6 p.m., Sun 1 to 5 p.m.

where to shop

Elkin Antiques and Collectibles Mall. 131 S. Bridge St.;(336) 526-3000; In addition to merchandise from more than 60 vendors there Is also a year-round Christmas shop located here. Built in the 1890's the building once served as the local shell station. Open Wed through Sat 10 a.m. to 6 p.m. and Sun 1 to 6 p.m.

where to eat

Fiddles Pub. 223 W. Main St.; (336) 527-4782. Providing Elkin's only palatable nightlife is this pub with what else but fiddles from around the world on the walls. Serving burgers, barbecue, and pub staples, it's a friendly bar that frequently schedules live music. Open daily 11 a.m. to 11 p.m. $$.

Southern on Main. 102 E. Main St.; (336) 258-2144; southernonmain.com. Collards, pimento cheese, and other southern staples are placed appropriately on the menu here. You might even try the more creative dishes like southern popcorn, a special fried okra app, or the fried green BLT. Open Sun and Tues through Thurs 11 a.m. to 9 p.m., until 9:30 on Fri and Sat. $$

boonville, nc

getting there

Boonville is located at the intersection of US 601 and SR 67 just off I-77 at exit 82. Founded in 1895 at the crossroads of a Catawba Indian trail and a Cherokee trail, oral history indicates frontiersman Daniel Boone hunted in this area frequently. Folktales say Boone slept in a hollow of a tree at the Booneville Baptist Church here; thus the town bears his name.

where to go

RagApple Lassie Vineyard and Guest House. 3724 RagApple Lassie Ln.; (336) 367-6000; ragapplelassie.com. An illustration of a championship show calf hanging out on a crescent moon makes its way onto every one of the wines coming out of this winery, featuring vinifera grapes. A historic guest house is available for a minimum 2-night stay and the welcoming Back Door Cafe allows guests to sip wine while enjoying a selection from the menu. Open daily noon to 6 p.m.

Sanders Ridge Vineyard Winery and Restaurant. 3200 Round Hill Rd.; (336) 677-1700; sandersridge.com. One of the most beautiful spots on the Yadkin River holds one of the best restaurants around. In the Shore family for more than 150 years, Sanders Ridge is a winery of more than 150 acres with a lake, nature trails, and a serene environment. Their award-winning wines are classic Cabernet, Chardonnay, Merlot, and more. Southern dishes come largely from the certified organic garden and become remarkable sandwiches and salads at lunch and as family-style dinners with variable in-season selections. Tasting room open daily noon to 5 p.m. Restaurant ($$) open Thurs through Sun 11:30 a.m. to 3 p.m. and 5:30 to 9 p.m.

east bend, nc

getting there

East Bend is located a few miles east of I-77 and Boonville on SR 67.

where to go

Carolina Balloon AdVentures. 3028 Black Diamond Ln.; (336) 699-3332; usaballoon .com. Float over pristine rolling hills, the graceful Yadkin River, and vineyard after vineyard during this high-flying adventure. Carolina Balloon offers morning and afternoon rides in hot air balloons from 4 launch sites conveniently located in Yadkin County. Flight selections can also include a low-level tour of a winery and dinner. Rates start at $225 per person. Call for reservations.

Cellar 4201. 4201 Apperson Rd.; (336) 699-6030; cellar4201.com. Oaky Chardonnay and sweet local-grape wines come from the Cellar. This smaller vineyard produces small quantities of high-quality fine wines. Sip from a glass on the patio. Open Fri through Sun noon to 6 p.m.

Divine Llama Vineyards. 4126 Divine Llama Ln.; (336) 699-2525; divinellamavineyards .com. Words that you don't hear together often (or ever) join up for one good experience here in Yadkin Valley. You can pet the llamas (and miniature horses) if you like, or even book them for an different trekking experience. Tastings of European-style wines are conducted in the rustic farmhouse nestled on 5 acres. Open Fri and Sat noon to 6 p.m., Sun 1 to 6 p.m.

Flint Hill Vineyards. 2133 Flint Hill Rd.; (336) 699-4455; flinthillvineyards.com. A 19th-century yellow farmhouse set among massive oak trees and colorful gardens serves as the tasting room for this winery. Only open since 2005, it offers 8 wines and an exquisite restaurant. The Century Kitchen ($$), located on the vineyard, is as critically acclaimed as its wines. Servings of seasonal selections are dished out family-style. Open Fri through Sun noon to 5 p.m.

where to eat

Kitchen Roselli. 105 E. Main St.; (336) 699-4898; kitchenroselli.com. Located in what was the historic Davis Brothers Store, this restaurant seamlessly blends Italian recipes with the fresh local foods they turn into fresh pasta and other dishes. The menu often features shrimp scampi and filet mignon. Open Thurs though Sun 5 to 9 p.m. $$–$$$.

lexington, nc

getting there

From East Bend, take SR 67 east and US 52 south to reach Lexington.

where to go

Childress Vineyards. 1000 Childress Vineyards Rd.; (336) 236-9463; childressvineyards .com. Racing guru Richard Childress leapt into the wine business with as much zeal as he exhibits in the racing business. The beautiful Italianate stone and stucco building sets the tone for a spectacular wine-tasting experience. A bistro also offers lunch. Open Mon through Sat 10 a.m. to 5 p.m., Sun 1 to 5 p.m.

Junius Lindsay Vineyard. 385 Dr. Zimmerman Rd.; (336) 764-0487; juniuslindsay.com. This farmland has been in the Zimmerman family since 1894, reopened in 2004 by Michael Zimmerman after traveling abroad. All wines are produced from varietals from the south of France. Open Fri through Sun 1 to 5 p.m.

Native Vines Winery. 1336 N. Hwy. 150; (336) 787-3688; nativevineswinery.com. This first winery to be opened by a Native American in the country specializes in producing wines from native grapes, blueberries, and even apples. A few bottles of vinifera wines are sold here, too. Open Mon through Fri 11 a.m. to 5 p.m., Sat 11 a.m. to 6 p.m. and Sun 1 to 5 p.m.

Weathervane Winery. 1452 Welcome Arcadia Rd.; (336) 701-5235; weathervanewinery .com. Focused on keeping as much of the production process by hand as possible, this winery produces good dry, sweet wines in small quantities. Open Tues through Sat 11 a.m. to 5 p.m., Sun 1 to 5 p.m.

where to shop

The Bob Timberlake Gallery. 1714 E. Center St.; (336) 249-4428; bobtimberlake.com. This gallery, retail store, and museum features the art, home furnishings, and accessories of artist and designer Bob Timberlake. Special events throughout the year highlight Timberlake and other artists. Open Tues through Sat 10 a.m. to 5 p.m.

day trip 43

food & drink

swan creek wine:
hamptonville, nc

hamptonville, nc

Swan Creek, which runs south out of the Yadkin River, is the second of the North Carolina areas to be designated by the federal government as an official American Viticultural Area. The rich soil in the area between the Brushy and Blue Ridge Mountains creates an environment much like the rolling hills of France and Italy. Though it encompasses nearly 180 square miles, there are few wineries here, three in the unincorporated community of Hamptonville. It's not unusual to see the buggies driven by people from the small Amish community on the country roads in this area.

getting there

Hamptonville is located in the southeast area formed at the intersection of I-77 and US 421.

where to go

Dóbbins Creek Vineyard. 4430 Vineyard View Ln.; (336) 468-4770; dobbinscreekvine yards.com. Outstanding views of the Blue Ridge Mountains highlight a trip to this vineyard. A rustic log structure houses the tasting room with hickory walls, cherry bar, and stone fireplace. Wines include Riesling, Chardonnay, and Merlot. Open Fri noon to 5 p.m., Sat 11 a.m. to 5 p.m., Sun 1 to 5 p.m.

Laurel Gray Vineyards and Winery. 5726 Old Hwy. 421; (336) 468-9463; laurelgray.com. A 75-year-old milking parlor and farm pond are at the center of this vineyard. The 84-acre estate is planted with 10 acres of European-style grapes that produce award-winning wines. Take a guided tour of the state-of-the-art winery Wed through Sat 10 a.m. to 5 p.m., Sun 1 to 5 p.m.

Shadow Springs Vineyard. 5543 Crater Rd.; (336) 468-5000; shadowspringsvineyard .com. The tasting room here overlooks the vineyard, a small pond, and a gazebo. Shadow Springs sells a large selection of vinifera wines for such a young vineyard, founded in 2005. Open Wed through Sat 10 a.m. to 5 p.m., Sun 1 to 5 p.m.

where to shop

Shiloh General Store. 5520 Saint Paul Church Rd.; (336) 468-4789. Run by the small community of Amish that settled here in the 1980s, in this store you'll find everything from candy to cheese and canned vegetables and from breads to soaps and soup mixes. A small deli serves prepared sandwiches and ice cream. Open Tues through Fri 9 a.m. to 5 p.m., Sat 9 a.m. to 4 p.m.

day trip 44

food & drink

barbecue battle:
lexington, nc; greensboro, nc; wilson, nc; goldsboro, nc; greenville, nc

Except for the great basketball rivalry between the University of North Carolina Tar Heels and the Duke Blue Devils, there may not be any issue more hotly debated or more intensely discussed than what makes good barbecue. Many words have been used to describe which is best and many a swine life has been lost in testing those sometimes unyielding positions. What's not within the bounds of reasonable debate is that North Carolina is one of the best places on Planet Earth to enjoy barbecue.

This day trip pits (pun intended) the epicenter of western barbecue against the towns more likely to serve eastern styles of barbecue. Geographically and theoretically speaking, any establishment in the Lexington area that claims to serve barbecue should probably be plating smoked pork cooked slowly over coals and served with a ketchup-based sauce. That would be western-style barbecue. In the eastern corner, generally centered on the Wilson area, both the white and dark meat of the pig would be used. And most distinctively, it would be served using a tangy vinegar, salt, and pepper mixture with absolutely no tomato base. The same other ingredients might be found in the dip or sauce of western barbecue— just not ketchup. Serve it all up with hush puppies, fries, and sweet tea.

Rolling out of wine country and into barbecue country, a stop in Lexington is a must for the barbecue foodie. Barbecue joints began locating here in the 1950s after they saw that barbecue sold really well out of tents. Since 1984 the city has conducted the Lexington Barbecue Festival in October, drawing more than 160,000 people to this mid-size city for the 2-day event. Now some 15 restaurants in and around the city of Lexington cater to the barbecue crowd. Barbecue here is characterized by inclusion of a tangy red slaw—even a slight difference from some other western barbecues.

The cultural and historical values of a day trip to Greensboro were covered substantially in day trip 4, but omitted was the additional value it brings to the culinary scene. Heading to an event at the Greensboro Coliseum? Want to check out the ACC Hall of Champions? A good plate of barbecue should be in your future, too. One of North Carolina's most highly acclaimed barbecue restaurants is right next door to the coliseum.

Goldsboro is best known as home of Seymour Johnson Air Force Base, but it also had some significance during the Civil War. Perhaps equally significant is the local legend that says that barbecue was actually born here. Though the origins of eating slow-cooked pork and corn bread can be traced back centuries, historians trace the tradition of cooking pork in a pit over hot coals to Goldsboro social functions prior to the 1920s.

lexington, nc

getting there

Lexington is located just off I-85 near the intersection of US 64, almost in the geographic center of the state.

where to go

Historic Uptown Lexington Walking Tour. 114 E. Center St.; (336) 236-4218 or (866) 604-2389; visitlexingtonnc.org. Before sitting down for a big plate of barbecue, work up an appetite with a self-guided tour of the historic downtown beginning at the visitor center. On the tour are 41 historic properties on the National Register of Historic Places within a 5-block area plus fringe sites dating from 1824 to 1948. Visit the Candy Factory, best known for producing Red Bird Peppermint Puffs, and listen to the player piano, then browse Lanier Hardware. Plus, see how many pigs you can count. The fiberglass porkers are pieces of art to promote barbecue and other businesses in town.

where to eat

The Barbecue Center. 900 N. Main St.; (336) 248-4633; barbecuecenter.net. The Barbecue Center is one of a dying breed—still using a real wood smoker and still offering curb service. In addition to typical chopped and sliced selections, the Barbecue Center offers great banana splits for dessert. Open Mon through Sat 11 a.m. to 9 p.m. $.

Smiley's. 917 Winston Rd.; (336) 248-4528. One of Lexington's originals, Smiley's serves the traditional sliced and chopped offerings as well as Brunswick stew that gets high marks. You can also get chicken but only Fri, Sat, and Sun. Open Tues through Sat 10 a.m. to 9 p.m. $$.

Speedy Lohrs. 8000 N. Hwy. 150; (336) 764-5509. The Lohr family has been smoking pig in the Lexington area for decades. They serve pork, chicken, and ribs right, plus this restaurant also makes a great chili dog and fried seafood on Saturday nights. Open Mon through Sat 6 a.m. to 9 p.m. $.

greensboro, nc

getting there

To get to the coliseum area in Greensboro, take exit 38 off I-85 Business, following the signs for the coliseum area. Merge onto US 220 North, which turns into Freedom Mill Road. Travel just over 1 mile and turn left on Coliseum Boulevard.

where to go

ACC Hall of Champions. 1921 W. Lee St.; (336) 315-8411; acchallofchampions.net. Located in the coliseum complex, the ACC Hall of Champions features interactive exhibits that highlight the achievements of the ACC athletes and sports programs over the past 6 decades. The centerpiece is a video globe that shows some of the conference's greatest moments. Other kiosks allow visitors to check out their favorite schools and athletes and to trace a time line of the ACC. The hall also includes championship trophies and other memorabilia. Admission is free Open Thurs through Sat 10 a.m. to 4 p.m.

Greensboro Coliseum Complex. 1921 W. Lee St.; (336) 373-7400; greensborocoliseum .com. The Greensboro Coliseum is a 23,500-seat center that's been hosting major events since 1959. It's been the home of the Atlantic Coast Conference's men's basketball tournament more times than any other venue. It also hosts Greensboro's major performing arts organizations, big-name concerts, and national touring acts. The complex here also includes the 2,500-seat War Memorial Auditorium and an events center.

where to eat

Stamey's. 2206 W. Gate City Blvd. (with a second location at 2812 Battleground Ave.); (336) 299-9888; stameys.com. Founder C. Warner Stamey received his barbecue training in Lexington, so this is barbecue in that same style. He bought a restaurant called Swicegoods there, renamed in Stamey's, and moved it here in 1953. In addition to succulent pit-cooked barbecue, don't leave Stamey's without trying one of their famous cobblers. Open Mon through Sat 11 a.m. to 9 p.m. $$.

wilson, nc

getting there

Wilson is located on I-95 at the intersection of US 264. Heading east, the sauce changes significantly; the cut of pork alters ever so slightly. US 70 underscores a giant swath of area that could be known as barbecue country. At its heart is the town of Wilson, where tobacco once sold more than barbecue sandwiches. Today it offers two of the state's best eastern-style barbecue restaurants.

where to shop

Wilson boasts antiquing at its best, so if you need an excuse to make your way here to dine on great barbecue, antiquing is it. Located along US 301 are several places to get started.

Bobby Langston Antiques. 2620 US 301 South; (252) 237-8224; langstonantiques.com. In addition to operating this traditional antiques location, Bobby Langston also conducts regular estate sales and auctions. Langston has been in business here for 50 years and now has wide-ranging American and European offerings that date to the 17th century. Open Mon through Fri 9 a.m. to 5 p.m.

Boone's Antiques. 2014 US 301 South; (252) 237-1508; boonesantiques.com. Boone's claims it is one of the largest antiques dealers on the East Coast with 4 acres of Chinese porcelain, paintings, oriental rugs, garden art, and more. Open Mon through Sat 10 a.m. to 5 p.m.

Boykin Antiques & Appraisals, Inc. 2013 US 301 South; (252) 237-1700. This is a distinctive collection of American and English decorative arts. Boykin specializes in Asian antiques including Asian dolls. Open Mon through Sat 10 a.m. to 5 p.m.

where to eat

Marty's Barbecue. 2643 Ward Blvd.; (252) 281-1709; martysbbq.com. Named for the late Marty Ellis, who served barbecue here for 30 years, the barbecue joint is back in business in an old convenience store with new owners. Cajun corn sticks are popular here. $

Parker's. 2514 US 301 South; (252) 237-0972. Doing business here since 1946, Parker's sweet tea ranks as the best in the state along with its Brunswick stew. And even though its barbecue ranks as tops in the state as well, customers recommend trying the fried chicken, too. Barbecue is served family-style with boiled potatoes and corn sticks, a close relative to corn bread. $–$$.

goldsboro, nc

getting there

From Wilson, Goldsboro is a few miles south on I-795 at US 70.

where to eat

Wilber's Barbecue. 4172 Hwy. 70 East; (919) 778-5218; wilbersbbq.com. Wilber Shirly purchased Hills Barbecue in 1962 and renamed it. Since then, both President George H. W. Bush and President Bill Clinton have eaten here. Wilber's Barbecue sauce is bottled and sold over the Internet. Open Mon through Sat 6 a.m. to 9 p.m., Sun 7 a.m. to 9 p.m. $–$$.

greenville, nc

getting there

Greenville is easy to reach via US 264 from east or west.

where to eat

Bs Barbecue. 751 Bs Barbecue Rd.; (252) 758-7126. Home of the East Carolina University Pirates, Greenville is an unusually big college town. Ample cultural opportunities are available, but one reason is good enough to visit—barbecue. When checking out a barbecue joint, one can't judge the quality of food by the appearance of the place it's served. This is especially true of Bs, a run-down-looking dive that serves the tops in eastern North Carolina barbecue. Located near the East Carolina University campus, Bs is open for lunch only, and when they run out of food, they close. Get there early. $.

day trip 45

food & drink

>>>

carolina seafood trail:
morehead city, nc; sneads ferry, nc;
ocean isle beach, nc; calabash, nc

From the fried little pieces of heaven at Calabash to the seafood festival at Morehead City and more than a select oyster or two in between, there's no question the Carolinas serve up the best seafood plates around. Fresh Carolina catches vary by season. Spring brings a generous selection of soft-shell blue crab, mackerel, and yellowfin tuna, while summer proffers a fair share of shrimp and snapper. Though oysters can be harvested from farms year-round, a wild variety is harvested beginning in fall along with flounder, mackerel, and grouper. The Carolina fresh fish experience shouldn't be confined to those prepared and served in restaurants. Venture into retail operations to take some home. Events honoring the delectable morsels and the people that harvest them are well worth the day-tripper's time, too.

morehead city, nc

getting there

Morehead City sits at the end of US 70 at the intersection of US 17. US 70 becomes Arendell Street, the main street in the waterfront port—which is a delightful mix of recreational boaters and anglers making a living off the sea.

where to go

NC Seafood Festival. Downtown; (252) 726-6273; ncseafoodfestival.org. Morehead City is North Carolina's only deepwater port north of Wilmington. Its downtown waterfront offers boardwalks on which to stroll and a big handful of places in which to dine, so each year on the first weekend in October, the city celebrates the sea and the bounty that comes from it during the NC Seafood Festival. The event, drawing an estimated 200,000 people, features nonstop musical entertainment, a boat show, fireworks, a sailing regatta, and the time-honored flounder fling.

where to shop

Blue Ocean Market. 2010 Bridges St.; (252) 726-4886; blueoceanmarketnc.com. Many locals buy their seafood at the Blue Ocean Market, where it is fresh up to 4 times a week. Blue Ocean uses its Facebook page to keep folks apprised of what fish is coming in. Open Mon through Fri 10 a.m. to 6 p.m., Sat 9 a.m. to 5 p.m.

Captain Jim's Seafood. 4665 Arendell St.; (252) 726-3454; captjimsseafood.com. A wide selection of fresh-caught seafood and shellfish is available seasonally. They will pack your purchase so it will make the ride home. Captain Jim's also supplies many of the local restaurants with its catches.

where to eat

The Sanitary Fish Market and Restaurant. 501 Evans St.; (252) 247-3111. After 63 years of serving seafood, the Sanitary continues to be a destination as well as a restaurant. Its famous hush puppies are on the table before the chairs are completely pulled in, and all dishes are served with coleslaw and French fries. Stop to browse the memorabilia before you exit. The restaurant is filled with comments of visitors since 1938, along with photographs of beauty queens and politicians. Lunch and dinner, generally fried or broiled, are served daily. $$.

where to stay

Buccaneer Inn. 2806 Arendell St.; (252) 726-3115. The Buccaneer Inn is a standard hotel accommodation outside downtown Morehead City. Its position on Morehead City's main street makes the hotel a convenient location for a day-tripper not planning on spending much time inside. The rooms, however, are clean and quiet, and it also has an outdoor pool. $.

sneads ferry, nc

getting there

Just over an hour from Morehead City lies the small town of Sneads Ferry. To get there, take SR 24 south through the southern portion of Croatan National Forest.

where to go

Sneads Ferry Shrimp Festival. 126 Park Ln.; (910) 327-3335; sneadsferryshrimpfestival .org. More than 385 tons of shrimp are caught and hauled into Sneads Ferry each year, so this festival honors that industry. Held the third weekend of October, this community festival features the Shrimp Ball, entertainment, arts and crafts, a shrimp-heading contest, and the crowning of Miss Shrimp. On the waterfront in Sneads Ferry, you'll find a half-dozen places to pick up fresh seafood.

where to shop

Seafood markets in Sneads Ferry include **Davis Seafood** (155 Davis Ln.; 910-327-4081), and **Grants Oyster House** (1148 Old Folkstone Rd.; 910-327-3351).

J&B AquaFood. 16 Bayshore Dr.; (910) 330-0737. This is possibly one of the best places in the state to pick up fresh oysters and clams. They come from the waters of Stump Sound between Topsail Island and Jacksonville.

where to eat

Riverview Cafe. 119 Hall Point Rd.; (910) 327-2011. Great views of the active waterfront with boats coming in with the day's catch are afforded at this seafood restaurant. It's been here since the 1950s, so while the building may not impress the fried flounder will. The most plentiful selections are fried. Everett Seafood is located behind the restaurant if you want to take home a catch yourself. Open Sun through Thurs 11 a.m. to 8:30 p.m., Fri 11 a.m. to 9 p.m., and Sat 11 a.m. to 9:30 p.m. $$.

ocean isle beach, nc

getting there

Ocean Isle Beach is about 2 hours from Sneads Ferry, driving along US 17.

where to go

NC Oyster Festival. (910) 754-6644; ncoysterfestival.com. Though oysters are harvested in the sounds, intertidal, and shallow waters all along North Carolina's coast, Brunswick County laid claim 3 decades ago to the NC Oyster Festival. Bands play throughout the 2-day festival held the third weekend of October. It features a tennis tournament, road race, an oyster stew cook-off, and the oyster-shucking contest with the winner having a chance of moving on to the international oyster-shucking championship in Galway, Ireland.

where to eat

Ocean Isle Fish Company. 65 Causeway Dr.; (910) 575-0902; oceanislefishcom. A tiki bar and deck overlook the causeway where fisherman arrive with the day's catch. On the menu are selections of simple fresh fish dishes as well as burgers and such for land lovers. Open 11 a.m. to midnight. $$$.

calabash, nc

getting there

In order to get to Calabash from Ocean Isle, make your way back across the Intercoastal Waterway to SR 179. The drive isn't more than about 20 minutes.

where to eat

Though the number of family-owned, family-style restaurants is diminishing in this quaint fishing village, the streets are still lined with establishments often claiming to serve the original calabash-style seafood. Fresh local seafood is delivered daily to these restaurants, but diners should note that often offerings, even the deep-fried calabash plates, might not be fresh fish while they are being treated to picturesque views of the waterfront.

Becks, The Original Calabash Restaurant. 1014 River Rd.; (910) 579-6776; becksrestaurant.com. Founded in 1940, this restaurant and its recipes have been passed down from generation to generation. The Becks were among the original restaurateurs to open here. In addition to the standard calabash-style offerings, look for crab legs and broiled selections on the menu. $$.

Captain Nance's Seafood. 9939 Nance St.; (910) 579-2574; captainnancesseafood.com. You'll be seated along with a basket of hush puppies and honey butter if Captain Nance's is among your dining choices. Fine selections of flounder, shrimp, and other seafood dishes follow those hush puppies. $$.

Ella's of Calabash. 1148 River Rd.; (910) 579-6728; ellasofcalabashnc.com. Founded in 1950, Ella's claim to fame is as an original, too, but it also claims more fresh fish than others. Open daily 11 a.m. to 9 p.m. $$.

day trip 46

food & drink

fresh food:
anderson, sc; spartanburg, sc;
hendersonville, nc

From peaches in the upstate of South Carolina to the sweet apples of the mountains of North Carolina, fresh Carolina foods are waiting to be picked. A burgeoning farm-to-table restaurant business, pick-your-own farms, and all the remarkably fresh agritourism opportunities in between provide the hungry day-tripper with opportunities aplenty.

South Carolina ships 90,000 tons of peaches annually, more than twice the amount exported by the state of Georgia, which claims status as the peach state. Hendersonville in the mountains of North Carolina produces the lion's share of apples in this state that ranks seventh in apple production. Delicate strawberries, plump blueberries, hearty pumpkins, watermelon, flowers, herbs, and vegetables galore are all waiting on literally hundreds of farms that in recent years have opened their doors (or gates) to the public. Even dairy, beef, and poultry farmers are participating. Tours, petting zoos, hayrides, gift shops, and restaurants are among the many amenities offered by these sites. A primer based on some of the Carolinas agri-locations follows, but for more comprehensive listings on the agritourism sites in the Carolinas, visit ncfarmfresh.com or pickyourown.org for South Carolina.

anderson, sc

getting there

Near Clemson University, where farmers find a multitude of agricultural extension services, make your way to Anderson via I-85 at exit 19 (US 76).

where to go

Denver Downs Farm. 4915 Clemson Blvd.; (864) 261-8638; denverdownsfarm.com. Denver Downs, a cotton farm in the 1860s, now produces vegetables grown for sale at Denver Downs Farm Market, located at Lakeside Road near here. On-site, daily 9 a.m. to 5 p.m., you can buy tomatoes, beans, cucumbers, watermelon, figs, and other items the family purchases for resale such as peanuts. Seasonally, vegetables are available to pick on your own. Each October, the farm develops a corn maze and pumpkin patch. Open mid-June to Jan 1, Mon through Fri 9 a.m. to 6 p.m., Sat 9 a.m. to 4 p.m.

Berry Acres. 232 Strawberry Rd.; (864) 224 5441;. Berries galore grow on this small family farm. Pick your own strawberries, blackberries, blueberries, raspberries, peaches, and muscadines mid-Apr through Sept. Local honey, ground corn, and other delicacies are available for purchase at the red barn shop; then relax by the shaded lake. In fall the farm celebrates with its play patch that includes hayrides, a corn maze, zip lines, and other family fun attractions.

worth more time

Split Creek Farm. 3806 Centerville Rd., Pendleton; (864) 287-3921; splitcreek.com. This dairy farm in the foothills of the Blue Ridge, not far from Anderson, includes milking and cheese operations, and a kid nursery. Split Creek Farm's certified Nubian goat herd produces all the milk used for its cheese, fudge, yogurt, and other items sold at the shop here. They even sell cuts of goat meat. Open Mon through Sat 9 a.m. to 6 p.m., Sun 2 to 5 p.m. Tours of the farm are offered with advance reservations and a $4 fee per person.

spartanburg, sc

getting there

Spartanburg is located at I-85 and I-26 about an hour's drive north on I-85.

where to go

John Smith's Hill Farm. 199 Dobson Heights Rd.; (864) 497-3271; johnsmithhill.com. Specializing in herbs, soaps, oils, and natural sweeteners as well as organically grown eggs, this farm is operated as a legacy to African-American John Hill, who founded it at the turn of the century. A number of multicultural events are conducted throughout the year, and tours are available by appointment. Tours cost $7 for adults and $5 for children.

Strawberry Hill USA. 3097 Hwy. 11; (864) 461-7225; strawberryhillusa.com. Located just north of Spartanburg is the Cooley family farm that produces Top of the Hill brand fruit, including peaches, strawberries, cantaloupes, and blackberries. Fall brings a celebration with a corn maze and hayrides. Their shed on Highway 11 in West Chesnee offers the full selection of fresh picks, while the cafe across the highway offers fresh-made biscuits, burgers, and desserts including hand-churned ice cream with fresh fruit. The shed is open daily 8 a.m. to 8 p.m. in season. The cafe is open 6 a.m. to 2:30 p.m. but serves ice cream 10 a.m. to 8 p.m.

where to shop

Abbott Farms. 140 Chesnee Hwy. Ext.; (800) 764-0076; abbottfarmsonline.com. Abbott Farms opened its first peach stand on a little country road in South Carolina in 1955. That country road is now I-85, and Abbott Farms has 6 markets from Gaffney to I-26 near Columbia. Each location is a little different, but all offer fresh peaches as well as peach and other popular flavors of cider. Open Mon through Sat 7 a.m. to 8 p.m.

Converse Deli. 551 E. Main St., Suite 105; (864) 585-5580. Easy on the cholesterol and calorie count are the lunch offerings at the Converse Deli. This popular lunchtime restaurant is part of a farm-to-table program that even has a small garden in front of the restaurant. The selections, however, resemble those of a traditional deli. Open Mon through Sat 10 a.m. to 9 p.m., Sun 11 a.m. to 3 p.m. $.

> ## · quirky carolina
>
> *A million-gallon water tank standing 4 stories tall between exits 90 and 92 on I-85 north of Spartanburg has been named by some "Moon over Gaffney" because of its resemblance to the human derrière. Regardless, this peach has done its job. Built in 1981, the Gaffney Board of Public Works commissioned an artist to paint the tank to resemble a peach, attempting to make clear that South Carolina produces more peaches than the state of Georgia.*

Hub City Farmers Market. 298 Magnolia St.; (864) 585-0905; hubcityfm.org. The Hub City Farmers Market is an active, engaged organization that works to ensure all products sold at the market are locally produced. The seasonal Saturday market, at the old railroad depot, includes music, children's activities, cooking demonstrations, and other events. On Wednesday the market is held in Morgan Square downtown in summer.

hendersonville, nc

getting there

Traveling from peach country to apple country in a day's time isn't out of the question. Nestled in the foothills of North Carolina's Blue Ridge, the state's apple capital of Hendersonville is only about an hour from Spartanburg via I-26 West to US 64 at exit 49.

where to go

Coston's Apple House. 3748 Chimney Rock Rd.; (828) 685-8352; costonfarm.com. Pick your own apples at this fourth-generation farm. Dozens of varieties of apples as well as

'tis the season

High in the hills of North Carolina is a giant swath from Banner Elk to the Virginia border north of West Jefferson with more than 25,000 acres of Christmas tree farms that produce $100 million of Christmas trees, mainly Fraser firs, annually. Fraser firs love the mountains, requiring good drainage and a colder climate—generally about 3,000 feet in elevation, making the state the number-two producer nationally. A growing segment of that business is the choose-and-cut experience that's become more significant in the past decade, as public demand for green, memorable experiences grows. Opting for any live tree is a green choice. Christmas trees are recyclable and renewable. They absorb carbon dioxide and produce oxygen; 1 acre of Christmas trees provides the daily oxygen requirement of 18 people. And growers are expanding on the experience, providing complete Christmas shops, petting zoos, farm tours, hayrides, inflatables, pipe slides, marshmallow roasting, and food and beverage services. For more information or to use the interactive tree farm locator map, contact the **NC Christmas Tree Association** *(828-262-5826; ncchristmastrees.com). Or just put your car on US 321 between Boone and Blowing Rock beginning in November, pick a sign, and follow the directions. There are dozens from which to choose.*

pumpkins and other gourds are available beginning August 1. A bakery and gift shop here offers fried apple pies, cider, apple cookbooks, and kitchen gadgets. Open daily 8:30 a.m. to 5 p.m. in season.

Grandad's Apples N' Such. 2951 Chimney Rock Rd.; (828) 685-1685; grandadsapples .com. This fun-filled apple farm is especially good for families. In addition to 20 different varieties of apples, it has a small petting farm of goats, llamas, and other animals. The cow train takes children on a short tour of the farm. A pumpkin patch, corn maze, and related activities round out the season. Don't forget to stop in at the shop located at the barn and silo for a caramel apple or other goodies. Open daily 9 a.m. to 5 p.m. Aug through Oct.

J. H. Stepp Farm and Hillcrest Orchard. 221 Stepp Orchard Dr.; (828) 685-9083; stepp apples.com. Take a tractor-pulled wagon ride through this 40-acre farm. Stop in the rustic store to buy apple butter, apple salsa, and mixes for your own apple products. Open Mon through Sat 9 a.m. to 5:30 p.m., Sun 10 a.m. to 6 p.m.

Justus Orchard. 187 Garren Rd.; (828) 685-8033; justusorchard.com. Apples, blackberries, pumpkins, and peaches are all available at the Justus Orchard. Sip on a warm cup of cider while sitting on the big front porch or stop in at the bakery to shop for apple cider doughnuts, apple chips, and everything else apple. Open daily 8:30 a.m. to 6 p.m. July through early Nov.

worth more time

Based in Asheville, **Wild Food Adventures** (828-209-8599; notastelikehome.org) takes participants out to eat—outside, that is. Owner and tour leader Alan Muskat leads tours usually within an hour's drive from Asheville to forage for wild food. The 3-hour tours are suitable for all ages and include a tasting or a meal. The cost is $75 for adults and $35 for children.

where to shop

Henderson County Farmers' Curb Market. Corner of 2nd Avenue and Church Street, Hendersonville; (828) 692-8012; curbmarket.com. Shoppers are assured of getting only homegrown produce and locally handmade items because all vendors at this farmers' market are required to be residents of Henderson County. It's been that way since 1924, and some of the vendors are descendants of the original vendors. Shoppers will find crafts, baked goods, jellies, plants, flowers, toys, and seasonal produce. Open Tues, Thurs, and Sat 8 a.m. to 2 p.m. Apr through Dec; Sat 8 a.m. to 1 p.m. Jan through Mar.

the great outdoors

day trip 47

the great outdoors

>>>
the blue ridge parkway:
asheville, nc; burnsville, nc; spruce pine, nc; linville, nc; blowing rock, nc

Driving from Cherokee in the west to the Virginia state line near I-77, the Blue Ridge Parkway is a 3.5-hour tour of some of the most majestic views and engaging attractions in the Carolinas. It's so incredible, in fact, it would be nearly impossible to travel it that quickly. At 469 miles long, the parkway has been one of the most popular destinations for people on the East Coast for 75 years. Although it's not a national park, the parkway is maintained on either side by the National Park Service and was constructed in part as a Works Progress Administration project with assistance from the Civilian Conservation Corps. It took 52 years to complete, including the spectacular engineering feat of the Linn Cove Viaduct, which takes travelers around Grandfather Mountain. The North Carolina portion runs about 252 miles through 25 tunnels and to the parkway's highest elevation of just over 6,000 feet near the city of Waynesville and at the Eastern Continental Divide near Spruce Pine.

There are no interchanges on the parkway, with access at strategic locations granted by short roads that connect it to other highways. Once on the parkway, signs simply indicate North and South and that the speed limit is a maximum of 45 miles per hour. Frequent overlooks with parking spaces, occasional picnic tables, and trail heads can be accessed, like the rest of the parkway, free of charge. The road isn't maintained in winter, so it can be closed without notice during common inclement weather. Access the parkway at the Cherokee Indian Reservation and the Great Smoky Mountains National Park at US 441, and plan a northerly route beginning at MP 469. Those Milepost markers will get smaller as we travel north.

cold mountain

At parkway MP 420.2 overlook is the Shining Rock Wilderness Area, the second-largest such protected area in North Carolina. It includes Cold Mountain, the basis of Charles Frazier's best-selling novel by the same name.

asheville, nc

getting there

Access the parkway at Tunnel Road (US 70). Pick it up from I-240 at exit 7 west of Asheville. US 70 runs parallel to I-40 from Black Mountain, so you can access it from the east at a number of points. Just follow the signs.

where to go

Blue Ridge Parkway Visitor Center. Blue Ridge Parkway MP 384; (828) 298-5330; nps .gov/blri. This visitor center (one of 9 along the Parkway in North Carolina) is a good place to start your exploration of the parkway, to pick up brochures, and to learn more about the area. Inside the LEED certified building, find a small exhibit hall, a 22-foot-tall interactive map wall, and a 25-minute film about the parkway and regional heritage. A multimedia wall provides information on places to visit along the parkway and a small shop carries books, T-shirts, hats, and the like. Open daily 9 a.m. to 5 p.m.

Folk Art Center. Blue Ridge Parkway MP 382; (828) 298-7928; craftguild.org. This center is the home of the Southern Highland Craft Guild, which represents generations of hundreds of craft artists from the 9 states of southern Appalachia. Their work, sold here at the Allanstand Craft Shop, is nothing less than exquisite. You'll be able to interact with artists producing their wares and peruse rotating exhibits as well as work available in the shop. Open daily 10 a.m. to 5 p.m.

North Carolina Arboretum. 100 Frederick Law Olmsted Way; (828) 665-2492; ncarbo retum.org. Art and cultivated gardens are parts of this exhibit that helps guests understand the importance of plants to our world. Among the most prominent exhibits is a display of bonsai, an exhibit greenhouse, an azalea collection, and a heritage garden. In all there are more than 400 acres on which to enjoy reconnecting to the natural world. Guided outdoor walks are held Sat in warm-weather months. The Baker Exhibit Center allows the garden ample opportunity to display art- and nature-based exhibits on a regular basis. It also hosts an orchid show early in the year and other events of horticultural interest later in the year.

Admission is $16 per vehicle. Open daily 8 a.m. to 9 p.m. Apr through Oct, 8 a.m. to 7 p.m. Nov through Mar.

burnsville, nc

getting there

Burnsville is a small town between Asheville and Spruce Pine with a big claim to fame—the tallest peak on the East Coast. Simply head north on the Blue Ridge Parkway from Asheville, stopping first at Craggy Gardens at MP 364.

where to go

Craggy Gardens. MP 364 Blue Ridge Parkway. Don't miss Craggy Gardens if you are along this part of the parkway in June or July. Located in the Great Craggy Mountains, it is covered during those midsummer months with pink and purple rhododendron. A small visitor center, Craggy Pinnacle Trail, and other trails are located here. In mid- to late summer, keep your eyes open for blueberries. This area has prime picking. Open weekends in early Apr through late May 10 a.m. to 4 p.m., 9 a.m. to 5 p.m. Memorial Day weekend through Oct 31. The eastern entrance may stay open through Nov, weather permitting.

Mount Mitchell. 2388 Hwy. 128; (828) 675-4611; ncparks.gov. At Mount Mitchell, 6,684 feet above sea level and the highest point on the East Coast, clouds often hover around the peak. Temperatures are much cooler than the surrounding landscape by as much as 10 degrees, and quirky weather has brought snow here in July. It's not right on the parkway, but you can find easy access to it at MP 355. A small visitor center has exhibits on the peak and its plant and animal inhabitants. Behind the center is an observation platform and the grave of Dr. Elisha Mitchell, who fell to his death while trying to confirm the mountain's height. Birds more characteristic of New England and Canada—including winter wrens, slate-colored juncos, red crossbills, and golden-crowned kinglets—nest at these high altitudes. Picnicking is welcome, but there is also a restaurant here. Typically open during daylight hours.

spruce pine, nc

getting there

Spruce Pine proper is located at US 19 and SR 226, but there is plenty to do right on the parkway about 5 miles to the south and in the community of Little Switzerland.

where to go

Emerald Village. McKinney Mine Road off Highway 226A; (828) 765-6463; emeraldvillage .com. Set like a real mining operation with abandoned equipment, dozens of different minerals, gems, and rocks have been found here, including aquamarine, emerald, garnet, and uranium. Attendants are on hand to help identify finds, as are artisans for cutting and mounting newly found stones. Also visit the North Carolina Mining Museum, located in an underground mine, where you can examine old mining equipment and displays on the area's mining heritage. Other village attractions include the Company Store and Discovery Mill, where you'll find more displays related to mining as well as souvenirs and gifts. Open 9 a.m. to 5 p.m. Mon through Fri and 9 a.m. to 6 p.m. Sat and Sun, Apr through Oct. Fees vary by activity.

Museum of North Carolina Minerals. 214 Parkway Maintenance Rd.; (828) 765-2761. More than 300 of the rocks, minerals, and gems found naturally in this area are showcased in this facility, a parkway visitor center off the parkway near MP 331. Visitors enter an exhibit hall through a cave-like entrance to discover more about the rocks and soil beneath their feet through push-button and other innovative displays. Interactive displays also allow visitors to trace when and where certain minerals were discovered throughout North Carolina. Free. Open daily 9 a.m. to 5 p.m.

Orchard at Altapass. 1025 Orchard Rd., Blue Ridge Parkway at MP 328.3; (828) 765-9531; altapassorchard.com. When the Blue Ridge Parkway was built, it split this historic orchard in two, but in the mid-1990s Kit Trubey and her brother and sister-in-law Bill and Judy Carson bought the orchard, with turning it into something special in mind. Bill, a retired NASA scientist, had had about all he could take of retirement, so in the fall he spins yarns on a hayless hayride. The half of the orchard south of the parkway thrives with apple trees where visitors can pick their own, but it also includes a host of activities including mountain musical events and a seasonal butterfly exhibit. Free with a charge for some activities. Hours are seasonal and vary by activity.

where to eat

Switzerland Cafe. 9440 Hwy. 226-A; (828) 765-5289; switzerlandcafe.com. Light items, soups, and salads make up most of the menu in an old-time general store atmosphere near the Blue Ridge Parkway MP 334. Mountain trout and a handful of meat and veggie dishes are also served. Open daily 10 a.m. to 4 p.m. mid-Apr through Oct, and Fri and Sat 5 to 9 p.m. $–$$.

where to stay

Big Lynn Lodge. 10860 Hwy. 226A; (800) 654-5232; biglynnlodge.com. This is a very nice country inn with rooms, cottages, and condos, all of which afford spectacular views from rocking-chair porches. There is also a restaurant on-site that serves breakfast and dinner included in the room rates. $$–$$$.

Skyline Motel. 12255 Hwy. 226; (828) 765-9394; skylinevillageinn.com. Legend says that moonshine revenue paid for construction of the Skyline in the 1940s. Located just off the parkway in the side of a mountain, it is complete with wood paneling, marble floors, and other extravagances. The Cavern Tavern restaurant is also located here and serves steak, barbecue, and other hearty meals. $$.

linville, nc

getting there

Continue north on the Blue Ridge Parkway for about 30 minutes. To the east is Linville Gorge, one of the largest wilderness areas in North Carolina. Grandfather Mountain is easy to locate off the parkway.

where to go

Grandfather Mountain. 2050 Blowing Rock Hwy.; (800) 468-7325; grandfather.com. One of the top scenic attractions in the North Carolina mountains, Grandfather Mountain is a great place to spend the day hiking and learning about nature. The 5,964-foot peak was named for its profile as it appears from about 7 miles north. As the name suggests, from this vantage point the mountain looks like a bearded grandfather. A globally recognized nature preserve, you can drive through much of Grandfather Mountain, but you'll have to park at the visitor center and walk to get to the top. You'll also find picnic and limited camping facilities here. Food is available at **Mildred's Grill,** named for the famous bear that spent much of her life on Grandfather Mountain. Also located here is a nature museum with a gift shop. The museum offers an unusual look at the area's natural past, with displays and films on nature and the mountains. You'll see gold nuggets, precious gemstones, a billion-year-old rock, and displays of rare plants and animals. Habitats with a variety of animals—including black bears and cubs, cougars, deer, and eagles—are on display. Many of these animals have been injured and will never be able to return to the wild. The highlight of a visit to Grandfather Mountain is a stomach-rumbling walk across the **Mile-High Swinging Bridge.** It extends majestically over a natural gorge filled with hardwood trees and rhododendron. You'll find overlooks on both sides of the bridge if you can't make the walk across. Open daily 9 a.m. to 5 p.m. during winter, 9 a.m. to 6 p.m. in spring and fall, and 9 a.m. to 7 p.m. in summer.

worth more time
linville falls

In the Linville Gorge Wilderness Area south of Grandfather Mountain off US 221, Linville Falls is located at 717 Gurney Franklin Rd. (MP 317.14; 828-765-1045.) It is a 3-tiered fall that plunges spectacularly into the gorge. There are several accessible, easy to moderate trails here, as well as 2 overlooks. For a more extensive experience in the Linville Gorge area, contact the Morganton-based Hike More Adventures (828-595-4453), which guides backcountry hikes and camping trips.

blowing rock, nc

getting there

Blowing Rock is between MP 298 and 292 on the Blue Ridge Parkway about 30 minutes from Linville.

where to shop

Moses H. Cone Memorial Park. 667 Service Rd.; (828) 295-7938. Located in the 1901 home of textile magnate Moses H. Cone, named Flat Top Manor, is a craft shop of the Southern Highland Craft Guild with baskets, quilts, iron work, old-fashioned toys, and other items for sale. Surrounding the home are hiking and equestrian trails, a lake, and other natural amenities. Open daily 9 a.m. to 5 p.m., mid-Mar through Nov.

where to stay

Julian Price Park. MP 297 Blue Ridge Pkwy.; (828) 963-5911. Located at the foot of Grandfather Mountain, this park provides tent camping sites as one of only 3 such sites on the parkway. Surprisingly it's often uncrowded, even in summer. Price Lake here offers an opportunity for fishing and canoeing with canoes for rent at the park office. Several trails are available for hiking with cool mountain streams for wading. $.

worth more time
beyond blowing rock

After passing through Blowing Rock, the Blue Ridge Parkway continues for another 80 miles, and there are stops along the way that are worth more time. One of the famous frescoes by artist Ben Long, *The Last Supper*, can be seen at **Holy Trinity Episcopal Church** in Glendale Springs at MP 258. Then at MP 238.5 is the entrance to **Doughton Park** and the 1885 **Brinegar Cabin,** spared from the construction of the parkway in the 1930s but purchased for the right-of-way. Park rangers do occasional demonstrations at the site.

Doughton Park continues to skirt the parkway for another 6 miles, providing ample opportunities for hiking and other outdoor activities. The parkway then runs along the northern border of **North Carolina's Stone Mountain State Park,** ending for the Old North State at **Cumberland Knob Recreation Area.**

day trip 48

the great outdoors

> ### golf capital of the world:
> ### pinehurst, nc; southern pines, nc

With nearly 15,000 holes and immense geographic diversity, the golf experience in the Carolinas is unmatched. From legendary courses at Grandfather Mountain Golf and Country Club to Tobacco Road Golf Course in eastern North Carolina's Sanford and south to the resorts of the South Carolina coast, the Carolinas offer at least a dozen of what *Golf Digest* calls America's Best Courses.

The true land of golf legend, however, is Pinehurst and Southern Pines of the North Carolina Sandhills—the land of the longleaf pine and the "golf capital of the world." Within this area, which boasts nearly 50 championship golf courses, are no less than 4 courses on *Golf Magazine*'s list of top 100 courses anyone can play. On that list is Pinehurst No. 2 at Pinehurst Resort, a course you can play that was selected for the 2014 US Open Men's and Women's Championships. Since 1962 the course has hosted nine US Golf Association Championships, including two other Men's US Open Championships in 1999 and 2005.

Add in luxurious accommodations, elegant, upscale shopping opportunities, and fine culinary experiences, and the day-tripper will soon see this isn't a bad place to spend the day—golfing or not. Pinehurst was founded in 1887 by a Boston soda-fountain magnate who sold 5,000 acres here to James Walker Tufts, who wanted to build a southern winter retreat and a health resort. Tufts built an inn and New England–style village, designed by landscape architect Frederick Law Olmsted. Originally, he called it Tuftstown, later changing the name to Pinehurst by selecting the name from a runners-up list in a town-naming contest in the New England coastal area. Pinehurst's evolution as a revered golf venue is rooted in the 1898 development of its first golf course. However, it was the hiring of Donald

fore!

The Pinehurst/Southern Pines area, which takes no longer than 15 minutes to navigate by car from one end to the other, has more than 165 miles of fairways, 2,900 bunkers, 1 golf hole for every 75 residents, and 80 horse farms.

J. Ross as a golf pro in 1900 that undeniably altered the focus of Pinehurst Resort. For more information, contact the Pinehurst, Southern Pines, Aberdeen Area Convention and Visitors Bureau, 10677 Hwy. 15/501, Southern Pines 28388. Call (910) 692-3330 or (800) 346-5362, or visit homeofgolf.com.

pinehurst, nc

getting there

Located an hour from Raleigh and Greensboro and 2 hours from Charlotte, Pinehurst is about as convenient as it gets. From Charlotte, travel on Highway 27 to I-73/I-74 South. Take a left on Highway 211 south. From Raleigh, US 1 is a straight shot, and from Greensboro, US 220 merges with I-74 South. At Candor, take SR 211 south.

where to golf

Pinehurst Resort and Country Club. 1 Carolina Vista; (910) 295-6811 or (800) 487-4653; pinehurst.com. Nestled among the pines, this 4-diamond resort has played host to travelers since 1895. Pinehurst is the world's largest golf resort with 9 signature golf courses plus the Pinehurst Golf Academy. **Pinehurst's No. 2** is a perennial favorite of those who rank golf courses, consistently standing in the top 10 among public courses. Opened in 1901, this course was called "the fairest test of championship golf I have ever designed" by architect Donald Ross. Players have to drive the ball well and hit long irons well. Most of all, players must have a razor-sharp short game because of small greens that fall off around the edge. **Pinehurst No. 4** opened in April 2000 and was dubbed Tom Fazio's "tribute to Pinehurst." Number 4 was built with crowned greens similar to those found on No. 2 and complemented by British-style pot bunkers and sand areas planted with native grasses. It also consistently ranks as one of the top 100 courses you can play. **Pinehurst No. 8** was the site of the 1997 and 1998 PGA Club Professional Championships. This is solid, straightforward golf, free from theatrics like artificial earth moments and forced carries. This par 72 course was created by Tom Fazio to celebrate the 100th birthday of the resort in 1996.

pay to play

In this region it is not uncommon for greens fees to be more than $200. You'll also want to hire one of the region's famous caddies for $50 plus tip.

Pinewild Country Club. 6 Glasglow Dr.; (910) 295-5145; pinewildcc.com. Designed by Gary Player, the Holly at Pinewild is a classic "risk reward" layout complemented by beautifully wooded terrain, rolling hills, ponds, and streams. Pinewild has hosted the PGA's Tour School Qualifying and the LPGA's Pinewild Championship, and continues to play host to various USGA Qualifying Events.

where to go

Sandhills Horticultural Gardens. 3395 Airport Rd.; (910) 695-3882; sandhills.edu. Ten major gardens, covering 27 acres, are featured here, including the Ebersol Holly Collection, which is said to be the largest on the East Coast; a specialized conifer garden; the formal English Sir Walter Raleigh Garden; Hillside Garden; Azalea Garden; and the Desmond Native Wetland Trail Garden. Horticulture students at Sandhills Community College, whose graduates have gone on to find notable horticultural jobs at such places as the White House, maintain the gardens. Free. Open during daylight hours.

Tufts Archives, Given Memorial Library. 150 Cherokee Rd.; (910) 295-3642; tufts archives.org. The story of Pinehurst unfolds in the displays of maps, letters, pictures, news clippings, and other documents that date from 1895 when Tufts first began to make this resort a reality. Free. Open Mon through Fri 9:30 a.m. to 5 p.m. and Sat 9:30 a.m. to 12:30 p.m.

where to shop

The Village at Pinehurst. 80 Carolina Vista Dr.; (910) 235-8507. Created with James Tufts's vision, the shops at the Village of Pinehurst have storefront windows that mimic a turn-of-the-century New England shopping district. Grab a bite to eat at one of a handful of restaurants and stroll the inviting streets. The centerpiece, the Theatre Building, is an enclosed mini-mall that houses a group of stores, ranging from clothing boutiques to gifts and collectibles.

where to stay

Pinehurst Resort. 1 Carolina Vista; (910) 295-6811 or (800) 487-4653; pinehurst.com. Pinehurst Resort offers a spectacular centerpiece hotel and 3 inns as well as condominium and villa rentals. All accommodations in Pinehurst are priced in the $$$ category. For reservations, call (800) 487-4653. Accommodations typically include meals and golf packages, but there are a host of other amenities including 3 full-size croquet courts, tennis courts, and a 31,000-square-foot spa with 28 private treatment rooms and 8 salon stations. The spa also showcases a golf fitness studio. Also available from the resort are 30-minute guided carriage tours of the village of Pinehurst for $15 per person.

The Holly Inn. 2300 Cherokee Rd. Originally opened on Dec 31, 1895, this was the village's first inn. The Holly Inn has 85 rooms with period furnishings. The inn offers 2 distinctive dining options in Pinehurst Resort's modified American meal plan. The 1895 Grille ($$$) is the resort's premier dining experience, featuring regional cuisine in an elegant southern grill, with a buffet breakfast and innovative New American–style cuisine for dinner. The cozy Tavern ($$–$$$), with its century-old, hand-carved, imported Scottish bar, working fireplace, and outdoor patio, is open daily for lunch and dinner.

The Carolina. 1 Carolina Vista. Built in 1901, this stately Victorian structure is the centerpiece of the resort, housing 210 guest rooms and 12 suites. The hotel's Carolina Dining Room ($$$) serves breakfast, lunch, and dinner, and the Ryder Cup Lounge ($$) is for lighter meals and cocktails.

Manor Inn. 5 Community Dr. With 45 rooms this inn has the intimate feel of a bed-and-breakfast and is a popular choice of golfing groups and families because of its value pricing and room configuration options.

Magnolia Inn. 65 Magnolia St.; (910) 295-6900 or (800) 526-5562; themagnolia inn.com. Old South hospitality can be found at this charming inn located in the center of the historic village of Pinehurst. Enjoy gourmet dinners ($$$), particularly the crab cakes, served in the dining room, on the porch, in the pub, or poolside. Golf packages are available. $$$.

southern pines, nc

getting there

To get to Southern Pines from Pinehurst, take the minutes-long drive on Highway 2, also known as Midland Road.

where to golf

Longleaf Golf & Family Club. 10 N. Knoll Rd.; (910) 692-6100; longleafgfc.com. Created by Dan Maples, this par 71 course is popular and challenging, but affable to even moderate players. It has retained the white fences, hedgerows, and rail posts—a tribute to its former past as a horse-training estate.

longleaf pine

The pine tree was named the North Carolina state tree in 1963, no doubt because of the ubiquitous nature of, among others, the longleaf pine. In fact, the world's oldest longleaf pine (467 years old) can be found near Weymouth Woods Sandhills Nature Preserve in Southern Pines.

Pine Needles Lodge & Golf Club. 1005 Midland Rd.; (910) 692-7111; pineneedleslodge .com. Restored in 2004, this Donald Ross–designed course has thrice hosted the US Women's Open Championship. This 100-year-old resort is located on 500 acres of longleaf pine, and the Pine Needles course was built here to contour with the natural surroundings.

Talamore Golf Resort. 48 Talamore Dr.; (910) 692-5884; talamoregolfresort.com. This 18-hole championship course was designed by Rees Jones. A long 7,000-foot course, Talamore is a newer course that has begun receiving accolades from the national media. It also grabs attention for its use of llama caddies.

where to go

Historic Shaw House Properties. Morganton Road and Broad Street; (910) 692-2051; moorehistory.com. Operated by Moore County Historical Society are 3 historic homes—the Shaw, Garner, and Bryant Houses—built during a 50-year period beginning in 1770. Each is furnished with plain-style furniture, depicting life in the Sandhills at the end of the 18th century. Also maintained by the historical society are the Britt Sanders and Joel McLendon Cabins (ca. 1760–90). Guests might be surprised at the rustic appearance of all the homes, but that is due in large part to the society's care in preserving them as accurately as possible. Free. Open Tues through Fri 1 to 4 p.m.

Weymouth Center. 555 E. Connecticut Ave.; (910) 692-6261; weymouthcenter.org. This 1920s Georgian mansion, situated on 24 acres with extensive gardens, offers arts and humanities activities. The former home of author James Boyd, it's listed on the National Register of Historic Places. The home holds a writers' lecture series, writers-in-residence program, and chamber music presentations. The North Carolina Literary Hall of Fame here pays homage to the most distinguished Tarheel men and women of letters. Find displays, photographs, and lists of works for such notable writers as Thomas Wolfe, O. Henry (William S. Porter), Paul Green, and James Boyd. Admission is $5. Open Mon through Fri 10 a.m. to 2 p.m.

Weymouth Woods Sandhills Nature Preserve. 1024 N. Fort Bragg Rd.; (910) 692-2167; ncparks.gov. Named for Weymouth, England, the 898-acre nature preserve of longleaf pine forest is home to the endangered red-cockaded woodpecker. A nature museum includes exhibits on the importance of the longleaf pine, prescribed burnings that have preserved it, as well as presentations of nature at night and underground. The preserve includes 4.5 miles of year-round trails, and staff conducts regularly scheduled guided tours and programs. Open daily 8 a.m. to 6 p.m. Nov through Mar, 8 a.m. to 8 p.m. Apr through Oct.

where to shop

Campbell House Galleries. 482 E. Connecticut Ave.; (910) 692-4356; mooreart.org. The Arts Council of Moore County preserves this historic home as display space for the work of a featured local, state, or regional artist each month. Most artwork is offered for sale. Open Mon through Fri 9 a.m. to 5 p.m. and select Sat 2 to 4 p.m.

where to eat

Ashten's. 140 E. New Hampshire Ave.; (910) 246-3510; ashtens.com. A winner of North Carolina's Best Dish for its asparagus strudel, Ashten's offers a comfortable fine dining atmosphere plus a pub atmosphere that serves great Angus burgers. Open Tues through Sun for dinner only. $$–$$$.

Chef Warren's. 215 Northeast Broad St.; (910) 692-5240; chefwarrens.com. This cozy French bistro presents mouthwatering menus that feature nightly specials, tapas, and seasonal dishes. Many dishes are prepared with the harvest of the chef's own garden. Open for dinner only on Tues through Sat. $$$.

Ice Cream Parlor. 176 Northwest Broad St.; (910) 692-7273. A popular spot with the lunch crowd, the Ice Cream Parlor specializes in old-fashioned handmade burgers served southern-style with mustard, chili, slaw, and onions. It also serves homemade chicken salad, cakes, and, of course, ice cream hand-scooped out of the freezer. Open daily. $.

Restaurant 195. 195 Bell Ave.; (910) 692-7110; 195pinehurstdining.com. Specializing in all-natural fusion cuisine, this restaurant features grilled swordfish, grilled free-range rack of

quirky carolina

A random collection of tools and practically every kind of preserved North Carolina wildlife along with messages of creationism make up the **Creation Museum, Taxidermy Hall of Fame of North Carolina, and Antique Tool Museum.** *It's located in the Christian Bookstore at 156 N. West Broad St. (910-692-3471).*

lamb, and items as simple as chicken quesadillas. Open for lunch and dinner Wed through Fri, lunch only on Tues. Closed Sun and Mon. $$.

Sweet Basil. 134 Northwest Broad St.; (910) 693-1487. It's a good sign when you see lines outside the door of a restaurant. And that's often the case at Sweet Basil, popular for its soups, salads, and sandwiches, particularly the grilled eggplant sandwich with sweet roasted peppers and arugula on focaccia. Open Mon through Fri 11 a.m. to 3 p.m., Sat 11:30 a.m. to 3 p.m. $$.

where to stay

Jefferson Inn. 150 W. New Hampshire Ave.; (910) 692-9911; jeffersoninnsouthernpines .com. Established in 1902 and renovated in 2009, the Jefferson Inn is a noted landmark in the historic district of Southern Pines. The inn has 15 luxurious rooms and extravagant 1-bedroom suites. Experience fine cuisine in the dining room of One Fifty West or slightly more casual dining at the Tavern and Courtyard. $$.

day trip 49

the great outdoors

> south carolina golf:
> myrtle beach, sc; kiawah island, sc;
> hilton head, sc

Just over the South Carolina border is the North Carolina community of Carolina Shores, where there is not much more than five massive golf courses. From that point south all the way to Hilton Head Island, golf courses dot the landscape like black spots on a Dalmatian. Sure there's a lot more to see and do, but don't tell the avid golfer that. In all, South Carolina offers some 370 golf courses, mostly amid the sun and sand of its coastal resorts. Six golf courses in this region alone rank among the best places in the country the everyday golfer can play. Among them are the famous Harbour Town Golf Links at Hilton Head and the oft-cursed-upon Ocean Course at Kiawah Island, not a bad place for duffers in its own right.

myrtle beach, sc

getting there

Myrtle Beach is located at the extreme northeastern corner of South Carolina and is accessible via US 17 from the north or south. From the west, make your way from wherever you are to US 501, which goes all the way to I-95 and beyond.

where to golf

Barefoot Resort. 4980 Barefoot Resort Bridge Rd.; (843) 390-3200; barefootgolf.com. With 4 golf courses designed by the likes of Davis Love III, Tom Fazio, Greg Norman, and

Pete Dye, this resort, technically located in North Myrtle Beach, is a popular stop for many of the 1 million people who play golf in the Myrtle Beach area each year. The wide-open Love course, named by *Golf Week* as a public top 10 course, integrates an old plantation home setting, while the Fazio course utilizes trees and water features to create a dramatic effect. Hazards and other pitfalls border the moderately difficult Dye course, and Norman's course is set among natural vistas along the Intercoastal Waterway.

Legends Golf Complex. 1500 Legends Dr.; (843) 236-9318; legendsgolf.com. The Heathlands course, one of 5 at Legends Golf Complex, has made the list of *Golf Week*'s top 10 public-access courses. Designer Tom Daok intended to shape it like the old-world Scottish courses such as St. Andrews. With relatively few trees, ocean breezes can heavily affect shots here.

Tidewater Course and Plantation. 1400 Tidewater Dr.; (800) 446-5363; tidewatergolf .com. Also technically located in North Myrtle Beach, this course situated on a bluff offers spectacular views of the ocean and Intercoastal Waterway. A saltwater marsh runs along much of the eastern side of the course while the Intercoastal Waterway flanks the west. The natural contours of the property were retained when the course was designed, making it suitably challenging.

kiawah island, sc

getting there

Kiawah Island is a barrier island south of Charleston. To get here, travel south on US 17 and take Bohicket Road from SR 700 near Charleston. Wadmalaw Sound prohibits direct access from the south.

where to golf

Kiawah Island Golf Resort. 1000 Ocean Course Dr.; (843) 266-4670; kiawahresort.com. Built in 1991 by designer Pete Dye, it was selected to host the 2012 PGA Championship. *Golf World* named Kiawah Island the number-1 golf resort in the U.S. and *Golf Digest* ranked the Ocean Course at Kiawah Island Golf Resort the toughest public course in America, and the number-4 public course. With 10 holes along the Atlantic Ocean, the golfer's game is substantially affected by wind. Kiawah Resort has 4 other courses and a host of other guest amenities, including clay and hard tennis courts and 10 miles of private beach. The Osprey Point Course, designed by Tom Fazio, and Oak Point, the newest of Kiawah's courses, are also public and receive consistent accolades from national media. Jack Nicklaus's Turtle Point and Cougar Point are also open to guests of the resort. Accommodations here include rooms and suites at the Sanctuary as well as condos and villas throughout the island. Minimum night stays may apply in-season.

hilton head, sc

getting there

Hilton Head is located south of Point Royal Sound at the southern tip of South Carolina. It is accessible via I-95 by taking US 278. From Kiawah Island, backtrack to US 17 and follow this east until it joins up with the interstate.

where to golf

Harbour Town Golf Links. 32 Greenwood Dr.; (866) 561-8802; seapines.com. Located at the luxurious Sea Pines Resort on the southern end of Hilton Head Island, Harbour Town offers play in a variety of terrains including wide fairways, pine and oak woodlands, marshes, and areas riddled with bunkers and ponds. Highly acclaimed, it is home to the Hilton Head Golf Academy.

May River Golf Course at Palmetto Bluff. 476 Mount Pelia; (843) 706-6580; palmetto bluffresort.com. The Jack Nicklaus signature course at Palmetto Bluff just outside the city limits of Hilton Head features 7,171 tough yards through live oaks and across scenic land-scapes. *Condé Nast* named Palmetto Bluff one of the best golf resorts in America, and it includes a wide-ranging host of amenities including a spa and access to recreational activities such as horseback riding and kayaking.

day trip 50

the great outdoors

>>> **start your engines:**
concord, nc; kannapolis, nc;
mooresville, nc

The Carolina cities of Darlington, Rockingham, and Wilkesboro are synonymous with the history of stock car racing. Each once held some of the sport's most prestigious races, but in modern times Charlotte and cities north of it have taken hold as veritable epicenters of the world of NASCAR. Wilkes County native Junior Johnson, who would go on to become one of the biggest early names in racing, got his start in the sport like many early drivers—running moonshine through the hills of North Carolina. During Prohibition, drivers using modified cars that possessed the speed to elude police would help moonshiners transport their goods to market. When Prohibition was repealed in 1933, moonshiners continued to make their illegal whiskey and continued to use those fast drivers to avoid revenuers. Concurrently, fast sports cars setting land speed records at Daytona Beach were all the rage. In 1936, 27 drivers gathered at Daytona Beach at an event that would become the first unofficial stock car race. Among those drivers was Bill France Sr., who in 1948 would establish the National Association of Stock Car Auto Racing.

NASCAR is still a France family business based in Daytona. It sanctions three major racing series that make it the number-two spectator sport in America, behind NFL football. Its corporate headquarters are in Daytona, but it also has North Carolina offices in Charlotte, Concord, Conover, and Mooresville. Its 75 million fans spend an estimated $3 billion on licensed products each year.

Charlotte Motor Speedway, built in 1960 in what is now the city of Concord, also includes a newer dirt track and dragway attracting visitors year-round. Since it began to develop, the city has grown by leaps and bounds with an economic impact from tourism quadrupling in the past two decades to more than $313 million. Concord Mills Mall is North Carolina's biggest tourist attraction with 17 million visitors per year. Also linked to the rich heritage of stock car racing is the city of Mooresville, home of more than 60 NASCAR teams and related companies. Kannapolis is popular among legions of race fans if for no other reason than it was the home to the man in the black 3 car—Dale Earnhardt, who would lose his life at Daytona. The icing on the cake in making this a true racing mecca was the opening of the NASCAR Hall of Fame in downtown Charlotte in 2009.

concord, nc

getting there

I-85 at times is heavily congested at exit 49, the location of Concord Mills Mall and a major exit for Charlotte Motor Speedway, located on US 29. It is, however, the easiest access to the city of Concord.

where to go

Morrison Motor Car Museum. 4545 Concord Pkwy. South; (704) 788-9500; backingup classics.com. A checkered sidewalk leads in to Backing Up Classics, where more than 50 classic, antique, 1950s, 1960s, and muscle cars are on display. The museum is owned by Morrison Motor Company, which also buys and sells collector cars, trucks, and motorcycles from a location on US 601 near here. At the museum it carries a wide selection of NASCAR merchandise representing a number of drivers and teams. Admission is $8 for adults and $6 for students or seniors. Hours are Mon through Fri (except Wed) 10 a.m. to 5 p.m., Sat 9 a.m. to 5 p.m., and Sun noon to 5 p.m.

Charlotte Motor Speedway. 5555 Concord Pkwy. South; (704) 455-3209; charlotte motorspeedway.com. NASCAR Cup, and Truck Series racing is conducted on this major 1.5-mile track throughout the year. Its biggest events, however, are the May and October races that feature activities that go on for 2 weeks at a time throughout Concord and Charlotte, which hosts a 3-day Memorial Day Weekend festival called Speedstreet. The Memorial Day Coca-Cola 600 is known as one of the longest and most brutal races in the championship series. In October the Bank of America 400 is also part of the NASCAR championship series. When the 167,000-seat track isn't used for racing, it hosts car shows, Legends Car, Bandolero, and Thunder Roadster Racing. Tours that include a lap around the track in a tour van are offered when big events aren't scheduled.

The Dirt Track at Charlotte Motor Speedway seats another 14,500 people around a half-mile track and offers dirt car racing and monster trucks. The zMAX Dragway hosts National Hot Rod Association events on a track that is 4 wide instead of the traditional 2. While the cars at the big track might flirt with 200 miles per hour, these roaring monsters head down a straight strip topping 300 miles per hour.

Garage Pass Tours. 810 Treva Anne Dr.; (704) 455-2819; garagepassshoptours.com. Stan Rabineau at Garage Pass Tours can spin a racing yarn with the best of them. After a long career working for race teams, he has taken a step back from the sport so that he can pass along his love for it to others. In fact, all guides have related backgrounds to give tourists an insiders' view of some of the biggest names in motorsports. Included on the tours are Hendrick Motorsports, Chip Ganassi Racing with Felix Sabates, Roush Racing, Gibbs Racing, Penske South, Robert Yates Racing, Dale Earnhardt Inc., museums, and motorsports galleries as well as dining at race-themed restaurants. Guides vary tours to give participants the best chance of catching action or even a NASCAR superstar. Tours start at $60 per person plus meals and entry fees and include both individual and group tours.

Hendrick Motorsports. 4400 Papa Joe Hendrick Blvd.; (704) 455-3400; hendrickmotor sports.com. Over 25 years Rick Hendrick has turned his racing business into a racing dynasty with 13 championships and dozens of major victories. As a tribute to those who made it happen, he opened the Hendrick Motorsports Museum with famous stock cars, sports cars, and championship hardware. It's located on the campus where Hendrick's team develops some of the most progressive technologies used in racing. On display are Jeff Gordon's Daytona 500 winning car, the Chevy Lumina driven by Tom Cruise in the film *Days of Thunder*, and videos and items depicting technology from the sport. Get a peek at the shop from numerous viewing windows. Open Mon through Fri 10 a.m. to 5 p.m. and Sat 10 a.m. to 3 p.m.

Richard Petty Driving Experience. 6022 Victory Ln.; (704) 455-9443; drivepetty.com. Richard Petty, "The King," is behind this driving experience. Like most of these operations, the schedule varies according to the NASCAR schedule here and at speedways across the country. The speedway experiences include up to 80 laps around the speedway. A 3-lap ride-along starts at $99, and driving experiences begin at $449.

Roush Fenway Racing Museum. 4600 Roush Place Northwest; (704) 720-4600; roushf enway.com. Take a self-guided tour of one of the most storied owners in NASCAR history. Its 31 championships include 5 in the top cup races. At the museum is a wall graphic with a time line of the organization, trophies, and team vehicles, including Greg Biffles's 2009 Daytona-winning Ford. Free. Open Mon through Fri 8 a.m. to 5 p.m.

where to shop

Afton Village. 360 Exchange St. Northwest; (704) 721-5337; aftonvillage.com. The modern, upscale ambience at Afton Village combines with new but friendly streets, homes, and storefronts to form a progressive community all its own. A village green and pergola are surrounded by a handful of shops and restaurants.

Concord Mills. 8111 Concord Mills Blvd.; (704) 979-5000; simon.com. More than 200 stores, anchored at one end by a Bass Pro Shops Outdoor World and a multiplex cinema at the other, are laid out in a speedway pattern with a pit stop food court. In addition to specialty stores are a variety of brand outlet stores from Gap to Eddie Bauer. It includes an outdoor NASCAR theme park with go-karts and other race car–themed attractions. A new aquarium is also located here. Open Mon through Sat. 10 a.m. to 9 p.m., Sun noon to 7 p.m.

Richard Petty Motorsports. 7065 Zephyr Place; (704) 706-2120; richardpettymotorsports .com. This is the home of the "The King" who would someday own a race team. Petty, who still holds a record 200 wins, retired in the mid-1990s and now owns several teams. The shop includes things that are wearable and memorable. Open Mon through Fri 9 a.m. to 5 p.m.

Sam Bass Gallery. 6104 Performance Dr.; (704) 455-6915; sambass.com. The late Sam Bass was to NASCAR what Norman Rockwell was to 20th-century American life. For more than a decade, Bass has painted scenes from the sport and has become the official artist of NASCAR. His gallery here offers more than 300 works including originals, prints, posters, and fine art. Open Mon through Fri 9 a.m. to 5 p.m.

where to eat

Cabarrus Creamery. 21 Union St. South; (704) 784-1923; cabarruscreamery.com. Choose from 25 flavors of homemade ice cream at Cabarrus Creamery, including sliced lemon or Moon Pie, inspired by the classic, southern, chocolate-covered graham cracker and marshmallow snack cake. It's a 1950s-themed place, for good reason. It's been serving scoops in Concord for 80 years, although in 3 different locations. $.

Louis' Grille. 5062 SR 49 South; (704) 455-3944. Meat and veggie dishes are offered in this popular breakfast and lunchtime destination. Many race teams visit the diner, which is decorated in a race motif. Open Mon through Fri 6 a.m. to 3 p.m., Sat 8 a.m. to 2 p.m. $$.

Punchy's Diner. 550 Concord Pkwy.; (704) 786-2222; Punchy's is a family-friendly and colorful '50s-styled diner, serving homemade meals, desserts, and ice cream from nearby Gastonia's Tony's Ice Cream at booths or at the soda fountain counter. Partake of Dale Earnhardt's favorite: a tomato sandwich with lettuce and Miracle Whip. Open Mon through Sat 6 a.m. to 9 p.m., Sun 7 a.m. to 9 p.m. $.

The Speedway Club. 5555 Concord Pkwy. South; (704) 455-3216; gospeedwayclub.com. Overlooking the 1.5-mile track, The Speedway Club's chef Pete Nowak creates culinary delights for the children's menu as well as a dinner menu that makes any race fan's evening special. Menu items are as simple as chicken wings and as elaborate as Bourbon Peach Pork served with an arugula salad. $–$$$.

kannapolis, nc

getting there

From the Concord Mills area, use I-85 North for the quickest route into Kannapolis. From downtown Concord, use Concord Parkway, which crosses I-85 and becomes Cannon Boulevard and leads to Dale Earnhardt Boulevard.

where to go

Adventures in Motorsports. (858) 748-6877. Based in Kannapolis, AIM is the exclusive tour operator for Charlotte's NASCAR Hall of Fame and packages events that include race tickets as well as Hall of Fame induction weekend events that give participants some exclusive access.

Curb Motorsport Museum. 600 Dale Earnhardt Blvd.; (704) 938-6121; mikecurb.com. The name Mike Curb might be more synonymous with country music than with NASCAR. Curb, whose country music label includes artists such as Tim McGraw, LeAnn Rimes, and Hank Williams Jr., is also a NASCAR and Indy car owner. He blends his passion for the 2 industries at this museum. Featured are dozens of NASCAR and Indy cars and other exhibits combined with gold records, autographed posters, and other items from country and pop music icons. Open Mon through Fri 9 a.m. to 5 p.m.

Dale Earnhardt Plaza. South Main and West B Streets at Cannon Village; (704) 938-3200. In the heart of Cannon Village in Dale Earnhardt's hometown is a permanent tribute to his life and career. Earnhardt, who drove the famous black number 3 car, was one of the best-loved drivers of all time. His aggressive driving made the sport exciting for his fans, but he died tragically in the 2001 race at Daytona. The plaza includes a 9-foot bronze statue and a granite monument sent by fans in Vermont and New York. The Cannon Village Visitor Center also has a series of works by Sam Bass on Earnhardt's legendary career.

hall of fame

*The **NASCAR Hall of Fame** (400 E. Martin Luther King Blvd., Charlotte; 704-654-4400; nascarhall.com) conducts its annual induction ceremony in late January. The event includes a full slate of events spanning several days in Charlotte and the surrounding area. Among the inductees are Bill France Sr, Bill France Jr., Dale Earnhardt, Richard Petty, and Junior Johnson, all of whom were admitted as the first class in 2010.*

The Dale Trail. 3003 Dale Earnhardt Blvd.; (800) 848-3740; daletrail.com. Just about any spot in Kannapolis is a starting point for the Dale Trail. The Dale Trail map with a total of 19 stops can be obtained at the Cabarrus County Visitors Center and takes fans to sites important to the legendary race driver, including Idiot Circle where he cruised in the 1960s and other hangouts such as his favorite restaurant. From Kannapolis the Dale Trail leads to other sites in Mooresville and Concord.

where to shop

Stewart-Hass Racing. 6001 Haas Way; (704) 652-4227; stewarthaasracing.com. Find apparel and keepsakes from Tony Stewart and Kevin Harvick at this shop that has garage-viewing windows, too. Open Mon through Fri 8 a.m. to 4:30 p.m.

mooresville, nc

getting there

Mooresville can be accessed by traveling north on I-77, but there are also easy connections to the Concord-Kannapolis area to the northeast. That's why it has become such a hot location for the racing industry. While there are fewer public locations, businesses on which race teams depend are economic staples of this community. From Kannapolis, use SR 3, also known as Dale Earnhardt Highway, north into Mooresville.

where to go

Dale Earnhardt, Inc. 1675 Dale Earnhardt Hwy. 3; (704) 662-8000; daleearnhardtinc.com. DEI is one of the largest teams on the NASCAR circuit, and its Mooresville facility is the area industry's largest and includes gift shops for Earnhardt merchandise and members of the DEI team as well as a showroom of Dale Earnhardt exhibits. On display here are all 7 of his championship trophies, his fire suits, and his race cars. As a corporation, the organization's contributions to racing are far-reaching, from technological advances to philanthropy with a foundation that makes significant contributions to children's programs, education, and wildlife preservation. Open Mon through Fri 9 a.m. to 5 p.m., Sat 10 a.m. to 4 p.m.

Doug Foley Drag Racing School. 149 A Byers Creek Rd.; (866) 372-4783; dougfoley .com. A half day of lessons is all it takes to get behind the wheel of a dragster. Foley is the only area school that offers this experience, ranging from ride-alongs at zMax Dragway to full lessons at the Mooresville facility. Ride-alongs start at $99, and driving lessons start at $399.

Memory Lane Motorsports Museum. 769 River Hwy.; (704) 662-2320; memorylaneauto museum.com. Of all the race shops and museums in the area, this is the one that should not be missed. More than 150 vintage cars and retired NASCAR vehicles are on display to tell the story of auto racing, from buggies to the moonshine runners that led to the founding of today's popular sport. Also here is the car driven by Will Ferrell in the movie *Talladega Nights: The Legend of Ricky Bobby* along with other cars of film and fame. Visitors find displays of a selection of soapbox derby cars, toys, tractors, and vintage motorcycles as well. Admission is $10 for adults and $6 for children ages 6 to 12. Open Mon through Sat 10 a.m. to 5 p.m. Winter hours may vary.

North Carolina Auto Racing Hall of Fame. 119 Knob Hill Rd.; (704) 663-5331; ncarhof .com. This should not be confused with Charlotte's NASCAR Hall of Fame. This is a much smaller facility that acts as a visitor center for tourists seeking all things racing. It includes a display of several dozen cars, a theater that shows a film on the history of racing in North Carolina, and an art gallery. Admission is $6 for adults, $4 for children ages 6 to 12 and for seniors. Open Mon through Fri 10 a.m. to 5 p.m., Sat 10 a.m. to 3 p.m.

where to shop

JR Motorsports. 349 Cayuga Dr.; (704) 799-4800; dalejr.com. This is Dale Earnhardt Jr.'s operation that also owns cars driven by members of his race team. The retail store here sells Junior's personal brand.

Kurt Busch Store. 151 Lugnut Ln.; (704) 799-2428; kurtbusch.com. Die-cast cars, hats, and T-shirts of this popular driver are available for purchase at the shop. A series of cars, including the first one he raced in and his 1964 Volkswagen Beetle from high school, are on display. Open Mon through Fri 9 a.m. to 4 p.m.

Kyle Busch Motorsports. 351 Mezeppa Rd.; (704) 662-8088; kylebuschmotorsports .com. At Kyle Busch headquarters is the facility where his fleet of Toyotas is maintained. A museum and race shop include displays of his cars, race hardware, and fire suits as well as various personal items. Open Mon through Fri 9 a.m. to 4 p.m.

Penske Racing. 200 Penske Way; (704) 664-2300; penskeracing.com. In addition to checking out the retail operation and museum for drivers who have been on this team, visitors can walk a catwalk over the garage area. Open Mon through Fri 8 a.m. to 5 p.m.

where to eat

Alino Pizzeria. 500 S. Main St.; (704) 663-0010; alinopizzaria.com. Seems everywhere you turn you see another accolade for this pizza place that wood fires pizza in 90 seconds. $$

Trackside Restaurant. 233 Broad St.; (704) 663-3955. This comfortable family-style restaurant is run by George Georgakis, who has had several culinary endeavors in the Charlotte area. Breakfast is typically southern, while lunch- and dinnertime selections range from salads to gyros. $$.

worth more time

Visit the **Richard Petty Museum** (142 W. Academy St., Randleman; 336-495-1143; rp museum.com) north of here. Race cars, awards, and photos honor the 7-time NASCAR champion. See highlights of The King's 35-year career in a full-length movie in the mini-theater and take home gifts for a favorite race fan. Admission is $12 for adults, $7 for children ages 7 and up, and free for children 6 and under. Open Wed through Sat 9 a.m. to 5 p.m. The Petty Compound, where his garage is located, is in Randleman, too.

day trip 51

the great outdoors

winter sports:
blowing rock, nc; banner elk, nc;
beech mountain, nc; mars hill, nc;
maggie valley, nc; sapphire, nc

Six ski resorts make the mountains of North Carolina one of the best winter sports destinations east of the Rocky Mountains. At elevations that exceed 3,000 feet, 60 to 100 inches of natural snow fall each year, which, when supplemented with modern snowmaking equipment, produce outstanding conditions even before Thanksgiving. The region spans from Blowing Rock west to Maggie Valley and south to near the Georgia and South Carolina state lines. **The High Country Ski Report** at (800) 962-2322 or the independent website skisoutheast.com can provide real-time information about conditions at each of the state's slopes. In addition to skiing, many of the slopes offer ice skating, tubing, snowboarding, cross-country skiing, and even snowshoe hiking trips.

blowing rock, nc

getting there

Blowing Rock is probably the most accessible resort, just off the Blue Ridge Parkway near US 321.

where to go

Appalachian Ski Mountain. 940 Ski Mountain Rd.; (828) 295-7828; appskimtn.com. The 50-year-old Appalachian Ski Mountain has 9 slopes, 5 lifts, and 3 terrain parks plus an outdoor ice arena. A large lodge has a big observation deck outside and fireplace inside where you can warm up with a cup of hot chocolate, in addition to a full-service restaurant. A handful of slopeside cabins are available for rent for $230 per night. Lift ticket rates (weekday nights) start at $22 for children and $29 for adults. Weekend and holiday rates are as high as $77.

banner elk, nc

getting there

From Blowing Rock, take US 221 north to SR 105 south and SR 184 west. It's a slow 30-minute drive up this mountain. The elevation in Banner Elk is slightly higher at 3,700 feet; the highest ski slope in this part of the country is here, making Banner Elk an apt candidate for a day trip.

where to go

Sugar Mountain Resort. 1009 Sugar Mountain Dr.; (828) 898-4521; skisugar.com. This is the area's largest ski resort with 125 acres that include 21 slopes, 8 lifts, and a terrain park. There is also an area for snow tubing and an outdoor ice skating rink. A snowshoe hiking program on Sugar Mountain has caught on in recent years. A lodge at the base of the mountain has a cafeteria and a lounge along with its ski shop. The season usually runs from the first week in Nov to late Mar. Lift tickets start at $21 a night during the week and top out at $80 for a full holiday. Rentals start at $13. Hours vary seasonally.

where to stay

Banner Elk Winery & Inn. 60 Deer Run Ln.; (828) 898-9099; blueberryvilla.com. This spectacular countryside villa overlooks rolling landscapes, a vineyard, and winery as well as a trout pond. It has 8 rooms named for the blueberries cultivated here. The winery is open for tours and tastings every day except Monday. $$$.

Inn at Elk River. 875 Main St. West; (828) 898-9669; elkriverinn.com. This Williamsburg-style inn appears to be historic, but in fact has only been here since the mid-1990s. Private treetop decks with spectacular mountain views overlooking Elk River are only part of the amenities offered at this conveniently located inn. Four of the 8 rooms have wood-burning fireplaces. $$.

worth more time
snow tubing

In the town of Seven Devils, south of Banner Elk, is a ski resort–turned–snow tubing center. **Hawksnest Tubing & Zip Line** (2058 Skyland Dr., Seven Devils; 800-822-4295; hawks nesttubing.com) provides an affordable opportunity to those who want to avoid the high cost of lift tickets and rentals. The park is especially good for families, even those with younger children. Weekday tubing tickets are $24, and weekend tickets are $32. A series of 20 zip lines take the adventurous over the park. Hours vary seasonally.

beech mountain, nc

getting there

Beech Mountain is about 30 minutes north of Banner Elk on SR 184.

where to go

Beech Mountain Resort. 1007 Beech Mountain Pkwy.; (828) 387-2011; beechmountain resort.com. Ski Beech is the highest ski area in the East with a peak of 5,506 feet. It has 17 slopes, 8 lifts, and a variety of terrain for skiing and snowboarding. The resort is a complete ski village with shopping, dining, and other amenities. It's one of 2 ski areas with its own microbrewery. In the middle of the village is a huge ice skating rink, and ski chalets surround the resort. Weekday lift tickets start at $26 and top out at $87. Rentals start at $22 for a half day. Hours vary seasonally.

Sledding Hill at Beech Mountain Town Hall. 403 Beech Mountain Pkwy.; (800) 468-5506. This sledding hill is for kids age 12 and under, although parents may ride with smaller children. Plastic sleds are required. Free.

mars hill, nc

getting there

From Beech Mountain, Mars Hill is just under a 2-hour drive via SR 184 and SR 194, which will deliver the driver to US 19. At I-26 take SR 213 north.

where to go

Wolf Ridge Resort. 578 Valley View Circle; (828) 689-4111; skiwolfridgenc.com. Wolfe Ridge is among the most family-oriented resorts with 15 slopes and 3 lifts that offer a lot of runs for beginner and intermediate skiers. Two lodges, each with full-service restaurants and big stone fireplaces, offer skiers a place to warm up and re-energize or to simply relax after a long day of skiing. Like Blowing Rock's Appalachian Ski Mountain, access to this resort is also easy. The resort offers a handful of cabins for rent at the top of the resort where guests can swim in a heated, glass-enclosed pool. Weekday night lift tickets are $23, and weekend or holiday lift tickets are $70.

maggie valley, nc

getting there

Maggie Valley is off I-40 west of Asheville, so begin by taking I-26 south from Mars Hill. At Asheville, take the I-240 loop to reach I-40 West. Take exit 103 for US 19 South for Maggie Valley.

where to go

Cataloochee Ski Area. 1080 Ski Lodge Rd.; (800) 768-0285; cataloochee.com. Though Cataloochee Ranch, located next to the ski area, offers wintertime ski packages, with its neighboring ski slope, all are welcome to ski here. With the help of snowmakers, the North Carolina ski season usually starts in early December. Cataloochee has 18 slopes and trails that range from gentle slopes for beginners to Upper Omigosh for expert skiers. Cat Cage Terrain Park is exclusively for snowboarders, while tubers will want to hit Maggie Valley Tubing Park, located about 4 miles from the ski area but operated by the resort. Weekday night tickets start at $23, while weekend and holiday tickets are $73 for adults.

sapphire, nc

getting there

From Maggie Valley, take US 23/74 south and west. SR 107 runs south to Sapphire. Located 30 minutes southwest of Brevard just off US 64 and fewer than 15 miles from the remote area where North Carolina, South Carolina, and Georgia meet.

where to go

Sapphire Valley Ski Area. 4000 Hwy. 64 West; (828) 743-1169; sapphirevalleyresort.com. This is North Carolina's smallest ski slope but it offers a great opportunity for beginners and children to learn skiing skills. It has 2 slopes and 3 lifts over 8 acres plus the 200-foot Frozen Falls tube run. The Four Seasons Grill is located in a large lodge that offers a range of amenities including a pool, hot tub, game room, and miniature golf. Several ski chalets surround the resort. Lift tickets start at $26 for children and top out at $83 for a full-day adult ticket.

where to eat

Sapphire Mountain Brewing Company. 50 Slicers Ave.; (828) 743-0220; sapphiremountainbrewingcompany.com. Located in the original clubhouse of Sapphire Valley National Golf Club, dozens of microbrews are offered in an old-time saloon setting. The flooring was actually reclaimed from a 19th-century saloon. The beers brewed here were passed down for generations, beginning when the original brewery opened here in 1888. The menu specialty is wood-fired pizzas. $$.

day trip 52

the great outdoors

>>> **palmetto recreation:**
catawba, sc; long creek, sc; hopkins, sc;
santee, sc; moncks corner, sc

From the Piedmont to the Blue Ridge Mountains to the black waters near Charleston, South Carolina's lakes and rivers provide wide-ranging outdoor activities. Come face to face with an alligator in a cypress swamp, fish the famous waters of the Santee River, brave the same rapids Burt Reynolds took on in the film *Deliverance* (cue dueling banjos here). Certainly these adventures can't be tackled in a single day trip, but taken in stride, they are guaranteed to fill many days of trips for the outdoor adventurer.

Many of South Carolina's outdoor destinations are in places less traveled. Creature comforts like restaurants and hotels are few and far between. Some GPS won't work, so bring a map, a full tank of gas, and a plan. Leave just a little to chance, and you are likely to stumble upon a favorable plate of barbecue or fish or even a lively bit of nightlife. The adventure begins in the upstate's York County, but then diverts west to follow South Carolina's rivers, dammed and converted to power-pumping lakes all the way from the Blue Ridge to the deep blue sea.

catawba, sc

getting there

Twenty minutes southeast of Rock Hill, just a few miles from I-77, is the town of Catawba. From points north or south on I-77, take exit 77 for US 21 South to get there.

where to go

Landsford Canal State Park. 2051 Park Dr.; (803) 789-5800; southcarolinaparks.com. Each May and June nature presents a spectacular showing of Rocky Shoals spider lilies, potentially the largest population of this particular flowering species in the world. From mid-May to mid-June these resilient flowers, capable of growing in the harsh conditions of the swiftly flowing Catawba River, spread rapidly. At their peak the flowers cover the water in a blanket of white. Remains of a mid-19th-century canal system include the lockkeeper's home, which is now a museum, a mill site, and burial sites. You can explore all this on the short hike here or canoe through the Class I and II rapids. Admission is $6 for adults, $3.75 for seniors and $3.50 for age 6 to 15. Open 9 a.m. to 6 p.m. daily.

River Town Kayaks and Canoes. 6361 Richburg Rd., Great Falls; (803) 482-3387; river-townadventures.com. Located just a few miles south of Landsford Canal State Park, River Town provides canoe and kayak rentals as well as instruction and guided trips along this part of the Catawba River. They offer 3-hour paddling trips as well as 2-day camping trips.

worth more time

Andrew Jackson State Park (196 Andrew Jackson Park Rd., Lancaster, SC; 803-285-3344; southcarolinaparks.com) is 20 minutes from Landsford Canal State Park on US 521 and was the birthplace of the seventh president of the US. At the park is a replica of an 18th-century schoolhouse and a museum on Jackson's childhood here in the upstate backcountry. Both tent and RV camping are permitted at the small campsite, and fishing is allowed in the 18-acre lake. The park is typically open during daylight hours. The museum and schoolhouse are open on weekends 1 to 5 p.m. Admission is $$3.50 for adults, $1.50 for seniors and $1 for children.

long creek, sc

getting there

Skirting across the northern portion of the upstate takes the outdoor adventurer to the southeastern edge of the Blue Ridge Mountains. The towns of Long Creek and Mountain Rest, an hour west of Greenville via US 123, provide a good base for outdoor adventure. The quickest route here using interstates takes the driver north into North Carolina via I-77 to I-85 South, where exit 11 at SR 24 West goes to Long Creek after it becomes US 123/76.

where to go

Chattooga Ridge Canopy Tours. 1251 Academy Rd.; (864) 647-9587; wildwaterrafting .com. More than a half mile of line split over 10 sections with stops at trees and platforms make up this zip-line canopy tour designed for ages 10 and up that also crosses over Academy Lake. Although it's located at the Wildwater Rafting center, the zip line is operated by a separate company that runs zip lines throughout the Southeast. The cost of a ropes and raft package is $129 per person. Hours vary seasonally.

Wildwater Ltd. 1251 Academy Rd.; (864) 9587; wildwaterrafting.com. Scenic rafting trips on the Chattooga River, which forms the South Carolina–Georgia border, originate from this center in the foothills of the Blue Ridge. This is the site of the 1970s film *Deliverance*. Trips range from a 4-hour outing for families to overnights on Class III and IV rapids. Slower-paced kayak trips on Lake Tugalo are also designed for families. Cottages and cabins in the $$ price range are available for rent at the center. Costs vary by activity.

worth more time

Oconee State Park (624 State Park Rd., Mountain Rest, SC; 864-638-5353; southcarolinaparks.com) provides a host of outdoor adventures in and around the town of Mountain Rest. Rustic cabins and a family campground with a swimming lake are all available at this outstanding park. Fish for bass or bream from around the lake or the campground dock, hike or bike on one of 6 trails, or play miniature golf at the campground entrance. Nantahala Outdoor Center (888-905-7238; noc.com) also conducts rafting adventures in this area. To the north, explore the town of Salem and Lake Jocasse.

hopkins, sc

getting there

Back down to the central part of the state, south of Columbia is the Congaree National Park where the Saluda River becomes the Congaree. Hopkins is the physical address for the park, but it spans southeast to the town of Eastover. From Long Creek it's a long haul of at least 3 hours. Start on US 76/123 West. At Greenville, use the I-185 loop to bypass the city to the south and connect with I-385. This merges with I-26 near Clinton and will deliver you to I-77 South at Columbia and the town of Hopkins off exit 5 (SR 48).

where to go

Congaree National Park. 100 National Park Rd.; (803) 776-4396; nps.gov. After joining the Saluda River at Lake Murray, the Congaree River ambles out of the southeastern corner of Columbia to Congaree National Park and one of the state's most pristine assemblages of flora and fauna. Declaration as a national park protects this 22,200 acres of North America's largest contiguous tract of old-growth bottomland hardwood forest. Interspersed among the hardwoods are towering pines that compose one of the tallest forests on the East Coast and plants and animals that provide fodder for research among students at the University of South Carolina. For the adventurer are more than 20 miles of hiking trails, including a boardwalk loop and places to canoe, kayak, and fish. The Harry Hampton Visitor Center, open daily 8:30 a.m. to 5 p.m., includes a well-done exhibit on the park's inhabitants and is a starting point for a boardwalk loop through the swamp. In wet seasons, rangers also offer free canoe tours, including equipment, beneath cypress and tupelo trees draped with Spanish moss. Advance reservations are recommended and can be made by calling the visitor center or by visiting the website. Owls, woodpeckers, otters, white-tail deer, and other wildlife frequent this protected area. Admission is free. Generally open during daylight hours. The visitor center is open daily 9 a.m. to 5 p.m. Oct 1 to Mar 31 with hours extended to 7 p.m. on Fri and Sat the rest of the year.

where to eat

Big T's Barbecue. 2520 Congaree Rd., Gadsen; (803) 353-0488; bigtbbq.com. Big T now bottles its barbecue sauce for sale in area grocery stores. It does boast the best barbecue in the state along with fried fish, pork chops, collards, and pigs' feet. There are 2 other locations in Columbia, but this one makes a perfect pairing with a Congaree trip. Open Wed 11 a.m. to 9 p.m., Thurs through Sat 11 a.m. to midnight. $$.

santee, sc

getting there

The town of Santee is conveniently nestled between Lakes Moultrie and Marion and has become a gateway to this great outdoor recreation corridor known as Santee Cooper. Here the Congaree becomes the Great Santee River. What began as the Catawba River in the North Carolina Piedmont and all the tributaries in between, including the Broad and Saluda Rivers, pours into the Atlantic Ocean through the Santee and Cooper Rivers. To get here, take I-95 from points north or south and access Santee at exit 98, SR 6. From Hopkins it's an hour-long drive taking SR 48 to US 601 South and SR 267 South.

santee cooper lakes

Lakes Marion and Moultrie at Santee are joined by a 6.5-mile canal to create a total of 170,000 acres of recreational lake. The world-record channel catfish, largemouth bass, black crappie, and several others were caught on these lakes in recent years.

where to go

Cajun Guide Service. Mill Creek Marina, MP 79 Hwy. 6; (803) 492-3381; santeecajunguide .com. A host of guides registered with the US Coast Guard operate charter fishing operations at Santee Cooper, and unless you have your own boat and are familiar with the lakes, you will want to use one of them. Cajun Guide Service has one of the only female guides in the area, Barb Witherell, who operates the service with her husband, Bob. Rates start at $400 for 1-4 adults for 8 hours.

Fisheagle Tours. 305 State Park Rd.; (803) 854-4005; fisheaglewildlifetours.com. Departing from Santee State Park on a 28-passenger boat, Fisheagle Tours takes 2-hour tours of Lake Marion that include the "sunken" forest—the cypress swamp flooded during the construction of Santee Cooper Power Plant. Tour guides tell entertaining but historically accurate stories of the Native Americans and other former inhabitants of this region, including early 20th-century moonshiners. Tours cost $30 for adults and $20 for children ages 4 to 12, and depart on Wed and Sat at 1 p.m., Fri 10 a.m.

Santee National Wildlife Refuge. 2125 Fort Watson Rd., North Santee; (803) 478-2217; fws.gov. This birders' paradise includes frequent wintertime appearances by the bald eagle and peregrine falcon as well as migratory waterfowl such as wood ducks and mallards. Throughout the year red-tailed and red-shouldered hawks can be viewed with occasional appearances by American alligators and endangered wood storks. Several trails including Wright's Bluff Nature Trail are open for wildlife observation, photography, and hiking. A visitor center contains a number of displays describing refuge wildlife and habitats and provides an excellent opportunity for visitors to become acquainted with the refuge before venturing out. For the history buff Fort Watson, located atop the Santee Indian Mound, is the site of a significant Revolutionary War battle. Free. Generally open during daylight hours. Visitor center is open Tues through Sun. 8 a.m. to 4 p.m.

Santee State Park. 251 State Park Rd.; (803) 854-2408; southcarolinaparks.com. Santee State Park offers 158 lakeside campsites ($15 per night) along Lake Marion and 20 lakefront cabins ($80 to $120 per night). Its extensive facilities include hiking and biking trails, fishing access, swimming access, boat ramps, a camp store, and a visitor center. Daytime admission is $3, $1.50 for seniors and $1 for children. Typically open during daylight hours.

where to shop

Santee General Store. 8932 Old Number 6 Hwy.; (803) 854-2105. This old-time general store sells a variety of souvenir items, peach cider, cobbler, jams and jellies, and other items. You can also get a scoop of ice cream or forgotten camping items.

where to stay

Clarks Restaurant and Inn. 114 Bradford St.; (803) 854-2141; clarksinnandrestaurant .com. First opened in 1946, this historic inn looks like a B&B, but accommodations look like traditional hotel rooms. Amenities include a pool and covered pergola alongside it. The restaurant on the property includes a warm fireplace and cozy English-style pub. $$.

Whitten Inn. 123 Mall St.; (888) 726-8337; whitteninn.com. The Whitten Inn is part of a small chain that also has properties in Texas and New Mexico. It's a simple hotel with an outdoor pool and casual restaurant on-site. $.

worth more time

Francis Beidler Forest. 336 Sanctuary Rd., Harleyville; (843) 462-2150; beidlerforest.com. Francis Beidler Forest is owned and operated by the Audubon Society of South Carolina just outside Moncks Corner. They say it is the largest virgin cypress-tupelo swamp forest in the world. Its 15,000 acres of sanctuary in the heart of Four Holes Swamp embrace 1,800 acres of ancient trees that tower over black-water streams, clear pools, and hundreds of species of wildlife. A 1.75-mile-long boardwalk, with 9 rest stops and 2 rain shelters, takes visitors into the heart of the old-growth cypress-tupelo swamp. Canoe trips, night walks, and other activities are available in season and by reservation. Admission is $10 for adults, $8 for seniors, $5 for ages 6 to 12. Open Tues through Sun 9 a.m. to 5 p.m.

moncks corner, sc

getting there

Moncks Corner is located at the southern tip of Lake Moultrie. Get there from Santee by taking SR 310 south to US 176. From there SR 311 will take you to Moncks Corner.

where to go

Cypress Gardens. 3030 Cypress Gardens Rd.; (843) 553-0515; cypressgardens.info. More than 170 acres of swamp and gardens were once part of a prosperous rice plantation. Meander along garden paths, which are actually dikes from the rice-growing era when these waters were impounded to flood the fields. Explore the black-water swamp with guides from bateaus (flat-bottom boats) or on your own. Cypress Gardens is home to numerous wildlife species from the mighty alligator to tiny mosquito fish. In the Butterfly House, native species thrive amid the abundant flowering plants that supply food for caterpillars and adult butterflies. A "swamparium" houses many animals from the swamp that visitors might not see in the wild, displayed in various tanks holding a total of 24,000 gallons of water. Terrariums are home to native venomous snakes, as well as other reptiles and amphibians, giving the visitor an opportunity to observe these animals in a safe and educational environment. Admission is $10 for adults, $6.50 for seniors, $5 for children 6 to 12. Open daily 9 a.m. to 5 p.m. Closed Thanksgiving, Christmas, and the month of January.

Old Santee Canal Park. 900 Stony Landing; (843) 899-5200; oldsanteecanalpark.org. Opened in 1800, this canal was a crowning engineering achievement for the state that saved considerable time and money getting crops to the port at Charleston. Much of its 22 miles lie beneath the water of Lake Moultrie, but some parts of the canal are still visible. The park here is located on a bluff at the headwaters of the Cooper River. The 1843 Stony Landing Plantation House has been restored and is used as a museum. Admission is $5 for adults, free for children ages 6 and under. Open daily 9 a.m. to 5 p.m.

Overton Park. Short Stay Road; (843) 761-8039; santeecooper.com. Preserved for swimming, picnicking, and other outdoor family activities, Overton Park is a Lake Moultrie beach access maintained by the state-owned utility company Santee Cooper. Fishing is not allowed. Admission is $2 for ages 4 and up. Open daily 10 a.m. to 6 p.m.

Santee Cooper Charters. 806 Bowfin Dr.; (843) 899-4325; santeecoopercharters.com. Go after stripers, largemouth bass, catfish, crappie, and trout with this well-known fishing charter group that includes a dozen experienced guides. Cost starts at $425 for up to 2 people. Additional charges apply up to 6 people in each boat.

where to eat

Gilligan's at the Dock. 582 Dock Rd.; (843) 761-2244; gilligans.net. Gilligan's operates several locations in the Charleston area, but this one is accessible to boaters on Lake Moultrie. Grab a fish sandwich or check out the raw bar at this island-themed location. Open Sun through Thurs 11 a.m. to 9 p.m., Fri and Sat 11 a.m. to 10 p.m. $$.

historic trips

day trip 53

historic trips

>>> **civil war—the beginning:**
charleston, sc; ehrhardt, sc;
florence, sc; columbia, sc

From the first shots fired at Fort Sumter to Sherman's fiery raid of Columbia, South Carolina has a lot of reasons to remember the Civil War. Having come to rely on slave labor at its rice and cotton plantations, South Carolina, committed to the precepts of states' rights, became the first to secede from the Union. Furthermore, Governor Francis W. Pickens and other state authorities viewed the presence of four US military installations in and around Charleston—Fort Moultrie, Fort Sumter, Castle Pinckney, and the US Arsenal—as an insult to South Carolina's sovereignty and a threat to her safety. Following its secession on December 20, 1860, tensions mounted, and the state seized three of the four forts and waited for the Union to respond. South Carolina was eerily quiet until the end of March as Confederate forces began to assemble and took responsibility for diplomatic relations. That silence ended when Abraham Lincoln decided to send supplies to Fort Sumter, to the Union forces remaining there. General P. G. T. Beauregard, the Confederate commander in Charleston, demanded that Union Major Robert Anderson surrender the fort. When he refused, Beauregard ordered the batteries surrounding the harbor to open fire. The first shells fell early on the morning of April 12, 1861, as Beauregard looked on from his downtown Charleston balcony. The Confederacy won that battle, but the war had begun.

Thereafter South Carolina was not a major battleground during the war, though it was often battered. The 60,000 South Carolinians who served during the war would stay in Charleston early on but would then spend much of the war in Virginia, Mississippi, Georgia, and Tennessee. Port Royal at Hilton Head fell early in the war and was occupied by the Union; it would serve as a base to impose attacks on Charleston throughout much of the rest of the war. In September of 1864 the Confederate government established a military prison at Florence, but it would only be a few months before General William Tecumseh Sherman would cross the Savannah River and march to Columbia. On February 16 Sherman reached Columbia, and on February 17 Charleston was evacuated. Later, in April, Federal troops under General Edward E. Potter made their way through Georgetown, Manning, Sumter, and Camden—the last significant military operation in the state.

charleston, sc

getting there

Charleston is located at the east end of I-26.

where to go

Battery Number 5. Take Highway 171 for 5 miles, and turn left onto Burclair Drive. Cross Secessionville Road to Seaside Plantation, then take the second road on the right; (843) 869-3223. Still largely intact, this Confederate earthwork was constructed in 1863 under the direction of General P.G.T. Beauregard, when he commanded the Departments of South Carolina, Georgia, and Florida. It was intended to anchor the Confederate defenses of James Island as it overlooked Seaside Creek and the Secessionville peninsula. Free. Typically open during daylight hours.

Fort Moultrie. 1214 Middle St., Sullivan's Island; (843) 883-3123; nps.gov. Undergoing upgrades throughout its existence, the fort that stands today is actually a third structure built in 1809. Major Robert Anderson and 85 Federal soldiers occupied the fort before they moved to Fort Sumter in December of 1860 and Confederate soldiers seized it. During the first battle of the Civil War, Confederates at Fort Moultrie fired on Union troops in Fort Sumter. Thereafter Confederate forces successfully used both forts to protect Charleston from a combined Union navy and army siege from 1863 to 1865. Now a national monument, a museum on the site includes items from all of those battles, a short film, and the stories of the men who were stationed here. Free. Open daily 9 a.m. to 5 p.m.

Fort Sumter National Monument. 340 Concord St.; (843) 883-3123; nps.gov. Fort Sumter is located in Charleston Harbor between Charleston, Patriots Point, James Island, and Sullivan's Island. Though visible from all shores, it is not accessible by vehicle. **Fort Sumter Tours** (843-722-2628; fortsumtertours.com) operates a ferry and 30-minute narrated trip to Fort Sumter from Liberty Square in downtown Charleston or from Patriots Point Maritime Museum in Mount Pleasant. Once on the island, visitors can get an informative interpretation of the fort and its history provided by national park rangers. Its construction began in 1829, but it still wasn't completed by the time the war began. General P. T. G. Beauregard ordered the fort attacked on April 12, 1861. During the siege of Charleston, it was reduced to one-third its original size and was never rebuilt. Admission to the park is free. Ferry fees are $30 for adults, $28 for seniors, $18 for ages 4 to 11. Hours vary slightly by season but are generally 9:30 a.m. to 2:30 p.m.

H.L. Hunley. Warren Lasch Conservation Center, 1250 Supply St.; (843) 743-4865; hunley .org. Scientists recovered the *H.L. Hunley*, a Civil War submarine, in 2000 after its being lost for more than 100 years. It is preserved in a specially designed freshwater tank at this former navy shipyard in North Charleston as scientists excavate and study its remains. Though the submarine played only a small role in the Civil War, it has larger significance in the development of submarine technology in that it launched the first successful submarine attack against an enemy vessel. Visitors take a tour of the Conservation Center for a look at the *Hunley* and details on its preservation. There is also a video, and artifacts that have been excavated from the vessel are on display. Tours cost $18 for adults and $10 for children ages 5 to 17. Tours offered Sat 10 a.m. to 5 p.m. and Sun 10 a.m. to 3 p.m.

Magnolia Cemetery. 70 Cunnington Ave.; (843) 722-8638; magnoliacemetery.net. Founded in 1849 on the banks of the Cooper River, this is the oldest public cemetery in Charleston. Buried here are generations of southern leaders that include governors Thomas Bennett, Langdon Cheves, Horace L. Hunley, and Robert Barnwell Rhett. The hundreds of Confederate soldiers buried here include 5 generals—Micah Jenkins, Arthur Manigault, Roswell Ripley, James Conner, and C. H. Stevens. More than 20,000 South Carolinians died in the war, but most didn't make it back for burial. Free. Typically open during daylight hours.

ehrhardt, sc

getting there

From Charleston, take US 17 south to SR 64 west. It's fewer than 75 miles to Ehrhardt.

where to go

Rivers Bridge State Historic Site. 325 State Park Rd.; (803) 267-3675; southcarolina parks.com. On February 2–3, 1865, during the final months of the Civil War, 1,200 Confederate soldiers made a stand against Sherman here at Robertsville and Lawtonville on the Salkehatchie River. Though the earthen fortifications are still intact today, they weren't stout enough to help thwart the invasion of a division of more than 5,000 Union soldiers. Today Rivers Bridge is on the National Register of Historic Places and is the only state historic site in South Carolina that preserves a Civil War battlefield. The site also includes the Memorial Grounds, where Confederate soldiers were interred and are remembered in memorial services that have been held annually since 1876. Interpretive panels tell the story of the night the war began to end in South Carolina. Monthly living history programs are offered the first

Saturday of each month at 10 a.m. The fee for the tour is $5 for adults, $3 ages 6 to 16. Site admission is free. Open daily 9 a.m. to 6 p.m.

where to stay

Broxton Bridge Plantation. 1685 Broxton Bridge Rd.; (803) 267-3882; broxtonbridge .com. This 5-bedroom plantation home was built in the 1850s and now serves as a sportsman's lodge. Unfinished longleaf pine boards surround every room. Guest rooms are all decorated in a hunting theme. Horseback riding and clay shooting are also offered on the plantation. $.

Ehrhardt Hall. 13764 Broxton Bridge Rd.; (803) 267-2020; ehrhardthall.com. This 1903 mansion with 12-foot ceilings and ornate moldings, and decorated with period antiques, provides an elegant historic experience. Southern city–themed rooms are spacious and bright, and 2 levels of front porch are well-equipped with rocking chairs. Breakfast is likely to include French crepes. $$.

florence, sc

getting there

Florence is located where I-20 runs into I-95. From Ehrhardt, take SR 217 north to SR 61, which delivers the driver to I-95. The drive to Florence is about 2 hours.

where to go

Florence National Cemetery. 803 E. National Cemetery Rd.; (843) 669-8783; cem.va .gov. Established in 1865 in conjunction with the Florence Stockade, a Union prisoner of war camp, the prisoner cemetery forms the nucleus of this cemetery. Nearly 3,000 Union soldiers who died in the prison—as many as 2,000 of them unknown—are buried here. Free. Typically open during daylight hours.

Florence Stockade. Stockade Road on the national cemetery site. A gazebo and interpretive markers along a walking trail mark the area where once stood the Florence Stockade. Built in September 1864, it held more than 12,000 Union soldiers transferred from prisons in Georgia as Sherman made his way to South Carolina in February of 1865. Free. Generally open during daylight hours.

War Between the States Museum. 107 S. Guerry St.; (843) 663-1266. The museum is a showcase of American life during the 1860s. It includes artifacts from battles and campsites, the CSS *Pee Dee*, photos of military personnel, and items from the Florence Stockade, the Union prison camp located here. The museum also houses a scale model of the stockade. Admission is $2 for adults, $1 for children. Open Wed and Sat 10 a.m. to 5 p.m.

columbia, sc

getting there

Columbia is located where I-77 ends and where I-26 and I-20 meet. From Florence, take I-20 west for the 90-minute drive into Columbia.

where to go

Elmwood Cemetery & Gardens. 501 Elmwood Ave.; (803) 252-2123. This 1854 cemetery overlooks the Broad River. Within it is a complete Confederate cemetery. Historical walking tour maps are available in the office, open Mon through Fri 9 a.m. to 5 p.m.

General Sherman's March on Columbia Self-Guided Walking Tour. 1717 Gervais St.; (803) 217-0071; shermansmarch.com. On February 17, 1865, following an 18-day march from Georgia, Union General William Tecumseh Sherman and his soldiers looted and burned the city in what has been described as drunken retribution for the city's role in starting the South's secession. Visitors to Columbia can follow that treacherous path to see the preserved ruins and other landmarks that signify that day. Mostly what remains are historical signs, but still to be seen are remnants of Saluda River Bridge; the South Carolina State House, which is now marked with stars where cannonballs struck it; the Horsehoe Buildings at USC; 1849 McCord House; Hampton-Preston House; Mills House; the 1853 First Presbyterian Church; the First Baptist Church where the secession convention met in 1860; and a handful of other sites. Some buildings are open to visitors.

Riverbanks Zoo and Garden. 500 Wildlife Pkwy.; (803) 779-8717; riverbankszoo.org. Not only is Riverbanks the capital city's most popular attraction, it also protects some of its most historically significant properties. It is listed on the National Register of Historic Places for structural remains dating back to the early 1800s. Found along the garden's river trail are the ruins of Saluda Mill, one of South Carolina's oldest textile mills set ablaze by Sherman and his troops. "Sherman's Rock," where Union troops camped and staged their attack on the city, remains at the site. An interpretive center includes artifacts, descriptions, and other historical exhibits.

South Carolina State Museum. 301 Gervais St.; (803) 898-4921; scmuseum.org. Exhibits created as part of the state's 150th anniversary have been added to the Confederate Relic Room at this heralded museum. Bibles, soldiers' letters, and other artifacts tell the story of how the war impacted their lives and the ones they left behind. Weapons, uniforms, audiovisual displays, and other exhibits also help tell South Carolina's Civil War story. Admission is $13.95 for adults, $12.95 for seniors, and $11.95 for children ages 3 to 12. Open Mon through Fri 10 a.m. to 5 p.m., Sat 10 a.m. to 6 p.m., and Sun noon to 5 p.m.

where to stay

Chesnut Cottage Bed & Breakfast. 1718 Hampton St.; (803) 256-1718; chesnutcottage
.com. Confederate President Jefferson Davis once addressed the citizens of Columbia from
the porch of Chesnut Cottage. Today there is more rocking going on here than speechmak-
ing. It was the home of author Mary Boykin Chesnut, but now it has guest rooms with period
antiques as well as a library with Civil War artifacts. $$$.

day trip 54

historic trips

>>>

civil war—the end:
atlantic beach, nc; new bern, nc;
kinston, nc; kure beach, nc;
four oaks, nc; salisbury, nc; durham, nc

From Stoneman's raid in the North Carolina mountains en route to the Confederate prison in Salisbury, to the effective end of the war in Durham, the indelible mark of the War Between the States remains in the Old North State. In North Carolina there were hundreds of battles, skirmishes, and historic events that would have some effect on the war. Today there are nearly 200 sites—some as simple as historic markers, others as complex as a complete museum—that tell the state's story of the American Civil War.

Early on, Union strategists realized the importance of the North Carolina coast, protected for much of its length by its barrier islands and its sounds. Union forces were quick to move in to occupy the islands to choke off critical shipping lanes to the Wilmington and Weldon Railroad. Realizing the importance of eastern North Carolina, Union General Ben Butler launched an amphibious attack against Confederate forts located on the Outer Banks and took control of them by February 1862. Nothing of the conflict remains, but historical markers give due note. Then, significantly, New Bern fell on March 14, 1862, and Federal troops would use the town as a base for the remainder of the war. Fort Macon, a brick structure guarding the approach to Beaufort, was surrendered by the Confederates on April 25. By late spring 1862, Union soldiers occupied the towns of Plymouth and Washington, though the Confederate forces managed to maintain control of the Great Dismal Swamp and recaptured Plymouth in 1864. Federal forces stopped there. Aside from a few raids from those newly established bases, the Union forces went no farther until the very end of the war when Sherman entered North Carolina. Protected by strong fortifications at the mouth of the

Cape Fear River at Kure Beach, the port at Wilmington remained open, shipping supplies to Lee's army in Virginia until the forts fell in early 1865.

atlantic beach, nc

getting there

Atlantic Beach is on North Carolina's Crystal Coast across Bogue Sound from Morehead City.

where to go

Fort Macon State Park. (252) 726-3775; ncparks.gov. Located on the east end of the island, surrounded by water on 3 sides at MP 0 on Highway 58, Fort Macon is a popular destination for the variety of activities available. The Civil War fort hides in the dunes to protect Beaufort Inlet. Built 1826–34 to protect the deep water port, the fort was taken by North Carolina militia in April 1861. Confederate occupation lasted a little more than a year. Fort Macon fell April 25, 1862, to a Union land-sea operation. From the fort walls, you can see the wreck site of Blackbeard's flagship, *Queen Anne's Revenge*, which lies in 20 feet of water just off the inlet and is being recovered by the state. Rangers offer guided tours to interpret the lives of the soldiers who lived here. A 1-mile nature walk from the fort leads to frequently good bird watching. Open year-round with interpretive programs offered daily, there are picnicking facilities, a bathhouse (user fees are $4 per adult, $3 for ages 5 to 12), and lifeguard services. The park is generally open during daylight hours. The swimming area is open in summer 10 a.m. to 5:45 p.m. The fort is open daily year-round, except for Christmas Day, 9 a.m. to 5:30 p.m.

new bern, nc

getting there

New Bern is located at the end of US 70 on the Neuse River. From Atlantic Beach, take US 70 west and arrive in New Bern in less than an hour.

where to go

New Bern Visitor Center. 203 S. Front St.; (800) 437-5767; visitnewbern.com. Begin a walking tour of downtown New Bern here. The center can provide maps (or download one in advance from the website) and background information on the city's engagement in the war. Many of the homes and buildings here are preserved due in part to the Union occupation of the city through much of the war. Among the significant buildings on the tour are the

Attmore-Oliver House (510 Pollock St.); John Wright Stanly House (300 block of George Street), headquarters of General Ambrose Burnside after the 1862 Battle of New Bern; and Jones House (Pollock and Eden Streets), used to house Confederate prisoners.

New Bern Academy Museum. 511 New St.; (252) 514-4874. This early 19th-century building, which served as a military hospital during the Civil War, now houses exhibits focusing on the history of New Bern, including much on the Civil War. Topics covered include the Confederate defense of the town in 1862, the Union occupation and battles, and the structure's role as a hospital. Admission is included with your Tryon Palace ticket. Open Frithrough Sun 12:30 to 4:30 p.m.

New Bern Battlefield Park. Park entrance near the intersection of Route 70 and Taberna Way; (252) 638-5773; newbernhistorical.org. The original historic battlefield, which has well-preserved earthen fortifications, is accessible for tours. Download a self-guided walking tour map from the historical society website. Union soldiers approached this strong Confederate position on March 13, 1862. A Union attack from land and sea by 12,000 troops the next day exploited a weak spot, flanking and carrying the position. Retreating Confederates set fire to warehouses full of military supplies and the Trent River Bridge as Northern forces closed in by land and water on March 14, 1862. After a brief period of bombardment and lawlessness, New Bern was occupied and became a Federal stronghold in eastern North Carolina.

kinston, nc

getting there

At the intersection of US 17 and US 258, find the city of Kinston, on the banks of the Neuse River, the longest river contained entirely in the state of North Carolina. From New Bern, Kinston is a 45-minute drive west on US 70.

where to go

Kinston-Lenoir County Visitor Center. 101 E. New Bern Rd.; (252) 522-0004; visitkinston .com. This visitor center stands on the site of the 1862 First Battle of Kinston and is a few miles west of the Battle of Wyse Fork, fought in the waning days of the war in 1865. Information and exhibits describe both battles. Also find information about the CSS *Neuse* and many of the area's Civil War resources. Sites include views of original Confederate earthworks, areas of fighting, and the bridge over the Neuse River into downtown Kinston, burned during the fighting. A highlight of the tour is a battlefield park, located at Meadowbridge Drive and Harriett Drive, which preserves the left flank of the Confederate final defensive line. The Battle of Wyse Fork, the second-largest battle in the state involving some 25,000 troops, was an attempt by Confederates to delay or block a Federal advance on Goldsboro.

CSS *Neuse* State Historic Site. 100 N. Queen St.; (252) 522-2107. The CSS *Neuse*, named after the river on which it was based, was constructed in 1863 amid Confederate hopes the ironclad could help them regain control over the rivers and sounds of eastern North Carolina. The *Neuse*, known as "the gunboat," is a 158-foot ironclad ship that looks somewhat like a river barge. In April 1864 the *Neuse*, not yet fully equipped, was launched in a hasty attempt to improve its faltering chances in the Civil War. Before it reached New Bern, the *Neuse* ran aground and eventually returned to its base. On March 12, 1865, the crew burned her to prevent capture. The wreck remained in the river until 1963 when it was raised, then set in its present site. A museum has been created where the boat rests to tell about its history and the role this river town played in the Civil War. The museum includes a slide show and artifacts from the vessel. The remains of the *Neuse* (much of its wooden lower structure and some of its iron plating) are displayed here. Admission is free. Open Tues through Sat. 9 a.m. to 5 p.m.

CSS *Neuse II* Replica. Corner of Heritage and Gordon Streets; (252) 560-2150; cssneuse foundation.com. The CSS *Neuse* Foundation built this replica of the *Neuse* to illustrate what a sailor's life was like during the Civil War. It rests on a grassy lawn near downtown. The foundation representatives who led fund-raising efforts to build it say it is the only full-size Civil War ironclad replica in the country. Admission is free. Open Mon through Fri. 9 a.m. to 2 p.m., Sat. 9 a.m. to 5 p.m., Sun 1 to 5 p.m.

where to eat

Chef and the Farmer. 120 W. Gordon St.; (252) 208-2433; chefandthefarmer.com. Chef Vivian Howard rose to prominence when her PBS series *A Chef's Life*, hit the airwaves across the country. Howard now operates this restaurant with a focus on creative dishes that celebrate regional cuisine made with local ingredients and an oyster bar called the Boiler Room. At Chef and the Farmer look for a frequently changing menu featuring fresh seafood, southern veggies, and more. Open Wed through Sat 4 to 9 p.m. $$–$$$.

King's Restaurant. 910 W. Vernon Ave.; (252) 527-1661; and 405 E. New Bern Rd.; (800) 332-6465; kingsbbq.com. King's acclaimed barbecue uses a vinegar and red pepper–based sauce. It's also hand chopped so that the sauce will be properly absorbed. Should you stop at King's, abandon all plans to count calories, and order the "pig in a pup," an oversize hush puppy stuffed with barbecue that goes for $2.50. Top it off with King's famous banana pudding or pecan pie. $–$$.

where to stay

The O'Neil. 200 North Queen St.; (252) 208-1130; the-oneil.com. Located in what was once the Farmers and Merchants Bank, this beautiful boutique hotel was completed in 1924. Its 16-ton vault, teller windows, counters and intricate plaster ceiling have all been preserved in the hotel's lobby and its well-appointed but unique rooms are located in the bank offices in the upper floors. The building had the state's first licensed elevator. $$.

kure beach, nc

getting there

Kure Beach is less than 2 hours from Kinston. The drive follows SR 11 south, which combines with SR 241, SR 111, and SR 41 along the way. At the town of Chinquapin, SR 41 peels off to the southwest, leading to I-40. Take I-40 east to bypass Wilmington, leading to Kure Beach via US 421.

where to go

Fort Fisher State Historic Site. 1610 Fort Fisher Blvd.; (910) 458-5538; nchistoricsites .org. "The last major stronghold of the Confederacy," this historic site includes interpretive exhibits and audiovisual presentations depicting the 2 major battles fought here. Only about 10 percent of the original fort remains, but what is left is impressive. Up until the final months of the war, Fort Fisher protected the blockade runners moving supplies inland to Confederate forces. Union forces overran the earthen fort in January 1865 and, in subsequent days, Wilmington, which sealed the fate of the Confederacy. Today the site includes a gun battery with examples of cannons used in the Civil War and a trail with markers and monuments. A museum traces the fort's history and the life of the soldiers who called it home, and technology is utilized for several interactive and audiovisual displays. The centerpiece of the exhibits is a large fiber-optic battle map featuring a three-dimensional model of Fort Fisher, thousands of moving lights, and dramatic narration and sound effects illustrating the final bloody hours of the engagement. In the days following, Fort Anderson near Southport fell as Union soldiers marched to Wilmington. Free. Open Tues through Sat 9 a.m. to 5 p.m. Free.

four oaks, nc

getting there

To get to Four Oaks from Kure Beach, make your way to Wilmington by using US 421/117 and then I-40 West. The total drive time of 2 hours will take you to exit 334 at SR 96 and to Four Oaks.

where to go

Bentonville Battlefield State Historic Site. 5466 Harper House Rd.; (910) 594-0789; nchistoricsites.org. By March 1865 Confederate General Joseph Johnson was desperate to stop Sherman's march through the Carolinas and was assembling all the men he could for a final attempt to save the Confederacy. Johnston saw an opportunity to attack Sherman's divided army here, and he struck hard on March 19, 1865. After heavy fighting, the biggest battle in North Carolina, Sherman was able to reunite his army and overpower the outnumbered Southerners. Johnston finally withdrew on March 21, and Sherman moved on to Goldsboro and his waiting supplies. This was the last major Confederate offensive of the war. Today a visitor center features a bookshop, an audiovisual program, and exhibits relating to the battle. The centerpiece of the exhibit is a large fiber-optic battle map offering a vivid portrayal of the first and bloodiest day of fighting at Bentonville. The historic Harper House, which served as a field hospital for the Federal Corp, still stands on the battlefield. The downstairs rooms interpret a functioning Civil War field hospital while the upstairs rooms feature period domestic furnishings. Admission is free. Open Tues through Sat 9 a.m. to 5 p.m.

where to eat

Four Oaks Restaurant. 203 W. Wellons St.; (919) 963-2289. This popular spot provides homestyle meals like pork tenderloin and gravy, fried chicken and more. Open Mon through Sat 6 a.m. to 8:30 p.m. and Sun 7 a.m. to 2 p.m. $$

salisbury, nc

getting there

From Four Oaks it is nearly a 3-hour drive on I-40, slipping beneath the Raleigh-Durham area and heading south on I-85. So unless you are set on visiting these Civil War sites in a chronological fashion, you could opt to stop in Durham first.

where to go

Historic National Cemetery & Confederate Prison Site. 202 Government Rd.; (800) 332-2343 or (704) 638-3100; visitsalisburync.com. On March 25, 1865, Union General George Stoneman left Tennessee with 6,000 cavalrymen and began a trek into western North Carolina and southwestern Virginia to disrupt the Confederate supply lines, destroy mines and ironworks, and to free prisoners at Salisbury. On April 12, 3 days after Robert E. Lee's surrender at Appomattox, Stoneman arrived in Salisbury, burning public buildings and the deserted prison camp. Though nothing remains of the Salisbury prison, you will find 3 monuments erected by the State of Maine, the Commonwealth of Pennsylvania, and the US government. A nearby log house, the former garrison for the prison, is still standing, though, and houses various antiques and artifacts. CDs to accompany a driving tour are available from the visitor center on Innes Street for $5 each.

Rowan County Courthouse Museum. 202 N. Main St.; (704) 633-5946; rowanmuseum .org. Stoneman's raid is described on a Civil War Trails sign in front of the county courthouse in Salisbury. North Carolina's governor when the war broke out, John W. Ellis, was the first judge in this 1855 Greek Revival–style structure. The building escaped destruction when Union General George Stoneman raided the town. Now the courthouse, one of the finest examples of pre–Civil War architecture in the state, serves as a museum. Artifacts from the Civil War are on display here. Free. Open Mon through Fri 10 a.m. to 4 p.m., Sat and Sun 1 to 4 p.m.

durham, nc

getting there

Durham is less than 2 hours north on I-85 from Salisbury. From other points, take I-40 to Durham. The interstates merge near here.

where to go

Bennett Place State Historic Site. 4409 Bennett Memorial Rd.; (919) 383-4345; historic-sites.nc.gov. It was at Bennett Place that the Civil War effectively ended. Union General William T. Sherman and Confederate General Joseph E. Johnston met at this farmstead in 1865, 17 days after Confederate General Robert E. Lee surrendered at Appomattox. Following other meetings in Hillsborough, the one in Durham set up the largest surrender of the war. Although fighting continued in the west, this was the conclusion to the bloody War Between the States. Today the farmhouse and outbuildings have been restored, and the grounds also include a museum and interpretive center. Exhibits of uniforms, flags, weapons, and more focus on North Carolina's role in the war. A surrender reenactment is presented each April. Free. Open Tues through Sat 9 a.m. to 5 p.m.

day trip 55

historic trips

>>> **mountain music:**
mount airy, nc; sparta, nc; wilkesboro, nc;
boone, nc; lenoir, nc

Stringed instruments from Africa combined with traditional lyrics from Europe in the southern Appalachian Mountains to spawn a uniquely American tradition. Almost religiously revered, old-time music developed in the mountains and the foothills along the North Carolina–Virginia border in the early part of the 20th century. To find its roots you have to dig deep into Georgia, but its traditions are maintained in the mountains of North Carolina unlike anywhere else.

This old-time music became bluegrass, folk, southern gospel, country, and what is now being called Americana. Though mountain music was influenced by English and Scotch-Irish ballads and the instruments brought to America by those immigrants and African slaves, early minstrel shows, early religious music, and even vaudeville would influence its development. But most mark recordings by Fiddlin' John Carson from Atlanta in 1922 as giving birth to this tradition. North Carolinians Roy Scruggs, Doc Watson, Tommy Jarrell, and Charlie Poole, however, are at the top of the list of musicians who helped this musical style develop, and their legacy still lives today in music halls, festivals, and even barbershops.

One could travel for weeks from the Blue Ridge Music Center in Galax, Virginia, at the North Carolina border near Sparta and Mount Airy, where this day trip begins, to the John C. Campbell Folk School in Brasstown, in extreme western North Carolina, visiting literally hundreds of locales that preserve mountain music, vocals, and dance. The best sampling of these music styles, however, can be found a couple hours from Mount Airy south to Lenoir and west to Boone. For information on current shows throughout the Blue Ridge, log on to blueridgemusictrailsnc.com.

mount airy, nc

getting there

Mount Airy is located in the northern central part of the state. Take I-77 to I-74 east to US 601 north.

where to go

The Earle Theatre. 142 N. Main St.; (336) 786-7998; theearle.org. The Earle Theatre is home to the second-longest running live radio show in America. Only the *Grand Ole Opry* has been running longer than WPAQ's *Merry Go Round*, which is broadcast live from the theater each Saturday morning from 11 a.m. to 1:30 p.m. Since 1948 the show has hosted a wealth of talent, and began broadcasting at the Earle in 1997. Although the Earle functions as a traditional movie house with first-run and classic films, it also includes the Old-Time Music Heritage Hall with exhibits, audio-guided tours, lessons, workshops, and a UNC-TV documentary hosted by David Holt, *Music of Surry County*, that is played continuously each day. It also hosts the Tommy Jarrell Festival each February in honor of the banjo player who was born in the Round Peak community near here. Heritage Hall is open Mon through Fri 11 a.m. to 3 p.m., Sat until 3:30 p.m., and Sun 1 to 3:30 p.m. Jam sessions are held Thurs at 7 p.m. and Sat at 1:30 p.m. Admission to jam sessions is free. Admission to Heritage Hall and the *Merry Go Round* is $6.

Mount Airy Blue Grass and Old Time Fiddlers Convention. Veterans Memorial Park; (336) 345-7388; surryarts.org. For almost 50 years the first full weekend in June has been dedicated to the music, dance, and singing that was born in part in Surry County. It's a family-friendly festival that revolves around individual and band competitions in which winners take home cash prizes that range from $10 to $800. Could it be more for bragging rights than the money? Admission is $10 per day.

sparta, nc

getting there

From Mount Airy, take SR 89 west to SR 18. Sparta is just on the other side of I-77.

where to go

Alleghany Jubilee. 25 N. Main St.; (336) 200-4949; alleghanyjubilee.com. Located in a deep, narrow storefront that was once a movie theater in downtown Sparta is the Alleghany Jubilee, a dance hall where foot-stompin' music is played twice a week. Adorning the walls of the hall are snapshots of patrons dancing, portraits of various bands that have appeared there over the years, and guests having fun in the family-friendly atmosphere where alcoholic beverages are strictly prohibited. Tues night admission is $7. Sat night admission is $8. Doors open at 6 p.m. with performances from 7 to 10 p.m. Line-dancing lessons are offered on Mon night.

where to eat

Brown's Café. 115 Jones St.; (336) 372-3400. Biscuits and gravy and other home cooking comes out of Brown's for breakfast, lunch, and dinner. Popular dishes include anything fried and anything with mashed potatoes. Open Mon 7 a.m. to 2 p.m., Tues through Sat 7 a.m. to 8 p.m. $$

where to stay

Harmony Hill Bed & Breakfast. 1740 Halsey Knob Rd.; (336) 209-0475. Though there's not much else offered in the small town of Sparta, this highly rated B&B is a jewel in the hills. Built around 1890, the Victorian home has Queen Anne influences. A generous library is offer by its owner, who is a former teacher and bookstore owner. $$.

worth more time

New River Traditions, a mural featuring two musicians—one playing a fiddle and the other a banjo—is one of 15 murals painted on the exterior walls of buildings in downtown West Jefferson. Though it denotes the importance of traditional music to this Ashe County town along the New River, you will want to venture outside the town limits to explore those opportunities. Phipps General Store (2425 Silas Creek Rd.; 336-384-2382) near the north fork of the New River near Lansing is the site of jam sessions on Friday at 7 p.m. Also near here is the Old Helton Hog Stomp, a dance and jam session held every Thursday at 7 p.m. at the Old Helton School (336-384-4707) in the town of Sturgills off SR 194 west of Helton.

wilkesboro, nc

getting there

Wilkesboro is less than an hour from Sparta. Head south on SR 18, which bypasses downtown North Wilkesboro to get you to Wilkesboro.

where to go

MerleFest. 1328 S. Collegiate Dr.; (800) 343-7857; merlefest.org. Held as a fund-raiser for Wilkes Community College on its campus in late April since 1988, MerleFest has become one of the state's largest festivals. It's held in memory of Merle Watson, the son of the late, great music legend Doc Watson who died tragically in a tractor accident at age 36. The festival includes 4 days of what Doc called "traditional-plus." It's 100 bands that play traditional, folk, Americana, country, bluegrass, and more, sometimes combining talent for incredible, once-in-a-lifetime performances on 14 stages. There's much to do in addition to the non-stop music, including taking nature hikes or shopping for art, crafts, musical items, and collectibles. The festival includes a songwriting competition, storytelling, and other fun events for everyone in the family. One-day tickets start at $45 and 4-day tickets can cost as much as $180 at the gate.

Wilkes Heritage Museum. 100 E. Main St.; (336) 667-3171; wilkesheritagemuseum.com. Located at this museum is the Blue Ridge Music Hall of Fame, a showcase of music from the mountains of north Georgia, North Carolina, and Virginia. Photos, posters, instruments, and other items help detail the development of old-time music and other related genres. A photo gallery recognizes inductees since 2008 and includes those who helped develop old-time music as well as musicians, singers, and writers from country, gospel, and bluegrass. Admission is $6. Children under age 5 are admitted free. Open Mon through Sat 10 a.m. to 4 p.m.

boone, nc

getting there

The route from Wilkesboro to Boone is an absolutely beautiful 30-minute drive west on US 421.

where to go

Harvest House. 247 Boone Heights Dr.; (828) 263-4171; hhcboone.org. In addition to a small performance venue, Harvest House operates a recording studio, an art studio, and a dance studio. It hosts frequent performances by local and regional artists with a portion of its proceeds befitting various charities in Haiti, Nicaragua, and Africa. Performances are typically held on Sat nights at 7:30 p.m. Admission is $18 for adults and $10 for students.

Jones House Community Center. 604 W. King St.; (828) 268-6280; joneshouse.org. A bronze statue of music legend Doc Watson is a block away from Jones House, a 1908 home listed on the National Register of Historic Places and overlooking downtown Boone. Operated by the city, it is the site of frequent concerts using the home's front porch as the stage. Old-time jam sessions are also held here on Thurs evenings at 7:30.

lenoir, nc

getting there

Take US 321 south for a straight shot from Boone to Lenoir, descending into the foothills from the High Country in about 30 minutes.

Drexel Barber Shop. 100 S. Main St., Drexel; (704) 907-8863. Between Lenoir and Morganton you'll find one of the state's more unusual and endearing jam sessions. World War II veteran Lawrence Anthony was the driving force behind the jam at this barbershop that he owned and operated from 1964 until shortly before he died in December 2009. His son Carroll continues the tradition of music at the barbershop at noon every Thurs, Fri, and Sat. Hanging on the wall, visitors can see the guitar Anthony took with him through World War II and on which he taught his son how to play.

where to eat

Hardee's Red Burrito. 670 Morganton Blvd.; (828) 758-9700. Not many fast-food chains have made it into *Day Trips The Carolinas*, but this Hardee's Red Burrito, the same brand famous for its flame-broiled burgers, gets a mention for its Bluegrass and a Biscuit with the Hardee's Gang. Every Wed morning from 6 to 10:30 a.m., the gang is here. $

Sims Country Bar-B-Que. 6160 Petra Mill Rd., Granite Falls; (828) 090-5811; simscountrybbq.com. Another gem located outside the city limits, Sims Bar-B-Que has a Granite Falls address, but is readily accessible from Lenoir on US 321. Hidden away from view down a half-mile dirt driveway, the sprawling barn-like structure with the leaky tin roof accommodates a full field of cars on Fri and Sat nights—the only times it's open. For $13.50 you eat barbecue buffet style and settle in for a full night of traditional music and dance. $$

worth more time

The city of Shelby is more than an hour away, driving south on SR 18, but fans of old-time music will appreciate the trip to the Earl Scruggs Center (103 S. Lafayette St.; 704-487-6233; earlscruggscenter.org), named in honor of the 5-string, 3-finger-playing banjo master who was born near Shelby and earned famed with his partner Lester Flatt. Part museum, part event space, the Scruggs Center tells the story of American southern music through well-done exhibits. Open Wed 10 a.m. to 6 p.m., Thurs through Sat 10 a.m. to 4 p.m., and Sun 1 to 5 p.m. Admission is $12 for adults, $10 for students and seniors, and $5 for ages 5 to 17.

day trip 56

historic trips

the shag:
north myrtle beach, sc; raleigh, nc;
charlotte, nc

The shag, a form of the swing dance whose origin is commonly associated with North Myrtle Beach, is one of the great historic institutions of the 20th-century Carolinas. But even today legions of fans are dancing to keep it alive. Commonly associated with beach music, which also has its roots in the beach communities of the Carolinas, the shag grew in popularity because listening to rhythm and blues and other "black music" was not permitted in the '40s and '50s Jim Crow South, and it certainly wasn't played on urban radio stations. Teenagers came to the beach to listen on juke boxes . . . and to dance. For Carolinians, even those who have never shagged, it's nostalgic. It's a cold beer and a warm wind on a steamy summer night. Early shaggers might have called their dance the jitterbug—for in the beginning the tunes more closely resembled big band—but by the 1950s it slowed to a much smoother, rhythmic pace.

Now couples dance expertly, sometimes improvising, with complex steps and footwork but always, always smoothly. There are more than 70 shag clubs in the Carolinas plus a full, yearlong schedule of competitive events sanctioned by the Competitive Shaggers Association. The World Shagging Championship is held in Myrtle Beach each winter and there is even a junior shaggers association for the under 21 crowd. Radio stations from Aiken to Virginia offer all beach all the time playlists, and the State of North Carolina, where the shag is the official state dance (in South Carolina, too), offers a "Shag Tag" license plate for automobiles. Once upon a time, shaggers danced to the Drifters and Dominoes, later to the Eagles and Lionel Richie, and today to Josh Turner, Lady A, and Akon. Like another music legend said, "the times they are a-changin'."

quirky carolina

Each year the Richard Nixon Memorial Service Award goes to a member of the Association of Beach and Shag Club DJs who has performed outstanding service outside his regular DJ duties for the shag community. The award has nothing to do with the 37th president of the US. It's named in honor of a deceased member of the Beach and Shag Club DJ Hall of Fame.

The obvious choice for a shag-themed day trip is North Myrtle Beach, but following, too, are primers to get you ready for the big time.

north myrtle beach, sc

getting there

To get to the shag capital of the world, head to North Myrtle Beach on US 17, which runs north to south along the Carolina coast.

where to go

Deckerz. 90 Hillside Dr.; (843) 280-1200; deckerznmb.net. Part sports bar, catering to Ohio State fans, and part shag club, patrons typically enjoy Deckerz from one of 3 outdoor decks. Open 11 a.m. to 1 a.m. Sun through Thurs, 11 a.m. to 2 a.m. Fri and Sat. $.

Duck's Beach Club. 229 Main St.; (843) 663-3858; ducksatoceandrive.com. This is a popular spot for the Society of Standers, a local shag club. It regularly features some of the region's most popular beach music bands. Duck's also serves a selection of bar food, including seafood baskets and burgers. $$.

Fat Harold's Beach Club. 212 Main St.; (843) 249-5779; fatharolds.com. Possibly the most popular beach and shag club, this is a North Myrtle Beach landmark. While it's made for dancing, with a big dance floor, people say Harold and cooks at the Shag City Grill here make the best cheeseburger and the best bologna sandwich on the beach. A sister site, Harold's on the Ocean (2301 N. Ocean Blvd.), is structured more for concerts. Open 11 a.m. to 1 a.m. Sun through Thurs, 11 a.m. to 2 a.m. Fri and Sat.

OD Arcade and Lounge. 100 S. Ocean Blvd.; (843) 249-6460; odarcade.com. Right in the middle of downtown, this is a smaller dance club that does a lot of business. In addition to serving as a place to dance, there are also designated karaoke nights and live music on weekends. Open daily 11 a.m. to 2 a.m.

where to stay

Ocean Drive Beach and Golf Resort. 98 N. Ocean Blvd.; (843) 249-1436; ocean driveresort.com. With partnerships with many of the area golf courses, this resort offers a variety of packages from 1 night to a full week. Accommodations range from simple rooms to condos, and amenities include a pool, the Shaggers Hall of Fame, and the popular night-spot Spanish Galleon, which is located here, as are the OD Beach Club Grill, OD Cafe, and a tiki bar. $$$.

raleigh, nc

getting there

Raleigh is located at I-40 west of I-95. It's a hefty 3-plus-hour drive from Myrtle Beach. Take US SR 905 north from the beach to connect with SR 131 near Whiteville. SR 131 merges with SR 87 and will take the driver to I-95 North. That connects with I-40 West and will take you straight to Raleigh.

where to go

Loafers. 3914 Atlantic Ave.; (919) 872-5335; loafersbeachclub.com. Home to the Capital Area Shag Club, Loafers offers lessons on Tues nights. Music is usually DJ driven, but Loafers occasionally hosts live entertainment. The club also hosts several shag contests and events during the year. It's a private club, so no food is served. Hours vary seasonally.

TJ's Night Life. 4801 Leigh Dr.; (919) 713-1300; tjsnightlife.com. The home of the Raleigh Shag Club, the city's second dance club, TJ's is also a private club. Shag lessons are offered Mon and Tues at 7 p.m. A separate stage is set up on one end of the dance floor near the DJ booth for live entertainment. TJ's is also the home of Rayz Deck Party every Thurs night at 9 p.m. featuring Carolina beach music's top bands.

charlotte, nc

getting there

Charlotte is a 3-hour drive from Raleigh. Take I-40 West to I-85 South.

where to go

Lynn's. 4819 S. Tryon St.; (704) 527-3064; thelynnsdanceclub.com. This home of the Charlotte Shag Club is a popular nightspot. Shag lessons for both adults and juniors are offered at this private club on Fri nights. The Charlotte Shag Club also sponsors many other events throughout the year, such as the yearly Flashback party, '50s Sock Hop, Halloween party, and fund-raisers for charitable organizations. Open Wed through Sat 6 p.m. to 2 a.m.

day trip 57

historic trips

lighthouses of the outer banks:
corolla, nc; coquina beach, nc; buxton, nc; ocracoke, nc; cape lookout, nc

Begin about as far north as you can at the Corolla Light and finish at Cape Lookout. You will have seen five lighthouses, but that's not all North Carolina's Outer Banks has to offer. This spectacular region affords some of the best views in the state and has been home to some the state's most riveting history, dating back to the 16th century when Spanish mustangs were abandoned here. Sir Walter Raleigh walked this ground and the pirate Blackbeard likely roamed these areas. The Civil War battered much of the Outer Banks and key strategic victims were the lighthouses here. German U-boats even attacked and sank 80 ships here during World War II. Throughout much of the banks, drivers navigate Highway 12 with the Atlantic Ocean on one side and the sounds on the other. Sand blows across the highway at the narrowest points, and nature is preserved along much of this region.

corolla, nc

getting there

Corolla is located at the extreme northern end of the Outer Banks on SR 12.

where to go

Back Country Outfitters & Guides. 107-C Corolla Light Town Center; (252) 453-0877; outerbankstours.com. Back Country Outfitters offers wild horse safaris in addition to other ecotours. The wild horse safari serves up a variety of experiences through the off-road neighborhoods to the Virginia state line to see the wild mustangs left behind by early explorers almost 500 years ago. Naturalist guides take guests over 30 miles of backcountry beach dunes, where these powerful horses roam free. Reservations are required. Prices vary according to activity.

Corolla Wild Horse Museum. 1126 School House Ln.; (252) 453-8002; corollawildhorses .com. This museum, dedicated to the preservation of the local wild horse population, is housed in the Old Corolla Schoolhouse, in the heart of historic Corolla Village. Visitors see interactive displays and learn about local history and the story of the horses that inhabit this area. Kids' programs are held on Tues and Thurs from 11 a.m. to 2 p.m. Open Mon through Thurs 11 a.m. to 4 p.m.

Currituck Beach Lighthouse. Highway 12 at Corolla Village Rd.; (252) 453-4939; obcinc .org. Highway 12 ends at the Currituck Beach Lighthouse, a redbrick tower built in 1875. It's distinct among its cousins to the south because it is unpainted. Its 214 steps are open for climbing thanks to the renovation efforts of the Outer Banks Conservationists over the past 2 decades. While the other lighthouses here suffered early damage and drama with everything from pirates to Civil War skirmishes to encroaching waters, Currituck Beach Lighthouse had an uneventful beginning and a slow decline. After World War II the lighthouse's usefulness waned and its remote location contributed to its falling into disrepair and assaults by vandals. Its keeper house and several other outbuildings have also been renovated. Admission to the grounds is free. There is a $10 fee to climb its steps. Open daily Easter through Thanksgiving 9 a.m. to 5 p.m. (until 8 p.m. on Thurs).

The Whalehead Club at Currituck Heritage Park. 1100 Club Rd.; (252) 453-9040; whaleheadclub.com. Built in the mid-1920s to satisfy industrialist Edward Collings Knight Jr.'s passion for hunting waterfowl, the Whalehead Club is a spectacular landmark on the Currituck Outer Banks. Knight and his wife used the Corolla home as their winter residence from 1925 to 1934. It still boasts Tiffany lamps, cork-tiled floors, and brass duck head and water lily hardware. This tour teaches participants about the history and art of the home and gives them a greater appreciation for the environment and geography of the area as well as some navigational skills. Open Mon through Sat 10 a.m. to 4 p.m. Some tours require advance registration.

where to eat

Spanky's Grille & Pizza. MP 3.5 Highway 12; (252) 261-1917; spankysnc.com. Spanky's is a great place for breakfast or a midday meal. Many say Spanky's turns out the best hot dogs in the state, but the burgers aren't bad either. Try either one with chili cheese fries. $.

where to stay

The Sanderling. 1461 Duck Rd.; (877) 650-4812; thesanderling.com. Just south of Corolla near Duck is this AAA 4-diamond resort named one of the best in the country by *Condé Nast Traveler*. Right on the beach, the resort includes a spa and racquet club as well as offering privileges at the nearby Currituck Golf Club. Bright, sophisticated rooms and suites are offered at 3 separate inns that are also surrounded by vacation homes. $$$.

coquina beach, nc

getting there

Passing through the bustling areas of Kitty Hawk, Kill Devil Hills, and Nags Head on SR 12 will take drivers south to Bodie Island. Coquina Beach is about 2 hours from Corolla.

where to go

Bodie Island Lighthouse. Highway 12, 8 miles south of juncture of US 158/64; (252) 441-5711. Bodie Island begins in the south at Coquina Beach, home of the Bodie Island Lighthouse. A visitor center, exhibits, and nature trail are open during daylight hours from Apr through early Oct. Thanks to recent repairs that stopped its decay, the lighthouse, built in 1872, is again open to climb. In 2009 the National Park Service began the first major renovation of the lighthouse since it was built. The project also enhanced the surroundings, an already pristine seascape area. Bodie Island, originally "Body," is named after the family who owned the land, but folklore would have it that the moniker resulted from the many shipwrecked bodies that washed ashore. Rising 165 feet and painted with striking black and white horizontal stripes, the picture-perfect Bodie Island Lighthouse is actually the third attempt to illuminate the perilous stretch of coast between Cape Hatteras and Currituck Beach. The first structure was so shoddily built, it was razed after 11 years of operation. A second structure was destroyed by Confederate soldiers. Finally, this current tower was lit in 1872. The National Park Service has owned it since 1953. Admission to climb is $10 for adults and $5 for seniors and children age 11 and under. Open daily 9 a.m. to 4:30 p.m.

Pea Island National Wildlife Refuge. 708 N. Hwy. 64; (252) 987-2394; fws.gov/pea island. Just north of Rodanthe begins the 5,915-acre Pea Island National Wildlife Refuge and part of the Charles Kuralt Trail, a series of refuges in coastal Virginia and North Carolina. Use the observation platforms that expand across brackish water, salt flats, and marshes throughout the area to view hundreds of species of local birds and any number of birds migrating to and from the refuge. The refuge also has a visitor center and nature trail, and bird walks and children's programs are held during the summer and fall. Open 9 a.m. to 4 p.m. daily Apr through Nov and weekends the rest of the year.

buxton, nc

getting there

Buxton is an hour drive south of Coquina on SR 12.

where to go

Cape Hatteras Lighthouse. Highway 12; (252) 473-2111; nps.gov/caha/index.htm. At 208 feet the Cape Hatteras Lighthouse is an international symbol for the North Carolina coast. Erosion from the treacherous sea began to threaten the 100-year-old lighthouse, and plans were undertaken to save it. As a result, in 2000 the lighthouse was moved about 1 mile inland. You can still climb the 248 steps to its top and get a spectacular view of the surrounding area from the outside. On the grounds of the lighthouse is the Cape Hatteras Visitors Center and Museum. It's the tallest of the lighthouses, in fact the tallest in America, serving vessels trying to navigate the dangerous Diamond Shoals, shifting sands 10 miles off the coast that have earned this area the name Graveyard of the Atlantic. The first lighthouse was built here in 1803, but it was inadequate—too short and not bright enough to see from beyond the shoals. In 1852 the tower was extended to 150 feet, but this structure was badly damaged in the Civil War and later destroyed to make way for the present lighthouse 600 feet to the north. Admission to climb is $10 for adults and $5 for seniors and children age 11 and under. Open daily 9 a.m. to 5:30 p.m. in summer and until 4:30 p.m. the rest of the year.

where to eat

Buxton Munch. 47359 Highway 12; (252) 995-5502; buxtonmunch.com. Fish and shrimp tacos, crabby patties and other beachy dishes suit this location well., but you can also get burgers and salads. $$

Diamond Shoals Restaurant. Highway 12; (252) 995-5217; diamondshoalsrestaurant .com. Diamond Shoals serves local seafood, and it's open for breakfast, too. Known for its clam chowder, crab bisque, and homemade crab cakes, even lunchtime might require a wait here. A fresh seafood market also operates from this location. Open daily 6:30 a.m. to 2:30 p.m. and for dinner at 5 p.m. The market is open 10 a.m. to 7 p.m. $$.

Orange Blossom Bakery & Cafe. Highway 12; (252) 995-4109; orangeblossombakery .com. Breakfast, including fresh baked goods and gourmet coffee, is the specialty here. Try the Apple Ugglies, sticky and sweet fried apple pies. Open daily 6:30 to 11 a.m. $.

where to stay

Cape Hatteras Motel. Highway 12; (800) 995-0711; capehatterasmotel.com. You'll find rooms, efficiencies, and apartments at this waterfront motel trimmed with wooden shingles.

The lighthouse is within view here, and a boardwalk leads to the beach. Or you can while away the time enjoying the view of the ocean from deck-top rocking chairs. $$$.

The Inn on Pamlico Sound. 49684 Highway 12; (866) 726-5426; Innonpamlicosound .com. Comfortable but elegant, this inn sits on a ridge overlooking the sound. Many rooms have waterfront views while others have balconies. $$$

Lighthouse View Motel. Highway 12; (252) 995-5680; lighthouseview.com. This is one of the larger and nicer accommodations in Buxton. Located on the ocean side of the island, in addition to lighthouse views, it offers rooms, efficiencies, and interesting octagonal 2-room villas. There is also a large, oceanside pool. $$$.

ocracoke, nc

getting there

Ocracoke is only accessible from either end by state-operated vehicle ferry. From the north near Buxton, depart from the town of Hatteras on SR 12; from the south, take the ferry from Cedar Island.

where to go

Banker Ponies. North of Ocracoke Village on Highway 12. These small horses ran wild on the island until the late 1950s, when they were penned at their current home. The ponies are descendants of horses brought to the New World by Spanish explorers as early as the 16th century and can be viewed and photographed from an observation deck just off the highway. Free. Typically open during daylight hours.

Ocracoke Lighthouse. Lighthouse Road; (252) 928-4531; ocracokepreservation.org. The white stucco Ocracoke Lighthouse is to the west of the village. Hike if the weather is nice because parking is extremely limited on the small street. Built in 1823, the lighthouse, only 75 feet tall, is the state's oldest still in operation. Its beam can be seen from 14 miles away, but the tower is not open for climbing. A nearby historic home has been moved to this location and converted to a museum with antiques, tools, and Civil War artifacts. Ocracoke's history is less eventful than that of other lighthouses in the area. Built to help mariners navigate between Ocracoke and Portsmith Island, it received minimal damage in the Civil War and still casts its steady beam at night.

where to eat

Back Porch. 110 Back Rd.; (252) 928-6401; backporchocracoke.com. This is one of the better seafood places on the island. Fresh catches of the day are combined with other specialties such as citrus-marinated calamari and crab cakes with lemon caper sauce. It has a children's menu and basket-size portions in case there are any other light eaters in the family. $$–$$$.

Howard's Pub and Raw Bar. Highway 12; (252) 928-4441; howardspub.com. This is one of the kid-friendlier places, offering an array of burgers, chicken, and pizza as well as oysters and the best onion rings. It has checkers, mind benders, and other assorted games for you to play while waiting for your meal. $.

where to stay

Anchorage Inn & Marina. Highway 12; (252) 928-1101; theanchorageinn.com. Located overlooking the picture-perfect Silver Lake, this is a pet-friendly place with rooms and some efficiencies. There is a small cafe, too, but it is also within walking distance to many Ocracoke attractions. $$–$$$.

Jerniman's Campground. Highway 12; (252) 928-4031; jernimans.com.com. Book your reservations early for this oceanfront campground, 3 miles from the village. The campground gets you away from the hustle and bustle of tourists and is quite scenic and nicely kept. $.

The Castle on Silver Lake. Silver Lake Road; (800) 471-8848; thecastlebb.com. This majestic inn offers very nice rooms and condos. A variety of amenities are provided, including private piers, bikes, and a game room. $$$.

cape lookout, nc

getting there

To reach the lighthouse, state ferry service is available from Harkers Island, Beaufort, Davis, and Morehead City. The landing at Harkers Island is the closest to the lighthouse. At Ocracoke, take the ferry from the south end of the island on SR 12.

where to go

Cape Lookout Lighthouse. 131 Charles St.; (252) 728-2250; nps.gov. The 21-mile stretch of Cape Lookout Shoals has been inhabited for centuries and is now a National Seashore. Because of opposing currents—the warm Gulf Stream mixed with the cool Labrador Current—it produces intense fog and dangerous shoals. The particularly treacherous area off Cape Lookout earned the name the "Horrible Headland." In 1804 Congress authorized a lighthouse here, but it wasn't until 1812 that the first Cape Lookout Light—a 96-foot tower— was completed. It was almost immediately apparent that the much-anticipated light was inadequate and visible only 11 miles in good weather—less than that in bad. By 1850 the lighthouse was in serious disrepair, and the keeper had to constantly shovel piles of sand that would build up against his quarters.

First lit on November 1, 1859, the second Cape Lookout Lighthouse proved to be a model for the other lighthouses that would be rebuilt along the Outer Banks—163 feet tall, the graceful new tower was just over 28 feet in diameter at its base with 9-foot-thick walls painted with a checkered pattern. The fixed white light is visible for 19 miles and can easily be seen above the almost opaque salt spray whipped up by fierce winds. In 1942 the US Navy responded to an attack near here by German U-boats, deploying anti-submarine vessels and initiating aircraft patrols. For decades, dredging operations have helped to stave off erosion from the tidal currents in Bardens Inlet, and the Friends of Cape Lookout National Seashore was formed in 2008 to partner with the National Park Service in preserving and interpreting the seashore. Repair work included stabilizing the spiral iron staircase that corkscrews up the lighthouse, adding a new handrail, improving accessibility to the lantern room, and installing a new guardrail around the outside gallery. The tower reopened for climbing in 2010. The visitor center in the keepers' quarters adjacent to the Cape Lookout Lighthouse is open from 9 a.m. to 5 p.m. from Apr to Nov. The tower is open for climbing from mid-May to mid-Sept. Tickets may be reserved for climbing from 9:30 a.m. to 3 p.m. on Tues through Fri by calling (252) 728-0708. Reservations can only be made for dates the same week and must be booked at least 1 day in advance.

index